STUDENT

CULTURAL

DIVERSITY

Understanding and Meeting the Challenge

Second Edition

Eugene García
University of California, Berkeley

HOUGHTON MIFFLIN COMPANY
BOSTON   NEW YORK

Senior Sponsoring Editor: Loretta Wolozin

Associate Editor: Lisa Mafrici

Project Editor: Anne Holm

Senior Manufacturing Coordinator: Marie Barnes

Marketing Manager: Pamela J. Laskey

Cover design: Rebecca Fagan
Cover image: © Eric Dinyer/Graphistock

Photo credits: page xviii, Stock Boston/Bob Daemmrich; page 32, Stock
Boston/Jean-Claude LeJeune; page 113, The Image Works/Sven
Marston; page 122, Stock Boston/Bob Daemmrich; page 132, The
Image Works/Elizabeth Crews; page 150, Stock Boston/Gale Zuker;
page 180, The Image Works/Elizabeth Crews; page 252, The Image
Works/Momatiuk Eastcott; page 261, Tony Stone Images/Loren
Santow; page 311, Stock Boston/Jean-Claude LeJeune; page 338,
Tony Stone Images/David Young Wolff.

Printed in the U.S.A.

Library of Congress Catalog Card Number: 98-72030

ISBN: 0-395-90419-6

123456789-QF-02 01 00 99 98

BRIEF CONTENTS

CONTENTS

TABLES

FIGURES

PREFACE

I remember the day one of my eldest brothers came home from school noticeably disturbed—physically and otherwise. He had been in a nasty fight. Like most younger brothers, I didn't hesitate to ask, "How bad does the other guy look?" After my brother yelled at me for asking such a dumb question, he told me why he had been in that fight.

It seems that some kid had called him a "dirty Mexican." I had heard those words myself. At the age of five, I had already begun to realize that I was different, and that some kids didn't seem to like that. My brother then made it quite clear why, to him, the words "dirty Mexican" were fighting words. He said we should be proud to be Mexicans—should allow no one to call us dirty. My brother said those were bad words aimed at our mother. She worked hard to keep us clean, he continued, and we should always be proud of that.

Since that day, I recognized that to be different—by culture and by language—was not a negative. My brother was absolutely clear about his conclusion. Sadly, many in our society have not yet arrived at this same conclusion.

This book is written in recognition of those children who are considered "dirty" by many other children, because of the color of their skin, their language, or their culture. Some of these children are my own, others are children of my brothers and sisters, but most are just children marked by society because they are outside the "preferred" boundaries. Diversity is a wonderful gift to our society, but often it's an unrecognized gift—at times easily discarded or even scorned. Just as the motto of our nation is stated to be "e pluribus unum," meaning "out of many, one," the motto of this book is best articulated by its variation "e diversitate unum"—out of many groups bonded by their humanity, yet distinct from one another, we form one nation.

It has always been the challenge of humankind to get along cooperatively and peacefully in the world. That challenge remains substantive and grows daily as our own existence becomes more and more dependent on our near and far neighbors' well-being. We know so much more today about meeting this challenge, especially in the domain of education. Educating all of our children to meet our highest expectation is possible. Like the fear of diversity, ignorance of how to meet the challenge is no excuse. This book's aim is to help eliminate both of these excuses.

Audience and Approach

Student Cultural Diversity: Understanding and Meeting the Challenge, Second Edition is an introductory core text for courses on teaching culturally diverse students. The text is for one-semester, junior, senior, and fifth-year courses in *Multicultural Education, Teaching Culturally Diverse Students, Diversity in Families and Communities,* and *Language and Culture in Schools.* The text can also be a supplement in a variety of education courses. Teachers taking such courses increasingly ask, "How can I teach the entire range of students that I will find in classrooms today?"

The Roots of Diversity

This book provides the basis for responsive teaching by exploring the roots of diversity. This basis consists of the social, cognitive, and communicative roots of diversity; how children of diverse backgrounds learn to think and communicate within their home, community, and school environments is the pivotal framework of this book. Language—from its early acquisition to its use to construct and communicate meaning—is treated fully as a key component of the roots of diversity.

The Responsive Teacher

An understanding of the roots of diversity in context helps teachers create classroom climates and instruction that are responsive to diverse students' needs. To connect concepts to active classroom practice, the theme of responsive teaching is integrated throughout the text narrative. Additionally, a feature called "Becoming a Responsive Teacher" presents practical classroom-oriented interludes in each chapter. Finally, helping teachers develop responsive pedagogy is the main topic of Part Three, "The Educational Response." Teachers who are truly effective learn to adjust their teaching strategies in response to the learning styles of individual students. The dual point consistently made by this book's approach is that (1) the roots of diversity provide understanding necessary for (2) meeting the challenge of responsive teaching.

Content and Revision in the Second Edition

The second edition of the text consists of nine chapters divided into three parts. **Part One, "Student Diversity in Context,"** assesses the breadth and complexity of America's culturally diverse student population. Chapter 1, "Cultural Diversity in America's Schools," explores demographics and immigration trends, identifying more clearly the students we will be teaching today and tomorrow and the cultural and language backgrounds they bring with them. Chapter 2, "Views of Culture and Education," provides a conceptual overview of culture: how the term is defined and what it means to be inside or outside of a particular culture. New coverage of "cultural capital" and new treatment of the impact of race, class, gender, and diversity on school culture have been added to this chapter. Chapter 3, "Educational Approaches to Students Cultural Diversity," examines past and present educational approaches to diversity. Where have we been successful, and where have we fallen short? How far have we come in providing equitable means and intellectual opportunities to a multicultural population? New coverage of "the constructivist perspective" has been added.

Part Two, "The Roots of Diversity," the core of the book, probes into the communication process itself and how teachers interact with their culturally diverse students and families. Chapter 4, "An Ecology of Family, Home, and School," describes methods of helping students build bridges between the sometimes incongruous worlds that they experience inside and outside the classroom.

Chapter 5, "Language and Communication," shows how language develops in early childhood and presents research on bilingualism and multilingualism; it also contains new coverage of non-standard dialects. Chapter 6, "Language, Culture, and Cognition," examines the effects of social contexts—peers, the family, and the community—on the individual child's learning style and how well he or she performs in school. Expanded coverage of instructional discourse for diverse students and the role of constructivism and cognition has been added to this chapter.

Part Three, "The Educational Response," focuses on concrete ways in which educators can address the needs of culturally diverse students. Chapter 7, "The Effective Teacher: Preparation, Assessment, and Characteristics," looks at the preparation and characteristics the teacher of culturally diverse students must have, and what assessment methods may be used to determine his or her effectiveness in the classroom. A new section on the school principal's role in effective schooling has been added. Chapter 8, "Effective Instruction of Linguistically and Culturally Diverse Children," examines the preparedness of the school itself, describing the qualities of some schools that have experienced success in educating multicultural populations. This chapter also makes recommendations on how other schools can share in this success. New to this edition, Chapter 9, "Educational Approaches at the Middle and Secondary School Level," addresses issues of diversity during the middle school and secondary school years. It is schooling during this critical adolescent period that sets the stage for high school completion and postsecondary education. This chapter provides real-life cases and examples to help meet the needs of readers who are going to be middle or high school teachers. Each chapter in this second edition has been completely updated with the latest statistics, research and coverage of key topics.

Special Learning Features

Student Cultural Diversity: Understanding and Meeting the Challenge offers a number of valuable features designed to help students easily grasp and learn the material in the text.

▼ *Focusing questions* at the opening of each chapter introduce the major topics to be explored.
▼ *"Becoming a Responsive Teacher"*—a unique feature appearing at least once in each chapter—presents classroom situations drawn from the author's experience and from current studies and research. As a departure point, questions and activities in "Meeting the Challenge," a section within this feature, encourage students to reflect, then to respond thoughtfully and creatively to the diversity in real-world classrooms.
▼ *Marginal notations* draw attention to central points throughout the text and provide helpful landmarks for review.
▼ *Key terms* appear in boldfaced type so that their meanings are reinforced and can be more easily located.
▼ A *summary of major ideas* at the end of each chapter helps the student further understand and clarify what has been read.
▼ *"Extending Your Experience"* questions prompt students to apply their new understanding of diversity to their own lives and to the outside world. These questions will be especially

helpful for students whose experience has primarily been among homogeneous populations.

▼ A list of *resources for further study* also appears at the end of each chapter, providing students with additional opportunities to read and learn.

▼ A *glossary* at the end of the book defines important terms.

▼ A *references* section provides background for books and studies cited in the text, which students may wish to explore further.

▼ *Teacher Education Station Web Site* (found at *http://www.hmco.com/college*, then click on "Education") provides additional pedagogic support and resources for beginning and experienced professionals in education, including the unique "Project-Based Learning Space." For more details on all that this web site offers, see the site map on the back inside cover of this book.

Acknowledgments

A number of reviewers made useful suggestions and provided thoughtful reactions at various stages in the development of the manuscript. I wish to thank the following individuals for their conscientiousness and for their contributions to the content of this text:

Gloria Contreras, University of North Texas

Janette Klingner, University of Miami

Helene T. Mandell, National University

Shane Martin, Loyola Marymount University

Carlos J. Vallejo, Arizona State University

Grateful acknowledgment is also given to my editors—Lisa Mafrici and Loretta Wolozin—for their guidance, patience, and assistance throughout the book's development.

I would like to give special thanks to Julie Figueroa for her assistance. And a very special thank you to my wife, Erminda, who served as assistant, critic, and supporter.

Eugene García
Berkeley, California

STUDENT

DIVERSITY

IN CONTEXT

In Part One we describe the scope and complexity of the population of culturally diverse students in the United States. In Chapter 1 we examine how the rapidly changing cultural and ethnic makeup of the nation as a whole affects our classrooms. Who are the children we will be teaching, and what cultural and language backgrounds will they bring to the classroom?

Before turning to our discussion of cultural diversity in the U.S. schools, we need to define what is meant by the term "culture." In Chapter 2 we provide such a conceptual overview. What does it mean to be a member of a particular culture, and how does cultural membership affect people's interactions both within and outside of that culture?

In Chapter 3 we supply a historical survey of American educational approaches to the teaching of culturally diverse students. What has been done? What remains to be done? Have we made significant strides in achieving educational equality?

CULTURAL

DIVERSITY

IN AMERICA'S

SCHOOLS

CHAPTER 1

Focus Questions

▼ What are some of the trends in immigration to the United States over the last two decades?

▼ What are the expected demographics of the U.S. student population in 2026?

▼ What changes in the economy can today's students expect?

▼ How do indicators of child and family well-being relate to educational achievement?

▼ What do the changing demographics of the U.S. student population imply for the training and assessment of teachers?

▼ How are language minority students defined, and what types of educational programs are designed to serve them?

▼ How do national and state policies affect language minority students?

"Not the best or worst of times, but times of challenge."
—Tomás Arciniega

An Introduction

During my recent assignment (1993–1995) in Washington, D.C., as Senior Officer and Director of the Office of Bilingual Education and Minority Languages Affairs in the U.S. Department of Education, I attempted to apply my professional experience and expertise as an educational researcher as well as my personal cultural and linguistic experiences to the task of addressing national educational policy. My professional identity was and continues to be nurtured in some of the best educational institutions of this country, whereas my nonprofessional identity was and continues to be rooted in a large, rural, Mexican American family—all speaking Spanish as our native language, all born in the United States like our parents, grandparents, and great-grandparents. I am one of ten children; five of us graduated from high school, and I'm the only one who has graduated from college.

I found the process of bringing my two *personas* (the Spanish term for "persons") together not as difficult as I might have expected. I even came to conclude that this intersection of my dual identities was quite helpful to me, my colleagues, and the wide variety of audiences with whom I interacted in my national role. In fact, I found that by integrating these personas, I was able to communicate with individuals in ways that would not have been possible if I had spoken only with one or two separate voices.

This book is my attempt to write about these intersecting but distinct voices in order to further our understanding of life in a diverse society, particularly as it relates to education in this country. There is no doubt that the historical pattern of education for culturally diverse populations in the United States is one of underachievement. This need not be the case in the future.

This book recognizes that multiple selves are a reality not just for me but for all Americans. Yes, it has been useful for me to recognize that I am walking in varied and diverse cultures. But this is an experience everyone shares to some degree. Diversity within each individual is as great as diversity between individuals and their many cultures. We all live with diversity, some of us more than others, and no one escapes this challenge or its advantages and disadvantages.

Cultural and social diversity is not a new issue, of course; it has been a challenge through the ages. Early Hebrew scholars debated the issue of "us versus them," or the *hom* versus the *goy*. Plato and Aristotle differed vehemently over whether social diversity or social homogeneity was preferable among peoples in a nation-state. Plato concluded that homogeneity minimized political tensions and favoritism, whereas Aristotle, his student, concluded that diversity fostered inventiveness and creativity as well as the political compromises necessary for a democracy. Saint Thomas Aquinas argued that a similarity in people's approaches to God promoted their unity, while Martin Luther opted to cultivate religious diversity.

Today, in our "shrinking" world, as the United States and other nations are pulled together by communications and economics, our diversity becomes more visible and harder to hide. In addition, more and more people are worried about it. For example, the movement known as "English First" is passionately concerned that multilingualism will result in violent confrontations, whereas indigenous peoples just as passionately mourn the loss of their languages and cultures. Thus, although diversity has always existed, our social institutions need to address it today more directly than they have in the past, and it is crucial that our educational institutions help us address it successfully.

At the core of this volume are two beliefs:

To honor diversity is to honor the social complexity in which we live—to give the individual and the culture in which that person developed a sense of integrity.

To unify is absolutely necessary, but to insist on unity without embracing diversity is to destroy that which will allow us to unite—our individual and cultural dignity.

A Portrait of Change and Challenge

Mrs. Margaret Tanner's classroom in a sunny, southern California elementary school looks much like any other fifth-grade room. The walls are brightly adorned with the children's work, and an aura of busy concentration prevails. The playgrounds outside and the cafeteria down the hall complete a picture repeated countlessly in communities all over the United States. Mrs. Tanner's school was built in the 1950s, and the number of students it serves has remained around six hundred since its opening. This changed briefly for a five-year stretch during the enrollment boom of the late 1970s, when it served over nine hundred students and operated "split" morning and afternoon sessions. Mrs. Tanner has had as few as 19 students in her classroom and as many as 35, but on the average her daily attendance is between 26 and 28 students.

Mrs. Tanner has taught fifth grade in this very classroom, in this school, in a suburb of Los Angeles, for 21 years. She is a dedicated and committed teacher. When she accepted her initial teaching assignment, her students and most of the other people in her community shared many demographic characteristics: they were almost all middle class, white, and English speaking— the descendants of people who had emigrated to the United States from Europe during the nineteenth and early twentieth centuries. In short, they were all very much like Mrs. Tanner herself.

Demographic Shifts

In that first decade of her professional career, however, demographic shifts began in her state. Los Angeles expanded and its suburbs multiplied, and her community became a haven for recently arrived Mexican immigrants and for other Spanish-speaking people coming to California from towns and cities in the southwestern United States. In that decade, the demographic makeup of Mrs. Tanner's fifth-grade class also began to change. Her white, middle-class students were joined by African American children whose parents had relocated from the southern United States, and by children who spoke Spanish in their working-class homes and commuted regularly between the United States and Mexico. The parents of these children, like the grandparents of her earlier students, had come to the United States to find employment and to achieve a higher standard of living for their families. Although these new students were not like her in some ways, Mrs. Tanner recognized their needs and abilities and felt just as committed to them as she had felt toward her first students.

Different Languages and Cultures

In the second decade of Mrs. Tanner's tenure, further shifts in the population continued to alter the demographics of her students dramatically. More and more, she is teaching children who speak a variety of languages in their homes and communities, including Spanish, Vietnamese, Russian, Hmong, Chinese, and Farsi. The communities in which these students live are made up of first- and second-generation Mexican immigrants, and first-generation Vietnamese, Hmong, Chinese, Iranian, Russian, and Central Americans. Many of these families have traveled to the United States to seek a better standard of living, but some were forced to escape politically unstable and other dangerous circumstances in their nations of origin.

Mrs. Tanner is quick to point out that her commitment and determination to serve these students is no less, and may be even greater, than it ever was. But she is also the first to admit that the diversification of her student body has challenged, to the very core, her own concept of her role as a teacher and her grasp of the skills necessary to teach effectively. As she sees it, the greatest challenge to her commitment as a teaching professional is the cultural diversity of her students, who come from different cultures, language backgrounds, and economic levels. Effectively teaching a classroom of over two dozen fifth-graders who come from radically different cultures and who speak different languages is not the job Mrs. Tanner was originally hired to do. Back in her first years as a teacher, she could fairly safely assume that all her students would respond similarly to a lesson and in ways that were familiar to her. Now, however, she can assume very little. In order to reach her diverse students while creating a cohesive learning environment, considerations of cultural and language differences must enter into her teaching strategies.

Teachers of the New Century

The changes and challenges Mrs. Tanner faces in her role as a teacher are being played out in classrooms all over the United States. Schools characterized by a culturally and linguistically diverse student population are soon to be the norm rather than the exception for new teachers of the twenty-first century. We need no crystal ball to see that the future for U.S. schools will mirror the changes that have occurred in Mrs. Tanner's classroom. The demographic shifts in our country's population are thoroughgoing and well documented. Groups of students once labeled minorities will become majorities, particularly in highly populated metropolitan areas where most of the student population is concentrated—areas where most of this country's students will either succeed or fail. Mrs. Tanner is a pioneer, a representative of things to come. And much like her own experience of self-examination regarding the practice of her profession, all of us will be required to take a fresh look at the assumptions underlying our current methods of teaching, learning, and schooling. Also, our commitment, like hers, to an increasingly diverse student population must never waiver.

This book is dedicated to all the Mrs. Tanners of this country. Moreover, it is an attempt to address the many complex forces and issues that are likely to demand the attention of teachers for years to come. I hope the insights it offers and the discussions it engenders will be of service to the dedicated individuals who devote themselves to children within a variety of educational settings.

In this chapter, we focus on the demographic attributes of culturally diverse students in the United States. Clearly identifying and defining this population has not been an easy task for educators, and most of the categories of definition reveal more about the definer than the defined. The educational initiatives targeted at culturally diverse students have been variously synonymous with programs for "poor," "lower class," "immigrant," "at-risk," "underachieving," and "dropout" students. As Gonzalez (1990) has documented, the children thus categorized are usually perceived as "foreigners," "intruders," or "immigrants" who speak a different language or dialect or who hold values significantly different from those of the American mainstream. These perceptions have led policymakers (including the U.S. Supreme Court) to highlight the most obvious demographic characteristic—a racial or language difference—in their attempts to address widespread academic underachievement in a population.

In this chapter we will see that there are many other demographic characteristics that help us understand academic underachievement among culturally diverse students. Specifically, this chapter will provide:

1. An overall demographic assessment of factors related to the schooling of culturally diverse populations, including issues of poverty, family stability, and immigrant status.
2. An in-depth discussion of academic performance, including comparative data on high school dropouts, academic achievement, and funding for education.
3. A particular analysis of the challenges associated with the growing number of language minority students—that is, students who come to school with no or limited proficiency in English.

In all this discussion of demographic information, it is easy to lose sight of the actual significance of the numbers. Keep in mind that as cultural and linguistic diversity in our schools increases arithmetically, the challenge to education increases geometrically and possibly exponentially. The schools of tomorrow will be transformed by our response today to a number of pressing variables and agendas. One of the most significant of these variables is the demographic reality of our school-age population.

The Extent of Cultural Diversity Among U.S. Students Today

Expecting a Different World

In contrast to the racial, ethnic, and linguistic diversity of U.S. students, the vast majority of teachers and administrators are white and speak English as their native—and only—language.

Many are experiencing the daunting personal and professional challenge of adapting in adulthood to a degree of diversity that did not exist during their childhood.

A Changing Nation

The average teacher and administrator in his or her thirties or forties grew up in the 1950s and 1960s. Those who were raised in this period before desegregation are likely to have attended school dominated by others of their own ethnic group. It was not until their teens that most encountered the effects of the civil rights movement and other expressions of ethnic presence on a national level. Nor did they experience the swift increases in diversity that have occurred recently. Thus many of today's teachers and their parents grew up expecting a much different world than they now face.

This is not to say that diversity did not exist. In fact, today's senior teachers began their education when the schools had a much larger proportion of foreign-born persons than they do today. To students of that era, however, diversity was probably not so evident, because of segregated ethnic enclaves in housing and schooling and because of the less developed nature of mass communications. In addition, the prevailing "melting pot" ideology matched people's own observations: the children of immigrants should and did abandon their native language and culture in order to become "100 percent Americans."

But the 30-year period straddling the mid-century mark was an anomaly in our history. Until the 1930s, the story of the United States was the story of immigration. The grandparents of today's teachers, who grew up in the early 1900s and were often immigrants themselves, experienced increasing ethnic and linguistic diversity in the society of their youth.

Immigration: The Historical Basis of Diversity

The United States has always been a multicultural, multilingual society. To many Americans, the immigration movement that brought our ancestors to this country is a closed chapter, part of our national past. But from the perspective of the entire spectrum of American history, immigration has been the norm rather than the exception. In this century two generations of adults have grown up in a period of atypically low immigration, an experience that has shaped our perceptions of our country. The new reality is that, in terms of immigration, the United States of 2000 will resemble the United States of 1900 more closely than the United States of 1950. Today's kindergartners will experience increasing population diversity over their lifetimes, just as their great-grandparents did.

A History of Immigration

From 1900 to 1910, nearly 9 million immigrants entered the United States, increasing the population by 10 percent. In the

Table 1.1 Immigration to the United States by Region, 1820–1990, with Special Emphasis on 1971–1980 and 1981–1990

REGION AND COUNTRY OF ORIGIN	1820–1990	1971–1980	1981–1990
All Countries	56,994,014	4,493,314	7,338,062
Europe	37,101,060	800,368	761,550
Austria-Hungary	4,342,782	16,028	24,885
Austria	1,828,946	9,478	18,340
Hungary	1,667,760	6,550	6,545
Belgium	210,556	5,329	7,066
Czechoslovakia	145,801	6,023	7,227
Denmark	370,412	4,439	5,370
France	787,587	25,069	32,353
Germany	7,083,465	74,414	91,961
Greece	703,904	92,369	38,377
Ireland	4,725,133	11,490	31,969
Italy	5,373,108	129,368	67,254
Netherlands	374,232	10,492	12,238
Norway and Sweden	2,145,954	10,472	15,182
Norway	801,224	3,941	4,164
Sweden	1,284,475	6,531	11,018
Poland	606,336	37,234	83,252
Portugal	501,261	101,710	40,431
Romania	204,841	12,393	30,857
Soviet Union	3,443,706	38,961	57,677
Spain	285,148	39,141	20,433
Switzerland	359,439	8,235	8,849
United Kingdom	5,119,150	137,374	159,173
Yugoslavia	136,271	30,540	18,762
Other Europe	181,974	9,287	8,234
Asia	5,019,180	1,588,178	2,738,157
China	914,376	124,326	346,747
Hong Kong	302,230	113,467	98,215
India	455,716	164,134	250,786
Iran	176,851	45,136	116,172
Israel	137,540	37,713	44,273
Japan	462,244	49,775	47,085

Table 1.1   Immigration to the United States by Region, 1820–1990, with Special Emphasis on 1971–1980 and 1981–1990 (*cont.*)

REGION AND COUNTRY OF ORIGIN	1820–1990	1971–1980	1981–1990
Asia (*cont.*)			
Korea	642,248	267,638	333,746
Philippines	1,026,653	354,987	548,764
Turkey	412,327	13,399	23,233
Vietnam	458,277	172,820	280,782
Other Asia	1,030,718	244,783	648,354
North America	13,067,548	1,982,735	3,615,255
Canada and Newfoundland	4,295,585	169,939	156,938
Mexico	3,888,729	640,294	1,655,843
Caribbean	2,703,177	741,126	872,051
Cuba	748,710	264,863	144,578
Dominican Republic	510,136	148,135	252,035
Haiti	234,757	56,335	138,379
Jamaica	429,500	137,577	208,148
Other Caribbean	780,074	134,216	128,911
Central America	819,628	134,640	468,088
El Salvador	274,667	34,436	213,539
Other Central America	544,961	100,204	254,549
South America	1,250,303	295,741	461,847
Argentina	131,118	29,897	27,327
Colombia	295,353	77,347	122,849
Ecuador	155,767	50,077	56,315
Other South America	668,065	138,420	255,356
Other America	110,126	995	458
Africa	334,145	80,779	176,893
Oceania	204,622	41,242	45,205
Not specified	267,459	12	1,032

Source: U.S. Bureau of the Census, *Historical Statistics of the United States, Colonial Times to 1970,* 1975, U.S. Bureau of the Census, *Statistical Abstract of the United States, 1991,* 1990, Washington, DC: Author.

1980s, about the same number of immigrants came to this country, but they accounted for only a 4 percent increase in a now much larger population. In the early decades of this century, and back as far as 1850, as many as 1 in 7 people in the United States were foreign-born. The current rate of 1 in 13 is high only in comparison to the low immigration rates of the 1950s and 1960s, when 1 in 20 Americans was foreign-born. By 2020, when today's kindergartners are in the workforce, the foreign-born population of the United States is again projected to be 1 in 7 people.

Because the United States is so closely identified with the English language, many people assume that Anglo-Americans have always formed the majority group in U.S. society. But the 1990 Census reveals that only 13 percent of Americans claim English ancestry. They are outnumbered by the 15 percent whose families originated in Ireland—and many of these families did not speak English as a native language. An additional 5 percent identify their ancestry as "American"; many of these are Scottish Americans whose families have been in the United States for 9 or 10 generations. Thus, at most, about one-third of all Americans trace their ancestry to the various cultures and languages of Great Britain.

Today, nearly one-fifth of Americans live in a household in which a language other than English is spoken. In half of these households that language is Spanish; the next most common languages are French, German, Italian, and Chinese. Educating students from these immigrant families may seem like an entirely new challenge, but it is not; such students have always been in American schools in large numbers. Throughout most of our history, one in four or five white Americans grew up in an immigrant family.

From 1981 through 1990, more than 7.3 million people immigrated to the United States—a 63 percent increase over the previous decade. Table 1.1 shows a detailed breakdown of immigration to the United States by country of origin. Apart from the sheer magnitude of numbers, what are the characteristics of this immigrant population? In relative terms, which are the significant countries of origin? Perhaps more importantly, what are the greatest changes in immigration patterns and emerging immigration trends?

Significant Countries of Origin

For more than two decades, Mexico has remained the country of origin for the majority of U.S. immigrants. As Table 1.1 shows, an estimated 1,655,843 Mexican citizens emigrated here between 1981 and 1990, exceeding the figure for any other nation by over a million. The Philippines were ranked second with 548,764, and China (346,747), Korea (333,746), and Vietnam

(280,782) followed close behind. Table 1.2, showing the most recent data available, indicates that the rankings changed slightly by the mid-1990s, but Mexico and the Philippines continued to head the list. Among the changes since the 1980s, the decline in immigration from Cuba is especially notable.

During recent decades, which countries of origin exhibited the greatest rates of growth in immigration to the United States? Looking at the two tables, we can see that the number of Salvadoran immigrants increased dramatically in the 1980s, as many Salvadorans fled their war-torn country. Irish immigrants increased 178 percent from the 1970s to the 1980s but declined again by 1995. The average yearly numbers of Iranian and Haitian immigrants have more than doubled since the 1970s. For Poland, the yearly rate in 1995 was nearly four times the average in the 1970s, and figures for other Eastern European countries have risen as well. The Vietnamese immigrant community in this country grew at a rate of 62 percent between 1971 and 1990, and the number of Vietnamese who arrived in 1995 was

Growth Rates in Immigration

Table 1.2 U.S. Immigrants' Country of Origin, 1995	
Mexico	86,960
Philippines	50,962
Vietnam	41,752
Dominican Republic	38,392
China	35,459
India	34,715
Cuba	17,932
Ukraine	17,432
Jamaica	16,335
Korea	16,034
Russia	14,560
Haiti	13,892
Poland	13,804
Canada	12,913
United Kingdom	12,311
El Salvador	11,563
Colombia	10,780
Pakistan	9,743
Taiwan	9,374
Iran	9,178

Source: U.S. Immigration and Naturalization Services, 1995, *Statistical Yearbook of the Immigration and Naturalization Services,* Washington, DC: U.S. Government Printing Office.

even higher than the average for the 1980s. Mexican immigration, however, shows the most significant growth. Immigration from Mexico almost tripled from the 1970s to the 1980s and continued at a high level in the 1990s. This, combined with the fact that Mexico ranks first in actual numbers of immigrants, translates into perhaps the greatest impact on the U.S. population.

These statistics describe a U.S. immigrant population, composed of vastly different peoples, that is both rapidly growing and rapidly diverging. We always have been and continue to be a nation of immigrants. As we will see, this feature of our national identity holds much significance for education.

Education for Immigrants in an Information Age

A basic mission for educators is to prepare young people for an occupational life. But the economic environment has changed dramatically in the past few decades, and even greater changes can be expected before today's students graduate and begin to seek employment.

Economic Changes

Manufacturing jobs used to provide a good living for U.S.-born ethnic minorities and for immigrants. Most jobs in the industrial sector required neither a high level of education nor academic competence in English. But those jobs have largely disappeared. The new economy demands workers who have more than basic skills; employees must be able to think critically and engage in group decision-making, communicate effectively in speaking and in writing, and adapt to changing conditions by learning new skills. In other words, a larger proportion of jobs in the future will require the kind of educational preparation that has traditionally been provided to only the top students.

The American economy is now intertwined with the global marketplace; workers who can interact easily with people of different cultural and linguistic backgrounds will be prized. Even the domestic workplace that today's students will enter is changing as employees and customers are becoming more diverse. Business leaders are well aware that most of their new employees will be minorities and women. Observers of American business trends comment that many companies have gone beyond debating whether they need to change; they are now actively managing diversity. If one of the purposes of education is to train young people to lead productive work lives, then schools will need to prepare all students for employment in a more ethnically, culturally, and linguistically diverse occupational environment.

Factors Affecting Immigrant Student Success. Students from immigrant families of all types are often defined by the one characteristic most of them share—a lack of English fluency. But such a definition masks their diversity and underestimates the challenge facing schools. Schools serve students who are new immigrants, ignorant of American life beyond what they have seen in movies, as well as African Americans, Mexican Americans, Asian Americans, Native Americans, and European Americans whose families have lived here for generations. Students representing dozens of native languages may attend a single school; in some school districts more than 125 languages are spoken by students. In many schools, a majority of the students come from immigrant or ethnic minority families, and these families may move frequently before they settle in one place. Student turnover is often high, and the ethnic mix may shift radically from year to year.

Diversity Among Immigrants

Along with linguistic diversity comes diversity in culture, religion, and academic preparation. Some immigrant students visit their home country frequently, while others lack that opportunity. Some immigrant students have had excellent schooling in their home country, whereas others have had their education interrupted by war, and still others have never attended school. Some are illiterate in their own language. Some speak languages that were only oral until recently; others come from cultures with long literary traditions.

The complexity of the task schools face can be illustrated by describing five hypothetical students from two families. The needs of each student are very different. The Escalonas immigrated from Colombia and the Nguyens from Vietnam. All four parents work together on an electronics assembly line. The Escalonas are both college graduates who taught high school math in their homeland. They have three children:

Maria Escalona (eighth grade): Maria had excellent schooling through the seventh grade in Colombia. The math and science curriculum in her school was more advanced than in the U.S. system. She studied English in Colombia for three years.

Raul Escalona (fifth grade): Raul had good schooling in Colombia, but had not yet begun to study English. Because he is only 10, his academic mastery of Spanish is incomplete.

Teresita Escalona (kindergarten): Teresita attended preschool in Colombia, and she knows the alphabet as well as songs, stories, numbers, shapes, and colors in Spanish.

Maria, Raul, and Teresita will have many language compatriots in their classes.

The Nguyens were farmers in their native country. Both parents attended school through the fourth grade. They have two children:

Binh Nguyen (tenth grade): Binh had a good education through the seventh grade, but has attended school only sporadically in refugee camps since then.

Tui Nguyen (third grade): Tui has had no formal education. Taught by her brother, she can read and write a little Vietnamese.

Binh and Tui have had little exposure to English. They will have a few classmates who speak their native language, but many whose first language is Spanish.

Clearly, the differences among these students—their ages at entry into the U.S. school system, the quality of their prior schooling, their native languages, the number of native language compatriots in their classes, their parents' education and English-language skills, and their family history and current circumstances—will affect their academic success much more than their common lack of English.

The Strategy of Assimilation. How can schools cope with the diversity presented by such students? Should they return to the model of education developed in the early 1900s to deal with the large influx of immigrant youngsters, a system intended to accelerate their assimilation into the American mainstream by replacing their native languages and cultures with those of the United States? In that era, educators confidently sought to fit newcomers into the American mold by teaching them English language and literature, a sugarcoated version of American history, and a respect for the U.S. political system and civic life. Some have recommended taking a similar approach today. Yet it is no longer possible even to describe American culture with confidence. If educators seek to fit all children into a single mold, what mold should that be? There is no single definition of American culture; multiple definitions have been informed by ethnic minority voices.

| Assimilation and Its Costs

The ultimate cost of this philosophy of educational assimilation has never been fully evaluated. How many children were estranged from their family and culture? How many grandparents of today's teachers lost their native language? How many worked a lifetime on the assembly line when they should have gone to college? How many became ashamed of who they were?

When immigrant students become shining academic stars, their success is often attributed to the values and habits of their native culture rather than to their assimilation. There is some evidence that assimilation may actually inhibit academic success. Studies of Mexican, Indian, and Vietnamese immigrants all suggest that those who maintain a strong identification with their native language and culture are more likely to succeed in school than those who readily adapt to American ways (Lucas, 1997; Olsen, 1997).

An Alternative to Assimilation: Giving Immigrants What Americans Take for Granted. Some advocates for students of immigrant families claim that they require special services, while others insist that these students would be better off if they were treated just like all other students. Another perspective would argue that what these students need is what white, native-born, English-speaking American students can take for granted—instruction in their native language, by teachers who share their ethnic and linguistic background, using books that celebrate the same values, heroes, and holidays that their parents celebrate.

Privileges of American Students

Typically, American students have been encouraged since infancy to enjoy books, to work independently, to assert their rights and defend their opinions, and to explore and express their individual feelings and thoughts—all qualities that enhance their potential for success in American schools. If American students were dropped into a Japanese classroom, where skills required for cooperation are valued, or a traditional Yoruba school, where the memorization of long oral passages is the primary learning method, they would have as much difficulty acquiring these new ways of behavior as learning the language.

Language learning itself is a more onerous task for children than is popularly assumed. Young children do not learn a second language effortlessly, and they do not learn faster with more exposure to the new language. Often their oral fluency outstrips their academic competence, and it may take many years for them to reach the appropriate grade-level academic ability in the new language. Contrary to common belief, helping students develop their first-language skills aids them in achieving competence in a second language. The more academic support students receive in their native language, in addition to high-quality instruction in English, the higher their overall achievement in English will be.

The task faced by a child of a non-English-speaking family is daunting indeed. Adults who move from one country to another, even temporarily, often suffer the disorientation of culture shock. Even adults who study a foreign language intensively often find their sense of personal and cultural identity shaken. Studies of speakers of Black English who write and speak in standard English show that they undergo shifts in cultural allegiance as they shift between languages.

Adults have developed sophisticated coping mechanisms, and immigrants can often derive comfort from staying within an ethnic enclave. But their children are thrust into the heart of an American institution—the school—with few resources for self-protection. In addition to having to cope with two languages and cultures, they are often rejected and ridiculed by their native-born American classmates. In the chapters to come we will explore these concepts as they relate to the education of immigrant and culturally diverse students in more depth.

Measuring Racial and Ethnic Diversity

To document the racial and ethnic heterogeneity of our country's population, the U.S. Bureau of the Census uses a set of terms that place individuals in separate exclusionary categories: white, white non-Hispanic, black, and Hispanic (the latter with some five subcategories). Unfortunately, these terms are simplistic and ambiguous and do not accurately represent the true heterogeneity of the U.S. population. It is therefore important to note at the outset of this discussion that these categories are useful only as the most superficial reflection of our nation's true diversity. Given the forced-choice responses allowed them in Census questionnaires, many U.S. citizens whose racial or ethnic identity crosses categories are compelled to answer inaccurately. Racially and culturally we are not "pure" stock, and any such measurement by the Census Bureau, by the Center for Educational Statistics, or by other social institutions that attempt to address the complexity of our diverse population is likely to result in only a vague sketch.

However, once we grant the inherent restrictions on efforts to document population diversity in the United States, we must note that an examination of the available data does provide a suggestive portrait of our society. We can discern a sketchy outline of the specific circumstances of various groups within our nation's boundaries. That sketch depicts consummate social and economic vulnerability for nonwhite and Hispanic families, children, and students. On almost every indicator, nonwhites and Hispanics are "at-risk," meaning they are likely to fall into the lowest quartile on indicators of "well-being": family stability, family violence, family income, child health and development, and educational achievement. The Census data also show that this specific population (usually referred to as the "minority"

Vulnerability for Some Populations

population) has grown significantly in the last two decades and will grow substantially in the decades to come. In the years ahead teachers in the U.S. schools will see increasing numbers of at-risk children in their classrooms.

Projected Trends for U.S. Schools

The most comprehensive report on the growing diversity of the student body in U.S. schools was published in 1991 by the College Board and the Western Interstate Commission for Higher Education. Entitled *The Road to College: Educational Progress by Race and Ethnicity,* this report indicated that the U.S. nonwhite and Hispanic student population would increase from 10.4 million in 1985–1986 to 13.7 million in 1994–1995. These pupils would constitute 34 percent of public elementary and secondary school enrollment in 1994–1995, up from 29 percent in 1985–1986. Enrollment of white students, meanwhile, would rise by only 5 percent, from 25.8 million to 27 million, and its share of the student population would drop from 71 percent to 66 percent in 1994–1995.

Projections for 2026

Figures 1.1 and 1.2 graphically display this astounding shift in student demographics. Figure 1.1 presents actual nonwhite and Hispanic K–12 public school enrollments from 1976 to 1986 and projected enrollments based on changes in enrollment from 1976 to 1986 by decade through 2026. Figure 1.2 presents simi-

Figure 1.1 ▼ **K–12 Public School Enrollment Projections, 1976–2026: Total Versus Nonwhite and Hispanic Enrollment**

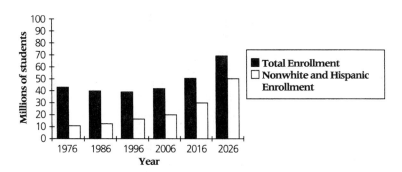

Source: U.S. Department of Education, Office for Civil Rights, *Directory of Elementary and Secondary School Districts and Schools in Selected Districts:* 1976–1977; and 1984 and 1986 Elementary and Secondary School Civil Rights Survey. As cited in U.S. Department of Education, National Center for Education Statistics, *The Condition of Education,* 1991, vol. 1, *Elementary and Secondary Education* (Washington, DC: Author, 1991), p. 68.

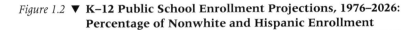

Figure 1.2 ▼ **K–12 Public School Enrollment Projections, 1976–2026: Percentage of Nonwhite and Hispanic Enrollment**

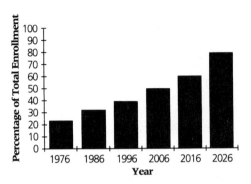

Source: U.S. Department of Education, Office for Civil Rights, *Directory of Elementary and Secondary School Districts and Schools in Selected Districts:* 1976–77; and 1984–86 Elementary and Secondary School Civil Rights Survey. As cited in U.S. Department of Education, National Center for Education Statistics, *The Condition of Education,* 1991, vol. 1, *Elementary and Secondary Education* (Washington, DC: Author, 1991), p. 68.

lar data but focuses on nonwhite and Hispanic student enrollments as a percentage of total enrollment. Each figure depicts a dramatic transformation projected for our nation's student body. Nonwhite and Hispanic student enrollment will grow from 10 million in 1976 to nearly 50 million in 2026. The percentage of those enrollments will rise from 23 percent to 70 percent of the total during this same time. Projections show that in 2026, student representation in our schools will be the exact inverse of what it was in 1990, when white students made up 70 percent of the enrolled K–12 student body.

It is of distinct educational significance that in 1986, 30 to 35 percent (3 million) of nonwhite and Hispanic students were identified as residing in homes in which English was not the primary language (August & García, 1988). Using these figures and extrapolating from the projections displayed in Figures 1.1 and 1.2, we find that by the year 2000 our schools will be educating 6 million students who have limited proficiency in English. By the year 2026 that number will conservatively approximate 15 million students, or somewhere in the vicinity of 25 percent of total elementary and secondary school enrollments. In the next few decades, it will be virtually impossible for a professional educator to serve in a public school setting, or even in any private school context, in which the students are not racially, culturally, or linguistically diverse.

Indicators of Child and Family Well-Being

As many researchers have discovered, educational concerns cannot be appropriately addressed without attending to related indicators of child and family well-being. Children who are healthy and who live in safe and secure social and economic environments generally do very well in today's schools. Students from poor families, on the other hand, are three times more likely to become dropouts than are students from more economically advantaged homes (National Research Council, 1993). Students who reside in economically disadvantaged and socially dangerous environments are at risk for academic underachievement in today's and tomorrow's schools. Our earlier discussion of expected demographic shifts and projected trends in student enrollments is sharpened by a consideration of some economic and social realities. As noted above, family income is correlated with academic performance. Family dislocations, uncertainty about one's future, and stress associated with poverty often undermine a child's ability to concentrate and to learn. Culturally and linguistically diverse students tend to live in situations that are not always compatible with a stable educational experience. Unfortunately, on a number of related measures of child and family well-being, the circumstances are bleak for this growing body of students.

Children Living in Poverty

According to the U.S. Bureau of the Census report *Poverty in the United States: 1995* (cited by National Center for Children in Poverty, 1995), 5 million U.S. children under the age of 18 resided in circumstances of poverty. This represents approximately 20 percent of the total population in this age group and was an increase of some 2 million since 1970. Of the children counted, 6.5 million, or 45 percent, were nonwhite and Hispanic. Table 1.3 presents exact numbers and percentages of children in poverty for 1975 and 1986 and related projections through 2026. These projections indicate that unless poverty is checked in very direct ways, the number of children in poverty will more than double by the year 2026. More than half of them will be nonwhite and Hispanic.

The overall family circumstances expected for these children over the next decades are also alarming. Most children of elementary school age presently reside in families headed by persons under the age of 30. Figure 1.3 provides evidence that these families will be economically disadvantaged. The figure shows median income from 1973 to 1986 and projected income through 2026 for families headed by persons under the age of 30. All families in this category have experienced and are projected to experience a decrease in economic capability. Again, particularly vulnerable will be families headed by persons who

Table 1.3 Children 18-Years-Old and Younger in Poverty, Projected to 2026

RACE OR ETHNICITY	1975	1986	1996	2006	2016	2026
Total students (in millions)	**12.3**	**14.2**	**16.4**	**19.4**	**23.1**	**27.9**
White, non-Hispanic	6.7	7.8	8.8	10.1	11.6	13.2
Total minority	**5.6**	**6.4**	**7.6**	**9.3**	**11.5**	**14.7**
Black	3.8	4.0	4.2	4.4	4.5	4.7
Hispanic	1.7	2.4	3.4	4.9	7.0	10.0
Total percent of poor children	**100**	**100**	**100**	**100**	**100**	**100**
White, non-Hispanic	54.8	54.4	53.6	52.1	50.0	47.2
Total minority	**45.2**	**45.6**	**46.4**	**47.9**	**50.0**	**52.8**
Black	31.5	28.5	25.5	22.5	19.7	16.9
Hispanic	13.7	17.1	20.9	25.4	30.3	35.9

Source: U.S. Bureau of the Census, *Current Population Reports,* Series P-60, *Poverty in the United States,* various years. As cited in the U.S. Department of Education, National Center for Education Statistics, 1991, *The Condition of Education, 1991,* Vol. 1, pp. 200–201, *Elementary and Secondary Education,* Washington, DC: Author.

are nonwhite and Hispanic. By 2026 the median annual family income for nonwhite and Hispanic families will drop to $10,000.

Implications of Poverty

What are the implications for education? Children in families with income below the poverty level are nearly twice as likely to be held back a grade level as their more advantaged classmates. Young people from low-income families also tend to leave school early and to enter the labor force to earn additional income for themselves or their families. While work experience during adolescence can have positive effects, recent research in-

Figure 1.3 ▼ **Meridian Annual Income for Families Headed by Persons Under Age 30 (in 1986 Dollars), Projected to 2026**

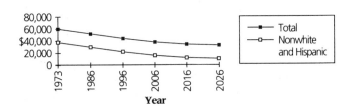

Source: C. M. Johnson, A. M. Sum, and J. D. Weill, (1988), Appendix: Table 3. As cited in National Center for Children in Poverty, School of Public Health, *Five Million Children: A Statistical Profile of Our Poorest Young Citizens* (New York: Columbia University, 1990), p. 47.

dicates that working more than half-time during the high school years can undermine academic performance (National Commission on Children, 1991). As for those students from homes in which English is not the primary language, over 90 percent in 1984 met poverty guidelines that allowed them to receive free or reduced-price lunches (Development Associates, 1984).

Much more eloquent than any quantitative analyses of this situation are the more intensive case studies that dramatically tell the disheartening educational stories of these underserved populations (Kozol, 1991; National Research Council, 1993; Rose, 1989; Wong-Fillmore, 1991). Numerous expository in-depth studies have found that serious disruptions of individual, family, and community functioning occur when young children from nonmainstream backgrounds encounter the schooling process. There is much evidence, both in hard figures and in personal testimony, that members of culturally and linguistically diverse populations in the United States face social, economic, and educational problems.

Student Diversity and Educational Vulnerability

The inevitable conclusion to draw from patterns evident in the preceding indicators of child and family well-being is that school-age children and their families, particularly those who are nonwhite and Hispanic, will continue to be placed in economic and social situations that increase their social, economic, and educational vulnerability. Today's educators and educators of the future will be challenged by a student body of increasing cultural and linguistic diversity. Many of our students will come to school from situations that are already identified as educationally disadvantageous. Even though as educators we have little power to ameliorate those situations, we must heed their effects in the academic setting.

Three important and much-debated variables are key to understanding the real human consequences of educational vulnerability: dropout rate, measures of academic achievement, and educational funding policies:

Dropout Rate. A major indicator of academic success in the United States is completion of high school. One of the national educational goals adopted by the 1990 Educational Summit in Charlottesville, Virginia, is to increase the U.S. high school completion rate to 90 percent by the year 2000. The dynamics of school completion are not well understood, however, and the cause-and-effect relationships involved are unclear (Fernandez & Shu, 1988). Much of the confusion stems from the variety of methods researchers have used to define what is meant by "completion." Fortunately, the National Center for Education Statistics (NCES) has begun to address this confusion. NCES issued two reports (Frase, 1989; Kaufman & Frase, 1990) that attempt to systematize our understanding of high school completion by defining the following set of dropout rates:

Types of Dropout Rate Reports

1. *Event rates report:* Compiled within a single year, an **event rates report** gives the percentage of students who left high school without receiving a diploma. This is a measure of the actual event of dropping out.
2. *Status rates report:* Compiled at any point in time, a **status rates report** gives the percentage of the population of a given age range who either (1) have not finished high school or (2) are not enrolled. This measure reflects the current status of a group in the whole population, including adults.
3. *Cohort rates report:* Compiled over a given time period, a **cohort rates report** describes what happens to a single group of students. This measure reflects changes in any given group over time.

Status and cohort reports provide a useful view of high school completion, since they take into consideration what happens to students after they leave school. These reports indicate that high school completion rates for all persons aged 16 to 24 have generally declined in the last 20 years. In 1989, about 4 million persons in the United States aged 16 to 24 were high school dropouts. In 1994, by contrast, 32.6 million persons aged 16 to 24 were high school dropouts (NCES, 1996). Prior to 1994, an average of 87 percent of all U.S. students received their high school diploma or its equivalent by the age of 24; by 1994 that figure had fallen to 85.8 percent (NCES, 1996).

Comparative Dropout Rates

Moreover, both event and status reports show that nonwhite and Hispanic students drop out of high school at two to three times the rate of white students. Hispanic youth have the highest national dropout rate, African Americans the second highest, and whites the lowest. During the period 1987–1989 about 8 percent of Hispanic students dropped out of school each year, an event rate almost twice as high as that for white students; 7 percent of African American students dropped out during that same period. More revealing are the status report data. In 1989, among the population aged 16 to 24, only 67 percent of Hispanics had completed high school or its equivalency, versus 86 percent of African Americans and 88 percent of whites (Kaufman & Frase, 1990). Using the most recent data available, NCES (1996) reported that in 1994, of persons aged 18 to 24, 61.8 percent of Hispanics had completed high school or its equivalency, versus 83.3 percent of African Americans and 90.7 percent of whites. In other words, there was a decline in high school completion for Hispanics and African Americans and an increase for whites. These same data indicate that high school completion rates are lowest in metropolitan areas, which have the highest concentrations of nonwhite and Hispanic populations. Completion rates are highest in suburban areas.

Academic Achievement. We have determined that high school completion is problematic for nonwhite and Hispanic students. How do these students do while they are in school? The NCES (1996) also has generated a set of data that addresses this question. The most revealing data concern grade-level achievement as measured by standardized tests of academic achievement over the years 1989 to 1995. This measure attempts to assess the relative number of students who are not achieving at the academic level considered normal for their age, which is called the **modal grade level.** Table 1.4 summarizes these data by showing the percentage of 8-year-olds and 13-year-olds who are performing one or more years below the expected grade level. The data are presented by gender, race, and ethnicity.

Performance Below Modal Grade

This table indicates that the percentage of students performing one or more years below modal grade level has increased overall for boys and girls and for whites, blacks, and Hispanics at each age level over the period reported. For 8-year-olds, the percentage of students performing below modal grade level increased from 18.1 percent to 20.2 percent; for 13-year-olds, the percentage remained the same at 31 percent. It is important to note that the percentage almost doubled for all groups for ages 8–10 to 12–14 years of age. In addition, an interesting pattern emerges for black and Hispanic students. At the age of 8 in 1995, there is little difference in below-level performance for whites (14.6 percent), blacks (14.8 percent), and Hispanics (17.5 percent). But by the age of 13, the discrepancy is quite significant. Whereas 29.0 percent of white 13-year-olds performed below grade level in 1989, the figure was 38 percent for blacks and 38.4 percent for Hispanics. From roughly third grade to eighth grade, academic achievement drops off significantly for all students and even more so for blacks and Hispanics as compared to whites.

The unfortunate result is that by the eighth grade 40 percent or more of black and Hispanic students are performing one grade

Table 1.4 Academic Performance of U.S. Students According to Modal Grade Level

PERCENTAGE OF 6- TO 8-YEAR-OLDS ENROLLED BELOW MODAL GRADE, BY RACE AND ETHNICITY, 1989–1995

Year	ALL STUDENTS			WHITE			BLACKS			HISPANICS		
	Male	Female	Average	Male	Female	Average	Male	Female	Average	Male	Female	Average
1989	21.4	25.1	18.1	22.4	26	18.6	19.6	21.7	17.5	21.9	23.7	20
1990	21.5	23.9	19.1	21.9	24.6	19	21.9	23.2	20.7	21.5	22.2	20.7
1991	21.2	24	18.2	21.3	24.4	18.1	21	22.9	19	21.8	22.7	20.8
1992	19.4	21.6	17.1	19.5	21.5	17.3	20.6	24.5	16.7	16.2	15.6	16.8
1993	18.7	21.2	16.3	18.8	21.4	15.9	20	21.8	18	18.9	19.1	18.9
1994	18.9	21.1	16.5	19.4	22	16.7	18.4	19.4	17.5	16.8	16.4	17.2
1995	17.5	20.2	14.6	17.7	20.5	14.7	16.8	18.8	14.8	14.4	11.4	17.5

PERCENTAGE OF 12- TO 14-YEAR-OLDS ENROLLED BELOW MODAL GRADE LEVEL, BY RACE AND ETHNICITY, 1989–1995

Year	ALL STUDENTS			WHITE			BLACKS			HISPANICS		
	Male	Female	Average	Male	Female	Average	Male	Female	Average	Male	Female	Average
1989	36.7	26.6	31.6	35	24.5	30	44.8	37.7	41.2	40	39.7	40
1990	36.2	25.7	31	33.3	23.2	28.2	52.7	39.3	46	40.2	34.9	37.5
1991	34.7	24.6	30	32.5	22.6	27.5	46.2	35	41	43.9	27.6	35.7
1992	37	24.6	31	35.8	23.2	29.5	44.5	31.2	38	42.5	25	33.7
1993	35.4	26.4	31	33.8	24.8	29.3	44.3	33.1	39	34.2	29	32
1994	35.6	26.7	31.1	34.4	25.7	30	39.9	32.3	36.1	36.3	28.5	32.4
1995	35.2	26	31	33.4	24.8	29.1	45	30.9	38	42.4	34.5	38.4

Source: National Center for Education Statistics, 1995, *The Condition of Education, 1995,* Washington, DC: U.S. Department of Education.

level or more below expected and normal achievement levels. These findings, in concert with the previously discussed high school completion and dropout data, raise important educational concerns. Clearly, as the population of nonwhite and Hispanic students increases to an estimated 70 percent of the total U.S. student population in 2026, this underachievement will be an extreme waste of intellectual potential—a waste that we cannot afford in the least. Intervention of some sort will be necessary to avoid squandering our nation's valuable human resources.

Educational Funding Policies. Educational financing in the United States is not without its national, state, and local complications. On the average, 90 percent of any educational expenditure consists of tax dollars flowing directly from local or state sources. Less than 10 percent of these expenditures come from federal sources. Although funding for education increased substantially in the United States during the 1980s, education spending actually declined slightly as a proportion of the gross national product to just over 3.5 percent, which is the lowest for all "developed" countries. In real terms, overall state and local spending rose 26 percent between 1980 and 1988, but the federal share actually decreased by 2 percent (Committee for Economic Development, 1991b).

Keep in mind that nonwhite and Hispanic children reside primarily in metropolitan areas in densely populated pockets of concentrated poverty and racial and ethnic segregation (Kozol, 1991). These children are likely to attend troubled schools with fewer resources and larger classes (Beyond Rhetoric, 1991). Moreover, these children have been more negatively affected than others by recent changes in educational funding policies. The reduction of federal assistance to education, including funds for providing compensatory education and desegregating school districts, has reduced the fiscal resources directly available for the education of these children (Levin, 1986). Districts that cannot be integrated because they lack white students are not eligible for enhanced funding available to establish science and math magnet schools, an emerging federal funding priority (Oakes, 1991). The educational personnel of such schools are not concerned with the educational buzzwords of recent years, such as "restructuring," "reform," "teacher empowerment," "site-based management," "teacher competencies," "outcome accountability," and "national goals." Instead, they are preoccupied with obtaining the bare necessities: windows, books, typewriters, classrooms with heat, working bathrooms, sufficient lighting, and long-overdue repairs and renovations (Kozol, 1991; Rose, 1989).

Loss of Federal Support

These schools have been transformed into institutions that must spend valuable time trying to secure the resources needed for basic survival. Much like developing countries, they seek alliances and petition for grants and loans from one source after another. These schools "beg" from city, state, federal, business, and charity sources. They do so only because the basic resources are not provided by present funding structures and formulas. In fact, those structures and formulas work to their disadvantage. These schools are in cities in which competition for tax dollars is great. These communities have high unemployment and underemployment and are pressed to provide a higher level of related social services. They are also competing to retain businesses. Such variables directly affect the resources that can be directed toward education.

Underfunding and "Fairness"

Most directly, students in these schools are underfunded, even in times that argue for "fairness" in school financing. As a society, we make it quite clear that we abhor the notion of social privilege. We strongly believe that an individual's financial background should not be a deterrent to educational success. Yet such a belief does not seem consistent with the ways in which we allocate educational resources. These fiscal disparities were identified over three decades ago. In 1968, in a now famous legal case, Demetrio Rodriguez, a parent in the Edgewood School District in San Antonio, Texas, argued that his children were underfunded relative to children in an adjacent school district only a few miles away. In the Edgewood School District (which was 96 percent nonwhite) residents paid a higher tax rate than did residents of the nearby district, which was predominantly white. Edgewood was able to generate only $37 for each pupil, and with additional resources provided by the state, spent $231 yearly per student. The neighboring school district generated $412 per student on its own, and with state resources spent $543 yearly per student. This amounted to a differential of over 100 percent.

Coons, Clune, and Sugarman (1970) documented the distinct differential funding between "rich white" districts and "poor minority" districts identified in this legal action as a national phenomenon. They argued that there is in such funding discrepancies something incongruous with the American ideology of fairness: "a differential of any magnitude the sole justification for which is an imaginary school district line" (p. 210). These boundaries and funding inequalities combined to make the public schools the institution that educated the rich and kept the poor uneducated (Coons et al., 1970).

Comparative Per-Student Spending

Preferential education for the rich and denial of education for the poor continues today. Table 1.5 provides an analysis of more recent educational funding differentials for school districts in New Jersey, New York, and Chicago. Arranged in order of per-

Table 1.5 Selected Per-Student Yearly Expenditures

SCHOOL FUNDING IN THE CHICAGO AREA (1988–89 SCHOOL YEAR)		SCHOOL FUNDING IN NEW JERSEY (1988–89 SCHOOL YEAR)		SCHOOL FUNDING IN SIX DISTRICTS IN THE NEW YORK CITY AREA (THREE-YEAR PERIOD)		
School or District	Spending per Pupil	District	Spending per Pupil	District	1986–87	1989–90
Niles Township High School	$9,371	Princeton	$7,725	Manhasset	$11,372	$15,084
New Trier High School	$8,823	Summit	$7,275	Jericho	$11,325	$14,355
Glencoe (Elementary & Junior High School)	$7,363	West Orange	$6,505	Great Neck	$11,265	$15,594
		Cherry Hill	$5,981	Mount Vernon	$6,433	$9,112
Winnetka (Elementary & Junior High School)	$7,059	Jersey City	$4,566	Roosevelt	$6,339	$8,349
		East Orange	$4,457	New York City	$5,585	$7,299
Wilmette (Elementary & Junior High School)	$6,009	Paterson	$4,422			
		Camden	$3,538			
Chicago (average all grade levels)	$5,265					

Source: Chicago Panel on School Policy and Finance; Educational Law Center, Newark, New Jersey; Statistical Profiles of School Districts, New York State Board of Education; *New York Times.* As cited in J. Kozol (1991). *Savage Inequalities: Children in America's Schools,* New York: Crown, pp. 236–237.

pupil yearly expenditure, these data show that school districts with the greatest proportion of nonwhite and Hispanic populations consistently spend the least amount per student.

Thirty years after research documented patterns in funding that were creating a "class" structure in education, with nonwhites and Hispanic students at the lower end, we have achieved no substantive remedy. Court actions seeking such remedies are being revisited by the Edgewood School District as well as by school districts in California, Illinois, New Jersey, and New York. Kozol (1991) sums up this situation best:

> These are Americans. Why do we reduce them to this beggary—and why, particularly, in public education? Why not spend on children here [in schools underfunded] at least what we would be investing in their education if they lived within a wealthy district like Winnetka, Illinois, or Cherry Hill, New Jersey, or Manhasset, Rye, or Great Neck in New York? Wouldn't this be a natural behavior in an affluent society that seems to value fairness in so many other areas of life? Is fairness less important to Americans today than in earlier times? Is it viewed as slightly tiresome and incompatible with hardnosed values? What do Americans believe about equality? (p. 41)

A Wasted Resource

The most pressing argument for our attention to the above signposts of educational vulnerability is the prospect of losing a significant body of our country's human resources at a time when we need all the resources we can muster. Added to this is the fact that young people lost from productive membership in our society often become a substantial resource liability. Estimates of fiscal resources diverted to high school dropouts throughout the United States in areas such as health services, unemployment, employment training, and social welfare reach billions of dollars yearly (National Research Council, 1993; National Commission on Children, 1991). Close to 85 percent of the people in the U.S. prison system are high school dropouts. Why can't our educational system invest in children so they become assets instead of liabilities? The irony of our predicament is most telling. The cost for a one-year stay in most state and federal prisons is nearly $30,000—the approximate cost, including tuition, fees, books, room and board, and miscellaneous, of sending a student to Harvard University for one year.

Costs of Low Educational Achievement

Recent efforts such as the Taylor Plan recognize the debilitating effect of educational vulnerability and work to find solutions.

Patrick Taylor, a Louisiana state legislator and the author of the
plan, has begun a campaign to revolutionize U.S. education. His
program calls for guaranteed free college tuition and fees for any
student who completes a high school education with a C-plus
average and scores well on college entrance exams. In 1992 Taylor convinced the Louisiana state legislature to adopt the plan,
which recognizes that keeping students in high school makes
economic sense. In Louisiana, the long-term cost (loss in tax-
payer revenue) associated with each individual who drops out of
high school is estimated at $250,000. This estimate does not in-
clude the extra cost associated with dropouts who become involved in the criminal justice system, which is an additional
$25,000 to $35,000 per person per year. In short, in terms of education the old adage seems to apply: pay now or pay later. We
will pay a lot more later.

**Loss of
Contribution
to Society**
    Besides its monetary costs to our society, dropping out involves
more intangible human costs. In my own family of ten siblings, the
children of migrant farm workers, only four graduated from high
school and only one—this one—had the opportunity to attend
college. As in so many other families, the members of our household had the native intelligence, motivation, and work ethic to
succeed in high school and beyond. Yet the circumstances of
poverty, cultural and linguistic difference, and the absence of a responsive educational system led to the direct underdevelopment
of the family's potential. This underdevelopment pertains not only
to each family member's individual educational, economic, and
personal growth, but to his or her potential contribution to the
family itself, to the community in which it is embedded, and to society at large. Considering the overall challenges faced by our
country and our planet, continued neglect of this potential is a
wastefulness we can no longer afford.

The Implications for Educators

The demographic information we have been discussing indicates
that the diversity in our schools is a recent but an explosive and
long-term phenomenon. Teachers, administrators, and other educational professionals who received their training over a decade
or two ago were not encumbered by the challenges facing preservice teaching candidates today. A readiness to respond to the
challenge presented by a highly diverse student body was not a
recognized part of their training. Indeed, a decade or two ago
relatively few individuals of minority status succeeded academically, with the result that even now the makeup of the teaching
profession does not match the demographics of the students it

serves. For the 1995–1996 school year, over 88 percent of the 2.6 million public and private school teachers and 103,000 school administrators were white. Less than 12 percent were nonwhite and Hispanic: 8 percent were African American, 3 percent were Hispanic, and less than 1 percent were American Indian, Alaskan Native, or Asian or Pacific Islander. In this same academic year, however, nonwhite and Hispanic academic enrollment was at 30 percent (NCES, 1996).

Effective Teaching

It appears that in the near future the vast majority of schoolteachers and administrators will be white, while the proportion of nonwhite and Hispanic students will continue to increase rapidly (NCES, 1991). What significance does this hold for the training of teachers? Although it is difficult to pinpoint specific attributes of teachers that have served a diverse student body effectively, recent research efforts have attempted to identify some. Unlike earlier reports that identified and described effective programs only, recent reports have sought out effective programs and/or schools and then attempted to describe the specific instructional and attitudinal character of the teacher (Carter & Chatfield, 1986; McLeod, 1996; Pease-Alvarez, Espinoza, & García, 1991; Tikunoff, 1983; Villegas, 1991).

Skills of "Good" Teachers

Dwyer (1991) identifies four domains of instruction at which "good" teachers excel: (1) teaching for content knowledge, (2) teaching for student learning, (3) creating a classroom community conducive to student learning, and (4) displaying teacher professionalism. Villegas (1991) has extended these four domains for teachers who serve a student population that is culturally and linguistically diverse. She suggests that "good" teachers in these classroom contexts incorporate culturally responsive pedagogy, meaning that they adjust their teaching strategies in response to the learning styles of individual students.

Concern for the effectiveness of teachers is not new. From the earliest days of education program evaluation, the quality of the instructional staff has been considered a significant feature (Heath, 1982). Unfortunately, for programs serving students of minority status, the evaluation of "effectiveness" has lately been consumed by an empirical concern for multicultural representation in the content of curriculum, at the expense of an examination of teaching strategies themselves. For programs dealing with students with limited English proficiency, interest has centered only on the use or nonuse of the students' native language and the development of English-language skills (August & García, 1988). Very little consideration is given to the attributes desired in the professional and paraprofessional staff members who implement the myriad of program types that serve students in compensatory education. Typically, staff evaluation deals with the number of years of service and the extent of formal educational training (Olsen, 1988). Yet most educational researchers will admit that the effect of any instructional intervention is directly related to the quality of implementation by the instructor. A recent report issued by the California Commission on Teacher Credentialing verified that because of high teacher turnover—and large numbers of misassigned teachers and classrooms staffed by teachers holding only emergency (that is, temporary and not state approved) credentials—a disproportionate number of poor and minority students are taught during their entire school career by the least-qualified personnel.

Little Focus on Staff Quality

Problems in Training and Assessment

It is important to note that professional teaching organizations such as the National Education Association (NEA), the American Federation of Teachers (AFT), and the National Association for the Education of Young Children (NAEYC)—to name a few of the largest—have specifically addressed the need for teachers to receive special training in teaching a culturally diverse student body. Certification agencies, such as the National Council for Accreditation of Teacher Educators (NCATE) and the California Commission on Teaching Credentialing, have included particular provisions related to "multicultural" education that institutions of higher

Special Training Recommended

BECOMING A RESPONSIVE TEACHER

Educational Backgrounds of Today's Immigrant Students

Over the past two decades, U.S. classrooms have undergone a dramatic change. Anyone coming into contact with the school system—whether educator, student, parent, policymaker, or service provider—cannot help but notice the profound and continuous diversification of every facet of the student population: racial, ethnic, religious, and social. This trend is hardly new, but its accelerated pace is having a tremendous impact on our educational system.

Each year, thousands of school-age immigrant children arrive in the United States seeking a better life. Each enters school with his or her own unique educational history and life experiences. Consider the following examples:

Somxai and Souphanh. Somxai and Souphanh Noum, a teenage brother and sister, spent the last seven years in a refugee camp in Laos waiting for resettlement in another country. After six years with no schooling in the refugee camp, they were provided with a few months of "survival" English to prepare them for life in a new land and a new culture.

Swetlana. Swetlana Borishkevich, a teenage Ukrainian, attended regular classes in the Soviet Union through the eighth grade, but she was not able to fulfill her wish to enroll in vocational training in the Soviet Union because her family fled to Italy. From there, they came to the United States, where she is enrolled in a large secondary school in New York City.

José. José Cardenas, a Mexican immigrant who came to the United States with his uncle, attended school in Mexico only occasionally, since he had to spend most of his time helping on the family farm. Although José is a very mature 16-year-old, he has completed only the third grade. He now

BECOMING A RESPONSIVE TEACHER *Cont.*

finds himself in an ESL program in Los Angeles with children who are much younger. He is embarrassed to be there and is quite bored with the endless drill. He can hardly wait to drop out of school and go to work in a fast-food restaurant.

Soo Jung Chu. Last year, Soo Jung Chu transferred from a prestigious Korean school to an American public school. Soo Jung Chu was at the top of his class in Korea. Now he feels intense frustration whenever he can't understand his schoolwork in English, but he is afraid to ask for help because it makes him feel dumb. He knows that the math class the school counselor placed him in is a "bonehead" class far below his mathematical abilities.

▼ Meeting the Challenge

1. Imagine you are one of the students described above. Write a journal entry expressing your thoughts and feelings about your first day of school in the United States. Which areas of the educational experience seem the most difficult? Which seem most exciting?
2. Select one of the young people described above and suggest two alternative ways in which a classroom teacher might introduce the student to his or her new school peers. Remember the importance of first impressions.
3. If you were the classroom teacher for one of more of these students, what would you want to know about their family backgrounds? What would you want to know about their languages and the cultures of their countries of origin?
4. What are the implications for these students' lives if their educational needs are not met by our schools? List the job opportunities available to each one of them if they drop out of high school.

education must implement in order to be accredited as teacher-training institutions and to ensure that their graduates will be considered viable candidates for state teacher credentialing.

Unfortunately, even though the need to train and assess teachers for competence in teaching culturally diverse students is a widely accepted idea, present modes of training and assessment remain highly problematic. The data quite clearly portray the problems in assessing individual professional competence. Present assessment practices can be criticized on several levels (McGahie, 1991; Shimberg, 1983; Sternberg & Wagner, 1986):

Criticisms of Current Assessment Practices

1. Although professional competence evaluations usually address only a narrow range of practice situations, teaching professionals engage in very complex planning, development, implementation, problem-solving, and crisis management. These endeavors usually require technical skills and knowledge that are not easily measured.

2. Professional competence evaluations are biased toward assessing formally acquired knowledge, likely because of the use of similar assessment for student academic achievement. We assess teachers the same way we assess students, even though we have differing expectations regarding these populations.

3. Despite the presumed importance of "practice" skills, professional competence assessments devote little attention to the assessment of enunciated practice skills. With regard to teachers of culturally diverse students, we do have some understanding of specific skills that might be necessary. Even so, because of the lack of specific research in this area, it remains difficult to articulate the exact skills to recommend for assessment.

4. Almost no attention is given to the assessment of what has earlier been identified as the "disposition" and "affective" domains of the teacher, discussed more specifically in Chapter 8. In recent analyses of "effective" teachers, these attributes were identified as being as significant for student learning, as are content knowledge and practice skills (Pease-Alvarez, Espinoza, & García 1991; Villegas, 1991).

In addition to the preceding concerns, professional assessment instruments are subject to severe violations of reliability and validity. Feldt and Brennan (1989) have demonstrated that components of measurement error are highly inconsistent in professional teacher assessment. Test validity is also a fundamental problem (Berk, 1986).

Keep in mind that inferences about a teacher's professional competence or ability to practice are actually inferences about what the researcher has decided is important to measure. Test-makers construct an assessment, and soon are willing to say that whoever scores at a certain level on that assessment is competent. Underlying the assessment, however, is the often questionable legitimacy of the constructs the test-makers defined. What if their list of "most important teacher attributes" is not, in fact, particularly pertinent to classroom realities? We presently lack any definitive body of research and knowledge regarding the constructs that define good teachers in general and good teachers of culturally diverse students in particular. That knowledge base is developing, but it is presently inadequate (García, 1991a).

Questionable Basis for Assessment

The Connoisseur Model

Given the inadequacies of the current means of assessment, what tools can we use? According to McGahie (1991), despite the appearance of objectivity in assessment instruments, at present teacher assessment is actually operating according to the **connoisseur model,** which carries certain presuppositions that are relevant to the education of our diverse student body:

Assumptions of the Model

1. Not all features of professional practice can be quantified.
2. There is no "one best answer" to a professional problem or question.
3. Connoisseurs are unbiased, are fair in rendering judgments, and—because of their demonstrated professional competence and commitment—are the most effective evaluators of teaching professionals.

The connoisseur model is routinely and explicitly used in a number of professional assessment endeavors, such as those in the visual and performing arts. We would never imagine using a "test" to determine the winner of an Academy Award. In fact, to determine "Teacher of the Year" honors at local, state, and national levels, connoisseurs are regularly called upon to serve as judges. They are asked to use their varying experience and expertise to identify the "best" teacher among the candidates nominated. Close examination of present methods of evaluating teacher-training programs indicates that the connoisseur model is the primary model in operation. In an NCATE accreditation review, "experts" are sent to evaluate the effectiveness of local teacher-training programs. In turn, instructors in those local programs, also acting in the role of connoisseurs, evaluate individual teacher candidates.

Might the connoisseur model be an acceptable way to train and assess the competencies of teachers who will face the challenges of an increasingly diverse student population? Unfortunately, due to the explosion of this diverse population and our own professional unpreparedness, we are learning how to apply the connoisseur model at the same time that we are using it as an assessment instrument. Because of the limited number of experts or connoisseurs available, and the diversity of students and the myriad programs that serve them, training and assessment of teachers remain highly problematic. Over time, as we develop a large corps of connoisseurs with special knowledge and experience regarding student cultural diversity, it will be possible to utilize this model—and it will likely be the only model appropriate. At present, however, it is not possible to implement the connoisseur model of evaluation on any large scale with the hope that it will be either reliable or valid.

We know now from both case-study observations and educational research data that the teaching expertise of professionals charged with meeting the challenges of diversity is not sufficient. The individual teachers held responsible for this gargantuan task have not been well prepared, and we are beginning to address

Challenge for New Teachers

that fact. You may be reading this book because of your interest, concern, and specific professional obligations in teaching or related educational professions. It is important to recognize that we are struggling together in this enterprise. We are far from achieving the instructional expertise that will effectively meet the growing challenges of diversity. Those challenges will not dissipate, and you will likely be called upon to assist directly in developing and implementing educational initiatives to meet them. You will not be just an actor on this stage. You will be strategically involved in writing the script.

The Language Minority Student

In our demographic discussion of student diversity, one distinctive subpopulation will receive selective attention because of its growing size, both relatively and absolutely, and its precarious situation within our educational institutions: **language minority students,** who come to the schooling process without the language skills through which that process is communicated. As the previous demographic data have indicated, in the next two decades in the United States, language minority students will comprise some 15 percent of K–12 enrollment. By 2026, these students are projected to make up nearly a quarter of our student body.

Language Diversity

Language minority students present a special challenge to our educational institutions because of their linguistic diversity. So much of what we do in the formal teaching and learning enterprise requires the effective communication of specific facts, concepts, ideas, and problem-solving strategies. Students with linguistic diversity encounter this teaching and learning enterprise not lacking in abilities but rich in communication skills that do not match those required in the classroom. If it is ineptly handled, this scenario is a formula for failure, despite the intellectual gifts such students might possess.

The education of students who come to our schools speaking a language other than English has received considerable research, policy, and practice attention in the last two decades. The U.S. Department of Education and several private foundations have supported specific demographic studies and instructional research related to these students, from preschool through college. Congress has authorized legislation targeted directly at these students on six occasions (1968, 1974, 1984, 1987, and 1994), while numerous states have enacted laws and developed explicit program guidelines aimed at meeting their needs. Moreover, federal district courts and the U.S. Supreme Court have concluded adjudication proceedings that directly influence the education of language minority students. This significant attention has allowed answers to some important questions that were unanswerable less than a decade ago. The following discussion will highlight these questions and their respective treatment in light of emerging information regarding language minority students.

Who Are These Students?

I was one of these students when I entered elementary school in 1952. Spanish was my first language as well as my home language, although my older brothers and sisters and I had achieved significant English proficiency. In the present system of labels for such children, I would have been classified as *limited English proficient* (LEP) and would have been referred to as a "language minority student," "a linguistically and culturally diverse student," or an "English-language learner."

Attempts at Definition

As one searches today for a comprehensive definition of such a student, a continuum of attempts unfolds. At one end of the continuum are general definitions such as "students who come from homes in which a language other than English is spoken." At the other end are such highly operationalized definitions as "students who scored in the first quartile on a standardized test of English-language proficiency." Regardless of the definition adopted, it is apparent that this sort of student comes in a variety of linguistic shapes and forms. Over 189 distinct languages groups have been identified in the language minority population in the United States.

Even in the largest of these groups—the "Hispanic" population—some members are monolingual Spanish speakers while others are to some degree bilingual. Other non-English-speaking groups in the United States are similarly heterogeneous. And these subpopulations are culturally as well as linguistically distinct.

Thus it is highly problematic to describe the "typical" language minority student. However, put simply, we might agree that such a student is one who:

▼ substantively participates in a non-English-speaking social environment;

▼ has acquired the normal communicative abilities of that social environment; and

▼ is exposed to a substantive English-speaking environment, more than likely for the first time, during the formal schooling process.

The various estimates of the number of language minority students compiled by the federal government (Development Associates, 1984, 1993; O'Malley, 1981; Waggoner, 1991) differ because of the particular definition adopted for identifying these students, the measure utilized to obtain the estimate, and the statistical treatment applied to generalize beyond the actual sample obtained. For example, O'Malley (1981) defined the language minority student population by establishing a specific cutoff score on an English-language proficiency test administered to a stratified sample of students. Development Associates (1984) estimated the population by using reports from a stratified sample of local school districts. Because of such differences in methodology, estimates of language minority students have ranged from 2,500,000 (Development Associates, 1993) to 4,600,000 (U.S. Bureau of the Census, 1991). Whatever its exact size, this population has the following attributes:

Statistics on Language Minority Students

1. Although these children reside throughout the United States, there is distinct geographical clustering. For example, about 75 percent of language minority children are found in Arizona, Colorado, California, Florida, New Jersey, New Mexico, New York, and Texas.

2. Of the language minority children in grades K–6 in 1993, 76 percent had a Spanish-language background; 8 percent were Southeast Asian (Vietnamese, Cambodian, Hmong, and so on); 5 percent were European; 5 percent were East Asian (such as Chinese and Korean); and 5 percent had language backgrounds designated as "other" (such as Arabic or Navaho).

3. In the 19 states most highly affected by the language minority issue in the national study done by Development Associates (1993), 17 percent of the total K–6 student population was estimated as language minority.

What Types of Educational Programs Serve These Students?

The staff of a school district with language minority students has many program options: "transitional bilingual education," "maintenance bilingual education," "English as a second language," "immersion," "sheltered English," "submersion," and so on (these are all the names of program types developed by the U.S. General Accounting Office, 1987a). Ultimately, most staffs will reject such labels and instead decide to answer the following questions:

1. What are the native-language and English-language characteristics of the students, families, and communities we serve?
2. What model of instruction is desired?
   a. How do we use the native language(s) and English *as mediums of instruction?*
   b. How do we handle the instruction of the native language(s) and English?
3. What staff and resources are necessary to implement the desired instruction?

School district staff have been creative in developing a wide range of language minority student programs that attempt to respond to these questions by addressing the needs of (1) different language groups (Spanish, Vietnamese, Chinese, and so on); (2) different grade levels within a school; (3) different subgroups within a classroom; and (4) different levels of language proficiency. The result has been a broad and at times perplexing variety of program models.

These program initiatives can be differentiated by the way they utilize the native language and English during instruction. Development Associates (1993) surveyed 333 school districts in the 19 states that serve over 80 percent of the language minority students in the United States. For grades K–5, they report the following salient features of the instruction of language minority students:

Features of Current Programs

1. Ninety-three percent of the schools reported that the use of English predominated in their programs; conversely, 7 percent indicated that the use of the native language predominated.
2. Sixty percent of the schools reported that both the native language and English were utilized during instruction.

3. Thirty percent of the schools reported minimal or no use of the native language during instruction.

Two-thirds of these schools chose to utilize some form of bilingual curriculum to serve this population of students. However, one-third minimized or altogether ignored the native language in their instruction of language minority students. Recall that approximately three-fourths of language minority students in this country are of Spanish-speaking backgrounds. Programs that serve them have been characterized primarily as **transitional bilingual education,** which means that they offer a transition from early-grade Spanish-emphasis instruction to later-grade English-emphasis instruction and eventually to English-only instruction.

For the one-third of the students receiving little or no instruction in their native language, two alternative types of instructional approaches likely predominate: **English as a second language (ESL)** and **immersion.** Each primarily uses English during instruction but does not ignore the fact that the students have limited English proficiency. However, the instructors in these programs do not need to be able to speak the native language of the students. Moreover, these programs are best suited to classrooms that have a heterogeneous non-English-speaking student population rather than those in which one non-English-speaking group predominates.

Federal and State Educational Policies

Now that we have identified the language minority student and examined how that student has been served, let us turn our focus to educational policy: first, federal legislative and legal initiatives, and second, state initiatives.

Federal Legislative Initiatives

The U.S. Congress set a minimum standard for the education of language minority students in public educational institutions in Title VI of the Civil Rights Act of 1964, which prohibits discrimination by educational institutions on the basis of race, color, sex, or national origin, and in the Equal Educational Opportunities and Transportation Act of 1974 (EEOA), which attempts to define a denial of constitutionally guaranteed equal educational opportunity. The EEOA provides in part that

no state shall deny equal educational opportunities to an individual on

account of his or her race, color, sex, or national origin, by the failure by an educational agency to take appropriate action to overcome language barriers that impede equal participation by students in its instructional programs.

The EEOA does not mandate specific education treatment, but it does require public educational agencies to sustain programs to meet the language needs of their students.

Bilingual Education Act

The Bilingual Education Act of 1967 (BEA) was designed to meet the educational needs of low-income students with limited English-speaking ability. This act was added to the larger and more comprehensive Elementary and Secondary Education Act of 1968 and became a continuing subcomponent of that act. Grants were awarded to local educational agencies, institutions of higher education, or regional research facilities to (1) develop and operate programs for bilingual education, native history and culture, early childhood education, and adult education, as well as programs to train bilingual aides; (2) make efforts to attract and retain teachers from non-English-speaking backgrounds; and (3) establish cooperation between the home and the school.

Five major reauthorizations of the BEA have occurred since its initial passage in 1968—in 1974, 1978, 1984, 1987, and 1994. As a consequence of the 1974 Amendments (Public Law 93-380), a bilingual education program was defined for the first time as "instruction given in, and study of English and to the extent necessary to allow a child to progress effectively through the education system, the native language" (Schneider, 1976: 125). The goal of bilingual education continued to be a transition to English rather than maintenance of the native language. However, students no longer had to be from low-income backgrounds to participate. New programs were funded, including a graduate fellowship program for study in training teachers for bilingual education and another program for the development, assessment, and dissemination of classroom materials for bilingual education.

In the Bilingual Education Amendments of 1978 (Public Law 95-561), program eligibility was expanded to include students with limited English academic proficiency as well as students with limited English-speaking ability. Parents were given a greater role in program planning and operation. Teachers were required to be proficient in both English and the native language of the children in the program. Grant recipients were required to demonstrate how they would continue the program when federal funds were withdrawn.

The Bilingual Education Act of 1984 created new program options including alternative instructional programs that did not require use of the child's native language. These options were expanded in 1987. State and local agency program staff were required to collect data, identify the population served, and describe program effectiveness.

The New National Educational Policy of 1994

From this broader context, specific changes in policy with regard to language minority students developed in the reauthorization of the BEA in 1994. Typically changes in national policy are related to crisis intervention: there is a problem, and it must be addressed quickly, usually with more political and philosophical rhetoric than action. In the past, national policy for serving linguistically and culturally diverse students and their families was driven to a large extent by this sort of "crisis" rationale. This meant that policies have been frequently short-sighted, inflexible, and minimally cohesive and integrated; they are not always informed by a strong knowledge base.

Titles I and VII of the Elementary and Secondary Education Act of 1965 (ESEA) are both prime examples of the disadvantages of a crisis-intervention approach to providing services to Hispanic language minority students. However, the 1994 reauthorization of the ESEA brought about the following concepts in developing new policy:

Policy Changes of 1994

1. The new knowledge base, both conceptual and empirical, must be central to any proposed changes.
2. Consultation with the professionals in the field is critical in order to profit from the wisdom of current policy, administration, curriculum, and instructional practice.
3. National, state, and local policies and programs must be cohesive in order to integrate services that are to be provided.
4. The demographic and budgetary realities of the present and of the coming decade must be acknowledged.

New policy directions, primarily those related to Titles I and VII of the ESEA, will be implemented according to these guidelines. (See *Teachers College Record*, 1995, for a comprehensive description of the policy foundations of this reauthorization.)

We will now explore each of these guidelines in more detail to understand this new policy more fully.

Knowledge Base. Recent studies have documented the effectiveness of various educational practices related to linguistically and culturally diverse students in selected sites throughout the United States. The case-study approach of this research has included examinations of preschool, elementary, and high school classrooms. Teachers, principals, parents, and students were interviewed, and specific classroom observations were conducted to assess the dynamics of the instructional process. The results of these studies provide important insights into general instructional organization, literacy development, academic achievement in content areas (like math and science), and the views of the students, teachers, administrators, and parents.

Use of Research Findings

In brief, the studies have found that effective curriculum, instructional strategies, and teaching staffs are rooted in the sharing of expertise and experience through multiple avenues of communication. Effective curricula provide students with abundant and diverse opportunities for speaking, listening, reading, and writing, along with scaffolding to help guide them through the learning process. Further, effective schools for diverse students encourage them to take risks, construct meaning, and seek reinterpretation of knowledge within compatible social contexts. Within this knowledge-driven curriculum, skills become tools for acquiring knowledge, not ends in themselves.

An effective curriculum recognizes that any attempt to address the needs of linguistically and culturally diverse students in a deficit or "subtractive" mode is counterproductive. Instead, educators must be "additive" in their approach to such students; that is, the teachers must add to the rich intellectual, linguistic, academic, and cultural attributes and skills the students bring to the classroom. Moreover, programs for these students should be integrated and comprehensive. They should not be segregated, and the development of English and academic content mastery must be seen as equally important. The same educational goals are to be articulated for these students and *all other* students. In addition, federal efforts to assist local school districts, particularly in programs that may be perceived by parents as inappropriate for their children, should be clearly explained to the parents, and the parents should voluntarily agree to their children's participation.

Wisdom of Practice. Too often, in the heat of legislation and the political process, policy development is highly centralized under the control of various interest groups and professional policymakers. Therefore, with the 1994 reauthorization of the ESEA, new national policy initiatives were crafted in consultation with diverse constituencies. For linguistically and culturally diverse communities, the "usual players" in this process included the National Association for Bilingual Education; the Mexican American Legal Defense Fund, which has made specific legislative recommendations of major proportion; and other educational groups.

Using Reform Expertise

This new legislation was also organized as a result of broader efforts at school reform. Of particular significance was the report by the Carnegie Foundation for the Advancement of Teaching, *The Basic School: A Community for Learning,* which acknowledged that there are key components of an effective school that need to be brought together in an integrated and cohesive manner. A good teacher in a good classroom is not enough to guarantee that effective learning will occur. Effective schools are those that reinforce the significance of the early school years and place a high priority on learning language and knowledge with cohesiveness. *The Basic School* is based on the concept of "best practice," a comprehensive plan for educational renewal that has as its goal the improvement of learning for every child. This same idea is at the core of new federal education policy.

The work of the Stanford Working Group was also significant in shaping the new policy. This group, funded by the Carnegie Corporation of New York, consulted widely with many individuals representing a broad spectrum of theoretical, practical, and policy expertise. In published reports and in various forums, it put forward a comprehensive analysis and articulated precise recommendations for policy and legislation related to linguistically and culturally diverse populations.

Thus, those who shaped the new policy proposals drew upon the shared wisdom from various established perspectives. Moreover, further changes, if they are to be effective, must be embraced by those individuals and organizations active in the field.

Cohesiveness. The new policy arising from the 1994 reauthorization of the ESEA also attempted to view provision of services to students in a comprehensive and integrated manner. Through the introduction of new legislation in Goals 2000, the U.S. Department of Education set the stage for the state-by-state development of standards. Then, with the 1994 reauthorization, an alignment of the goals initiative with specific goals and of the standards initiatives with specific resource allocation policies was accomplished. This alignment recognizes that federal, state, and local government efforts must be integrated if they are to be effective and efficient. Moreover, the federal role must allow for flexibility at the state and local levels while requiring that all children achieve at the highest levels.

Cohesiveness of Policy

The Title VII reauthorization of services to students with limited English proficiency is also highly congruent with the alignment principle. As such, Title VII is not seen as yet another intervention aimed at meeting an educational crisis in American education but rather as a key component of the integrated effort to address effectively the educational needs of students. Specifically, Title VII will continue to provide for leadership and increase national, state, and local educational services, professional development, and research related to linguistic and culturally diverse populations. Other programs, particularly Title I of the ESEA, will more directly increase the services needed by all students living in poverty, including those with limited English proficiency.

Demographic and Budgetary Realities. Over the last decade, large increases in the number of LEP students in our schools have occurred. In the last six years, that increase was nearly 70 percent, or approximately 1 million students. There is no reason to believe this trend will subside. Rather, it is important to recognize that the national presence of this population as well as its diversity are substantial. In the last decade 10 states have been added to the list of those with more than 2 percent of their student population designated as LEP. Today there are 20 such states, half of them with LEP student populations between 5 and 25 percent. Moreover, these LEP students are quite diverse, with over 180 language groups represented in programs funded under Title VII.

Pressures of Numbers and Money

Unfortunately, the fiscal resources needed to meet the growing and diverse demands of this population are not likely to be increased in any significant way. National, state, and local funding for this population has not grown in proportion to the increase in the number of students. Critics such as Linda Chavez (past presidential advisor to Ronald Reagan) and Congressman Bill Light of New York have indicated that bilingual education costs taxpayers between $5.5 and $15 billion yearly. How they arrive at those figures is a mystery, since federal funding for bilingual education in the last decade has ranged between $125 and $200 million yearly. A 4 percent increase in federal funds was requested by the Clinton administration in 1996, but no major increases are likely to be requested in the near future. Although new legislation in the Improving American Schools Act (IASA) regarding the distribution of Title I funds to high-poverty areas should bring more resources to Hispanic language minority students, such funding will still be limited. This means that present resources must be utilized more efficiently.

Changing Title VII to Ensure Effective Schooling for Language Minority Students. The Title VII legislation of 1994 was part of a cohesive change in policy direction from the U.S. Department of Education. Title VII will continue to provide leadership and build the capacity of educational services, professional development, and research related to linguistically and culturally diverse populations. However, programs for language minority students will be packaged in a comprehensive manner that recognizes the significance of Goals 2000, Title I and other ESEA programs, and state and local education efforts. This new federal legislation not only recognizes but also directly responds to the needs of linguistically and culturally diverse children. Title I legislation, for example, will be opened up to serve as a major source of federal educational programming for language minority students.

Improvements in Title VII

Within this framework, Title VII has undergone several changes. Direct assistance to local and state educational agencies has been the core federal service to LEP students. Under the new legislation, existing programs would be replaced by development and enhancement grants, comprehensive school grants, and comprehensive district grants. This new configuration recognizes the complexity of educational responses for language minority students as well as the necessity for locally designed and integrated programs. State review of proposals will reinforce the implementation of state plans for these students.

Other changes that relate to research, evaluation, and dissemination have been made in response to input from the field. Research activities will be developed by the U.S. Office of Bilingual Education and Minority Language Affairs, with required consultation from the field and enhanced coordination with other U.S. Department of Education research activities. Program evaluation requirements will be simplified to be more "user friendly" and directed at program improvement, assessment of student English proficiency, and academic outcomes and dissemination. To showcase the success of existing Title VII programs, there will be added emphasis on academic excellence programs that have effectively disseminated and demonstrated their expertise locally, regionally, and nationally. The work of Multifunctional Resource Centers and the Evaluation Assistance Centers will be merged with new comprehensive technical assistance and professional development efforts of the U.S. Department of Education.

After 20 years of efforts to develop a teaching force prepared to meet the needs of LEP students, this area remains a major challenge. Professional development programs will place renewed emphasis on such work, including a new career-ladder program. In addition to continuing attempts to prepare LEP teachers, opportunities for professional development through doctoral fellowships remain, and postdoctoral opportunities have been created to continue the development of a strong research and theoretical base.

These changes are framed by a commitment to the value of bilingualism and the belief that all children can meet high standards. The new policy will strengthen federal services for language minority students not only through Title VII but also through Title I and related federal K–12 education funding, thus opening the possibility of an additional several million dollars.

Over $1 billion in federal funding has been appropriated through Title VII legislation for educational activities (program development, program implementation, professional training, and research) for language minority students. In addition, other congressional appropriations (for vocational education, Chapter I, and so forth) explicitly target language minority students.

Federal Legal Initiatives

The 1974 U.S. Supreme Court decision in *Lau v. Nichols,* the landmark statement of the rights of language minority students, declares that LEP students must be provided with language support:

> There is no equality of treatment merely by providing students with English instruction. Students without the ability to understand English are effectively foreclosed from any meaningful discourse. Basic English skills are at the very core of what these public schools teach. Imposition of a requirement that, before a child can effectively participate in the education program he must already have acquired those basic skills is to make a mockery of public education. We know that those who do not understand English are certain to find their classroom experiences wholly incomprehensible and in no way meaningful.

Legal Rights of LEP Students

Castaneda v. Pickard of 1981 set three requirements for an appropriate program for language minority students:

1. The program be based on a sound educational theory.
2. The program must be "reasonably calculated to implement effectively" the chosen theory.
3. The program must produce results in a reasonable amount of time.

The courts have also required appropriate action to overcome language barriers."Measures which will actually overcome the problem" of limited English proficiency are called for by *U.S. v. Texas* (1981), and "results indicating that the language barriers confronting students are actually being overcome" are mandated by *Castaneda.* Therefore, local school districts and state education

BECOMING A RESPONSIVE TEACHER

California: The "Minority Majority" State

O ver the period 1987 to 1997, student diversity in California changed significantly. The number of students identified as LEP increased by a startling 20 percent (see Figures a–c). In fact, a major milestone was reached by 1988, when the majority of students in California's public schools were from ethnic and racial "minorities." Non-Hispanic white students now constitute the minority of students in the schools and, based on demographic projections, will continue to do so.

The extent of the changes in the diversity of California's student population can be best appreciated by comparing the composition of the student population in 1987 with the "new" students who entered school between 1987 and 1990 (actually, new students who entered minus existing students who left). The accompanying graphs illustrate these differences. In 1987, 48 percent of all students were from ethnic and racial minority groups, and 13 percent were LEP. But of the new students who entered the schools in 1986–90, 92 percent were from ethnic and racial minority populations, and 65 percent were LEP. Clearly, the new students entering California's schools are much different from previous students.

Figure a ▼ **LEP Students in California Public Schools, Kindergarten through Third Grade, 1987–1997**

Source: California Department of Education, *Language Census Report for California Public Schools.* Sacramento: Author, 1997.

BECOMING A RESPONSIVE TEACHER *Cont.*

Figure b ▼ **LEP Students in California Public Schools, Fourth through Eighth Grade, 1987–1997**

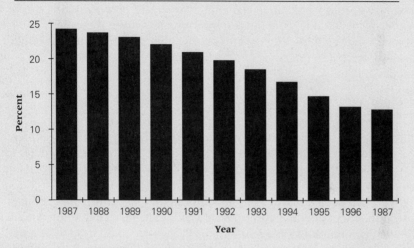

Source: California Department of Education, *Language Census Report for California Public Schools.* Sacramento: Author, 1997.

Figure c ▼ **LEP Students in California Public Schools, Ninth through Twelfth Grade, 1987–1997**

Source: California Department of Education, *Language Census Report for California Public Schools.* Sacramento: Author, 1997.

BECOMING A RESPONSIVE TEACHER *Cont.*

Enrollment projections by the California Department of Finance suggest that these trends will continue throughout the 1990s. Total elementary and secondary enrollment is projected to increase by 47 percent during the next decade, or by 200,000 students per year, which is about three times the rate of growth in the 1980s. The proportion of students from minority populations is projected to increase from 54 percent to 63 percent during the same period.

▼ Meeting the Challenge

1. Research the comparable elementary and secondary school enrollment data for your own state or city for 1986–1990. Are the trends similar to or different from those described for California? Construct a graph from the data if you can.
2. If you had been a teacher in the California schools during this dramatic shift in student demographics, what types of in-service training would have been helpful to you?
3. How might the social life of a school be affected by a significant increase in LEP students? As a teacher, what classroom methods would you use to encourage communication among students with different language backgrounds?

agencies have a responsibility to assess the effectiveness of special language programs on an ongoing basis. Other court decisions have delineated the requirements of professional training and the particular role of standardized tests.

State Initiatives

Twelve states have mandated special educational services for language minority students. Another twelve explicitly permit these services, and one state prohibits them. Twenty-six states have no legislation that directly addresses language minority students.

State policies for language minority students can be characterized as follows:

Variations by State

1. Implementing programs that allow or require instruction in a language other than English (17 states).
2. Establishing special qualifications for the certification of professional LEP instructional staff (15 states).
3. Providing school districts with supplementary funds to support LEP educational programs (15 states).
4. Mandating a cultural component of LEP programs (15 states).
5. Requiring parental consent for enrollment of students in LEP programs (11 states).

Eight states (Arizona, California, Colorado, Illinois, Indiana, Massachusetts, Rhode Island, and Texas) impose all of these requirements concurrently. Such a pattern suggests continued state attention to issues related to language minority students (for details see García, 1991b).

Of particular interest is a subset of states that together are home to almost two-thirds of this nation's language minority students: California, Florida, Illinois, New York, New Jersey, and Texas. In these states, bilingual credentialing and ESL or some other related credentialing/endorsement are available. However, in only three of these six states is such credentialing mandated. Therefore, even in states with high numbers of language minority students, there is no direct concern for the establishment of specific professional standards. As Valencia (1991) suggests, because language minority students tend to be concentrated in a few districts within a state (as is particularly true of Chicanos in the Southwest), their presence does not exert a great deal of pressure statewide.

Conclusion

Sometimes making sense of demographic data from the realm of education is like trying to make sense out of baseball by picking through the vast array of statistics printed in tiny type at the back of the sports pages. No one can develop a genuine feel for the game merely by examining the statistics, no matter how comprehensive, strategic, or ingenious those numbers are. Numbers may never be able to fully convey the excitement experienced in the stands or on the field. Think for a moment about how you would describe your own formal schooling activities if you could answer only the statistical questions "How many?" "How much?" and "How long?" These questions allow you no room to tell the story of your educational experience.

We utilize demographic statistics in education, much as we use baseball statistics, to help us summarize the nature of the enterprise by describing the status of the groups and individuals involved. The demographic analysis in this chapter has presented specific status indicators with the warning that such description can add some depth to, but not total understanding of, the challenging issues that today's and tomorrow's educators face. To understand the quality of the educational experience of most culturally and linguistically diverse children, we will have to go beyond the numbers. For that we will need imagination—and a feel for the game.

Where do we start? What can these descriptive data tell us about the challenges facing us? It is undeniable that the students who will populate our schools, who will play the "game," will soon differ radically with regard to race, culture, and language. In less than two decades, one-half of the students in U.S. schools will be nonwhite and Hispanic—and half of them will speak a language other than English on their first day of school. Teachers who receive their credentials today will likely be responsible for the education of a student body that is more diverse than at any other time in the history of U.S. formal education. This will be true at all levels of education.

The growing population of diverse students will begin their schooling with several strikes against them. They will be coming to the plate from social and economic circumstances that will leave them most vulnerable to the various pitches they will be asked to hit. Those pitches carry two powerful spins: a globally competitive climate in which educational success is an absolute must and a world in which our fundamental knowledge base is growing exponentially.

These students are likely to be equipped not with the best that money can buy but with the least that society is willing to allow them. They are likely to be "coached" by individuals who do not meet the highest standards or who themselves are learning to play the game as their own responsibilities and commitments change and increase. Many of these players will require coaching in a language not their own. They will need to acquire knowledge of the game along with facility in the language and culture in which the game is immersed.

Meeting the Challenge

Despite the immensity of their task and the difficulties stacked against these students, the data unequivocally indicate that the future of education rests with them. As they grow to represent the majority, their success will be our success, and their failure will be our failure. They—and we—must succeed. We have no other alternative short of calling off the game. But education, unlike baseball, is not an endeavor we can cancel or postpone when the weather looks bad. The U.S. educational system must rise to the challenge and accommodate students it has historically underserved.

Mrs. Tanner believes this is true. She is living this challenge and is not about to give up. There is no doubt that as a nation we have the resourcefulness we need to succeed. The remainder of this book will address ways of identifying those resources and applying them to the task at hand.

SUMMARY OF MAJOR IDEAS

1. Educators in the U.S. schools face the challenge of teaching increasing numbers of children who are culturally and linguistically diverse. The education of these children must take into account demographic factors, issues of academic performance, language background, and child and family well-being.

2. From 1989 to 1990, immigration to the United States has increased 63 percent over the previous decade. Mexico has remained the leading country of origin, with the Philippines, China, Korea, and Vietnam close behind. The rate of immigration from places such as El Salvador, Ireland, Iran, Haiti, and Eastern Europe has dramatically increased, but immigration from Mexico has nearly tripled since 1980.

3. The racial and ethnic makeup of the United States is more diverse than Census data indicate. The nonwhite and Hispanic population, which is growing, is most at risk on indi-

cators of child and family well-being: family stability, family violence, family income, child health and development, and educational achievement.

4. It is projected that nonwhite and Hispanic enrollment will grow to approximately 70 percent of total school enrollment by 2026. And at this time nearly 25 percent of students will come from homes in which English is not the primary language spoken.

5. Today's students must be well prepared to meet the demands of a changing economy that requires workers with more than the basic skills. In addition, the increasingly diverse U.S. and global marketplace will place a premium on those who can interact easily with others of various cultures and languages.

6. Students living in poverty are three times more likely to drop out of school than are students with economic advantages. It is projected that the number of children in poverty will greatly increase by 2026.

7. The dropout rate is one indicator of educational vulnerability. The 1990 Education Summit proposed the goal of increasing the U.S. high school completion rate to 90 percent by 2000.

8. Event and status rates reports show that nonwhite and Hispanic students drop out of high school two to three times more often than white students.

9. The percentage of all 8-year-old and 13-year-old students performing below modal grade level increased between 1983 and 1989. By eighth grade 40 percent or more of black and Hispanic students were performing one or more levels below expected standards.

10. Most nonwhite and Hispanic children are likely to attend schools with fewer financial resources and larger classes. Funding discrepancies between "rich" and "poor" school districts raise questions of fairness in education.

11. Effective teachers of students who are culturally and linguistically diverse excel in five domains: (a) mastering content knowledge; (b) teaching for student learning; (c) creating a classroom community for student learning; (d) teacher professionalism; and (5) incorporating culturally responsive pedagogy.

12. Professional teaching organizations, such as the National Education Association and the American Federation of Teachers, and some certification agencies have addressed the need to train educators to teach culturally diverse students. Nevertheless, the training and assessment of teachers of culturally diverse students remain problematical.

13. The connoisseur model is a method of teacher assessment whereby experienced and knowledgeable educators train and judge other educators. It may be the best way to improve the instruction offered to culturally diverse students.

14. The language minority student is one who substantively participates in a non-English-speaking social environment, has acquired the normal communicative abilities of that social environment, and is regularly exposed to an English-speaking environment only during the formal school process. Roughly three-fourths of language minority children in the United States are from Spanish-speaking backgrounds.

15. Since the mid-1960s, a series of national policies have attempted to address the needs of language minority students. More recent changes in federal law have recognized the importance of developing programs that capitalize on the wisdom in the field, are cohesive and well integrated, and consider demographic and budgetary realities. The various state policies that focus on language minority students, even in states with high numbers of such students, are uneven in their approach and their requirements.

EXTENDING YOUR EXPERIENCE

1. Describe the physical facilities, programs, and student demographics of your high school. What special materials were available for student use, such as computers, art and music supplies, and sports equipment? Research the school district expenditures for your state. How does your high school rank statewide in terms of per-student spending?

2. Design an elementary school whose sole purpose would be to respond to a student body of maximum cultural and linguistic diversity. As creator of this school, what are your requirements for staff credentials and experience, educational materials, and curriculum? Describe a typical classroom in your dream school.

3. Reflect on your regular personal interactions with people who are fluent in languages other than English. Is language diversity part of your daily experience? If not, how might you prepare yourself to teach in a linguistically diverse classroom?

4. Your best student has just informed you that she has to drop out of high school and get a job to help support her family. Part of her earnings will go to support her brother, who is in

college. Her parents seem unconcerned and claim that since she will be getting married, it is not so important that she finish high school. What will you say to this student and her parents? What will you need to know about them before offering them helpful counsel?

5. You have 26 students in your fourth-grade language arts class, but only 20 textbooks are available, and your school has no budget for more. How will you make sure all of your students have the necessary materials for learning?

RESOURCES FOR FURTHER STUDY

August, D., & García, E. (1988). *Language minority education in the United States: Research, policy, and practice.* Chicago: Charles C. Thomas.

This publication advances the discussion of issues pertaining to language minority students and how researchers, practitioners, and policymakers can utilize this dialogue to address the issues that affect these students. The authors present and analyze legal precedents that have affected the education of language minority students.

National Commission on Children (1991). *Beyond rhetoric. A new American agenda for children and families: Final report of the National Commission on Children.* Washington, DC: Author.

The commission took over two years to investigate, analyze, and recommend changes in national, state, and local policy toward children and families. The agenda calls for action to reinvest and reinforce the care, education, and protection of children. The commission estimates that it would take about $60 billion to bring its recommendations to reality. The point is clearly made that if our nation is to compete, succeed, and grow, it needs citizens who are capable. Particular attention is given to students who are poor, who are from minority groups, who are limited English speakers, and who have single parents.

Wong-Fillmore, L. (1991). When learning a second language means losing a first. *Early Childhood Research Quarterly, 6,* 323–346.

The author argues that children's loss of a primary language, particularly when it is the only language spoken by the parents, can be very costly to the children, their families, and society at large. There is no question about the benefits children from diverse backgrounds receive when they learn English. The problems arise in how students come into contact with English and in how learning English affects the family consciousness. Wong-Fillmore argues that the goal of education for new immigrants should not be limited only to learning English.

VIEWS

OF CULTURE

AND EDUCATION

CHAPTER 2

Focus Questions

▼ What are some of the social and economic changes that have resulted in new contexts for education in the United States?

▼ What are the group-oriented and the individual-oriented concepts of culture?

▼ How does the concept of culture prevalent in U.S. schools affect which practices are deemed appropriate for teaching culturally diverse children?

▼ What are some of the cultural demands of U.S. schools, and how might students respond if the demands of their home culture are different?

▼ What are the three ingredients for teaching effectively in a context of student cultural diversity?

▼ What is cultural capital? How do schools deter or enhance its development?

"A text without a context is a pretext."

The subject of this book is the increasing numbers of young people all over the United States whom I have referred to as culturally or linguistically diverse. In all our coming discussions of educational theories and practices, we must keep these children firmly in mind. They are our *students,* and, in a sense, they are our "text"—we will open the book of their educational experiences and read the signs of change that we as educators must follow. We will consider both the stories of individuals and the broader trends that generalize to groups of individuals. We will approach our "text" informed of a full range of social and educational issues that will help us be better readers of what is in store for schools in the United States.

This chapter lays out some of the contexts for education in the years to come. Social, economic, and cultural changes in the United States have raised questions about the proper role for our schools. The answers to these questions require a clearer understanding of our assumptions regarding culture and the individual and the part our schools are to play in transmitting culture to children. We will also look at the culture of school itself and examine the qualities that will be important for teachers of culturally diverse students.

New Contexts for Education

The accomplishments of all societies rest on the fundamental educational capabilities of their individual members. We must examine our past educational practices for successes and failures and use the present to rework and reenvision our goals for teaching and learning. We must look ahead and prepare our nation's children for the future. We will talk much in this book about change. Fortunately, continuing attention to educational reform in this country provides us with some solid information about changing social and economic circumstances that affect education. A variety of reports are produced yearly about our country's schools, ranging from preschool to higher education. The analyses and related reforms these reports suggest have focused our attention on many significant variables that influence our educational institutions today and others that will do so in the future. The following list highlights several of these new contexts for education:

▼ Economically, the United States finds itself at a significant competitive disadvantage relative to the growing emphasis on what is termed the "global marketplace." International trade will be the arena for economic growth in the next century. At the present, only 10 percent of U.S. jobs are related directly to international trade. However, it is estimated that over the next two decades, this figure will increase to more than 50 percent. As activity in the global marketplace increases, the economic stability of our country will depend on how well we prepare the next generation for participation in this context.

Global Marketplace

▼ Education has become a major activity of institutions that are not primarily educational in nature. Only one-third of formal education occurs within primary, secondary, and postsecondary educational institutions. One example of this is the education the business sector provides to employees.

Career Flexibility

▼ Today's sixth-graders will likely average 7 to 10 job changes in their lifetime and 2 to 3 changes in career. My father was an agricultural worker and died an agricultural worker. I have had four jobs but only one profession: teaching. My daughters may change jobs 10 times and experience 2 or 3 shifts in profession.

▼ Only 8 percent of tomorrow's jobs will require less than a high school education. Thirty-five percent will require at least a high school education, and a whopping 60 percent will require three or more years of postsecondary education.

▼ Eighty percent of new jobs will be in the information and service sector of the economy. This has been the fastest-growing part of our economy for the past decade. Employees in this field must be flexible, computer literate, creative, and highly skilled at communication (preferably in more than one language), with good "people" skills.

▼ Major shifts in values over the past three decades have broadened the educational prospects for women in the United States. No longer limited to traditionally "female" professions such as teaching and nursing, young women are now training in large numbers for a broad spectrum of careers in business, law, and technical fields. The demise of gender-based barriers to economic participation has been accompanied by changes in a host of other issues, including sexual behavior, health and environmental concerns, and family priorities.

The Role of Schools

What is the role of the school in the midst of these new and developing circumstances? It seems evident that schools cannot provide adequate job training skills. The job market described above will be much too volatile, and employers themselves already find it necessary to provide their employees with job training tailored to specific tasks and functions. It thus appears that schools must take on several responsibilities, some similar to and others significantly different from the ones they have now:

1. Schools must serve children well with regard to the development of academic skills: "readin', writin', and 'rithmetic." Our society needs all its members to be able to communicate well and to be linguistically, mathematically, and technologically literate.
2. Schools must focus on the development of what I call "living" processes, involving students in curricula that enhance human relationships, critical thinking, and civic responsibility. An emphasis on process means attending to means as well as ends—that is, examining how individuals think through their ideas and actions and make decisions in addition to examining the ideas and decisions themselves.

Schooling for the Future   In the new curriculum of the twenty-first century, schooling must become collaborative, highly social in nature, and process oriented. The lives of the young people now in school, even more than our own, will be characterized by continuous and dramatic social, economic, and technological change. As adults, these students must be able to react flexibly to these changing situations. They must be equipped with enough understanding, knowledge, and skill to act as well-informed members of society. They must be able to reflect on and analyze the perplexing array of social and individual problems that are part of modern life.

Cultural Change and Disruption

Change is never easy. The cultural shifts our nation is now undergoing take their toll on our individual and collective experience. Disruptions in the social fabric often lead to misunderstanding, miscommunication, and tension among people. In the most stressful situations, especially ones that involve economic hardships, people can feel pitted against one another, and old **Growing Pains** hatreds and old ignorances may rise to block progress and growth. We will undergo more growing pains as the demographics of the U.S. population are transformed. In fewer than 20 years, 70 percent of California's students will be nonwhite and Hispanic, and one-half will speak a language other than English on their first day of school. As we saw in Chapter 1, this same scenario is transforming schools in other states, including

New York, New Jersey, Florida, Michigan, Illinois, and Texas. Such states will represent over 50 percent of the U.S. population in the near future.

We are a country of incredible cultural and linguistic diversity. We are singularly nationalistic—"American" to the core—but are still unaccepting of the diversity among us. Recent data on sociological perception suggest that over the past three decades the white majority of the U.S. population has not changed its stereotyped view of minority groups. The majority continues to perceive minorities as less intelligent, lazy, and of lower moral character. These findings are absolutely frustrating considering that within these same three decades our country has witnessed a civil rights movement, a women's movement, and an equal educational opportunity initiative. Millions of dollars and, more significantly, millions of person-hours have been dedicated to addressing the inequalities and human injustices of our age.

Renewed Debate

The publication of *The Bell Curve* (Herrnstein & Murray, 1994) has reinvigorated a bitter public debate on significant scientific and societal issues, including a set of interrelated theories regarding the influences of genetic and environmental factors in the development of human intelligence; arguments over racial, ethnic, and group differences in intelligence; concerns about possible test biases; and questions concerning the implication of scientific research on these issues for education and public policy. Essentially the same argument—that race is related to innate intelligence—often coupled with the suggestion that African Americans and other selected people of color are genetically inferior, has continued for many years (Wigdor & Garner, 1982). Laosa (1995) suggests that, like a refractory strain of retrovirus, these issues tend to remain latent and from time to time resurge brusquely into the public consciousness.

At the political and policy levels, events in California and Texas are further examples of negative reactions to immigrant and minority students. In California, the passage of Proposition 187 in 1994 and Proposition 209 in 1996 set the stage for the development of a state policy that attempts to eliminate K–12 public education for undocumented immigrant students and that abolishes the use of affirmative action as a tool for providing equal educational opportunity in admission to public higher education. Following the decision in *Hopwood v. Texas* (1996), Texas no longer allows race, gender, and ethnicity to be used as criteria for offering scholarships or grants for higher education. These public policy intrusions, which rescinded the educational opportunities afforded immigrants and minority students (including women), have created a very different political climate for this population.

Language at Home and School

The context of "us versus them" is exemplified in the educational experience of many language minority children. In a nationwide survey of families, Wong-Fillmore (1991) found evidence of serious disruptions of family relations when young children learn English in school and lose the ability to use the language spoken at home. The study revealed that parents of language minority students fully recognize the importance of English and want their children to learn it at school, but they do not want this to happen at the expense of the home language. Many such parents expressed concern that their children would lose their native language and thus become estranged from their families and cultural heritage. Others reported that their children had already lost or were losing the home language.

Children's Loss of Home Language

An interviewer quoted in this study told the story of a Korean immigrant family whose children had all but lost the ability to speak their native language after just a few years in American schools. The parents could speak English only with difficulty, and the grandmother, who lived with the family, could not speak or understand English. She felt isolated and unappreciated by her grandchildren. The parents spoke to the children exclusively in Korean, refusing to believe that their children could not understand them. They interpreted the children's unresponsiveness as disrespect and rejection. Only when the interviewer, a bilingual Korean-English speaker, tried to question the children in both languages did the parents finally realize that the children no longer spoke or understood Korean. The father wept as he spoke of not being able to talk to his children. One of the children commented that she had never understood why her parents always seemed to be angry.

Systematic lack of support for students' home language has been pervasive in U.S. schools during most of the twentieth century. And difficulties caused by a family's inability to communicate are not manifested only in the home. On the contrary, family problems form the basis of children's problems, and those problems follow children into school, into the streets, and later into their work lives. When enough individuals have problems, our whole society has problems.

It may be years before the harm done to families by this situation is fully assessed. The experience of one family that had been in the United States for nearly 20 years displayed how breakdowns in communication can lead to the alienation of children from parents. As teenagers, the four children had completely lost their ability to speak or understand Spanish. They reportedly were ashamed of Spanish, and did not acknowledge it when their parents spoke it, even though it was the only language their parents knew. The mother indicated that her 17-year-old son was having problems in school. He was often truant and was in danger of dropping out. She had tried to talk with him, but he didn't understand her. Their attempts at discussion ended in physical violence, with mother and son coming to blows when words failed them (Wong-Fillmore, 1991).

When we think about the numbers of families facing similar difficulties, the gravity of our national predicament becomes apparent. To prosper, we must find a way out of this situation and embrace the great and rich diversity of our culture. In the next section we shall discuss two different theories of culture and their implications for education in the United States.

What Is Culture?

When we speak of the **culture** that an individual belongs to, we are generally referring to the system of understanding characteristic of that individual's society or some subgroup within that society. This system of understanding includes values, beliefs, notions about acceptable and unacceptable behavior, and other socially constructed ideas that members of the culture are taught are "true." This is the common definition of culture employed by many anthropologists, who analyze the behavioral patterns and customs of groups of people. The word "culture," however, can have a variety of connotations in general usage.

An Experiment in Definition

I recently asked a class of university juniors and seniors preparing for careers in education to break into small groups and identify very specifically attributes of their individual cultures. It was no surprise to me that one student responded, "I'm white. I have no culture." Such responses occur all too frequently. "Of course you have a culture," I answered as the other students scrutinized our interaction. "Everyone has a culture." They all went off, some a bit reluctantly, to complete the assignment.

At the end of the exercise, each group reported their findings and analysis. Yes, they all had a culture, but with a diverse set of students it was not easy to discuss individual cultural characteristics. These students, like most of us, usually do not sit down and expose their culture. They live it. They can recognize it when they see it. And they can determine when they are not in it, and that usually distresses them. These students also seemed distressed in speaking openly about their culture to one another, as if exposing it would leave them vulnerable to criticisms about who they were or what they might represent.

My students all survived their initial distress and discovered in a few minutes the basic tenets of the science of anthropology. To define a culture by its attributes might be a start, but this in itself is not particularly useful. The students did identify cultural attributes. They indicated that their cultures were made up of many distinguishable attributes: familial, linguistic, religious and spiritual, aesthetic, socioeconomic, educational, dietary, gender,

Problems of Definitions

and so on. The list was quite long. But what seemed quite evident was that they all came to the conclusion that this thing—culture—was not easy to define. To do so meant (1) defining these attributes in relation to specific individuals who live in distinct physical and social contexts and (2) taking into consideration the previous histories of those individuals and those social contexts. In short, they determined that culture is both complex and dynamic, yet for individuals living their cultures, it is quite recognizable.

We began this discussion with the ideas of novice educators and their conceptualizations of culture. Let us now turn to the "experts." Even professional anthropologists struggle with the same questions that bedeviled my students, but their thinking is more systematic, and that will help us.

The Group-Oriented Concept of Culture

The **culture concept,** with its technical anthropological meaning, was first defined by Edward Tylor in 1871 as "that complex whole which includes knowledge, belief, art, law, morals, custom, and other capabilities and habits acquired by man as a

Culture Is Learned

member of society" (Kroeber & Kluckhohn, 1963, p. 81). Since Tylor's time, anthropologists have advanced many other definitions of culture. These definitions, like Tylor's, commonly attempt to encompass the totality (or some subset of the totality) of humanity's achievements, dispositions, and capabilities. Virtually every anthropologist considers culture to be something that is learned and transmitted from generation to generation.

Culture Is Shared

Most definitions of culture include another dimension, the notion that culture is something that members of a group share. An anthropology textbook states, for example, that behaviors and ideas may be considered cultural only insofar as they are shared among members of a social group (Nanda, 1990). This formulation is useful for anthropological comparisons between societies or subgroups within societies. Its basic assumption, however, is that of uniformity among the cultural attributes of individual members of societies and subgroupings of societies. In this formulation, the primary focus of culture is some kind of group.

Anthropologists do acknowledge that members of all societies display individual differences in their behavior and thinking. That is to say, societies are characterized to some extent by intercultural heterogeneity. But these differences are not significant for anthropologists and usually are noted only insofar as they determine the "looseness" or "tightness" of a society's cultural system. When researchers in anthropology write their ethnographies, or their deep descriptions and analyses of any group, they tend to ignore individual variations and to abstract what they apparently consider "an essential homogeneity from the background noise of insignificant diversity" (Schwartz, 1978, p. 419).

Along these lines, anthropologist Ralph Linton defined culture as "the sum total of ideas, conditioned emotional responses and patterns of habitual behavior which the members of a society have acquired through instruction or imitation and which they share to a greater or less degree" (quoted in Kroeber & Kluckhohn, 1963, p. 82). Although ideas or learned behavioral habits need not be totally shared by everyone in a group, it is nevertheless this property of sharing, the commonality of attributes, that defines the domain of culture.

Educational Considerations. Some emphasis on shared traits is basic to any conceptual understanding of the role of culture in education. However, such an emphasis leaves little if any room for the recognition of each student's individuality within the framework of the culture concept. Individuality becomes the domain of psychology, relevant only to discussions of personality, while "culture" is used to refer to ideas and behaviors that prevail in the individual's group. Using the culture concept as a basis for theories of education might be appropriate if the goal is to educate (or reeducate) a group, as in modernization programs applied by developing countries to their peasant populations. But the focus of most education, as all who have taught for any time know, is the education of the individual student, not the education of his or her ethnic group.

Consequences for Teacher-Student Interaction

The relevance of this problem lies in the possible consequences of the **group-oriented concept of culture** for the perceptions and expectations of teachers in their interactions with culturally diverse children. A group-oriented concept may serve to distract the teacher's attention from the student's particular experience of culture-generating processes, in and outside of school. The culture concept adopted by the teacher greatly affects teacher-student interaction. The assumptions a teacher makes about the student's culture, whether right or wrong, may stereotype the student and thus preclude the flexible, realistic, and open-minded teacher-student interaction needed for effective instruction. The effect of this stereotyping on students is significant, since the educational process is fundamentally a process of social interaction, with socialization as a primary goal.

Let's consider an example of how the group culture concept might operate in a teacher-student interaction. Picture a situation in which the teacher is perplexed by some action or response by a student of minority status. A teacher who has studied some anthropological descriptions of the student's ethnic culture may leap to an interpretation of the student's behavior based on idealized characteristics anthropologists have attributed to that culture. The teacher may mean well, but to construe an individual's behavior solely on the basis of generalizations about group traits is to stereotype the individual, no matter how valid the generalizations or how well meaning one's intentions.

Stereotyping of Students

It would be better for the teacher to encounter the student in the way anthropologists most often come to understand the people they study. Although they write about cultures in collective terms, anthropologists build their understandings through observations of individuals. The teacher's efforts to understand the individual student could (and should) be supplemented by knowledge of cultural attributes widely held in the student's ethnic community. But this fund of knowledge should be viewed only as background information. The question of its applicability to the particular student should be treated as inherently problematical. Many studies (for example, Cole, 1995; Rodriguez, 1989; Tharp & Gallimore, 1988) also caution educational personnel against hasty "ethnographic/cultural" generalizations on the grounds that all linguistic-cultural groups are continuously undergoing significant cultural changes.

Individual Differences

Even teachers who are of the same minority status as their students may be considered in some ways culturally different from those they are teaching. This observation is not recent. Guerra (1979) points to linguistic and other cultural variations both within (student-student) and between (student-teacher) generations of bilingual populations. Cuellar (1980) argues that one's understanding of the meaning and value of culture and language must take into account the fact that "a community's characteristics reflect the composition of the different generational cohorts in the different age strata" (p. 198). What this means is that the individual variation within cultures should be of particular importance to educators.

The Individual-Oriented Concept of Culture

The group culture concept is not the only instrument available for understanding individuals and groups. Fortunately, anthropological theory contains an **individual-oriented concept of culture** developed and used by a number of anthropologists with interests in psychology. As Schwartz (1978) notes, these theorists criticized the group culture concept for the way it can "lead one to imagine culture as floating somehow disembodied in the noösphere or, at best, carried by human beings as a conductor might carry an electric current containing information" (p. 434). Rather than work with an abstract idea of culture, these theorists were interested more in how culture was manifested in the lives of individual human beings.

An early expression of the individual-oriented concept of culture is seen in the work of anthropologist J. O. Dorsey. The American anthropologist Edward Sapir (quoted in Pelto & Pelto, 1975) wrote the following description of Dorsey's approach:

> Living as long as he did in close touch with the Omaha Indians, [Dorsey] knew that he was dealing, not with a society nor with a specimen of primitive man but with a finite, though indefinite, number of human beings who gave themselves the privilege of differing from each other not only in matters generally considered as "One's own business" but even on questions which clearly transcended the private individual's concerns. (p. 1)

Culture as Variable

Advocates of the individual-oriented concept of culture frequently describe a society's culture as a "pool" of constructs (rules, beliefs, values, etc.) by which its members conceptually order the objects and events of their lives. The participation of individuals in this pool is seen as variable. Spiro (1951), for example, distinguished between the cultural "heritage" of all members of a society (that which has been made available to them by their predecessors) and each individual's particular cultural "inheritance" (that portion of the group's heritage that the individual has effectively received, or "internalized," from the past). Schwartz adds that the individual also manipulates, recombines, and otherwise transforms these inherited constructs. This process of transformation, together with the outright creation of new constructs, is a major source of culture change (Schwartz, 1978). The individual's own portion of a society's culture is termed by Goodenough (1981) as a "propriocept," by Wallace (1970) as a "mazeway," and by Schwartz (1978) as an "idioverse." All of these specialized terms are variations on a core nature of culture: each individual assembles his or her own version of the larger culture.

For some of the anthropologists who employ an individual-oriented concept of culture, "the private system of ideas of individuals is culture" (Pelto & Pelto, 1975, pp. 12–13). Other anthropologists of like mind reject the implication in such a notion of individual cultures. As they see it, the contents of one subjective system alone cannot be considered a culture. Like Schwartz, these theorists consider a cultural system to consist of all the constructs available to a society's members. Nevertheless, the society is itself not the locus of culture; its individual members are. The culture thus is a distributive phenomenon in that its elements are widely distributed among the individual members of a society. A major implication of this **distributive model of culture** is a rejection of the traditional assumption of cultural homogeneity—that is, the idea that all members of a culture share all that culture's attributes. The distributive model instead implies that each individual's portion of the culture differs in some ways from that of any other.

According to Schwartz (1978), Wallace's antidote to the homogeneous view of culture is an overdose, leading to the opposite malady of ignoring the degree of cultural sharing that does occur between individuals. Schwartz's own model of culture takes into account both the sharing and nonsharing of cultural constructs between members of a society, and he argues that both are fundamentally essential to a society's viability. Diversity, he argues, increases a society's cultural inventory, whereas what any individual could contain within his or her head would make up a very small culture pool. Commonality then permits communication and coordination in social life. In Schwartz's (1978) own words:

> It makes as little sense to depict the distribution of a culture among the members of a society as totally heterogeneous and unique in each individual as it did to argue for complete homogeneity. We must dispense with the a priori assumption of homogeneity, but, similarly, we are not served by an a priori assumption of heterogeneity. (p. 438)

Educational Considerations. I view Schwartz's formulation of the distributive model of culture as the most appropriate for addressing issues of cultural diversity in the schools. This formulation permits, within the framework of culture, simultaneous recognition of a student's "ethnic" culture and those characteristics that define the student as a unique individual. Students share with their ethnic peers constructs they do not share with others, but all individuals are in some ways different from their ethnic peers. The distributive model also permits recognition of traits that members of subgroups share with members of the larger culture, such as those acquired through acculturation.

Schooling is a major variable in **acculturation,** the process by which the members of a society are taught the elements of the society's culture. The acculturation process is a crucial considera-

Variety in Acculturation

tion in the analysis of ethnic minorities in pluralistic societies. Variety in acculturation also contributes significantly to the heterogeneity of ethnic cultures. Writing about the U.S. cultural subgroup labeled "Hispanic," Bell, Kasschau, and Zellman (1976) note that among Chicanos, "many have ancestors who came to North America several centuries ago, but others are themselves recent immigrants. Hence, a simple cultural characterization of [this] ethnic group should be avoided" (p. 7). These authors also caution against a simplistic view of the process of acculturation, noting that it "may not be linear, in the sense that one simply loses certain Mexican attributes and replaces them with Anglo attributes" (pp. 31–32). In other words, acculturation may be characterized by more complex combinations of attributes—and by ongoing recombination—rather than by simple substitution of Anglo attributes for the original ethnic ones.

Additive or Subtractive Acculturation

With regard to the effect of U.S. schooling, as Gibson & Obgu (1991) suggest, acculturation can be understood as either additive or subtractive. In her work with Punjabi Sikh immigrants, Gibson (1995) finds these immigrants to be quite eager to have their children succeed in U.S. schools. Yet she also reports that these same parents are just as anxious about their children's loss of important Punjabi cultural attributes. They would thus like to see an *additive* acculturation for their children—the acquisition of knowledge and skills of a new culture without rejection of the old. Yet in the schools these students attend, little or no attention is paid to the Punjabi culture. These schools practice a *subtractive* acculturation, often identified as assimilation, aimed at replacing the old culture with the new. Too often, U.S. schools adopt such subtractive acculturation practices, often without being cognizant of their effects.

Customs and Culture

The result of these various acculturation processes is wide differences among students within the same ethnic group. "But what about customs?" some people may ask. "If the family maintains certain ethnic customs, don't they help to minimize the effects of acculturation?" Chicanos, for example, might point out that nearly all members of their group recognize certain *costumbres* (customs) that distinguish them from the larger society. Yet customs occupy a realm of culture that is more likely to belong to the public sphere than to form a specific part of an individual's subjective orientation. Referring to the "layered" nature of culture, anthropologist Benjamin Paul (1965) has observed that "what we call customs rest on top and are most apparent. Deepest and least apparent are the cultural values that give meaning and direction to life. Values influence people's perceptions of needs and their choice between perceived alternative courses of action" (p. 200).

BECOMING A RESPONSIVE TEACHER

Influential Teachers, Influential Students

These students will change American society.

American society is not the same as it was a century ago, or even a decade ago, partly because of the different peoples who have come to our shores. Without the contributions of individual groups, we would not have such American icons as the Christmas tree, the log cabin, labor unions, and jazz. Jewish immigrants in the early part of this century made a key contribution—they demanded entry to college in such numbers that they transformed what had been a finishing school for the wealthy into an opportunity for individual advancement.

Those college-bound students were fortunate to have teachers dedicated to their success, even if the teachers never anticipated that their efforts would have the far-reaching effect of helping to democratize higher education. Teachers of that era were selected not only for their formal credentials, but for their suitability as role models for the young. The impact of teachers on the life of young people can hardly be overestimated. Teachers represent a link to the adult world of educated, successful professionals. Especially for children from a different culture and language, teachers have a tremendous impact; they are their link to American society. Without the caring guidance of teachers, the immigrant and minority youth of today will readily learn how to eat at McDonald's, play video games, and watch MTV. But they will have great difficulty getting to college and becoming engineers, playwrights, or teachers themselves.

▼ Meeting the Challenge

1. Write a letter to a young relative or friend. In this letter, describe some of the changes that have occurred in the world since you were his or her age. You might mention specific political or social events or trends and your thoughts about them. Feel free to refer to any types of changes you have encountered that you feel have affected your life. Then, given your

BECOMING A RESPONSIVE TEACHER *Cont.*

perspective as an older mentor for this young person, provide some suggestions about which aspects of schooling might help prepare him or her to confront change constructively. If you decide to send this letter, consider sharing any response from the addressee with your classmates.

2. Find out what student cultural centers are on your college or university campus, and then visit each one. If possible, also visit cultural centers in the local community outside your campus. Gather leaflets and flyers and take some notes about the activities these cultural groups are planning. In class, compile a master list of events to attend over the semester and decide which ones interest you the most. Volunteer to attend an event and review it for your classmates.

3. You have been granted the opportunity to spend an entire day with a 10-year-old child doing anything you want, wherever you want. This child is from an ethnic and linguistic background that is radically different from yours. In fact, you may not even have a shared language. What would you want this child to teach you about his or her world?

I purposely emphasize the problematic nature of cultural variability and sharing. The variable nature of acculturation and the individual uniqueness that it engenders are, I believe, no less important for the education of culturally diverse students than are the "real" cultural differences between ethnic groups. Education must deal with both the individual and the culture.

I hasten to add that teachers who work with children from culturally diverse populations must be not only keenly aware of the instructional objectives of education but also knowledgeable about and sensitive to the impact that culture has on the student.

Culture as Central to Development and Education

Some scholars have made a persuasive case that typical definitions of culture do not appropriately address its significance in our understanding of human existence. Geertz (1973), for example, has suggested that culture is part of our continuous human endeavor to construct meaning out of life: "Humans are

Constructing Culture

animals suspended in webs of significance that they spin. Culture is those webs, and the analysis of it is not an experiment in search of law but an interpretive one in search of meaning" (p. 83). According to this interpretation of culture, we are all similarly *constructing* culture in response to our own need to understand our circumstances and seek meaning for them. In this sense there will likely be many more similarities than differences in the ways in which individuals and groups construct culture. The specific context will vary, but not the basic goal.

Luria's (1928) and Vygotsky's (1929) notions of child development, cognition, and learning in relation to culture are also very

Cultural Basis of Cognition

instructive. They argue that cognition and learning emerge through culturally mediated, historically developing, practical activity (Cole, 1995). In the most basic sense, human psychological processes arise simultaneously with forms of behavior and "tools" or artifacts that are utilized to modify material objects as a means of regulating human interactions with both the physical and the social world. These "tools" include tangible goods as well as communicative, cognitive, and other processes that allow knowledge of the use of tools to be transmitted to others (Luria, 1928). In this view, culture is the entire pool of tools accumulated by a social group in its historical existence. Individuals use these artifacts as they interact with their own world, and in doing so they continue to construct culture.

This view that human cognition and psychological processes have a social origin—artifact development in culture—has great implications for our construction of schooling. Vygotsky (1981) would go so far as to conclude that all forms of cognition and learning are social and therefore cultural in origin:

> Any function in children's cultural development appears twice, or on two planes. First it appears on the social plane and then on the psychological plane. First it appears between people as an inter psychological category and then within the individual child as an intra psychological category. . . . Social relations or relations among people genetically underlie all higher functions and their relationships. (p. 63)

In his research on child development, Cole (1995) follows this conceptual framework for understanding culture and human development. He concludes that teachers can be very important in organizing a child's environment so as to enhance the types of social experiences that lead to optimal development. He suggests that "it is the foundation upon which, in an ideal world, the education of children would be organized" (Cole, 1995, p. 111). We will explore this concept in Chapter 6, when we address specific roots of cognitive functioning and education.

Culture and Disabilities

It is important to note that as culture becomes more central to our analysis of development, learning, and schooling, all forms of cultural experience that generate diversity in our student populations need to be recognized. For example, children who are challenged by a physical and/or mental disability are exposed to cultural conditions different from those experienced by children who are not living with such challenges. Deaf populations have suggested that they develop in bilingual/bicultural social circumstances that are often not understood or addressed in our schools. The same can be said for children who are raised by caregivers whose sexual preference differs from that of the majority, or children who themselves express nonmajority sexual preferences. These examples suggest the importance of realizing that such students are immersed in a different cultural milieu and that issues of cultural diversity must be broadly defined. If culture in this sense comes to the center of our understanding of development and learning, it cannot be ignored in the classroom.

Race, Class, Gender, and Cultural Diversity

There are important issues in U.S. education concerning the relationships among race, class, gender, and cultural diversity. It is still quite apparent that the United States continues to struggle with the facts of racism (Weinberg, 1990), classism (Nieto, 1992), and sexism (Weis, 1988). In each of these cases, the basis for discrimination is the belief that those of one race, social class, or gender are either inherently superior or inferior.

The existence of such beliefs and the individual or institutional behavior that springs from them is not disputed here. Clearly, all educators must be vigilant with regard to these debilitating ideologies, especially within schooling practices. For example, the fact that students of one race, class, or gender are overrepresented in less challenging curricula (through the use of tracking or classroom grouping) and have consistently high dropout rates, poor attendance, and of course low achievement can be seen as potentially related to racism, classism, or sexism.

Culture and "Isms"

What is different about my attention to culture as the central variable in schooling is a more comprehensive and useful understanding of these "isms." Racism serves as a good example. In the United States, most people are actually a mixture of races. Sometimes we even coin terms to indicate this mixture, such as *mulatto* (referring to someone of European and African background) and *mestizo* (referring to someone of European and indigenous American ancestry). Such individuals are not just examples of the racial mixture of this country. They also demonstrate the existence of new culture-creating groups whose characteristics may be either similar to or different from their ambiguous racial identities. Is it more useful, then, to focus on these individuals' "racial" character or on their cultural character? I suggest that an emphasis on their culture will be both more useful and more conceptually sound in education. This approach does not ignore the existence of racism or other "isms," of course; rather, it incorporates such factors into the cultural analysis.

The Role of Cultural Capital

A person's entire set of cultural relationships, not just in the family but across all the key social spheres, has been called his or her **cultural capital.** In effect, it is the cultural fund that the individual draws upon to support all the activities of life. Not only does it help protect and nurture the individual in family or family-like settings, it also plays a similar role in nonfamily-like institutions, especially the school. For healthy human development to occur, caretakers and other social agents (including teachers) must offer children systematic opportunities to construct the relationships that build cultural capital (Valenzuela & Dornbusch, 1994).

But what of children who live in diverse cultural contexts? Is their cultural capital sufficient to protect and nurture their development, in school and elsewhere? Does school help them develop such capital, or does it in fact undercut the process?

Sociologists have not been particularly encouraging in their answers (Mehan, Villanueva, Hubbard, & Lintz, 1996; Mirón, 1996; Romo & Falbo, 1996). Stanton-Salazar (1997) summarizes a set of issues that all too often obstruct the development of the cultural capital of culturally diverse students:

Barriers to Developing Cultural Capital

1. Values based on social status, ethnicity, language, and gender may lead to such situations as the overrepresentation of white males in gifted classes and of black and Latino males in learning disability programs.

2. Barriers such as the inability of the school staff to communicate effectively in languages other than English may make school an uncomfortable experience for certain students.

3. Schools may use evaluation processes that hinge on the willingness of students, families, and the community to adopt the standards of the dominant group. For example, a state's new assessment activity for students of beginning reading may focus only on English and thereby ignore the fact that many children in the state are learning to read in a language other than English.

4. Distrust and detachment may be institutionalized. For example, a school may require teachers to report to the Immigration and Naturalization Service (INS) any students and families they suspect of being in the country illegally. The parents may respond by keeping their children away from school because of their fear of deportation (regardless of whether they are indeed legal residents).

5. Ideological mechanisms may limit the ability of people to seek and give help in the school, particularly in terms of the achievement of high academic standards. For example, the presence of the "*el pobrecito* syndrome" ("this poor kid syndrome") among instructional staff expresses the notion that children who are poor, immigrant, non-English-speaking, or from troubled families need the school as a protective and insulating environment. This frequently leads to lower academic expectations for the students. "What these kids need is a safe and loving place, not a challenging curriculum," teachers may think—when in fact the children need both.

This sociological analysis speaks volumes about how the school can impede the development of cultural capital among diverse student populations. But this need not always be the case.

Overcoming the Barriers

Various studies have documented how specific schools have attempted to overcome such barriers and promote cultural capital (August & Hakuta, 1997; García, 1997; Miramontes, Nadeau, &

Commins, 1997; U.S. Department of Education, 1998). August and Hakuta (1997) comprehensively reviewed schools and classrooms in which linguistically and culturally diverse students have achieved high academic performance. Through their analysis of some 33 case studies, they identified the following factors as contributing to the students' success:

> a supportive school-wide climate, school leadership, a customized learning environment, articulation and coordination within and between schools, use of native language and culture in instruction, a balanced curriculum that includes both basic and higher-order skills, explicit skills instruction, opportunities for student-directed instruction, use of instructional strategies that enhance understanding, opportunities for practice, systematic student assessment, staff development, and home and parent involvement. (p. 171)

The Culture of the School

The school has many, if not all, of the characteristics that anthropologists and sociologists tell us belong to culture. It has tacit rules, patterns, formal structures of organization, and an ecological component. Most important are the tacit dimensions. We tend to think that school is all about learning "the three R's." Parents and children, and sometimes teachers themselves, do not recognize that the school makes cultural demands on students in addition to the intellectual ones.

Competing Concepts of School

As in our earlier discussion of culture, a distinction must be made between competing concepts of the nature and purpose of school. Recent research acknowledges that schools are social situations that are constructed through the interactions between individuals (Feldman & Shen, 1971; Gardner, 1983). More traditional views represent schools as institutions with stable traits generally impervious to individual influence. It is important for educators to understand how our society views the concept of school, which underlies how we approach the teaching of students in schools. If we see teaching and learning as embedded within a cultural context, we are more likely to recognize that performance will vary as a function of that context.

Student Response to School Culture

Some examples from research into the cultural demands of school will demonstrate this point. Observing the classroom performance of Native American students, Phillips (1983, 1984)

Observations of Students

found that these students appeared to conform exactly to the stereotype of "the silent Indian child." Phillips was puzzled, however, because her observations outside the classroom indicated that in this context these children were certainly not silent. She identified what is now considered an important aspect of school culture: **participant-structured demand,** or the demands of instruction that are imposed by the organization of the learning environment itself. She was able to make this discovery only because she observed the children across a number of situations—in community settings, in their homes, and in school.

Phillips found that classroom lessons imposed varying demands on the children. The classrooms were organized in an individualistic, competitive way. Children were expected to stand up alone in front of the classroom and to respond competitively to the teacher's questions. The Native American children were not doing

Contrasting Demands of Home and School

well in this arrangement. Phillips contrasted the demands of the school with the demands of the home. There were definite demands in each culture. In the homes of the Native American children, she found a culture in which children were working cooperatively in groups, not competitively. For an individual to stand out, to act on his or her own, independent of the group, was to violate the norm of the home. Conversely, it was to violate the norm of the classroom not to stand out. The children were thus caught in a bind between the competing demands of home and school.

Other studies have compared home and school cultures. Heath's (1982) work, conducted in a number of different areas, contributes a good deal to our knowledge base. In her study of low-income black and white Appalachian children, she found that their teachers, who came from different economic and cultural backgrounds, talked to children differently than did the

Language Use

children's parents. Heath described a difference in language used between home and school. The school placed a great demand on children to display their knowledge. Children would often be asked a question for which the teacher already had the answer. If, for example, a child correctly answered the question, "What time is it?" the teacher would respond not with "Thank you" but with "Very good," indicating that the child's knowledge had been tested. The teacher did not need the information. At home, however, when a child was asked, "What time is it?" the underlying assumption was that the child had information needed by another member of the family. Interestingly, middle-income parents often use a questioning strategy similar to the teacher's. They play games such as peek-a-boo that also have a dimension of information. But Heath found that in low-income families there was little imitation of the conversational demands of school. These children were not gaining practice at home with a linguistic device essential to their school performance.

The School's Response to Children

The school must allow cultural elements that are relevant to the children to enter the classroom freely. Some refer to this practice as **scaffolding.** With scaffolding, the school provides a set of supports that utilize the child's home language, discourse style, participation orientation, and so on, thereby enabling the child to move through relevant experiences from the home toward the demands of the school as representative of the society. It is not a subtraction of culture, and it is not an attempt to reproduce home environments in the context of the school. Instead the idea is to encourage the child to respect the demands of the school culture while preserving the integrity of the home culture.

Importance of Scaffolding

We must first comprehend the fact that children—all children—come to school motivated to enlarge their culture. But we must start with *their* culture. We need not regard them, certainly not initially, as organisms to be molded and regulated. We look first to determine how they seek to know themselves and others and how their expertise and experience can be used as the fuel to fire their interests, knowledge, and skills. We look first not at their deficits—at what they do not know—but at what they need to know. Far from having deficits, they are rich in assets. As teachers, we enter their world in order to aid them and to build bridges between two cultures (Sarason, 1990).

Teaching in a Cultural Context

If educators better serve culturally diverse students by understanding cultural diversity and respecting individuality, have they fulfilled their obligations as teachers? I believe they have not. Our culturally diverse populations continue to be highly vulnerable in today's society and today's schools. We examined this social, economic, and educational vulnerability in the previous chapter. It is in the best interests of all of us for culturally diverse students to succeed. They will carry us all to either a bright or a beleaguered future.

Respect Is Not Enough

Given the present circumstances and the magnitude of this challenge, what must we do? Sensitivity to "culture," while necessary, is not sufficient. Earlier we saw how even well-meaning teachers may stereotype students when trying to allow for cultural differences. There are three additional ingredients needed for effective teaching in a context of student cultural diversity:

▼ Personal commitment
▼ Knowledge of what makes a difference
▼ Educational leadership

Let's look more closely at these elements and take an inventory of them in our schools today.

Personal Commitment

We need not be fooled by liberal or conservative rhetoric. We have not achieved educational equality for our culturally diverse populations, and substantive progress in this area requires further resolve. It is often trumpeted that Head Start, school choice, restructuring, site-based management, cooperative learning, the whole language approach, educational technology (computer-assisted instruction), and so forth have already or will soon reverse the pattern of underachievement among linguistically and culturally diverse populations. Clearly these contributions are important, but our own part in the U.S. educational system suggests that we as teachers should resist the notion of a miracle cure. No new methodologies, reorganizations, or curricula will satisfactorily address the problem of underachievement unless the individuals who implement these initiatives are deeply committed to the enterprise. The change that is necessary must be fueled by the type of social energy that our nation has tapped in the past. As in the eras of President Kennedy's "New Frontier" or President Johnson's "War on Poverty," we must grasp the spiritual importance of this new educational challenge.

No Miracle Cures

More than two decades after President Carter warned of a crisis of spirit in America—a warning that proved politically disastrous for him and a boon to rival Ronald Reagan—and with President Clinton having urged a national discourse on issues of diversity and unity, a broad spectrum of the nation's social and intellectual leadership is concluding that such concepts are as critically important now as they were in the 1960s. In fact, they say, the crisis has deepened. We are losing the faith that our children's days will be better than our own, and it is no longer possible to deny this fact—even to ourselves.

A consensus has emerged that a lack of confidence among Americans in the future and in one another lies at the heart of the nation's ills. A nation that passed much of the 1970s, in the aftermath of the Vietnam War, in search of its soul and self spent the 1980s and 1990s in what many see as a self-consuming materialism. We now enter the twenty-first century in a cynical, dispirited mood. "There is disturbing evidence to suggest that most forms of responsibility toward others have eroded in recent decades" (p. 101), asserts Derek Bok, former president of Harvard University, in his 1990 book *Universities and the Future of America*. The percentage of people who feel that most individuals in power try to take advantage of others has doubled over the past two decades and now exceeds 60 percent.

Importance of Inspiration

It is difficult to believe that the picture is truly so bleak. Most of us know people who are generous and creative in their interactions with others—even heroic in small ways, considering the multiple stresses and strains of modern life. They work hard, tend to their families, and contribute to their communities. Many people care deeply about individual and collective welfare in the United States. It is possible that our current cynicism is simply a measure of disappointed idealism, of surprise and dismay that our work as a nation is not done and may never be done, and that we must continue to call upon the inspiration, resolve, commitment, and passion of everyone.

Some have argued that we have lost the ability to inspire our children. Others say we have lost the ability to inspire ourselves. But inspiration is the spark that leads to resolve and commitment, and we cannot afford to be without it. Borrowing from Jaime Escalante, the noted California educator depicted in the popular 1988 film *Stand and Deliver,* we will need *ganas*—the desire that fires the will to overcome great challenges.

Knowledge of What Makes a Difference

Individual Uniqueness

We will also need a new knowledge base. Recent research has pinpointed the problem of educational vulnerability. It has destroyed stereotypes and myths about the educational needs of culturally diverse students and laid a foundation upon which to reconceptualize present educational practices and to launch new initiatives. As we saw earlier in this chapter, the basis for change is a new understanding of individual uniqueness within a cultural context. No one set of descriptions or prescriptions will suffice for all students of a given cultural background.

Attributes of Successful Teachers

We should pay attention to what seems to work. As noted above, recent research summarized by the U.S. Department of Education (1998) and August and Hakuta (1997) has documented educationally effective practices with linguistically and culturally diverse students in selected preschool, elementary, and high school classrooms throughout the United States. The results show that the teachers of these classrooms were highly committed to the educational success of their students. They perceived themselves as instructional innovators utilizing "new" learning theories and instructional philosophies to guide their practice. Most of these teachers were involved in professional development activities such as small-group support networks with other educators. They had a strong, demonstrated belief in the importance of communication between the school and the home (several teachers were interacting weekly with parents), and felt they had the autonomy to create or change the instruction and curriculum in their classrooms, even if it did not exactly meet district guidelines. They had high academic expectations for all their students ("Everyone will learn to read in my classroom") and served as advocates for their students. They rejected any suggestion that their students were intellectually or academically disadvantaged.

This and other research shows that effective curriculum, instructional strategies, and teaching staffs are rooted in sharing expertise and experiences through multiple processes of communication. Abundant and diverse opportunities for speaking, listening, reading, and writing, along with home-to-school bridges that help guide students through the learning process, constitute an effective curriculum. Effective schools also encourage culturally diverse students to take risks, construct meaning, and reinterpret the knowledge they acquire as it applies to their lives. Within this curriculum, skills are taught as tools for acquiring further knowledge. Research into such effective programs should continue. The more we know about what makes them effective, the more equipped we will be to educate diverse student groups.

Educational Leadership

The leadership necessary to mobilize this growing commitment and knowledge will recognize four interlocking domains that pertain especially to teachers.

Retraining Teachers

Knowledge Dissemination. We will need to disseminate knowledge about effective practices to those who can utilize it. This requires training, retraining, and more retraining of teachers. Individually and institutionally, new knowledge must be appropriated by people working in the field of education. It is of no use to students if researchers share their knowledge only among themselves. New avenues for knowledge dissemination and appropriation along with leadership in this domain are required.

Professional Development. New knowledge alone does not automatically lead to a new set of pedagogical or curricular skills ready for use by practitioners. Knowledge must be transferred to teachers and adapted for use in specific instructional contexts. Time and energy must be devoted to the collaboration required between teachers and researchers to develop new skills. Moreover, these new pedagogical and curricular skills must be evaluated in the field—they must prove themselves effective for students. We will need to hold ourselves and others automatically accountable. This requires leadership in both knowledge dissemination and professional skill development.

| **Risk and Collaboration** |

Disposition for Leadership. Many are called, but few will self-select. We need a generation of educational leaders who are willing to sacrifice, work very hard and very long, take risks, learn from failure, rise above frustration, rethink existing paradigms, and support and collaborate with their colleagues. Those who do not possess this set of dispositions must step aside, minimize obstruction, and otherwise admit that if they cannot be part of the solution, they will not be part of the problem.

Affective Engagement. We will need leadership that welcomes, adopts, nurtures, celebrates, and challenges our culturally diverse students. "They" must become "we." Anything short of raw advocacy every minute of every day will not suffice. Too many of these students have given up hope in themselves. We must not give up hope.

Mostly, educators need to act. Presidents and governors proclaim and set national educational goals. Educators need to move beyond such proclamations. The task at hand is not only to see the future but to enable it. With commitment, knowledge, and leadership, educators can enable the future for our culturally diverse society.

Conclusion

In this chapter, I have tried to set the context for a more thorough discussion of the educational challenges facing this country's educators. The challenge stands for all students and specifically for those who are culturally diverse. This country's educational future will be much different from its educational past. We will have to be capable of responding to transformations in social structures and institutions, in global organization, and in values. Historically, our schools' efforts to merge diverse groups into a homogenized "American" culture have not resulted in academic success for culturally diverse students. However, new insights into educational concepts, research, and practices suggest that we can meet this challenge successfully.

In the chapters that follow, I will more clearly define the notions of culture outlined here and describe the interrelationships among social, cultural, and linguistic contexts for education. We must continue to build a knowledge base regarding children, families, communities, and schools. Research studies that add dimension to what we already know about culturally diverse students will be valuable pieces of the puzzle. However, as the preceding discussion has indicated, merely building this knowledge base is not enough.

I want to point out, before you turn another page, that the information in this book will not make a critical difference in the lives of many of our most educationally needy students. Even with all its theoretical underpinnings and its comments on research, pedagogy, curriculum, and educational philosophy, it is still only a book. It is a forum through which knowledge can be developed, examined, and transmitted. But this knowledge must be combined with action on the part of educators if the challenges I have articulated are to be met head-on and successfully overcome.

SUMMARY OF MAJOR IDEAS

1. Ongoing social and economic changes, in this country and worldwide, have produced new contexts for education in the United States. We need to prepare students for participation in the global marketplace and for flexibility in their future careers. Projections show that in the near future 60 percent of all jobs will require some postsecondary education and 80 percent of new jobs will be in the information and service sector.

2. It is not the role of the schools to prepare students for specific jobs. Rather, schools must teach academic skills that develop students' intellectual abilities and that involve students in learning activities that enhance human relationships, critical thinking, and civic responsibility.

3. Despite its undeniable cultural and linguistic diversity, U.S. society still demonstrates an "us versus them" relationship between the white majority and minority populations. This pattern of thinking is reflected in schooling practices, with negative results especially for language minority students. For example, recent policy changes in Texas and California have eroded the educational opportunities offered to immigrant and minority students.

4. Culture is a system of values, beliefs, notions about acceptable and unacceptable behavior, and other socially constructed ideas characteristic of a society or of a subgroup within a society. The group-oriented concept of culture describes culture as a set of attributes that are shared by all the members of a group. The individual-oriented concept of culture describes culture as a set of attributes that are made

available to members of a group but may not be shared by all members. The group concept of culture emphasizes cultural homogeneity, and the individual concept of culture emphasizes cultural heterogeneity.

5. Criticism of the group-oriented concept of culture as a basis for educational theory centers on the assumption of cultural homogeneity. It may lead to stereotyping children in terms of their cultural group identification, rather than addressing children as unique individuals.

6. The distributive model of culture, which is based on the notion of cultural heterogeneity, implies that each individual's portion of a culture differs from that of any other individual. Because it recognizes the uniqueness of the individual, who is the focus of educational efforts, this concept may serve as a useful basis for educational theory.

7. Acculturation is the process by which the members of a society are taught the elements of the society's culture. There is much variety in the acculturation process within all societies. Variety in acculturation contributes to cultural heterogeneity.

8. Educational theory must be founded on the acknowledgment that individuals of similar cultural backgrounds may share some attributes but are also unique from one another. Educational practices must respond to the individual student first, within the context of the student's culture.

9. As culture becomes a central variable in the concept of schooling, the definition of cultural diversity must be expanded in order to promote the development of students from all types of backgrounds. Issues of race, class, gender, and disability, which clearly form part of an individual's culture, can then be incorporated into the cultural analysis.

10. Schools must strive to promote the development of the cultural capital, or set of cultural relationships, of their diverse student populations.

11. An important aspect of school culture is participant structured demand, a term that describes the demands of instruction that are imposed on children by the organization of the learning environment. Students for whom the cultural demands of home do not mesh with the cultural demands of school may not perform well academically. Different attitudes toward cooperation and competition and different uses of language at home and at school are two possible cultural variables.

12. Scaffolding is an educational practice that provides support for children as they move between disparate home and school cultures. The goal is to keep the home culture intact while the child learns to function within the demands of school.

13. Children enter school motivated to enlarge their culture. Building on what they already know instead of focusing on what they do not know is the goal of effective teaching.

14. Effective teaching in a context of student cultural diversity requires personal commitment, knowledge of what makes a difference, and educational leadership. Initiatives proposed by the educational leaders of tomorrow will focus on transmitting knowledge to teachers and developing new teaching skills. These leaders will be risk-takers who support one another's ideas and who celebrate student diversity in the schools.

EXTENDING YOUR EXPERIENCE

1. The text suggests that future job markets will require workers who are flexible and creative, skilled at communicating, and technologically literate. Outline some curricula that you think would develop these attributes in young people. As a further step, design a course for any grade level that focuses on developing children's awareness of three factors: human relationships, critical thinking, and civic responsibility.

2. Using your own words, and referring back to the chapter if necessary, explain the concepts of cultural homogeneity and cultural heterogeneity. Now list all your group memberships, both formal and informal: sets of friends and acquaintances, clubs, teams, and organizations in which you participate. Select one of these groups and describe what all its members have in common. Then describe how the members differ from one another. Write a few sentences introducing yourself to a new member of the group. Do you emphasize what you share with others, what makes you different, or both?

3. Using the categories listed in the text (familial, linguistic, religious and spiritual, aesthetic, socioeconomic, educational, dietary, and gender) and any others you can think of, characterize your cultural heritage—the systems of belief and thought in which you were raised. What portion of this heritage have you actually "inherited," or consciously incorporated into your own life? What portion, if any, have you rejected? Why?

4. Define participant-structured demand in your own words and describe how it operates in two of the courses you are taking. How do the cultural demands of these two class environments differ? Characterize your learning experience in each one. Write three serious recommendations to your in-

structor for altering the class culture to benefit your own particular style of learning.

5. Review the comments on cynicism by Derek Bok quoted in the chapter. Realize that if you are younger than 24, these comments refer to you. Do you feel that they accurately portray your vision of human nature? Interview five friends and describe their opinions on Bok's remarks. Using verbatim quotes from your friends, who may remain anonymous if they wish, present your findings to the class.

RESOURCES FOR FURTHER STUDY

Cole, M. (1996). *Cultural psychology: A once and future discipline.* Cambridge, MA: Belknap Press of Harvard University Press.

This volume touches very directly on the centrality of culture in the formation of the individual. The author traces the historical intellectual trail that has led to the prioritization of the ways in which culture serves the needs of individuality and thus argues that we cannot ignore the influence of culture on individual student development.

Goodenough, W. H. (1981). *Culture, language, and society* (2nd ed.). Menlo Park, CA: Benjamin/Cummins.

The essay looks at how humans expand their linguistic knowledge and cultural base. The study is based on research conducted in South America in a remote area of the Amazon River. The author points out that language and culture result directly from what individuals and groups do collectively for their own benefit and knowledge. All their decisions are made within the boundaries of what they had, have, or think they might have. This microscopic view of language and culture allows us to clarify the relationship between culture and society and to begin to grapple with a general theory of cultural stability by observing our commonalties, gains, and knowledge.

Kroeber, A. L., & Kluckhohn, C. (1963). *Culture: A critical review of concepts and definitions.* New York: Vintage Books.

The authors argue that culture is a general descriptive category of human nature. This definition allows cultures to have similar distinctive designs; however, the only changes culture can have are initiated by individuals, because individuals create organisms that operate in groups. These groups or cultures are a direct result of individuals interacting at the concrete level. In short, cultures begin, continue, or change as the result of individual action.

Rodriguez, C. E. (1989). *Puerto Ricans born in the U.S.A.* Winchester, MA: Unwin Hyman.

This book is an extensive discussion of American citizens of Puerto Rican descent. The discussion primarily supports the theory that their individual and group contributions have not brought prosperity to the Puerto Rican community. The theory is well supported by detailed Census data and socioeconomic trends. One area of particular interest is education. Puerto Ricans, like most Hispanic students in the United States, lag behind academically, are rapidly dropping out, are segregated, and have overall low academic achievement. The author presents some of the arguments traditionally used to validate the low educational attainment of Hispanic students and offers recommendations to improve the educational situation of Puerto Ricans.

Rose, M. (1995). *Possible lives: The promise of public education in America.* Boston: Houghton Mifflin.

This author accurately describes the lives of students and educators who are confronting the challenges of cultural diversity and rising above expectations of failure. A touching, thoughtful, and highly articulate account of real people in real schools who are beating the odds against them, it is a must read for any future teacher.

Schwartz, T. (1978). Where is the culture? Personality as the distributive locus of culture. In G. Spinder (Ed.), *The making of psychological anthropology* (pp. 197–218). Berkeley: University of California Press.

The author presents a model of culture that is neither homogeneous nor heterogeneous but instead a conglomeration of similarities and differences. Both culture and individual are constantly changing, but it is essential to recognize that even while changing, both are still stable and inherent. The author argues that individuals are the driving force behind cultural change, yet that such change affects other individuals and creates and re-creates culture.

Valdés, G. (1996). *Con respeto: Bridging the distances between culturally diverse families and schools: An ethnographic portrait.* New York: Teachers College Press.

This volume traces the development of Mexican American migrant children and their families as they confront the world both inside and outside the family, with a particular emphasis on how schooling intersects with this process. Through in-depth case studies, the reader comes to know each family and the intricate ways in which they address their own cultural practices and those they are facing through contact with the schools.

EDUCATIONAL

APPROACHES

TO STUDENT

CULTURAL

DIVERSITY

CHAPTER 3

Focus Questions

▼ What is Americanization, and what concept of culture underlies it?

▼ How have legal reforms in educational equity and the movement toward multicultural education in the U.S. schools affected the education of culturally and linguistically diverse children?

▼ What are the shortcomings of educational equity and multicultural education as approaches to understanding the educational needs of diverse populations?

▼ What are two new theoretical perspectives that attempt to explain why culturally diverse children often fail academically?

▼ How does the constructivist approach to knowledge provide the basis for a new pedagogy?

"Equity and pluralism in schools do not address diversity."

In our efforts to understand the effects of cultural diversity in the schools, we use theories of language, learning, thinking, teaching, socialization, and culture (García, 1993). Research pertinent to education has expanded its scope in recent decades. What was once considered the study of values and behavior (Mead, 1939a; Skinner, 1957) has become today an interlocking study of elements from linguistics, psychology, and sociology. Findings in each of these areas are independently significant, but together they help us understand the nature of the cultural experience at both micro and macro levels. Educators, for example, can focus on smaller units of social analysis, such as a speech event, for insight into a student's experience. We can also broaden the view to a larger unit of social analysis, such as social class, for vital contextual information. For teachers of culturally and linguistically diverse students, the issue of culture—what it is and how it directly and indirectly influences academic learning—is the crux of research interest.

This chapter concentrates on the schooling initiatives that have been targeted at culturally diverse students in the United States. In so doing, it discusses the way in which educational research, theory, policy, and practice of significance to these students converge. We will look beneath the variety of action plans and programs that have been devised for culturally diverse students and reveal the educational concepts and theories used as a foundation. We will find that definitions of culture and assumptions about cultural differences largely determine past and present educational practices.

A Historical Survey

Within the past few years, educational approaches related to culture and education have shifted from an early focus on "Americanization" (Dewey, 1921) to concerns about educational equity (Ramirez & Castaneda, 1974) and then to multicultural education (Banks, 1981; Banks, J., & Banks, C. A., 1995; Gay, 1997; Grant & Sleeter, 1988). More recent approaches center on the "effective" instruction of children from culturally and linguistically diverse groups (August & Hakuta, 1997; García, 1991c, 1995; Purkey &

Smith, 1983; Tharp, 1989). This section introduces these earlier educational approaches and explains how they developed from past theory and data on culture and education. Later sections will discuss newer approaches based on a broader understanding of cultural diversity as it relates to schooling. You will see that the linguistic, cognitive, social, and educational research and theory developed over the past two decades have dramatically reshaped our view of cultural "difference" in education.

Americanization

As I described in Chapter 1, at various times in its history—including its recent past—the United States has been a major destination for immigrants. The 1990 U.S. Census, for example, identified some 20 million immigrants, with nearly 6 million children living with immigrant parents and another 2 million foreign-born children (Smith & Edmonston, 1997). By 1996, the immigrant population had grown to 25 million, with an even greater increase in the number of children (Rambaut, 1997). According to Rambaut (1997):

1. Mexicans are by far the largest legal and undocumented immigrant population in the United States. They also have the lowest educational levels of any major ethnic group, native- or foreign-born.
2. Since the 1960s, Filipinos have formed the second largest immigrant population. They have the lowest poverty rate of any sizable ethnic group in the country.
3. Since 1975, immigrants from Vietnam, Cambodia, and Laos have formed the largest refugee population. Compared to refugees from Central America, the Balkans, or the former Soviet Union, they have the highest rates of poverty and welfare dependency in the country.

In short, the student diversity in the United States has been and continues to be driven by these dramatic increases in immigration, which in turn have driven the educational responses to this diversity.

Historically, **Americanization** has been a prime institutional education objective for immigrant and culturally diverse children (Elam, 1972; Gonzalez, 1990). Based on the sociological theory of **assimilation,** Americanization is an approach to acculturation that seeks to merge small ethnic and linguistically diverse communities into a single dominant national institutional structure and culture. Traditionally recognized as a solution to the problem of immigrants and ethnicity in the modern industrialized United States, Americanization is the "melting pot" solution.

Americanization schooling practices were adopted whenever the population of culturally and linguistically diverse students rose to significant numbers in a community. The government established special programs and applied them to both children and adults in urban and rural settings. The desired goal of Americanizing students was to socialize and acculturate the diverse community. In essence, the reasoning went, if schools could teach these students to speak standard English and to accept "American" values, then educational failure could be averted. Ironically, social economists have argued that such efforts to assimilate immigrant populations were coupled with systematic attempts to maintain disparate social and economic conditions between them and majority populations. Indeed, more than anything else, past approaches to addressing the educational problems of minority populations have actually preserved the political and economic subordination of these communities (Spencer, D., 1988).

Many immigrant populations have come to the United States in the last century. In 1921, Thomas and Park (1921b) argued that the "Old World" consciousness of immigrants would eventually be overcome by modern American values. Recent analysis by Gonzalez (1990) and D. Spencer (1988) shows, however, that Americanization did not evenly affect all immigrant groups. There are a number of reasons for this. According to Gonzalez (1990, 1994), there are important distinctions between the experience of European immigrants and that of other immigrant groups:

Different Immigrant Experiences

1. The Americanization of the non-European community has been attempted in a social context that continues to be highly segregated. Black, Hispanic, and other nonwhite students are more segregated today than they were three decades ago.
2. The assimilation of these nonwhite groups had both rural and urban aspects, whereas the European immigrant experience was overwhelmingly urban.
3. Assimilation was heavily influenced by the regional agricultural economy, which retarded a "natural" assimilation process.
4. Slaves and immigrants from Africa, Mexico, Puerto Rico, and other Latin and Asian countries could not escape the economic and political stigma assigned by the United States, an advanced industrialized nation, to their semi-industrialized, semifeudal lands of origin. Many such immigrants came from regions under U.S. domination. This relationship led to a very constrained immigration pool, with only farm and low-skilled labor immigrating continuously to this country. None of the

European nations had such a relationship with the United States, and thus their national cultures tended to be perceived as being relatively equal to that of the United States. This factor alone would have significantly affected the manner in which Americanization was applied to immigrants of non-European background.

American Indians: An Example

Although many immigrant groups have been subjected to the Americanization phenomenon, the effects of this process can be seen most dramatically on the indigenous population of the United States during the late nineteenth and early twentieth centuries. After the American Indians had been segregated on federal reservations, boarding schools were established for their children. At an early age, sometimes as young as 4 or 5, Indian children were removed from their families and placed in schools hundreds or thousands of miles away. The clear goal of such removal was to wash these children clean of the native and tribal influences regarded as negative by the majority of U.S. society.

As students in these boarding schools, Indian children were forbidden to speak their native languages, to practice their native religions or traditions, or to wear their usual dress. They were often forbidden to return to the reservation for visits. At the same time, they were taught English, "proper" manners of behavior, and other standard school content, and were subjected to Christian missionary efforts. In short, this major national effort at education, requiring significant economic and social resources, was built on a policy designed to rid these children of "negative" cultural attributes while instilling new "positive"— that is, "American"—cultural attributes. The goal was to rehabilitate a problematic cultural group over time through the use of the U.S. schools. The focus was on the young. The actual result, many American Indians have argued, was the anguish of young children and their families at separation, the loss of tribal responsibility and authority over the young, and the accelerated loss of the culture and language of indigenous peoples (Banks, C. A., & Banks, J., 1995).

Elimination of Differences

It can be argued that Americanization still underlies many programs aimed at culturally diverse students (Nieto, 1992; Rodriguez, 1989; Weis, 1988). For these students Americanization unfortunately still means the elimination not only of linguistic and cultural differences but of an "undesirable" culture. Americanization programs seem to be based on the incorrect assumption that in the United States a single homogeneous ethnic culture is in contact with a single homogeneous nonethnic one, and that the relationship between the two is not one of equals. The dominant community, enjoying greater wealth and privileges, claims its position by virtue of cultural superiority (Ogbu, 1987a). In one way or another, nearly every culturally diverse child, whether born in the United States or elsewhere, is likely to be treated as a foreigner, an alien, or an intruder.

In 1923 the superintendent of the Los Angeles schools voiced an eerily familiar complaint in an address to district principals: "We have the [Mexican] immigrants to live with, and if we Americanize them, we can live with them." Unfortunately, even today the objective is to transform the diversity in our communities into a monolithic English-speaking, American-thinking-and-acting community. As many have done throughout the century, this attitude was echoed in 1990 by Ken Hill, a superintendent in the California schools who has received national and state distinction for his efforts to serve a large number of African American, Mexican American, and Asian American students: "We've got to attend to the idea of assimilation and to make sure that we teach English and our values as quickly as we can so these kids can get in the mainstream of American life" (quoted in Walsh, 1990, p. B14). (It is important to note that at the time Hill made his statement, the dropout rate for nonwhite students in his district was over 40 percent [Matute-Bianchi, 1990].)

The Americanization solution has not worked. Moreover, it depends on the group-oriented concept of culture, which as we saw in Chapter 2 leads to mistaken notions about cultural difference. The Americanization philosophy presumes that culturally different children are as a group culturally flawed. To "fix" them individually, we must act on the individual as a member of a cultural group. By changing the values and language of the group, we will have the solution to the educational underachievement of students who represent these groups. In essence, the groups should "melt" into one large and more beneficial so-called American culture. Research has shown, however, that this "melting" does not in fact occur.

Children as Culturally Flawed

Our educational efforts have been responding quite ignorantly with regard to the processes by which individuals and groups actually come together to form culture. The challenge facing educators with regard to culturally diverse students is not to "Americanize" them but rather to understand them and to act responsively to their specific diversity in order to achieve academic success for *all* students. In recent decades, this realization has led directly to issues of educational equity.

Educational Equity

No one argues about the significance of education in this country. We are all quite convinced that an educated society is beneficial for enhancing individual well-being, improving our standard of living, and maintaining a democratic society (Dewey, 1921). Moreover, education is perceived as a vehicle for achieving the "American Dream." It is not surprising that many organizations in the United States, from large businesses to small community groups, have attempted to initiate and maintain educational endeavors in conjunction with efforts in the public schools. In fact, what with the many courses, workshops, seminars, conferences, and other structured learning opportunities available today, people are exposed to more formal educational experiences outside of the typical K–12 system than within it. Clearly in our society, education, from cradle to grave, is important to our citizens.

If this is so, then equal access to educational opportunities must be a corollary to this basic value. This was clearly brought home by the U.S. Supreme Court decision of 1954 in *Brown v. Board of Education*. This landmark case concluded that the separate, segregated education provided for black Americans was unequal to the education provided for white Americans. The Court argued that every effort must be made to address equal access to education regardless of race. Significant congressional actions during the 1960s and 1970 reinforced this decision for Hispanic Americans, Asian Americans, Native Americans, and women. The major legislative piece was the 1964 Civil Rights Act. Title IV of that act banned discrimination on the grounds of race, color, or national origin in any program receiving federal financial assistance (Title VII addressed educational equity across gender). Not coincidentally, the Elementary and Secondary Education Act (ESEA) of 1965 began to provide millions of federal dollars in assistance to state and local school systems. If these schools were to use these federal funds, they were to be held accountable to the standard of nondiscrimination.

This legislation directly banned recipients of federal resources from "restricting an individual in any way in the enjoyment of any advantage or privilege enjoyed by others receiving any service, financial aid or benefit under the [federally] funded program." Importantly, the recipient of federal funds was also prohibited from using criteria or methods that would have the effect of undermining the objectives of the federally funded program for individuals of a particular race, color, or national origin.

Legal Redress Allowed

Other provisions of this legislation provided the possibility of a private cause of action (a lawsuit) against a federally funded institution to rectify issues of discrimination. This meant that students and their parents were not required to wait until the federal government noticed that a funded program was out of compliance. Instead they could independently move the courts to seek relief. And they did. A barrage of legal action aimed at correcting educational inequities soon followed.

The 1994 overhaul of the ESEA (which is now known as the Improving America's Schools Act, or IASA) redirected some $11 billion in federal yearly appropriations to educational institutions, mostly K–12, throughout the country. The terms of the reauthorization, while acknowledging the acute need to serve the diverse student population, also recognized the following:

Central Points of IASA

1. The new knowledge about which programs are effective and why must be central to any proposed changes.
2. New policy must capitalize on the wisdom of current policy, administration, curriculum, and instructional practice.
3. Policies and programs must be cohesive in order to integrate the services that are to be provided. This cohesiveness should reflect the partnership among national, state, and local educational policies and programs.
4. The very limited amount of money for new programs that is available today and for the near to distant future must be acknowledged. Therefore, federal resources must be utilized in systemic reform efforts that minimize the notion of "compensatory" education and instead help educators to formulate and implement programs that allow *all* children to achieve to high academic standards.

(For a broader discussion of the policies, see Chapter 1; for a comprehensive description of the policy foundations of the 1994 reauthorization, see García & Gonzalez, 1995.)

In these 1994 legislative initiatives, the emphasis on *all* children is particularly relevant to the country's diverse student population, and it reflects an awareness that some children were systematically not benefiting from their educational experiences. Through the introduction of new legislation in Goals 2000, the U.S. Department of Education had already set the stage for the state-by-state development of educational standards. Then, with the passage of the IASA, the goals-and-standards initiative was aligned with the allocation of resources for specific policies. This alignment recognized that federal, state, and local government efforts must be coordinated to enhance effectiveness and efficiency. Moreover, the federal role must allow flexibility at the state and local levels while requiring that all children achieve at the highest levels.

This new policy is a first attempt to use federal support to unite equity and excellence in state and local educational endeavors. It is also one of the first instances in which federal policy has attempted not only to emphasize equal educational opportunity but also to focus on educational achievement outcomes that are based on high academic standards for all students. The results of this new policy are yet to be assessed.

Language Barriers Must Be Overcome

Other administrative and legislative actions have addressed further aspects of equal educational opportunity. For example, in 1970 the U.S. Department of Health, Education and Welfare issued a memorandum, later referred to as the **May 25 memorandum,** that clarified the mandate of the 1964 Civil Rights Act with respect to non-English-speaking students: "Where a liability to speak and understand the English language excludes national origin minority group children from effective participation in the educational program offered by a school district, the district must take affirmative steps to rectify the language deficiency in order to open instructional programs to these students." The Equal Educational Opportunities and Transportation Act of 1974 converted this administrative protection for language minority students into formal law. The act makes "the failure by an educational agency to take appropriate action to overcome language barriers that impede equal participation by its students in its educational programs" an unlawful denial of equal educational opportunities.

Taken together, these legal and legislative initiatives directly related the value placed on education in U.S. society to the educational needs of culturally diverse populations. Every child, regardless of race, color, national origin, or language, is legally entitled to the benefits of equal educational opportunity. This movement toward equal educational opportunity pervaded our schools for over a decade and still drives many initiatives designed for culturally diverse students. But equal access to education has not been the only stimulus behind our attention to culturally diverse students.

Multicultural Education

During the late 1970s and early 1980s, the educational establishment and representatives of minority groups themselves began to confront another important educational issue of particular consequence to culturally diverse students. Mostly aimed at curriculum reform, this debate suggested that the content of curriculum taught in U.S. classrooms should reflect the diverse character of the nation's population. A **multicultural education** was recommended for several reasons. First, advocates argued that the curriculum should better represent the actual contributions made by various cultural groups to this country's

Goals of Multicultural Education

society. They criticized prevailing curriculum for its unbalanced perspectives emphasizing only Western European values, history, literature, and general world view (Banks, 1982). The

United States is not one monolithic culture, these critics claimed, and the curriculum should reflect its true cultural diversity. Second, a multicultural curriculum would educate children of majority status as to the many accomplishments and contributions to U.S. society by individuals of minority status. This would at the same time reaffirm the significance of the minority group to the larger society and help develop positive self-esteem in children of minority status (García, 1983b). Third, multicultural education was perceived as a school reform movement aimed at changing the content and process of education within schools. Its goal was not to stop at merely providing equal educational opportunity but to go further and enhance the schooling experience for all students (Grant & Sleeter, 1987).

Focus on Curriculum

The concept of multicultural education gave rise to several distinct approaches to the instruction of students in general and of culturally diverse students in particular. However, the major impact of this reform movement has been in the area of **curriculum**—that is, the area of schooling that addresses the content of instruction. In essence, this major reform attempted to address what students should be learning. The movement made it quite clear that we needed to know more about this country's diverse cultural groups and that after we had uncovered such knowledge, we needed to dispense it in our everyday schooling endeavors.

Disparate Goals of Multicultural Education. The overall agreement about the importance of including curriculum that addressed diversity was quite significant, since there was some disagreement about the goals of curriculum reform. Sleeter and Grant (1987) and Gay (1997) have provided an excellent review of the varied goals and the overall limited consequences of the multicultural education reform movement on American education.

A Bridge to Success

Within a model described as "Teaching the Multiculturally Different," one goal was to assist educators charged with helping culturally different students succeed in mainstream schooling. Although this model did not directly cite the need to assimilate children of different backgrounds into the mainstream, this seemed to serve as its major goal. The prescription for success was usually subtractive in nature. That is, children with different cultures and languages were asked to leave behind these attributes through the assistance of bridgelike educational programs that promised access and success in academics and later in other societal domains. This type of multicultural education was regarded as a temporary, highly directed educational endeavor that would lead to a melting pot of a successful and more homogeneous student population.

Early versions of the federal program known as Head Start reflected this multicultural approach. For preschool children aged 3 and 4, Head Start, and its extension for the early elementary student, Follow Through, were perceived as bridges to the mainstream academic environment. Other compensatory education programs, such as Title I programs that address underachievement directly, were also meant to provide underachieving students with bridges to achievement. They are, however, still too often perceived as temporary and compensatory means of helping unsuccessful students make the transition to success through a process likened to natural cultural assimilation. In such assimilation, immigrants with very diverse cultures and languages come to embrace mainstream American values and to acquire English as their main mode of communication. Schools were asked to serve, positively, as an organized vehicle to hasten this natural process.

It must be noted that this perspective on multicultural education did stress the importance of cultural diversity among the students, families, and communities served. In this way, it was definitely distinct from earlier educational strategies of Americanization. The practice of taking American Indian youngsters from their families and placing them in boarding schools far from their homes was not meant primarily to serve as a bridge to American society. It was devised instead to be a direct break with a child's original but negatively perceived language and culture (Phillips, 1983).

Enhancing Human Relations

The bridging goal of some multicultural education efforts was at times combined with the goal of enhancing human relations (Banks, C. A., & Banks, J., 1995; Colangelo, Foxley, & Dustin, 1982). Such a result was seen as best achieved by learning about and with each other. In so doing, the members of diverse populations would be able to understand one another, and as a corollary improved communication and social relations would develop. Distinct from programs of assimilation and bridging, educational programs reflecting this approach to multicultural education asked students to learn about other groups not like their own and to utilize this new knowledge to enhance social accommodation of diversity—"Let's learn to get along better."

The most dramatic example of a large-scale program of this type comes from Canada. In the province of Quebec, French-speaking populations (Francophones) were in constant social and economic dispute with English-speaking populations (Anglophones). The solution to this problem in social relations was Bilingual-Bicultural Immersion Education. Anglophone children were placed in French-only schooling programs for the first three years of their educational experience. The goal of the program was for children to acquire knowledge of both the lan-

BECOMING A RESPONSIVE TEACHER

Assimilation Doesn't Equal Success

How can schools cope with the diversity presented by their students? Should they harken back to the model of education developed in the early decades of this century to deal with the huge numbers of immigrants, when educators responded to increasing cultural and linguistic diversity among their students by attempting to accelerate their assimilation into the American mainstream? Their mission was to Americanize immigrants by replacing their native language and culture with those of the United States. Educators confidently sought to fit newcomers into the American mold by teaching them the English language and literature, a sugarcoated version of American history, and a respect for the U.S. political system and civic life.

Although some recommend a similar approach today, it is no longer possible even to describe American culture with confidence; into what mold should educators seek to place all children? There is no single definition of American culture; multiple definitions have been informed by ethnic minority voices.

We also have never counted the cost of the Americanization philosophy. How many children were estranged from their family and culture; how many grandparents of today's teachers lost their native language; how many worked a lifetime on the assembly line when they should have gone to college; how many became ashamed of who they were?

When immigrant students become shining academic stars, their success is often attributed to the values and habits of their native culture rather than their Americanization. There is some evidence that assimilation may actually inhibit academic success. Studies of Mexican, Indian, and Vietnamese immigrants all suggest that those who maintain a strong identification with their native language and culture are more likely to succeed in school than those who readily adopt American ways (Rambaut, 1997).

BECOMING A RESPONSIVE TEACHER *Cont.*

▼ Meeting the Challenge

1. Research seems to indicate that assimilation does not serve culturally diverse students. Since it nevertheless persists as a response to cultural difference, who or what might it serve?

2. How would you define the culture in which you live? Develop a list of at least 10 highlights of this culture that most accurately characterize it. Your list may include values, events, people, places, or things both past and present that you consider culturally significant. Compare your list with those of your classmates. Make a separate list of all the items others selected that are surprising or unknown to you. Why were these items not on your list?

3. Consider these three Filipino children:
(a) Renaldo has recently arrived in the United States from the Philippines with his parents and three brothers.
(b) Carlo and his three brothers were born in the United States, as were both of their parents. Carlo's grandparents emigrated from the Philippines when they were in their twenties.
(c) Joshua was born in the Philippines but was adopted at birth by Anglo-American parents. His three adoptive brothers are also Anglo-American.
Explain the variety in acculturation these three children have experienced. Describe how an approach to education based on assimilation might affect each child. Alternatively, if you had all three of these children in class, how would you build on each one's specific relationship to language and culture?

guage and the culture of Francophones, with the expected product of better human relations. Evaluation of these programs indicates that these expectations were achieved without any loss in academic achievement resulting from children learning in a language other than their own home language (Swain & Lapkin, 1991). Swain & Lapkin (1991) point out that in Canada French speakers and English speakers are socially equal. This is not true of language-diverse groups in the United States.

Respecting Diversity

Yet another approach to multicultural education has been much more activist in nature. Its goals serve to promote respect for diversity. In addition to acquiring and disseminating information about the cultural diversity of the U.S. population, this approach is aimed at developing intellectual and societal acceptance of cultural diversity as a goal in and of itself (Banks, 1981, 1984; Fishman, 1990; García, 1997; Garcia, R., 1979; Gay, 1975, 1997; Gollnick & Chinn, 1986; Grant, 1977b, 1998).

Most popular and influential in the past decade, work in this area has attempted to bring together issues of race, ethnicity, gender, and social class. The thrust of such initiatives has been to permeate the curriculum with issues of diversity—in literature, social thought, scientific approaches, historical construction, and so on—while at the same time serving up criticism of "standardized" curriculums, particularly those that reflect Western European

A Focus on Social Injustice

contributions as the norm. A corollary of this approach is the overall multicultural and social reconstructionist perspective (Appleton, 1983; Suzuki, 1984). In this view, students are asked to become social critics, particularly in terms of issues of social injustice. Proponents argue that adoption of this multicultural educational approach would rid society of pervasive social injustices inflicted on the basis of race, ethnicity, and gender.

Such a proactive stance toward multicultural education is exemplified by programs in U.S. bilingual education. In the past decade, **double immersion** programs have been introduced into large Latino school districts in California, New York, Texas, Illinois, and Florida. The goal of a double immersion program is to produce a student population that is bilingual and bicultural. For non-Latino, English-speaking students, the goal is English and Spanish language and literacy. Beginning in kindergarten, these students are exposed to Spanish-language instruction in classrooms with Spanish-speaking students and to a curriculum that addresses bicultural concerns. For Latino students in the programs, the goals are the same. These aims are in concert with the notion of actively promoting cultural diversity, with a healthy academic respect for the linguistic and cultural attributes of the diverse students involved (Lindholm & Christiansen, 1990).

Similar programs in the public schools of San Francisco, San Diego, Detroit, New York, and Chicago are housed in **magnet**

schools. The purpose of a magnet school is to attract a highly diverse set of students around a thematically designated curriculum that is multilingual and multicultural. Such programs attempt to integrate African American, Latino, Asian, and other culturally diverse student populations by recognizing diversity as a positive ingredient in addressing the agendas of equal educational opportunity and multicultural education (Grant, 1991, 1998).

An Appraisal of Progress. Attention to multicultural education in this country over the past two decades has fired numerous debates and resulted in substantive accomplishments. Publishing companies have launched new curriculum efforts to address claims by proponents of multicultural education of bias in publishing (Gollnick & Chinn, 1994). Teacher-training programs have been required to provide specific training in student cultural diversity at the preservice level (California Commission on Teacher Credentialing, 1991). School-based programs such as the magnet and double immersion bilingual education programs described above find their roots, at least partially, in the values and goals of multicultural education.

The above discussion has attempted to locate multicultural education in three broad categories based on distinct but not necessarily exclusive goal agendas. We have seen that these goals range from bridging and assimilation for culturally diverse students, to enhancement of human relations, to active promotion of cultural diversity as a societywide goal. Keep in mind that all the goals of multicultural education build upon previous and ongoing initiatives that address the basic issue of equal educational opportunity: no child should be denied the benefits of education. These two educational approaches have provided an alternative to the traditional response of Americanization to the growing presence of cultural diversity in our schools.

Beyond Multicultural Education

Since the time of Socrates, educators and philosophers have argued for a kind of teaching that does more than impart knowledge and teach skills. Knowledge and skills are important enough, the argument goes, but true education and real teaching involve far more: helping students understand, appreciate, and grapple with important ideas while developing a depth of comprehension of a wide range of issues.

Yet teaching aimed at these important goals is presently most notable for its absence from U.S. classrooms. Goodlad (1984), for example, reports that:

> A great deal of what goes on in the classroom is like painting-by-
> numbers—filling in the colors called for by numbers on the
> page. . . . [Teachers] ask specific questions calling essentially for stu-
> dents to fill in the blanks: "What is the capital city of Canada?" "What
> are the principal exports of Japan?" Students rarely turn things around
> by asking questions. Nor do teachers often give students a chance to
> romp with an open-ended question such as "What are your views on
> the quality of television?" (p. 108)

If this portrait is true in mainstream American classrooms, it is even more true in classrooms with low-income, linguistically and culturally diverse children. Because of the perception that these students fundamentally require drill, review, and redundancy in order to progress academically (Brophy & Good, 1986), their learning opportunities are likely to be excessively weighted toward low-level skills and factually oriented instruction. As important as skills and facts undoubtedly are, no less important are more cognitively demanding learning opportunities that promote, as the philosopher Mortimer Alder (1982) has written, the "enlarged understanding of ideas and values" (p. 23).

Low-Level Skills

The lack of attention to higher-level cognition is only one of the systemic problems that continue to exist despite decades of efforts for equal educational opportunity and multicultural education. As much as they have contributed to changing demands in U.S. schools, these efforts have failed to address a number of important educational concerns. For the most part they have lacked a strong theoretical foundation. They have addressed curriculum only—not instructional methods or pedagogy. They have produced many single case studies of ethnic groups but little empirical data to substantiate the positive effects of implementation.

As described in Chapter 1, academic achievement in many culturally diverse populations has not been enhanced significantly over the past decades. Action for equal educational opportunity has generated legislative and legal policy along with concomitant resources to address this core societal value. But such action has not considered, in any comprehensive manner, how educational equity should be achieved. Educational attention in and around multicultural education has espoused important societal values and has led to advances in a number of educational fronts. But still it has not produced a set of comprehensive strategies that address the educational concerns it has raised (Sleeter & Grant, 1987). Essentially, the result of these initiatives in educational equity and multicultural reform has been to raise even more issues. This is no small feat, considering the many-headed character of U.S. schools.

The era of equal educational opportunity and multicultural education has left us a clearly identifiable legacy: educational endeavors related to culturally diverse students have been pragmatically oriented. That is, they have focused on a set of problems—discrimination, segregation, underachievement, low self-esteem, and non-English proficiency, to name a few—and have forwarded programs to address them. These pragmatic efforts tended to lack any substantive theoretical underpinnings. The proposed solutions were driven by somewhat ambiguous social values associated with educational equity and pluralism. Conversely, a more theoretical approach would still consider the problems of discrimination, underachievement, and segregation but would first attempt to understand why such problems exist. We could then develop solutions from a storehouse of understanding (Cole, 1996; García, 1991c; Tharp, 1991).

Lack of Theory

Another legacy of the past three decades of educational activity, particularly in the area of multicultural education, is the extended case study approach to cultural diversity (Nieto, 1992). The educational community has produced an extensive research literature on the characteristics of different racial, ethnic, and ethnolinguistic groups. The goal of this work was to document the cultural and linguistic attributes of various groups in the United States so that these attributes could be better understood and utilized to serve students. It was not uncommon to learn from these research studies, for example, that American Indian children were nonverbal (Appleton, 1983), that Asian American children were shy (Sue & Okazaki, 1990), that Mexican American children were cooperative (García, 1983b, 1995), that African American children were aggressive (Boykin, 1983), and that Anglo children were competitive (Kagan, 1983b).

Stereotypes Promoted

Although this case study work was meant to advance our understanding of culturally diverse students, it often had the effect of promoting stereotypes. Moreover, it did not recognize the axiom implicitly understood by social scientists who study culture: there is as much heterogeneity within any cultural group as there is between cultural groups. (See Chapter 2 for an extended discussion of this issue.) Unfortunately, descriptively useful indicators began to take on explanatory values: if that student is Mexican American, she must be cooperative, and speak Spanish. The problem arose when educators tried to apply case study information in the classroom. They developed educational programs to address the cultural attributes identified only to discover, for example, that many Mexican American children were not cooperative and did not speak Spanish. If all Mexican Americans are not alike, if all African Americans are not alike, if all American Indians are not alike, then what set of knowledge about those groups is important educationally? What overarching conceptualization of culture is truly useful for understanding the educational framework of culturally diverse groups?

New Theoretical Perspectives

Before we address the preceding questions directly, it seems appropriate to frame this discussion in terms of a continuum of educationally relevant theory. At one end of this continuum, theorists argue that serving culturally diverse populations calls for a deeper understanding of the interaction of a student's culture and the prevailing school culture (Tharp, 1989). At the other end, theorists claim that any population of students, no matter what their cultural background, will achieve academically if the appropriate teaching methods are implemented. Next we shall examine these two perspectives and other ideas that fall in between them.

A Continuum of Theories

The claim that culture plays a role in educational underachievement is supported by a wealth of research suggesting that the educational failure of diverse student populations is related to a "culture clash" between home and school. Evidence for this claim comes from Boykin (1986) for African American students; from Heath (1983) for poor white students; from Wiesner, Gallimore, and Jordan (1988) for Hawaiian students; from Vogt, Jordan, and Tharp (1987) for Navaho students; from García (1988) for Mexican American students; and from Rodriguez (1989) for Puerto Rican students. In essence, these researchers have suggested that educational endeavors that do not attend to the distinctiveness of

Cultural Dissonance

culture are likely to result in failure for certain students. Theoretically, these students do not succeed because the difference between their school culture and their home culture creates an educationally harmful dissonance—a home-to-school "mismatch." Sue and Padilla (1986) directly enunciate this position by asserting that "the challenge for educators is to identify critical differences between and within ethnic minority groups and to incorporate this information into classroom practice" (p. 62).

Using What "Works"

At the same time, however, other research supports the theoretical position that the academic failure of any student rests on the failure of instructional personnel to implement what is known to "work." In other words, it is not a mismatch of cultures that is to blame so much as the failure of instructional programs to utilize appropriate general principles of teaching and learning. Using the now-common research tool of **meta analy-**

sis, which is a method of analyzing and summarizing large numbers of research studies, Walberg (1986b) suggests that a synthesis of educational research identifies robust indicators of instructional conditions with academically significant effects across various conditions and for various student groups. Other meta analytic reviews (Baden & Maehr, 1986; Bloom, 1984; Slavin, 1989) agree. Among the specific instructional strategies proposed as candidates for "what works with everyone" are direct instruction (Rosenshine, 1986), tutoring (Bloom, 1984), frequent evaluation of academic progress (Slavin, Karweit, & Madden, 1989), and cooperative learning (Slavin, 1989).

Motivations and Expectations

This research also identifies expectations as significant factors in underachievement. Levin (1988) and Snow (1990) have suggested that students, teachers, and school professionals in general have low academic expectations for culturally and linguistically diverse students. Again, as popularized in the film *Stand and Deliver,* raising student motivation in conjunction with enhanced academic expectations and challenging curriculum is a prescribed solution. The assumption of theorists at this end of the continuum is that the educational failure of culturally diverse populations can be reversed by the systemic and effective implementation of general principles of instruction understood to work with "all" students.

Explanations for Lower Achievement

Interspersed within this continuum are other theoretical approaches that attempt to explain the academic underachievement of culturally and linguistically diverse students. Friere (1970) has argued that educational initiatives cannot expect to lead to academic or intellectual success under social circumstances that are oppressive. He and others (Cummins, 1986; Pearl, 1991) suggest that social oppression experienced by students taints any curriculum or pedagogy, however "successful" it is in general, and that only a pedagogy of empowerment can fulfill the lofty goals of educational equity and achievement.

Similarly, Bernstein (1971), Laosa (1982), and Wilson (1987) address underachievement by pointing to socioeconomic factors that influence the way schools and instruction are organized. When a group of people is exposed, over generations, to poverty and debilitating socioeconomic conditions, the teaching and learning process for children at home, in the community, and in the schools will suffer. The result is disastrous, long-term educational failure and social disruption of family and community. Ogbu and Matute-Bianchi (1986) offer a broader sociological perspective. They describe this country's present social approach to several immigrant and minority populations as "caste-like." In this attempt to explain underachievement, these theorists claim that certain populations are perceived as forming a layer of U.S. society that is not expected to excel academically or economically. These social expectations are reinforced until they become self-perceptions adopted by the members of "caste-like" populations, with academic underachievement and social withdrawal as the inevitable result.

So far we have discussed some of these new theoretical perspectives in only a general way. Throughout the rest of this book we will examine them more comprehensively. You should realize, however, that the continuum of theories I have represented as ranging from "cultural mismatch" to "general principles" is not a set of incompatible approaches. Instead, as this brief introduction has indicated, a wide variety of scholars have seriously attempted to understand why so many culturally and linguistically diverse students are not well served by educational institutions in the United States today. These conceptual contributions are not limited to espousing the principles of multicultural education or recommending policies of educational equity. They go farther, and they dig deeper. The theoretical approaches useful to us address the issues of educating a culturally diverse population by searching out explanations for the present unsatisfactory situation.

Broader Approaches

These contributions take into consideration the work of Friere (1970), Cummins (1979, 1986), Ogbu (1987a), Rose (1996), and Tharp and Gallimore (1988). This research suggests that the educational vulnerability of culturally diverse students must be understood within the broader context of the circumstances for children in U.S. society. No quick fix is likely under social and schooling conditions that mark students for special treatment according to a category of cultural difference without consideration for the psychological and social circumstances in which each student—as an individual—resides. These theorists warn us against isolating any single attribute (poverty, language difference, learning potential, etc.) as the only variable of importance. More comprehensive views of the schooling process urge an understanding not only of the relationship between home and school but of the psychological, sociological, and cultural incongruities between the two, and the resulting effects on learning and achievement (Cole, 1996).

The Constructivist Perspective

How do we as educators begin to understand such a complex set of interactions? One framework for understanding is founded on the concept of **act psychology.** First formulated at the end of the nineteenth century, this concept proposes a model for human cognitive processes, or how we come to know. It focuses on the assertion that the mental functions of perceiving, remembering, and organizing—ultimately, knowing—are all acts of

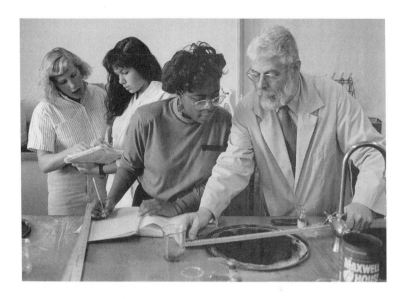

construction (Barlett as cited by Cole 1996). It also asserts that what we know is closely related to the circumstances in which we come to know it.

The term "construction" is particularly apt. Have you ever watched a large building evolve under construction? Scores of people and tons of material are marshaled and organized, and a structure rises seemingly out of chaos. Remember, though, that the process is not without its glitches. Days of rain may halt or alter construction, and the entire project is subject to the availability of supplies, not to mention the willingness of people to work together. The architects must consider features of the surrounding terrain and adjust their designs accordingly. In short, construction has a context, a set of local circumstances in which it happens. These circumstances greatly affect the final form of the building.

Construction of Knowledge

The **constructivist perspective** is rooted in the notion that human knowledge is the result of continual building and rebuilding. Our "construction materials" consist of the give-and-take between the organization and content of old information and new information, processes of organizing that information, and the specific physical and social circumstances in which this all occurs. We come to understand a new concept by applying our knowledge of previous concepts to the new information we are given. For example, in order to teach negative numbers, a math teacher can use the analogy of digging a hole: the more dirt you take out of the hole, the greater the hole becomes; the more one subtracts from a negative number, the greater the negative number becomes. But a math teacher cannot use this example with children who have no experience digging holes. It won't work. As you can see, this theory of how the mind works implies that continual revisions (or "renovations," as an architect might say) are to be expected. Therefore, when we organize teaching and learning environments, we must recognize the constructivist nature of those environments. As educators, we "build" teaching and learning environments out of what we know and how we come to know it. And we must continue to build. To ignore that is to discount the relevance of previous educational environments to the ones we are considering now. They got us to today, but that does not mean they will get us to tomorrow.

A New Pedagogy

Embedded in the constructivist approach to education is the understanding that language and culture, and the values that accompany them, are constructed in both home and community environments (Cummins, 1986; Goldman & Trueba, 1987; Heath, 1981). This approach acknowledges that children come to school with some constructed knowledge about many things (Goodman, 1980; Hall, 1987; Smith, 1971) and points out that children's development and learning are best understood as the interaction of past and present linguistic, sociocultural, and cognitive constructions (Trueba, 1988b). A more appropriate perspective on learning, then, is one that recognizes that learning is enhanced when it occurs in contexts that are socioculturally, linguistically, and cognitively meaningful for the learner. These meaningful contexts bridge previous "constructions" and present "constructions" (Diaz, Moll, & Mehan, 1986; Heath, 1986; Scribner & Cole, 1981; Wertsch, 1985).

> **Meaningful Contexts**

Such meaningful contexts have been notoriously inaccessible to culturally diverse children. On the contrary, schooling practices often contribute to their educational vulnerability. The monolithic culture transmitted by the U.S. schools in the form of pedagogy, curricula, instruction, classroom configuration, and language (Walker, 1987) dramatizes the lack of fit between the culturally diverse student and the school experience. The culture of the U.S. schools is reflected in such practices as:

1. The systematic exclusion of the histories, languages, experiences, and values of these students from classroom curricula and activities (Giroux & McLaren, 1986; Ogbu, 1982b).
2. "Tracking," which limits access to academic courses and justifies learning environments that do not foster academic development and socialization (Duran, 1986; Eder, 1982; Oakes, 1991) or perception of oneself as a competent learner and language-user.

3. A lack of opportunities to engage in developmentally and culturally appropriate learning in ways other than by teacher-led instruction (García, 1988).

This rethinking of the pedagogy of the U.S. schools has profound implications for the teaching and learning enterprise, especially as it relates to culturally diverse students (García, 1991d). The new pedagogy is one that envisions the classroom as a community of learners in which speakers, readers, and writers come together to define and redefine the meaning of the academic experience. Researchers variously describe it as a pedagogy of empowerment (Cummins, 1986), cultural learning (Heath, 1986; Trueba, 1987), or a cultural view of providing instructional assistance and guidance (Tharp & Gallimore, 1988). Whatever its designation, it allows for respect and integration of the students' values, beliefs, histories, and experiences and recognizes the active role that students must play in their own learning. This responsive pedagogy utilizes students' present knowledge and experiences as a foundation for appropriating new knowledge. For language minority students, this means using instructional strategies that incorporate the student's native language or bilingual abilities. Language is a substantial part of the social network within which children construct knowledge.

A responsive pedagogy for academic learning also requires a redefinition of the instructor's role. Instructors must become familiar with the cognitive, social, and cultural dimensions of learning. We need to recognize the ways in which instructional, assessment, and evaluation practices affect learning. We should become more aware of the purpose and degree of implementation of the classroom curriculum and understand its full impact on students. Specifically, we need to be alert to the configuration of the classroom environment and the ways in which students interact with one another and with teachers. Instructors must also recognize that helping students learn often requires allowing them to display their knowledge in ways that suggest their competence as learners and language-users. Once we begin to rethink all these dimensions of our role as educators, classrooms in U.S. schools will be equipped for the task of ensuring academic success for culturally diverse students.

Finally, teachers must question myths about learning processes and about the potentially underprepared student. In particular, we must debunk myths about students who come from households of lower socioeconomic status or ones where English is not the primary language. For educators who embrace the concept of a responsive pedagogy, new educational horizons for themselves and their students are not only possible but inevitable.

Community of Learners

Redefining the Teacher's Role

Table 3.1   Conceptual Dimensions of a Responsive Pedagogy: Addressing Cultural and Linguistic Diversity in High-Performance Learning Communities

SCHOOLWIDE PRACTICES

- A vision defined by the acceptance and valuing of diversity—Americanization is *not* the goal
- Treatment of classroom practitioners as fellow professionals and colleagues in school development decisions
- An atmosphere of collaboration, flexibility, and enhanced professional development
- Elimination (gradual or immediate) of policies that apply categories to diverse students that render their educational experiences inferior or limiting for further academic learning
- Reflection of and connection to the surrounding community, particularly the families of the students

TEACHER PRACTICES

- Bilingual/bicultural skills and awareness
- High expectations of diverse students
- Treatment of diversity as an asset to the classroom
- Ongoing professional development on issues of cultural and linguistic diversity and practices that are most effective
- Curriculum development that addresses cultural and linguistic diversity through the following means:
  1. Attention to and integration of home culture and practices
  2. Emphasis on maximizing student interactions across categories of English proficiency, academic performance, length of time in the United States, etc.
  3. Regular and consistent attempts to elicit ideas from students for planning units, themes, and activities
  4. Thematic approach to learning activities that integrates various skills, events, and learning opportunities
  5. Focus on language development through meaningful interactions and communications rather than grammatical skill-building that is removed from its appropriate context

Responsive Learning Communities

The Learning Environment

The learning environments that we consider essential to the development of a responsive pedagogy have been referred to as "effective schooling" (García, 1997) and "high-performance learning communities" (Berman, 1996). Regardless of the specific term used, these environments must address issues of student diversity in order to maximize their potential and to sustain educational improvement over time. To examine the challenge presented to today's schools by the social, cultural, and linguistic diversity of their students, Table 3.1 summarizes the conceptual dimensions that must be reflected in high-performing, responsive learning communities.

Conclusion

A focus on the content of specific cultures, such as that advocated in the multicultural education reform movement, is useful but will not be enough to attain educational equity for culturally diverse students. Similarly, the search currently under way for general principles of learning that work for all students must be redirected. Educational researchers and teachers themselves need a broader view that provides some explanation for pervasive underachievement among culturally diverse student populations. How do individuals with diverse social, cultural, and linguistic experiences construct knowledge—or "make meaning"? How do they communicate and extend that meaning, particularly in the social contexts we call schools? These are the vital questions for today's and tomorrow's educators, and finding answers will require a solid theoretical framework.

We must develop an in-depth understanding of the "meaning-making" process. We need to couple a grasp of socialization processes in and out of schools with a clear-eyed examination of our present pedagogy. Our mission is first to understand the relationships among language, culture, and the learning process. Only then will we be ready to transform our understanding into recommendations for a responsive pedagogy and curriculum. The rest of this book pursues these two goals.

SUMMARY OF MAJOR IDEAS

1. Approaches to the education of diverse student groups in the United States have shifted from Americanization to a focus on educational equity and multicultural education. More recent approaches are based on broader theoretical frameworks that consider the role of language and culture in education.

2. Americanization, or the "melting pot" solution to cultural diversity, seeks to assimilate, or merge, small ethnic and linguistically diverse communities into a single dominant national culture. It is an approach to acculturation that is based on a group-oriented concept of culture and the notion of cultural homogeneity as a desirable goal.

3. Members of non-European immigrant groups experience the process of Americanization differently than do members of European immigrant groups. This is because, comparatively, non-European immigrant groups are (a) subject to more ongoing segregation in the United States; (b) concentrated in both urban and rural areas; (c) more dependent on the U.S. regional agricultural economy; and (d) stigmatized by the low economic and political status of their countries of origin.

4. Native American children were subjected to Americanization on a large scale early in this century. Americanization

underlies any educational approach that assumes that some children are culturally flawed and have undesirable cultural attributes that should be eliminated or "fixed."

5. The U.S. Supreme Court decided in 1954 in *Brown v. Board of Education* that separate educational facilities for black students were not equal to educational facilities for white students and that U.S. schools must provide equal access to education regardless of race. The 1964 Civil Rights Act, the Elementary and Secondary Education Act of 1965, the May 25 memorandum of 1970, and the 1974 Equal Educational Opportunities and Transportation Act together legally require equal educational opportunity for every child in the United States regardless of race, color, national origin, or language.

6. New policies emerging from the 1994 reauthorization of the Elementary and Secondary Education Act have recognized the acute need to serve the culturally diverse student population in a comprehensive and integrated manner.

7. The concept of multicultural education began as a criticism of school curriculum that focused only on Western European values, history, literature, and general world-view. The movement toward multicultural education advocated reform of curriculum to reflect more accurately the truly diverse nature of the nation's population. Multicultural education was expected to highlight contributions to U.S. culture by individuals of minority status in order to offer children of majority status alternative perspectives and improved self-esteem.

8. As a reform movement, multicultural education had three main emphases, which sometimes were contradictory: (a) to provide a bridge to success for culturally diverse children through programs such as Head Start, by which they would be assimilated into the mainstream academic environment; (b) to enhance human relationships by teaching students from different cultures how to understand one another; and (c) to promote respect for diversity by portraying cultural diversity as a desirable social goal.

9. Two multicultural educational approaches that promote diversity and oppose the notion of assimilation are double immersion programs in bilingual education and magnet schools. Double immersion programs produce students who are bilingual and bicultural. Magnet schools offer a thematically designated curriculum that is multilingual and multicultural.

10. Because they lack a strong theoretical foundation, initiatives in educational equity and multicultural education have only partially addressed educational issues of concern to culturally diverse students. They have focused on developing programs to address educational problems at the expense of fully understanding why the problems exist. The extended

case study approach, favored by researchers who sought to document the attributes of different cultural groups, often had the unintended effect of promoting stereotypes.

11. New theoretical perspectives on the educational needs of culturally diverse populations span a broad continuum. Some researchers claim that educational failure is related to a mismatch between home and school cultures. Others claim that students fail academically because schools do not utilize principles of effective teaching and learning. Still other theorists point to social oppression, socioeconomic status, and social expectations for certain groups as keys to understanding educational underachievement.

12. More comprehensive perspectives on education focus on both the psychology of the individual student and the sociocultural context in which the student lives. These theories attempt not only to explain the relationship between home and school but also to reveal how learning and achievement are influenced by psychological, sociological, and cultural variables.

13. The constructivist approach to education is based on a specific model of how humans come to know and to understand. It proposes that humans gain knowledge by constructing it—by comparing and organizing old and new information within a surrounding local context or environment that greatly affects the final form the knowledge will take. This approach acknowledges that children come to school with constructed knowledge about many things.

14. In U.S. schools, culturally diverse children often are confronted with contexts for education that do not allow them to apply and extend their constructed knowledge. Such students are vulnerable to failure when faced with schooling practices that exclude their histories, languages, experiences, and values; that feature tracking; and that limit opportunity to learn in ways other than by teacher-led instruction.

15. A pedagogy that is responsive to culturally diverse students utilizes their constructed knowledge as a foundation for appropriating new knowledge. It also incorporates the students' native languages or bilingual abilities. In order to respond effectively to these students, teachers must become more familiar with the cognitive, social, and cultural dimensions of learning.

EXTENDING YOUR EXPERIENCE

1. Research the history of school desegregation efforts in your state during the 1960s and 1970s. Outline the results of any major state court cases you uncover. Look back through the

magazine and newspaper coverage of the time, and characterize the nature of the national public debate over educational equity. Prepare a list of three comments to report to the class about your findings.

2. Interview an older friend or relative who immigrated to the United States as a young person. Keeping in mind what you learned in this chapter about Americanization and assimilation, create a list of questions to ask this person about his or her experience in a new culture. What aspects of the original culture did he or she have to give up or change?

3. What role do you think teacher expectations play in students' accomplishments? How have high or low expectations from teachers influenced you? Create a written portrait of a particularly inspiring teacher you have had, exploring the possible sources for the inspiration you felt. Share your portrait with your classmates.

4. Reflect on a time in your own experience—whether in school or in a particular social situation—when you felt most like a foreigner or an outsider. Describe your feelings. What about the situation made you feel this way? Was it the way other people treated you? Was it something you were expected to do that you did not know how to do? What might have made you feel less excluded? As a teacher in a classroom of culturally diverse students, how can you be sensitive to a child's experience of outsiderness?

5. Is school the proper forum in which to discuss social issues centered on race, ethnicity, gender, and social class? Should students be encouraged to develop a critical, analytical perspective on social injustice? What types of questions do you yourself have about the unfairness and inequities you perceive in our society? List as many of your questions as you can, and then be prepared to share them in class.

6. Imagine that you are suddenly immersed in a culture completely different from the one in which you grew up. What aspects of your constructed knowledge about your own culture will be helpful to you as you join this new culture?

RESOURCES FOR FURTHER STUDY

Appleton, C. (1983). Cultural pluralism in education: Theoretical foundations. New York: Longman.

The author argues that the central task in education for a culturally diverse student population is to find an equilibrium between the differences and commonalities of individuals. The author discusses the historical, theoretical, ideological, and legal aspects of pluralism, and provides assessments and suggestions to ease the conflict pluralism presents, particularly for the educational system.

Banks, J., & Banks, C. A. (1995). *Handbook of research on multicultural education*. New York: Macmillan.

This volume offers a wealth of information related to multicultural education. An excellent resource tool, it addresses theoretical as well as practical issues along with an extremely comprehensive set of articles by leading authors in this field.

Cummins, J. (1986). Empowering minority students: A framework for intervention. *Harvard Educational Review, 56*(1), 18–35.

The author offers a theoretical framework for analyzing the school failure of minority students and the relative lack of success of compensatory education, bilingual education, and LEP programs, arguing that these attempts were unsuccessful because of the inflexibility of teachers, students, schools, and minority communities.

Oakes, J. (1990). Multiplying inequalities: The effects of race, social class, and tracking on opportunities to learn mathematics and science. Santa Monica, CA: Rand Corp.

This publication assesses the opportunities given to underrepresented and low-achieving groups of students to succeed in scientific and technological domains. Statistical reports and economic trends paint a dismal picture for the future. This deficiency can affect the economic well-being of the nation, since our educational system loses important human capital.

Sleeter, C. E., & Grant, C. A. (1987). An analysis of multicultural education in the U.S. *Harvard Educational Review, 57*(4).

The authors provide a framework to educators who are interested in dealing with misunderstandings about multicultural education. The term "multiculturalism" is examined and described, and various other definitions for it are criticized.

Weis, L. (Ed.). (1988). *Class, race, and gender in American education*. Albany: State University of New York Press.

The volume is a compilation of the work of various authors whose main goal is to engage in a more concise and interrelated discussion of how race, class, and gender harbor inequality. Some writers document the ways in which schools promote inequality, and others describe how cultures or groups outside the school stay out of school.

PART TWO

THE ROOTS

Tow much do we really know about the communication process, specifically in relation to the culturally diverse student? Part Two addresses teaching and learning as they relate to research into children's linguistic, cognitive, and social development, as well as schooling.

OF

What do current research findings indicate about the relationship between linguistic and cognitive development? How does the process of a child learning one language differ from that of a child learning two languages simultaneously? Chapter 4 describes the relationships between students'

DIVERSITY

family, school, and peer cultures and suggests how they combine to affect their engagement with learning. Which aspects of the school environment help students bridge the gap between home and school? Which aspects impede such bridge-building? Chapter 5 traces the steps in language development and discusses research into multilingualism and use of dialect.

Finally, what role does culture play? Chapter 6 examines the social context of learning and the role of the family, the peer group, and the community in the school achievement and psychology of individual learners. It also describes instructional strategies that can help all students become more effective communicators.

AN ECOLOGY OF FAMILY, HOME, AND SCHOOL

CHAPTER 4

Focus Questions

▼ What might prevent children from making successful transitions between their multiple cultures?

▼ What is the role of the family in the socialization of culturally diverse children?

▼ What are ethnic images, and how might they influence a child's concept of self?

▼ How does the cultural systems approach account for persistent educational underachievement among culturally diverse populations in the United States?

▼ What is the difference between voluntary and involuntary minority population?

▼ How can schools develop and sustain their partnerships with students' family and community?

▼ What are the advantages of scaffolding and the disadvantages of tracking and ability grouping?

"In the seed lies critical ingredients for future growth, but the initial nurturance of that seed also determines the same growth." —Conrad Lorenz

In any culture, important socialization practices formed within the context of family and home circumstances set the stage for a child's development for years to come. This chapter focuses on understanding students' multiple cultures and the transitions between them. It is my hope it will also provide information that will assist educators and others who work with students to build bridges between these cultures. We will look at family, school, and peer cultures, at the interrelationships among them, and in particular at how these cultures combine to affect children's engagement with learning. Of particular interest to us are the features in school environments that either aid or impede students' transitions between home and school.

The Meeting of Cultures

Before we can discuss the bridges we want to build across students' multiple cultures, we must identify the nature of the lines that separate these cultures. Some such boundaries are neutral in that sociocultural components experienced by the people on each side of the boundary are perceived as equal. When boundary lines are neutral, movement between cultures occurs with relative ease because the social and psychological costs to the individual are minimal. Alternately, when cultural borders are not neutral and when separate cultures are not perceived as equal, then movement and adaptation across borders are frequently difficult because the knowledge and skills in one culture are more highly valued and esteemed than those in the other. Although it is possible for students to navigate nonneutral borders with apparent success, these transitions can produce psychological effects that are invisible to teachers and others. Moreover, when the psychosocial consequences of adaptation across borders become too great for individuals to face, cultural boundaries become impenetrable barriers.

Cultural Boundary Lines

Earlier research generally has focused on families, peers, and schools as distinct cultural entities. We know that any one of these components can powerfully affect the direction in which students are pulled. For example, dynamic teachers, vigorous schools, and educational programs targeted to override the negative effects associated with low socioeconomic status, limited motivation, and language and cultural barriers can produce committed, interested, and academically engaged individuals (Abi-Nader, 1990a; Edmonds, 1979a; García, 1997; Heath, 1982; Joyce, Murphy, Showers, & Murphy, 1989; Slavin, 1989; Vogt, Jordan, & Tharp, 1987; Walberg, 1986a). Likewise, research on peer groups has described the potency and force with which members pull young people toward the norms of groups (Coleman, 1963; Eckert, 1989; Romo & Falbo, 1996; Ueda, 1987). We know too that family indices, such as socioeconomic status and parents' educational levels, are important predictors of students' engagement within educational settings (Jencks et al., 1972), as are cultural expectations and beliefs (Banks, C. A., & Banks, J., 1995; California Tomorrow, 1997; Clark, 1983; Erickson, 1987; Fordham, 1988; Gibson, 1987; Hoffman, 1988; McDermott, 1987; Ogbu, 1983, 1987a; Spindler, 1987; Spindler & Spindler, 1989; Suarez-Orozco, 1985, 1987; Trueba, 1982, 1988a; Trueba, Moll, Diaz, & Diaz, 1982; Valdés, 1996). In other words, we know a great deal about how aspects of families, schools, teachers, and peer groups independently affect educational outcomes. But we need to know how these worlds combine in the day-to-day lives of students to influence their engagement within school and classroom contexts.

As we attempt to create optimal school environments for increasingly diverse populations, educators need to know how students negotiate borders successfully—or, alternatively, how they are impeded by barriers that prevent their successful negotiation not only within an institutional context but with peers who are different from themselves. Figure 4.1 attempts to portray graphically the interaction of cultures that students must learn to negotiate.

Although we still have much to learn about the complex interactions of culture, socialization, and education, at least now we are asking the right questions. That is, recent research focuses on understanding and facilitating successful interaction among cultures rather than on discounting the attributes of minority cultures to accommodate those of majority cultures. Sadly, this has not always been the case. In Chapter 3 we saw that for a long time U.S. schools have considered the unique language development of culturally diverse children as a limitation. The social attributes of these children's family and home environments likewise have been viewed as detrimental to the students' social, economic, and educational success.

The desired effect of "Americanizing" students and adults was to socialize the culturally different community into the dominant culture. The early response was an attempt not only to

Influence on Students

Difference Seen as Negative

Figure 4.1 ▼ **A Model of Children's Multiple Cultures**

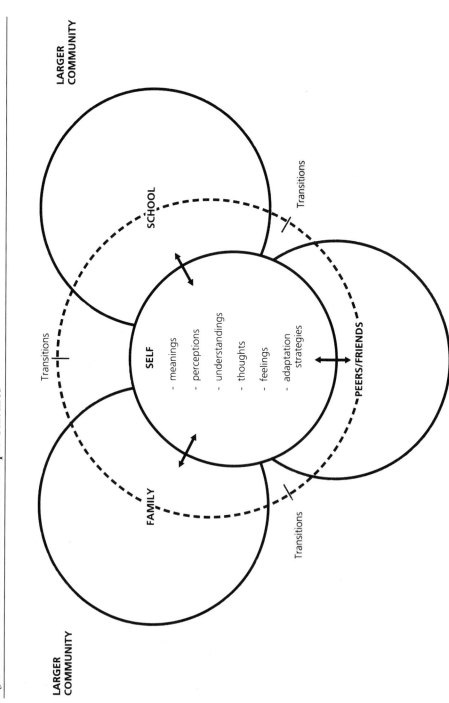

Source: Adapted from *Students' Multiple Worlds: Negotiating the Boundaries of Family, Peer, and School Cultures* (p. 56), by P. Phelan, A. L. Davidson, and H. T. Cao, 1991, Stanford, CA: Center for Research on the Context of Secondary Teaching.

**Socializing
Difference**

change but also to segregate culturally diverse student populations to better serve these children while not contaminating the
others. Legally segregated schools thus arose for blacks, Mexicans, Chinese, Jews, Germans, Poles, and others. Chapter 3 also
described how American Indian students were segregated into
government schools many thousands of miles away from their
families and communities. The belief was that if schools could
serve as the social institution that taught students English and
instilled "American" values, then the negative social and economic conditions of these populations could be eradicated.

Americanization continues to be the goal of many programs
aimed at culturally diverse populations in the United States. For
students, Americanization means the elimination not only of linguistic and cultural differences but of an undesirable culture.
This schooling approach does not recognize the significant
boundaries that exist between a student's family, community,
and school and the necessity of providing students with transitions and bridges across these borders. Instead, it considers only
the most negative perceptions of these differences while ignoring
the positive effects of the interaction that always have and always will occur when cultures meet.

*The Role of the Family
in the Socialization of Children*

Although the concept of Americanization has predominated in
U.S. society, educational research during the last two decades has
begun to regard ethnic culture as more than a target for elimination. Building on a foundation established by the noted anthropologist Margaret Mead (1937), more recent researchers have
begun to explore socialization as a means by which cultural differences can be understood as opposed to eliminated (notably Gallimore & Tharp, 1989; Kagan, 1983b; Lave, 1988; McClintock,
1974; Nieto, 1979, 1992; Soto, 1997; Valdés, 1996; Valsiner,
1989).

One of the most significant functions of **socialization** is the
transmission of values. By socialization, Mead (1937) and Mc-
Clintock (1972) refer to the process through which prescriptions
(ideas about what one should do) and prohibitions (ideas about
what one should not do) are transmitted to members of the so-

**Agents of
Socialization**

cial group. The traditional view of socialization generally presented in the literature has emphasized the family, including siblings and members of the extended family, as important agents

BECOMING A RESPONSIVE TEACHER

How Home Life Shapes Classroom Behavior

Maria was identified by her first-grade teacher as very quiet. She hardly ever participated in classroom discussions. Even when the teacher specifically invited her to participate, she was very reticent. She did very well on individual activities, but the teacher worried about her shyness.

A videotaping project was scheduled for her classroom as part of a larger research project exploring the language development of the children. The teacher made a request to make a special effort to video-tape Maria's interactions during specific whole-group lessons. These videotapes indicated that Maria was paying close attention to the teacher, but never volunteered to participate and at times avoided eye contact with the teacher when the teacher attempted to make eye contact with her.

Another aspect of the videotaping captured students working together in small groups at "learning stations" that the teacher had throughout the room. During one of those tapings, Maria was observed leading a group of five students through the exercises at the station. She was quite verbal, asking the other students questions and directing their activity. In addition, the students in the group looked to her for guidance, overtly requesting her assistance. Subsequent video recordings of similar small-group interactions in which Maria participated always showed Maria playing an active or even a leading role. Yet, on the very same days, Maria continued to be nonparticipatory within any lesson activity led by the teacher.

The teacher was very interested in these contrasting behavior patterns. She watched the videotapes herself and was deeply puzzled by the distinct ways in which she saw Maria behave. Here was her shy Maria acting not shy at all—in many cases actually looked upon as a leader by her peers.

The teacher decided to ask Maria about her family circumstances and was not surprised by the answers. Maria was one of eight children—five older than she and two younger. Her parents and older brothers worked in the local fields, and Maria took major responsibilities for caring for her younger brother and sister whenever her mother was unavailable. Her family lived in a two-bedroom house that required sharing of space and related resources. "Mom and Dad made the rules and enforced them," Maria said—

BECOMING A RESPONSIVE TEACHER *Cont.*

you respected their wishes; you knew they knew best. When Maria was asked if she was ever consulted regarding her opinions, impressions, or suggestions, she politely indicated that Mom and Dad knew best: it would be disrespectful to offer any opinions.

The teacher now understood Maria's hesitancy in responding to her during group lessons. The teacher as adult was a person to be respected—she knew best. Maria would likely never volunteer opinions or in any way challenge the authority of the teacher. However, in small-peer-group circumstances, she seemed to be making use of her caretaking skills—those practiced and appropriately regarded in her family. Without the necessary attention of the teacher, this culture clash could have had negative educational consequences for Maria. The teacher's perceptions of Maria's choice not to respond during formal instruction could have led to an impression that Maria could not participate—that she was uninterested, unmotivated, or lacked the ability to handle the academic content in the lessons.

Needless to say, the teacher appreciated the new-found information. She understood that Maria worked best in small groups and that she needed to develop the ability to participate in larger groups led by adults.

▼ Meeting the Challenge

1. Share the above story about Maria with a few of your friends outside of this class. Describe the teacher's observations about Maria's two different behaviors, and ask your friends why they think she would act so differently. After they offer some ideas, explain to them the concept of home-school culture clash and how it may influence children's learning experience. Report the results of your discussion to your classmates.
2. If the above-described small "learning stations" had not been an established part of Maria's classroom, what impression would her teacher continue to have about her?
3. What is shyness? Compare your definition with those of your classmates. Describe learning environments that have made you feel reticent to participate and why.

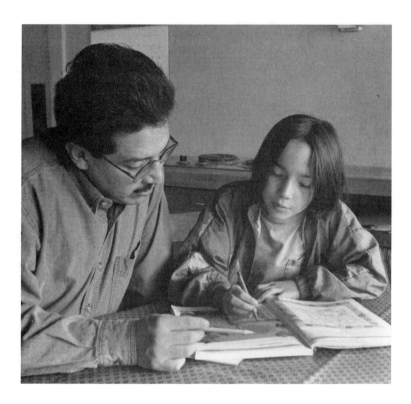

of socialization. More recent conceptualizations (e.g., Hetherington & Parke, 1988) have considered socialization agents outside
the family, such as teachers, peers, the media (especially television), and other persons with whom the child regularly comes
into contact.

Several authors have discussed the variables associated with
family background, family structure, and the broader social ecology that influence the socialization experiences of culturally diverse children (Keefe & Padilla, 1987; Knight, Bernal, & Carlos,
1988; McClintock, Bayard, & McClintock, 1983; Whiting & Edwards, 1988). The variables of family structure shown to be related to the parents' socialization goals include: (1) the strength
of familial interdependence, (2) the pattern of status in relationships within the family, and (3) family size (see McClintock et
al., 1983, for more details). Strength of familial interdependence
consists of feelings of family solidarity as well as attachment and
commitment to the family.

There is some empirical evidence of particularly close family
ties among Mexican American families (Keefe, 1979; Keefe,
Padilla, & Carlos, 1979b). For example, research comparing Hispanic families with Anglo-American families suggests that Hispanic families demonstrate closer relations and greater loyalty

**Family
Variables**

among members, more frequent visits among relatives, parental encouragement of family-centered interactions, fewer opportunities for children to invite friends into the home, less freedom for children to play away from home, greater disapproval of children who contradict authority, and fewer decision-making opportunities for children. Similarly, Johnson, Teigen, and Davila (1983) found parents of Mexican backgrounds to be relatively demanding and restrictive of children compared to Anglo-American parents. While we must be cautious of stereotyping all Hispanic families as showing strong interdependence among family members, McClintock et al. (1983) have speculated about the implications of this characteristic for a child's exposure to nonfamilial peers. Because of the greater emphasis on family-oriented interactions and within-family competition, it may be less relevant for a Hispanic child to compete with Anglo-American peers for recognition and rewards.

A related study of individual and cooperative socialization values explored the links between individuality and family connectedness in European American, Chinese American, Filipino American, Vietnamese American, and Hispanic American adolescents (Cooper, Baker, Polichar, & Welsh, 1991). Members of the three Asian American groups and the Hispanic American group reported much more concern for familial values than for the individual. In addition, members of these groups were much more likely to consider their siblings and peers, rather than their parents, as major sources of assistance and advice. By contrast, Anglo-American adolescents were much more individualistic in their perception of themselves in the family and more likely to seek out parents and adults for critical advice or support. Similarly, Seginer's (1989) study of the socialization of Arab adolescents found that older sisters play a key role in this process. These adolescents see their sisters as important consultants regarding the outside world, future plans, social relations, and education. Mothers are consulted only about pubertal changes, and fathers are consulted about permission, money, and political issues.

Still further evidence of cultural diversity in socialization practices comes from research on Native Alaskan families (Henze, Regan, Vanett, & Power, 1990). Interviews with Yup'ik families yielded a pattern of socialization that was centered not on the family but instead around those activities that are required for survival: the "men's house" provides instruction for boys in all aspects of community life, and the home is where women transmit information to girls. This gender-separate social structure evolved over many years as the functions of each gender were organized to meet the harsh survival challenges of the group's environment. The concept or structure of a core nuclear or extended family is nonexistent in this culture. Moreover, as other studies of American Indian cultures have revealed (Tharp, 1989), Yup'ik children are expected to learn by carefully observing adults or older peers and siblings, without asking questions or interrupting activities. Such diverse socialization practices have too often been interpreted as deviant instead of merely different. We review these examples here to reinforce the overall thesis that the environment of children outside of school sets the stage for their lifelong patterns of social relations, including those that are important in the schooling process.

The Concept of Ecology

In this chapter, we shall use the concept of ecology to gain an understanding of the family, community, and school environments of children. **Ecology** is the study of the relationships between an organism and its environment.

Ecology of the Family. Valdés (1996), Delpit (1995), García and McLaughlin (1995), and Soto (1997) have documented in great detail the ecology of minority families as it relates to the schooling of their children. The findings can best be summarized by the conclusion that these families are under siege (Soto, 1997). Interviews with parents, children, and teachers revealed that, in general, these families seem to be immersed in hostile educational and community settings. Even in communities that have rich ethnic traditions of language and culture, poor families from diverse linguistic and cultural backgrounds, as well as some immigrants and certain other minorities who are socially well established, report feeling that they are perceived as a threat to the status quo (Nieto, 1992; Soto, 1997; Valdés, 1996). As Soto (1997) reports of Puerto Rican families in Pennsylvania, many parents have adopted a "swallowing hard" approach to these circumstances. Particularly harmful is the educational system's preference for advocacy by parents combined with the Puerto Rican parents' adaptive stance of passivity. In general, the parents know very well that their children are not doing well at school and that they are not welcomed there as other children are welcomed. Yet the parents believe that by not advocating (some would say, not complaining) and by "swallowing hard," they are actually improving their children's situation in school.

There are, however, certain attributes of linguistically and culturally diverse families that can help promote children's success in school (Soto, 1997; Valdés, 1996). In a "successful" family, for example, the children are often raised bilingually with a clear appreciation for being bilingual and bicultural. Such families devise strategies to ensure that the children can use *both* languages in the home and community, and great importance is attached to such ability. These families also foster the children's pride in their culture's traditions through a variety of means, including intergenerational contacts, extended family interactions, and observance of special traditions (such as making *pasteles* and *tamales* at Christmas)—all of which require regular commitments of time and space.

Moreover, "successful" families support and nurture an appreciation of education for all family members. A micro learning community flourishes in the home, with parents teaching children, children sometimes teaching parents, and siblings and extended family members teaching one another. There is an overarching respect for each person's potential and actual contribution to the family. As Valdés (1996) indicates, these families are built on the notion that members act *con respeto* (with respect) toward one another.

Social Ecology

Besides the ecology of the family and the community, the broader social ecology has also been suggested as an important determinant in the socialization of children (Kagan, 1984; Keefe & Padilla, 1987). The social ecology includes such factors as the urbanization level of the community in which the child lives, the socioeconomic status of the family and the community, the nature of the minority status of other cultural groups in the community, and prevailing views about these cultural groups in the larger society.

Factors in Social Ecology

In many ways, a more rural environment and/or an environment of relatively low socioeconomic status may lead to socialization experiences that foster interdependency, respect for others, and more sharing of resources. In contrast, a more urban environment may lead to socialization experiences that cultivate independence, competitiveness, and more reliance upon social supports that are external to the family. There has been some empirical demonstration of a relationship between the social behaviors of children and urbanization level (e.g., Kagan, Knight, Martinez, & Espinosa-Santana, 1981) and socioeconomic status (Knight & Kagan, 1977). Minority status may lead to considerable variability in socialization experiences simply because children from a minority population generally have direct contacts with members of the minority group as well as with members of the Anglo-American majority (Ogbu, 1982a, 1987a).

The model of socialization briefly presented here suggests that characteristics of family background and structure and the broader social ecology are important determinants of the socialization practices to which children are exposed. We have barely scratched the surface of the many cultural differences that exist in socialization practices. Nonetheless, such conceptual rethinking of the child, the family, and the broader society as an ecological system is a far cry from the traditional tendency to regard cultural difference as a negative social attribute to be eliminated. Enlightened understanding of diverse student cultures cannot be founded on the Americanization strategy of taking all who are not "American" and making them "American." We will gain a clearer picture of the future for culturally diverse students in this country if we set aside issues of Americanization and instead concentrate on examining the nature of social variables and their relationship both to "cultural differences" and to educational practices and outcomes.

Ethnic Image and Its Effects

In recent decades, American society has made considerable progress in the area of race relations. Today many white Americans are more supportive of integration and racial equity than in the past (Jaynes & Williams, 1989; Schuman, Steeh, & Bobo, 1985; Smith, 1990; Smith & Sheatsley, 1984). Federal and state governments have instituted numerous programs to promote integration and to assist members of minority groups in their efforts to attain educational and economic equality of opportunity (e.g., through busing, affirmative action, and minority contracting). In the next section we will discuss the findings of research studies that explore the ethnic images that continue to prevail in our society despite this progress toward equity.

Ethnic Images in Society

Recent research has explored shifts in racial tolerance and in people's images of different ethnic groups. This work has addressed two questions: (1) What are people's images of several major ethnic groups along various dimensions? (2) Do these images influence attitudes and behaviors toward those groups?

In this discussion, **ethnic** is used as a general term to refer to seven groups of people (whites, Jews, African Americans, Asian Americans, Hispanic Americans, Native Americans, and white Southerners) who are differentiated partly by race, religion, nationality, and region of origin. **Ethnic images** describes people's general beliefs about cultural groups, in particular beliefs about group characteristics and attributes. We use the term *images* rather than words such as *stereotypes* or *prejudices* to avoid some of the baggage that is frequently associated with these words. For example, stereotypes and prejudice are often considered to contain a component of irrationality and to involve such fallacious thinking as improper generalization, excessive categorization, and rejection of counterevidence (Allport, 1954; Jackman, 1973; Schuman & Harding, 1964).

Contemporary relations between cultural groups in the United States cannot be understood without an examination of the images members of these groups have of themselves and of other groups. The notion that Americans are creating a color-and-creed-blind society is easily disabused by the data on ethnic images collected in the 1990 General Social Survey (Smith, 1990).

Rating of Ethnicities

First, these data indicate that people are willing and able to rate others on the basis of their ethnicity. Second, with one exception, minority groups were evaluated more negatively than whites in general. The one exception among minority groups was Jews, who were rated more favorably than whites on each characteristic except patriotism. No other group scored above whites on any characteristic. In this study, Jews were rated most positively overall (first on wealth, industry, nonviolence, intelligence, and self-support, and third on patriotism). Asian Americans and white Southerners were ranked next (second or third) on almost every dimension. Finally, African Americans and Hispanic Americans were ranked last or next to last on almost every characteristic.

Desired Social Distance

Ethnic images also are associated with the social distance that people wish to maintain between themselves and the members of other groups. As the rating scale for each group moves from positive to negative, people are less favorable toward living in a neighborhood where half of their neighbors are from particular groups and toward having a close relative marry a member of one of those groups. All the groups showed a significant relationship between ethnic images and desired social distance, but the relationship between these factors for Jews and white Southerners was modest, whereas the relationship for African Americans, Asian Americans, and Hispanic Americans was strong.

This research shows that images about ethnic groups are significant predictors of support for racial integration and desired social distance. Despite the demonstrable progress in tolerance of cultural difference over the last several decades, ethnic images are still commonplace in contemporary U.S. society. On the whole these images are neither benign nor trivial. Most members of the majority population in the United States see most minority groups in a decidedly negative light on a number of important characteristics. African Americans and Hispanic Americans in particular receive very low ratings. These negative ethnic images in turn help shape people's attitudes toward civil rights and racial integration. Ethnic images remain important determinants of public opinion on affirmative action, school desegregation, and many other group-related issues.

Effects of Ethnic Images on Children

How do ethnic images shape a child's personality? Following from the work of Smith (1990), personality may be understood as a structure that reconciles children's interpreted experiences and emotional states. Those experiences and emotions, in turn, are shaped by the social attributes ascribed to an individual by others. A sense of ethnic identity is part of that synthesis. In a world populated by people of many different ethnic backgrounds who often interact and conflict with each other, a child's developing sense of ethnic group identity is an important social issue. Several studies of the development of ethnic identity have focused both on children's ability to identify their own ethnic group and on their attitudes toward their own and other groups (McAdoo & McAdoo, 1985).

Research performed by Clark and Clark (1939) was perhaps the most famous inquiry into the development of ethnic identity, because the results became evidence that led the U.S. Supreme Court to declare racially segregated education illegal. In the Clarks' work, African American and Anglo-American children aged 3 years and older were presented with pairs of dolls

Negative Self-Concept

representing each ethnic group. On successive trials the children were asked to choose "which boy [doll] you would like to play with" or "which girl [doll] you don't like." The Clarks reported that most of the youngest children distinguished between the gender categories of the dolls and that both the African American children displayed a preference for the Anglo-American dolls. These results were interpreted by the justices of the Supreme Court as evidence that segregation resulted in the development of a negative sense of self among African American children. Studies conducted since the 1950s both confirm the Clarks' original findings (McAdoo & McAdoo, 1985; Spencer, M. B., 1988) and extend them to other minority ethnic groups, including Native Americans (Beauf, 1977). In all of these studies, children of minority groups were more likely to prefer Anglo-American dolls.

Importantly, these same studies have cast doubt on the notion that children from minority ethnic groups acquire a generalized

Recognition of Inequalities

negative self-concept. Beauf (1977), for example, reports incident after incident in which Native American children who display a preference for Anglo-American dolls also demonstrate with devastating accuracy an understanding of the economic and social circumstances that make their lives difficult in contrast with the lives of Anglo-Americans. Five-year-old Dom was given several dolls representing Anglo-Americans and Native Americans (whose skins were represented as brown) to put into a toy classroom.

> Dom: (holding up a white doll) The children's all here and now the teacher's coming in.
>
> Interviewer: Is that the teacher?
>
> Dom: Yeah.
>
> Interviewer: (holding up a brown doll) Can she be the teacher?
>
> Dom: No way! Her's just an aide. (Beauf, 1977, p. 207)

In Beauf's view, the choices children make when presented with pairs of dolls that represent different ethnic groups are less an expression of their self-concept than of their desire for the power and wealth of the Anglo-Americans with whom they have come into contact.

Other recent research has shown that when psychologists attempt to test the social concepts and self-concepts of young children, their expressed ethnic preferences change according to the

Environment and Self-Concept

circumstances. McAdoo & McAdoo (1985) report that the degree to which African American preschoolers show a preference for Anglo-American dolls has decreased relative to the results obtained in studies performed prior to the 1960s. She does not speculate on the reasons for these trends, but the end of racial segregation and several decades of political and cultural activism in the African American community are likely candidates. This conclusion is reinforced by Beauf's (1977) finding that young Native American children whose parents were active in promoting Native American cultural awareness and social rights chose dolls representing Native Americans more often than children whose parents took little interest in Native American affairs.

Additional evidence of the power of the environment to shape children's ethnic preferences comes from an experimental study that rewarded children aged 3 to 5 for choosing black versus white pictures of animals and people (Spencer & Horowitz, 1973). Initially all the children showed a preference for white stimuli (both animals and people), but after training sessions in which they received symbolic rewards (marbles that could be traded for cookies) for either choice, all children displayed a marked preference for black stimuli, and that preference remained intact over a period of several weeks.

In sum, the results of studies on ethnic identity indicate that children are aware of differences by the time they are 4 years old. At the same age, or not long after, they also become aware of and form judgments about their own ethnicity. These views, as well as their attitudes toward other people's ethnicity, seem to depend on both the beliefs of their adult caregivers and the perceived power and wealth of their own ethnic group.

A Cultural Systems Account of Underachievement

So far in this chapter we have discussed the relationship between culture and education by concentrating on issues of family, home, and socialization practices experienced by individual students. By its very nature, such a "micro" approach focuses on an individual student's social contact with parents, siblings, peers, and other representatives of social institutions. These interactions are seen as forming and guiding the student's communicative, cognitive, social, and educational development. In short, these interactions prepare the way for either educational success or educational failure.

An alternative to this intense focus on the individual student is the "macro" approach proposed by a number of anthropologists and sociologists. This approach broadens the examination to the cultural system. A system is a network of interrelating elements that form a complex whole. A cultural system, then, is a group of interacting cultural elements. The **cultural systems approach** to education considers the organization of a society, specifically the roles and status assigned to cultural groups within a society, to be a major determinant of educational underachievement (Gibson & Ogbu, 1991; Ogbu & Matute-Bianchi, 1986; Ogbu, 1982a, 1987b, 1992b; Solorzano, 1997b; Stanton-Salazar, 1997). Known by such names as the *structural inequality theory* (Gollnick & Chinn, 1990), *institutional racism* (Ovando & Collier, 1985), the *perceived labor market explanation* (Erickson, 1987), and most notably the *secondary cultural systems theory* (Ogbu, 1992a), this approach suggests that the specific social placement of a cultural group within the broader social fabric will directly affect the values, perceptions, and social behavior of members of that group.

Broader Approach

As it pertains to the education of culturally diverse groups in the United States, the cultural systems approach suggests that members of minority groups become convinced by the overall social order that their "place" in society is distinctively disadvantaged. In essence, students from minority backgrounds recognize that they are generally perceived as less intelligent, lazy, and dependent, and begin to take on these attributes themselves, particularly in response to perceptions held by social groups that wield political and economic power. As we saw in the previous section, the ethnic images that label some cultural groups as "lesser" have long persevered in our society despite outward signs of progress.

Types of Minority Groups

Ogbu (1992a) has been an important spokesperson for the cultural systems approach to understanding the disproportionate school failure of some minority populations in the United States and throughout the world. His analysis carefully distinguishes between immigrant or voluntary minorities and nonimmigrant or nonvoluntary minorities (also called "castelike," "outcast," or "pariah" minorities). The term *minority* suggests a group that is smaller numerically. When considered in a social context, however, minority usually refers to a group that is subordinate to a dominant group by a negative power relationship. Numerical majority does not guarantee a group dominant status. In Latin America, India, and Africa, for example, millions of native peoples historically were in a subordinate position to a minority of colonial powers (Gollnick & Chinn, 1990).

Ogbu's (1992a) analysis suggests that members of voluntary and involuntary minority groups may live in the same society and experience the same circumstances: prejudice, discrimination, residential segregation, inferior education for their children, and exclusion from desirable jobs. However, voluntary minorities often do well in school and sometimes are more successful academically than students in the dominant group. In the United States, for example, East Asian students often test higher on standardized testing than Anglo-American students. By contrast, involuntary minorities such as African Americans, Hispanics, and American Indians consistently have problems in school, perform below grade level, and have high dropout rates.

Ogbu and Matute-Bianchi (1986) have begun to elaborate on a conceptual framework regarding the distinction between voluntary and involuntary minority groups. Table 4.1 defines these two types of minority status. Tables 4.2 through 4.5 further describe these groups and chart their responses to and interpretations of prejudice and discrimination, based on a synthesis of Ogbu and Matute-Bianchi (1986) and Ogbu (1992a).

Table 4.1 Terms of Minority Status

VOLUNTARY MINORITY	INVOLUNTARY MINORITY
1. **Moved voluntarily to host society**	1. **Involuntarily incorporated through slavery, conquest, colonization, birth, and relegated to menial status**
2. **Chose to emigrate for**	2. **Did not choose to emigrate**
a. greater political freedom (including escaping death, imprisonment, or torture in homeland)	3. **Experience in "host" society is one of prejudice, discrimination, and exploitation in the form of**
b. economic well-being	a. residential segregation
c. better overall opportunities	b. inferior education for their children
3. **Experience in host society may include prejudice, exploitation, and discrimination in the form of**	c. job ceiling: exclusion from jobs even when qualified (particularly desirable jobs)
a. residential segregation	d. low wages
b. inferior education for their children	e. cultural and intellectual derogation
c. job ceiling: exclusion from jobs even when qualified (particularly desirable jobs)	4. **Secondary cultural discontinuities (cultural and language barriers)**
d. low wages	a. arose as coping mechanisms after minority group was subjected to the power of dominant group
e. cultural and intellectual derogation	b. are perceived as markers of social identity to be maintained
4. **Primary cultural discontinuities (cultural and language barriers)**	c. are general; have to do with "style" (interaction, communication, cognition, learning)
a. existed before minority group came into contact with dominant group	d. cause problems that do not tend to diminish over time; are attributed to social opposition and negative personal characteristics
b. are perceived as barriers to be overcome to achieve goals of immigration	
c. are specific; have to do with "content"	
d. cause initial problems for teachers, peers, and learning but diminish over time; are attributed to deficiencies in cultural assumptions	

Ogbu (1992a) proposes that the cultural models for voluntary and involuntary minorities differ in five key elements:

1. A frame of reference for comparing present status and future possibilities (see Table 4.2)
2. A folk theory of how to succeed, especially through education (see Table 4.3)
3. A sense of collective identity (see Table 4.4)
4. A cultural frame of reference for judging appropriate behavior and affirming group membership and solidarity (see Table 4.5)
5. An assessment of the extent to which one may trust members of the dominant group and the institutions they control

Table 4.2   Frame of Reference for Comparing Present Status and Future Possibilities

VOLUNTARY MINORITY	INVOLUNTARY MINORITY
1. Positive dual frame of reference:	**1. Negative dual frame of reference:**
a. compare life in host society to that in homeland ("there")	**a.** compare life to that of members of dominant group
b. perceive position "here" to be much better	**b.** perceive position to be much worse
c. perceive themselves as foreigners, outsiders, guests	**c.** perceive themselves as denigrated and subordinated members of dominant society
2. Believe that "foreigners" must tolerate prejudice and discrimination of dominant group to achieve emigration goals; not highly influenced by such negative factors.	**2.** See no justification for dominant group's belief that minorities are biologically, religiously, socially, and culturally inferior; highly influenced by such a negative attitude
3. View situation as temporary because	**3.** View situation as permanent and institutionalized because
a. they can return home	**a.** they have no other home
b. they can emigrate elsewhere with wealth and credentials	**b.** they cannot leave present circumstances
c. it will improve through education and hard work	**c.** it will not improve through education and hard work
4. Perception of job ceiling:	**4. Perception of job ceiling:**
a. menial position "here" compared with worse position at home	**a.** menial position compared with jobs held by dominant group members
b. exclusion from better jobs is caused by "foreigner" status, inability to speak the language, education elsewhere	**b.** exclusion from better jobs is caused by the fact that they are a disparaged group relegated to menial position

According to Ogbu (1992b), "the different cultural models resulting from these differing theories and frameworks are learned by the children and shape the attitudes, knowledge and competencies they bring to the school" (p. 141).

As a theoretical framework, this conceptualization of educational underachievement allows us to begin to understand the reasons for different educational outcomes for different populations of students. For example, Suarez-Orozco (1987) proposes that the different Hispanic American groups—Mexican Americans, Puerto Rican Americans, and Americans of Cuban, Central American, and South American descent, as well as recent refugees from Central America—are distinct populations and should be understood as such. They face different issues and have different patterns of educational adaptation. Suarez-Orozco (1985) reports that whereas nationwide one-fourth of Mexican Americans aged 25 or older had less than five years of schooling, the same was true for only 6 percent of other Hispanics. In the

**Different
Educational
Outcomes**

Table 4.3 Folk Theory of How to Succeed

VOLUNTARY MINORITY	INVOLUNTARY MINORITY
Value education, hard work, and individual effort as a means of "making it" and diminishing discrimination. As a result, 1. accept parts of the mainstream dominant culture 2. adopt the challenge of assimilating into the dominant culture	Do not perceive education, hard work, and individual effort as a means of "making it"; believe discrimination is permanent. As a result, 1. reject the value system of the mainstream dominant culture 2. develop a folk theory in opposition to the values of the dominant group

Table 4.4 Sense of Collective Identity

VOLUNTARY MINORITY	INVOLUNTARY MINORITY
Maintain a sense of the social identity they had before emigration, at least through the first generation. Thus, 1. may not approve of certain aspects of dominant culture or want to be like dominant group members, but do not develop oppositional identity	Form a new sense of peoplehood or social identity in opposition to the "oppressor." Thus, 1. identity is forged from group's ancestral heritage and present interpretations of discrimination and denial of equal treatment

Table 4.5 Cultural Frame of Reference for Judging Appropriate Behavior and Affirming Group Membership and Solidarity

VOLUNTARY MINORITY	INVOLUNTARY MINORITY

1. **Alternation model: group members**
  a. believe it is possible and acceptable to participate in two different cultures or two different languages for different purposes, alternating one's behavior to the situation
  b. become acculturated without assimilating; dominant culture is not seen as threatening; believe it is necessary to cross cultural boundaries to achieve emigration goal
2. **Stress cultural values of the homeland in family and community, but believe that members**
  a. must accept the rules of the host society
	1. **Cultural inversion model: group members**
	  a. assume it is not possible or appropriate for the same individual to participate in cultures of the dominant group and of the minority group
	  b. experience linear acculturation; crossing cultural boundaries is seen as threat to minority identity, culture, and language
	  c. communicate disapproval for "acting white"
	2. **Stress collective efforts and struggle, so members**
	  a. legitimate civil rights activities as well as rioting to change rules because the rules don't work for them

southwestern states, only 60 percent of Mexican Americans were reported to have graduated from high school compared to 86 percent of Anglo-Americans. Many Central American refugees, however, are experiencing school success.

An ethnographic study of two hundred Central American refugees at two schools in San Francisco found that the ideas these new immigrants had developed about the nature of opportunity in this country allowed them to succeed academically. This success was surprising. These students "were routinely routed to overcrowded, understaffed, poor inner city schools, into a poisonous atmosphere of drugs and violence," where teachers were afraid of their students (Suarez-Orozco, 1985, p. 125). They learned English quickly but were tracked into low-level classes they had already completed in their own countries. Yet many were highly motivated to persevere and to succeed in school. The Central American immigrants were perceived by their teachers as desirable students—eager to learn, appreciative, polite, respectful, and hard-working.

According to Suarez-Orozco (1987), these recent Central American immigrants developed a dual frame of reference in which they compared their situation in the United States with that in their homeland. Most perceived that they had more and better opportunities here. The students believed it was self-evident that the future was open to them. Their parents overlooked the difficulties and emphasized the positive: the United States was fairer; schools, hot lunches, and libraries were free; and teachers seemed sincerely interested in their students. These immigrants developed a folk theory of "making it" in which education became the single most significant factor in getting ahead. This was in contrast to the method of getting ahead at home, which was based on connections: "who you know." In the United States, they felt, getting ahead was based on "what you know." The students believed their parents were doing everything they could for them and in turn felt a duty to succeed and to remove other loved ones from dangerous situations in the homeland. No matter how bad things were here, they were not as bad as at "home."

With a similar interest in distinctions between minority groups, Matute-Bianchi (1990) focused on diversity within a population of students of Mexican descent at Field High School on the central coast of California. Conducted between 1983 and 1985, her ethnographic research included interviews with teachers, counselors, aides, administrators, students of Mexican descent, and her own observations. From this research she distinguished among five major categories or "cultural" groups of students of Mexican descent:

How to Get Ahead

1. *Recent Mexican immigrants:* Self-identify as "Mexicanos"; have arrived in the last three to five years; refer to Mexico as home; came to the United States for economic opportunity; considered "unstylish" by other students; proficiency in Spanish (oral and written) tends to be an indicator of school success.

2. *Mexican-oriented:* Maintain a strong identity as Mexicano; frequently Mexican-born, but have lived in the United States most of their lives; parents are immigrants; tend to be bilingual; adept at academic work in English, having received most schooling here; speak English with school personnel, Spanish and English with peers, Spanish at home; active in Sociedad Bilingüe (Bilingual Society); proud of Mexican heritage; many students with Spanish surnames who are in college prep from this group.

3. *Mexican Americans:* U.S.-born English speakers who are much more U.S.-oriented than previous groups; may not speak Spanish at home unless necessary; participate in mainstream activities; tend not to call attention to their ethnicity; include some of the most esteemed students of Mexican descent in the school; described by staff as "totally acculturated."

4. *Chicanos:* At least second generation of their family in the United States of Mexican descent; loyal to their own group and avoid school activities; call themselves "homeboys" and "homegirls," call academically successful students "schoolboys" or "wannabes" ("want to be white"); among the most alienated students in the school.

5. *Cholos:* Smallest group in the school; noted for culturally distinct style of dressing that represents an identity that is neither Mexican nor American; "gang-oriented" or "gang sympathizers"; "low riders" (vintage and modern automobiles that are altered to sit low on the ground and decoratively painted to reflect cultural ideologies) perceived to be gang members; feared and held in contempt by other students of Mexican descent and mainstream Anglo-American students.

Patterns in School Performance

Matute-Bianchi emphasized the different forms and functions of ethnic labels and self-identity in immigrant and nonimmigrant Mexican groups in the United States. She traced the relationships among these factors to variations in school performance and discovered a pattern of school success among immigrant Mexican-oriented students and of school failure among nonimmigrant Chicanos. The two groups were perceived differently by teachers and students, and members of the groups themselves had different perceptions of what their futures held in terms of employment.

According to Matute-Bianchi, the successful students of Mexican descent were achievement- and goal-oriented. They saw a connection between high school success and adult success. They defined success as having a nice car, a nice house, a good job, and no money worries. They wanted to go to college, although they were not sure of a career choice. They had both Anglo-American and Mexican role models in school. Most stated that interest and support from their parents were essential to their school success, which they defined as the result of attending school regularly, doing homework, asking for help, getting along with teachers, and working "as hard as you can." Some had received support from teachers and counselors.

The Chicanos and Cholos expressed the desire to get good jobs but did not have an idea of how that was accomplished. They did not feel a connection to the future in a positive way and lived for the moment or the weekend. They doubted that they would graduate, even though they wanted to. They had little exposure to occupations other than the menial and physically difficult jobs of low status at which their parents worked. They could not think of one successful adult of Mexican descent whom they knew well. Although they expressed desire to do well, they exhibited behaviors that resulted in school failure: truancy, disruptive behavior, failure to bring books and homework, poor performance in class, failure to pass enough classes to maintain academic standing. They were apathetic and defiant of school culture.

In Gibson and Ogbu (1991) similar findings in fieldwork carried out in Saint Croix (U.S. Virgin Isands) during the 1970s to study the relationship among ethnic identity, immigrant status, and school performance are described. Her results were similar to those of Matute-Bianchi (1990). In the Saint Croix public schools, immigrants were more successful than natives, even though they were similar in class status, color, and cultural background. This pattern shows up in other settings. In the United

States, for example, "Asian Americans (Koreans, Japanese, and Chinese) are the only minority group whose academic achievement surpasses that of whites" (Lee, 1991, p. 3). They exhibit higher college attendance rates and higher achievement scores than the Anglo-American majority. But Korean students, who in the United States achieve as well as Japanese students, do not fare as well in Japan, where they have much lower achievement rates than Japanese students. In Japan the college attendance rate of Korean high school graduates was less than 60 percent of the rate of Japanese high school grads. Lee (1991) suggests that the historical experience of Koreans in these two host societies provides valuable insight into the effect of cultural systems on academic achievement.

Specifically, Lee argues, Koreans have had an increasingly positive image in the United States for two reasons: (1) Korea has become of strategic and economic importance to the United States, and (2) most Koreans in the United States are educated people with middle-class backgrounds. With the exception of physicians, however, Koreans have found it difficult to enter the U.S. middle-class mainstream because of the language barrier, their inability to transfer skills acquired in Korea, and discrimination against them in large businesses.

Korean Students in Japan

In Japan, Koreans have been legally entitled to public education since 1965. By 1981, 80 percent of Koreans were attending Japanese rather than Korean schools, hoping a Japanese education would contribute to upward mobility and integration. Korean schools do not have the status of Japanese schools, and their graduates are turned away from qualifying exams for universities and are not eligible to attend barber, beauty, and chef schools. In Japanese schools, Korean students are discriminated against by staff, by other students, and even by textbooks, which portray Korea in a negative way and distort its history. Japanese children are brought up to consider Korean culture a "lower" culture. More than half of the Koreans in Japan use Japanese names to avoid harassment by Japanese students. Japanese teachers often treat Korean students with contempt and feel very negatively toward them. Korean parents must pledge to the schools that their children will not disturb order, and if tuition is required, Koreans must pay more than Japanese. According to Lee (1991), Koreans are perceived as having a disadvantaged role in Japanese society and they have indeed assumed this role.

Korean Students in the United States

In the United States, however, teachers, students, and parents see Koreans in a completely different light. American teachers welcome Korean students and praise them for qualities that many teachers feel are lacking in Anglo-American students. Koreans have proven themselves to be highly successful academically. Educators attribute this to the high standards held by East Asian parents and to their strict discipline and close management of their children's time. They believe that once East Asians overcome the language barrier, they will get good jobs. American parents perceive East Asian children as setting good examples for their own children and welcome them as friends (Ogbu, 1992a).

As we saw above, Koreans living in the United States have higher college attendance rates and higher achievement scores than Anglo-American students. Korean parents value education and have high expectations for their children, often teaching them at home before they are of school age. In Japan, Koreans are a castelike minority with little power in their host society. In the United States, Koreans are one of the most successful immigrant minorities.

Although some claim (Erickson, 1987) that Ogbu (1986) sees "a social revolution" as the only way out of the situation involuntary minorities find themselves in, Ogbu (1992c) does not in fact reach that conclusion. What he does stress is that educational practices and programs must be based on appropriate research. He points out that many intervention programs are based on the idea that ethnic minorities are "culturally deprived," "culturally deficient," or "socially disadvantaged" and that the school's role is to "redeem" them. He differentiates between "improvement research" and "explanatory research." He is interested in providing explanatory research, in particular comparative ethnographic research, "the long range goal of which is to provide knowledge for better and more effective educational policy as well as for preventative and remedial efforts" (Ogbu, 1987a). He cautions against instigating educational change without first understanding both the "micro" and the "macro"—the individual and the societal—aspects of underachievement in ethnic minority populations.

Research That Explains

Educational Implications

A distinction can be made between ethnic studies (the study of ethnic groups) and a sociocultural approach to language, culture, and education (Mehan, 1987). This distinction does not diminish the significance of ethnic studies. From the point of view of schooling practices, however, approaching contexts of learning for culturally diverse youth with a focus on ethnic studies poses difficulties—and in fact can be dangerous. Because it is impossible for educators to acquire complete ethnological knowledge of the student groups they will encounter, the knowledge they do acquire tends to be laden with stereotypes. These stereotypes in turn often lead to the assumption of cultural deprivation: because a culture is different, it is deficient. Educators should focus on understanding the intersection of the school context with the student's family, home, and community contexts, not only on understanding the differences among ethnic cultures.

Ethnic Studies Alone Are Insufficient

Educational Implications of Family Diversity

Soto (1997) has offered advice that can help schools serve the families of culturally diverse students. In Soto's study, the families themselves articulated the need for schools to move away from paradigms of shame to paradigms of compassion—that is, the need for schools to overcome an oppressive climate that devalues the language and culture of the home. When culturally diverse families were asked, "What advice do you have for schools?" the following themes emerged:

Families' Advice for Schools

1. *Provide culturally diverse students with access to quality programs.* Families envisioned "quality programs" as those in which the following conditions prevail: children's linguistic and cultural gifts are valued; expectations are high; academic learning is the norm; humanistic and democratic approaches are implemented; culturally diverse children are well represented in gifted programs; leaders are created; teachers care about the children; the classrooms are clean and brimming with colorful materials; children learn about technology; creativity is appreciated; communication between school and family takes place; problem-solving is evident; all children experience a world of equity and justice.

2. *Implement programs that preserve home languages and cultures.* Parents valued highly those instances of schooling that acknowledged parental language and culture. Parents were

most appreciative when the teachers communicated with them in Spanish and regarded the use of Spanish in the class-room as a positive educational attribute.

3. *Integrate caring and humanistic approaches to learning.* Early, painful educational experiences of culturally diverse students who had done well in school led parents of these "success stories" to conclude that children find it difficult to overcome oppressive educational climates. Parents reported that their children had done well academically despite the system, not because of it.

4. *Accept the fact that institutions of learning are not the only knowledge brokers in society.* Schools must become respectful of the knowledge and wisdom families can impart.

5. *Model ways of encouraging linguistic and cultural integrity at school.* Celebrating culturally relevant holidays and customs was particularly appreciated. Similarly, the school's understanding of extended family responsibilities, such as grandparents' or siblings' role in caretaking, was valued by the families in the study.

6. *Initiate mentoring relationships for minority students.* The mentoring roles described by the families were often quite simple and mechanical in nature. Helping students with college applications was one suggestion. In addition, establishing "ways of relating" to children that reflect high expectations and value persistence was important for parents.

7. *Interact and communicate in ways that value the linguistic and cultural background of families.* If children see that the adults in their learning environment value the language and culture of their homes, it stands to reason that they will gain pride in their families. The human relations and communicative patterns children observe in the "worlds of childhood" can have a long-lasting impact on how they regard themselves, their family, and their nation.

8. *Provide ethical and knowledgeable advice.* The parents raised such issues as: Is it ethical for schools to encourage families to speak only English at home? Is it ethical for schools to devalue children's home language and culture? Are schools offering knowledgeable advice about the optimal education practices for diverse learners? The families interviewed perceived schools as being neither knowledgeable nor ethical on matters affecting the daily educational realities of their children.

In terms of this *consejo* (advice), Epstein (1995) has provided important contributions related to parental involvement. Put simply, these researchers suggest that the way schools care about their students is reflected in the ways they care about the students' families. Proactive efforts to involve parents always seem to be on the agenda of elementary schools, but the effort tends to waver in later years of schooling. In addition, parent involvement is unfortunately often more rhetoric then reality in schools that serve a highly diverse population. But as Edwards (1995) and Epstein (1995) point out, this need not be the case, and they have identified several important components related to developing a strong and functional partnership between home and school:

1. *Development of parenting:* Educational and related agencies can organize ways in which basic information on parenting and child and family development can be conveyed to families. Since all parents are learning while doing, support for that learning process can be useful for the parents, the children, the family, and the educational staff.

2. *Family-school communication:* Systematic and ongoing communication between the family and school is critical. This can be accomplished both formally and informally, utilizing school events, teacher-parent conferences, home visits, parent journals, and student portfolios. Communication from the school in the language of the family lays the groundwork for developing a trusting relationship, which in turn will allow parents to become more aware of and involved in their important role in the education of their children.

3. *Parental participation in school governance:* Most local, state, and federal education policies require some sort of parental involvement in the governance and/or decision-making activities of the school. Yet such participation is too often peripheral (Edwards, 1995), selective, and constrained. Although parental participation does not mean that parents should "control" the school, it ought to be more than window dressing.

4. *Families and cultural groups in the school:* Many schools actively recruit volunteers or instructional assistants from their students' families or from representatives of linguistic and/or cultural groups that reside in the community. Such efforts do much to enhance the partnership opportunities and involve families directly in the educational process. This is particularly useful for immigrant families and communities, who can begin to learn about the educational process first-hand through such participation in the schools.

5. *Home support for teaching and learning:* Too often, poor and non-English-speaking parents come to the conclusion that they cannot help their children with homework or related

academic assignments. They themselves have likely not had the same educational experiences as their children or have had a history of educational failure. Yet even if this is the case, they can be a critical motivational and structural support for their children's academic success. As indicated earlier in this volume, parents of successful students and parents of those who are less successful display little difference in their aspirations for their children's school achievement. Often the difference lies in the parents' instrumental knowledge, not their academic knowledge, as it relates to helping their children become academically successful. Instrumental knowledge refers to those understandings about what is expected, required, and acceptable at school. All parents, once armed with this type of knowledge, can play a key role in their children's school success, even if they cannot directly assist them with academic subject matter. More direct efforts at enhancing family participation in teaching and learning, such as family math and family literacy programs, have quite effectively involved parents in content-area instructional support for their children.

Epstein (1995) has elaborated on many of these areas of parental and family involvement. Table 4.6 provides an excellent summary of the types of involvement and related practices that she has identified in her national studies of school/ family/community partnerships; Table 4.7 offers challenges and redefinitions of these sorts of partnerships.

Building Bridges Between Diverse Cultures

In Chapter 2 we saw how school and the classroom arrangements within it can be seen as analogous to a culture. The classroom has many explicit cultural elements, but it also has hidden cultural dimensions that Phillips (1984) and others have described. Children themselves often feel deeply the numerous cultural demands of the school.

Some of the classic work on this issue has been done by Labov (1972b), who studied the same group of children across different social domains of the school culture. Specifically, he observed educational testing encounters arranged in a number of ways. The theme of school culture is clear in his work: depending on the context in which one observes a child, one obtains a different view of that child. For example, in one intelligence testing situation (using a test such as the Weschler), the tester (who is white) places an object (e.g., a toy airplane) in front of the child (in this case a third- or fourth-grade African American student).

Effect of School Culture

Table 4.6 School/Family/Community Partnerships: Types and Sample Practices

TYPE 1 PARENTING	TYPE 2 COMMUNICATING	TYPE 3 VOLUNTEERING	TYPE 4 LEARNING AT HOME	TYPE 5 DECISION-MAKING	TYPE 6 COLLABORATING WITH COMMUNITY
Help all families establish home environments to support children as students.	Design effective forms of school-to-home and home-to-school communications about school programs and children's progress.	Recruit and organize parent help and support.	Provide information and ideas to families about how to help students at home with homework and other curricumum-related activities, decisions, and planning.	Include parents in school decisions, developing parent leaders and representatives.	Identify and integrate resources and services from the community to strengthen school programs, family practices, and student learning and development.
Sample Practices	Sample Practices	Sample Practices	Sample Practices	Sample Practices	Sample Practices
Suggestions for home conditions that support learning at each grade level.	Conferences with every parent at least once a year, with follow-ups as needed.	School and classroom volunteer program to help teachers, administrators, students, and other parents.	Information for families on skills required for students in all subjects at each grade.	Active PTA/PTO or other parent organizations, advisory councils, or committees (e.g., curriculum, safety, personnel) for parent leadership and participation.	Information for students and families on community health, cultural, recreational, and social support, and other programs or services.
Workshops, videotapes, and computerized phone messages on parenting and child-rearing at each age and grade level.	Language translators to assist families as needed. Weekly or monthly folders of student work sent home for review and comments.	Parent room or family center for volunteer work, meetings, and resources for families.	Information on homework policies and how to monitor and discuss schoolwork at home.	Independent advocacy groups to lobby and work for school reform and improvements.	Information on community activities that link to learning skills and talents, including summer programs for students.

Parent education and other courses or training for parents (e.g., GED, college credit, family literacy).	Parent/student pickup of report card, with conferences on improving grades.	Annual postcard survey to identify all available talents, times, and locations of volunteers.	Information on how to assist students to improve skills on various class and school assessments.	District-level councils and committees for family and community involvement.	Service integration through partnerships involving school; civic, counseling, cultural, health, recreation, and other agencies and organizations; and businesses.
Family support programs to assist families with health, nutrition, and other services.	Regular schedule of useful notices, memos, phone calls, newsletters, and other communications.	Class parent, telephone tree, or other structures to provide all families with needed information.	Regular schedule of homework that requires students to discuss and interact with families on what they are learning in class.	Information on school or local elections for school representatives.	Service to the community by students, families, and schools (e.g., recycling, art, music, drama, and other activities for seniors or others).
Home visits at transition points to preschool, elementary, middle, and high school. Neighborhood meetings to help families understand schools and to help schools understand families.	Clear information on choosing schools or courses, programs, and activities within schools. Clear information on all school policies, programs, reforms, and transitions.	Parent patrols or other activities to aid safety and operation of school programs	Calendars with activities for parents and students at home.	Networks to link all families with parent representatives.	Participation of alumni in school programs for students.
			Family math, science, and reading activities at school.		
			Summer learning packets or activities.		
			Family participation in setting student goals each year and in planning for college or work.		

Source: Joyce Epstein, May 1995, "Epstein's Framework of Six Types of Involvement and Sample Practices" from *Phi Delta Kappan*, p. 704. Reprinted by permission of Joyce Epstein.

Table 4.7 Challenges and Redefinitions of the Types of School/Family/Community Partnerships

TYPE 1 PARENTING	TYPE 2 COMMUNICATING	TYPE 3 VOLUNTEERING	TYPE 4 LEARNING AT HOME	TYPE 5 DECISION-MAKING	TYPE 6 COLLABORATING WITH COMMUNITY
Challenges	Challenges	Challenges	Challenges	Challenges	Challenges
Provide information to *all* families who want it or who need it, not just to the few who can attend workshops or meetings at the school building.	Review the readability, clarity, form, and frequency of all memos, notices, and other print and nonprint communications.	Recruit volunteers widely so that *all* families know that their time and talents are welcome.	Design and orgnaize a regular schedule of interactive homework (e.g., weekly or bimonthly) that gives *students* responsibility for discussing important things they are learning and helps families stay aware of the content of their children's classwork.	Include parent leaders from all racial, ethnic, socioeconomic, and other groups in the school.	Solve turf problems of responsibilities, funds, staff, and locations for collaborative activities.
Enable families to share information with schools about culture, background, and children's talents and needs.	Consider parents who do not speak English well, do not read well, or need large type.	Make flexible schedules for volunteers, assemblies, and events to enable parents who work to participate.		Offer training to enable leaders to serve as representatives of other families, with input from and return of information to all parents.	Inform families of community programs for students, such as mentoring, tutoring, and business partnerships.
Make sure that all information for and from families is clear, usable, and linked to children's success in school.	Review the quality of major communications (newsletters, report cards, conference schedules, and so on).	Organize volunteer work; provide training; match time and talent with school, teacher, and student needs; and recognize efforts so that participants are productive.	Coordinate family-linked homework activities, if students have several teachers.	Include students (along with parents) in decision-making groups.	Assure equity of opportunities for students and families to participate in community programs or to obtain services.
	Establish clear two-way channels for communications from home to school and from school to home.		Involve families and their children in all important curriculum-related decisions.		Match community contributions with school goals; integrate child and family services with education.

156

Redefinitions	Redefinitions	Redefinitions	Redefinitions	Redefinitions	Redefinitions
"Workshop" to mean more than a *meeting* about a topic held at the school building at a particular time. "Workshop" may also mean making information about a topic available in a variety of forms that can be viewed, heard, or read anywhere, any time, in varied forms.	"Communciations about school programs and student progress" to mean two-way, three-way, and many-way channels of communication that connect schools, families, students, and the community.	"Volunteer" to mean anyone who supports school goals and children's learning or development in any way, at any place, and at any time—not just during the school day and at the school building	"Homework" to mean not only work done alone, but also interactive activities shared with others at home or in the community, linking schoolwork to real life. "Help" at home to mean encouraging, listening, reacting, praising, guiding, monitoring, and discussing—not "teaching" school subjects.	"Decision-making" to mean a process of partnership, of shared views and actions toward shared goals, not just a power struggle between conflicting ideas. Parent "leader" to mean a real representative, with opportunities and support to hear from and communicate with other families.	"Community" to mean not only the neighborhoods where students' homes and schools are located but also any neighborhoods that influence their learning and development. "Community" rated not only by low or high social or economic qualities, but by strengths and talents to support students, families, and schools. "Community" means all who are interested in and affected by the quality of education, not just those with children in the schools.

Source: Joyce Epstein, May 1995, "Challenges and Redefinitions for the Six Types of Involvement" from *Phi Delta Kappan*, p. 705. Reprinted by permission of Joyce Epstein.

The tester says, "Tell me everything you can about this." There is a twelve-second silence, which can be a very long time during an IQ test or in a classroom environment. So the tester then changes the question: "What would you say it looks like?" The child says nothing for eight seconds. When one reviews the transcript and the testing results from such an event, one is likely to conclude that the child lacks critical cognitive and linguistic abilities.

But Labov did not stop there. He looked at the same child in a number of domains. He thought that this outcome might have something to do with the relationship between the African American child and the white tester, so he brought in an African American tester from the neighborhood to remove the racial boundary. When he repeated the test, but still with the tester on one side of the table and the child on the other side, the results were not much different. Then Labov did something that is now famous: he removed the trappings of power from the situation. He took the child away from table, removed the adult, and observed the child interacting with other children on the floor. The child's verbal production increased incredibly. Much like Phillips (1982), who found communicative differences between American Indian students and their school, Labov found significant communicative differences between the various domains of the school itself. In short, if you look at a child in only one situation, you get only one kind of picture.

Moll and Diaz (1986) contributed to this understanding of context specificity. They observed children, not at home and at school, but under different constraints of instruction. The children were enrolled in a bilingual program designed to allow Spanish-speaking children to acquire English as quickly as possible. In this program, the children had two teachers, one for English and another for Spanish. Moll and Diaz videotaped lessons in both settings and asked each teacher to watch the videotapes of the other. The Spanish-speaking teacher was appalled when she saw the children in the English-speaking teacher's classroom: they were not reading but were engaged in drill-and-practice exercises in which very little cognitive activity was taking place. By contrast, in the Spanish-speaking classroom, where the children were being given comprehension activities, they were reading in Spanish. Moll and Diaz discussed this situation with the Spanish-speaking teacher and hypothesized that reading is specific to the domain of language. So they performed some experiments. They had the children apply the reading comprehension skills they had acquired in Spanish to read in English. In doing this, by the way, they violated one of the basic

Effect of Instructional Constraints

tenets of bilingual education: keep the two languages separate. But when they let the children call upon all the intellectual resources they had available, their progress was remarkable. The students began to comprehend written English very nicely, even though they did not have complete mastery of the language. A bridge between the two cultures was thereby developed in support of the goals of the school.

Gallimore et al.'s (1986) study of the Kamehameha Early Education Program, or KEEP, is another example of how bridges can be built. One recommendation is to allow cultural elements that are relevant to the children to enter the classroom. This is the practice of scaffolding, which was introduced in Chapter 2. Scaffolding enables children to use relevant experiences from the home to move toward the demands of the school. For example, in the KEEP project, teachers incorporated cultural elements into the classroom at the beginning of reading lessons, which were divided into three parts. The first part centered on the children's experiences. Before reading a book, the children talked about their home experiences and things they knew about in the world. Then the teacher made transitions from those experiences to the book and directed the children to read the text. For example, the teacher would say something like, "We are going to read this article. As you read, can you think of three things that the writer says are important about culture?" The students then read the text silently, not aloud, in order to avoid pronunciation difficulties. Now the children have been oriented toward the text. In the end, the children's home experiences are linked with the text reading.

Close discourse analyses of lessons that utilize scaffolding reveal that the questioning structures change during the instruction. In the early part of the lessons, questioning structures are open-ended. Joint responses and joint progressions of narrative are allowed. By the end, however, the lessons very closely follow the traditional format. The children have been slowly guided through the instruction in a very microgenetic way, so they can decide what is important. The teaching is done so that the children's culture, interest, and experiences are preserved.

Scaffolding (margin)

Tracking and Ability Grouping

Ability grouping is managed by elementary school teachers within classrooms, and tracking distributes students among classrooms, usually in secondary schools. Both of these practices bring together groups of children with similar perceived academic abilities—for example, slow readers versus fast readers,

Patterns in Student Distribution (margin)

BECOMING A RESPONSIVE TEACHER

A Community of Learners

Every day, during a one-and-a-half-hour science segment in a self-contained sixth-grade class, and in two seventh-grade and one eighth-grade science classrooms, students engage in collaborative research in which they participate in designing their own curriculum. The class is organized into small research groups. Each group is responsible for investigating and writing about one subtopic from a larger content area. For example, different groups chose to study condors, whales, otters, and wolves during a sixth-grade unit on endangered species.

The students conduct their research with the aid of an extended community that includes all members of their own classroom, students and teachers in other project classrooms, research staff and scientists at the University of California at Berkeley, and various experts, such as forest rangers, furriers, and zoo personnel, whose work is related to the students' research. The project provides a core set of resources on environmental science (including books, articles, newspaper and magazine clippings, videotapes, and videodiscs), which the students and teachers supplement with other materials.

As the students gather information, adults guide them in note-taking, outlining, and writing, as well as in learning how to read technical material. Adults also intervene when students appear to need help working together on group tasks.

To aid students in their research, the project provides a computer environment based almost entirely on commercially available software. Each classroom contains six or seven Macintosh computers and a laser printer. Students are provided word-processing, spreadsheet, database, and graphics applications; access to a scanner; Internet access; and a computer-based index to the core set of resources (known as a "browser") to help students locate research materials.

An electronic mail package allows students to send messages and requests for help or information to their peers, their teachers, students and teachers in other classrooms, and even to project staff at the university. When appropriate, these questions are forwarded to university scientists who have agreed to be available for occasional consultation.

BECOMING A RESPONSIVE TEACHER *Cont.*

Once the students have recorded the results of their research, they re-assemble into "jigsaw learning groups" composed of one "expert" from each research group. Students then take turns leading discussions on their areas of expertise, using the materials prepared by their respective research groups.

This collaborative research approach differs from more traditional approaches to teaching in several ways. The approach intentionally favors depth over breadth and the process of learning over the learning of content only. Given the rate at which knowledge is changing, particularly in the sciences, we believe that a student who merely acquires current knowledge will be inadequately prepared for future demands in school, at work, and as a responsible citizen.

▼ Meeting the Challenge

1. Working with a few of your classmates, draw a diagram of this community of learners from the point of view of one of the students. Draw connecting lines to all the major groups of people the student can call on during the research process. Draw dashed lines to the research materials and technology available, showing the pathways by which the student would gain access to them. Compare your group's diagram with diagrams drawn by other groups.
2. With your whole class, discuss the extent of organizing, planning, and networking that was required by the educators who established the learning community described above. What barriers to education are being crossed here? How have some of these interconnections between groups been set up?
3. Develop a list of broad content areas that would be amenable to the process of learning in such a community. For each area, brainstorm with your whole class all the resource groups that could contribute to the learning network.
4. As a teacher of the students described above, how comfortable would you be with the hardware and software used daily in your classroom? List the items you would need to learn more about. See if one of your classmates can shed light on your questions.

and high achievers versus low achievers. Many studies (Mirón, 1996; Oakes, 1984a; Rueda & Mehan, 1987) indicate that there is a pattern in the distribution of children between different tracks: children from low-income and minority backgrounds invariably end up in lower tracks, and children from middle- and upper-income backgrounds are in upper tracks. Educational practices are also differentially distributed between these tracks. Students in higher tracks receive challenging educational opportunities; students in lower tracks receive much more practice and drill.

If children were also given equal opportunity to change tracks, this finding would not be quite so troublesome. But children get locked in: if a child is placed in a low-ability group in first grade, he or she will most likely remain there throughout elementary school. If a student is in a vocational track in seventh grade, that student is unlikely to change to a college-preparatory track. Instead of supporting the democratic ideal of a classless society, the school tends to reproduce the divisions within society.

The question is, why do the practices of tracking and ability grouping continue? Most of these activities are organized as practical solutions to very difficult problems: too many children in class, not enough resources, and the existence of distinct levels of student ability. But recent research supports heterogeneity, as opposed to homogeneity, as the basis for grouping students. There is extensive evidence that mixed groupings have a particularly beneficial result for those who need it the most: students from low-income backgrounds who have trouble with

Benefits of Mixing Ability Levels

school. In Kagan's (1986) review of the literature, study after study shows that children who do not perform well academically succeed best in heterogeneous groups. That idea resonates very well with parents of culturally diverse students but not with middle- and upper-income parents (Oakes, 1989), who think their children will suffer academically under those arrangements. However, recent research demonstrates that middle- and upper-income children from majority populations are also more likely to succeed in heterogeneous groupings than in homogeneous groupings (Slavin, 1989). That wonderful adage—that the best way to learn something is to teach it—truly does work in practice. When children are involved in the teaching process, they learn as well.

The extent to which tracking and ability grouping have become institutionalized practices is demonstrated by a poignant account related by Trujillo (1989), who was a high school principal. He tells of two counselors, advising two almost identical youngsters in preparation for tenth grade. Both students were Filipino, both had parents with limited English-language skills, and both had nearly identical records and test scores. As Trujillo watched, the first counselor talked the first student and his parents out of the academic program they had originally chosen. He took the youngster out of algebra and talked him into another year of remedial math. In the other conversation, however, the second counselor began describing the courses that the second youngster would need when he enrolled in college. The student was trying to avoid taking the harder classes, but the counselor promised that she would meet with him once a week to check on his progress. The father protested, saying, "We are very poor people. College is not one of the goals we have for our child. We could not afford that, and we don't want to deceive him." The counselor replied, "Don't worry about that, we'll get him a scholarship."

Beliefs That Limit Students

Both counselors were probably trained in the same program with the same methodology. The techniques and rationale the first counselor used to talk the student out of taking a college-prep curriculum were classic; they would make a beautiful chapter in the counseling textbook. In technique, there was nothing the counselor did wrong, and he could use the test scores to prove that the youngster belonged in the remedial classes. However, whereas the first counselor was still very much part of the belief system he had been taught, the second counselor had moved beyond this system; in short, there seemed to be two belief systems operating. Trujillo (1989) concludes that although the majority of U.S. educators know their subject matter and are fairly well steeped in the appropriate methodologies, they do not understand the students they are teaching: "In other words, the people who do well with children are those who understand them—who don't demean them" (Trujillo, 1989).

Conclusion

Educators must realize that children, all children, come to school motivated to enlarge their worlds. Educators start with the many cultures of students. Educators should not look at them, certainly not initially, as organisms to be molded and regulated. Instead they should observe their students to determine what they know, what they seek to know, and which of their experiences can be used to fuel the process of enlarging their interest, knowledge, and skills. Educators must not look at their students in terms of their deficits—what they do not know but need to know— for in fact they are rich in assets.

SUMMARY OF MAJOR IDEAS

1. Students must learn to negotiate the boundaries between the multiple cultures of family, school, and peers. Depending on the nature of the boundary, culturally diverse students may face great psychological and social consequences when making the transition from one culture to another. Sometimes the psychosocial costs are so great that a boundary becomes a barrier students are not able to cross. A complete understanding of underachievement among minority populations requires a full consideration of the interactions among culture, socialization, and education.

2. Socialization is the process through which prescriptions and prohibitions are transmitted to members of a social group. The family is a major agent of socialization, along with teachers, peers, and the media, especially television. Research shows much diversity in socialization practices across cultures. A child's socialization sets the stage for lifelong patterns of social relations, including those important in schooling.

3. Ecology is the study of the relationships between an organism and its environment. The socialization of children is determined not only by the ecology of the family and the community but also by the broader social ecology, which includes such factors as the urbanization level of the community, the socioeconomic status of the family and community, and societal views about cultural groups. The ecology of the minority family is characterized by its immersion in a hostile educational and community setting. However, many linguistically and culturally diverse families have devised ways of nurturing an appreciation of education and of individual achievement.

4. Ethnic images are people's general beliefs about cultural groups. Research indicates that ethnic images are tenacious in the United States and that people are willing and able to rate others on the basis of their ethnicity. Ethnic images are significant predictors of support for racial integration and desired social distance and for public opinion on affirmative action, school desegregation, and other group-related issues.

5. Personality is a structure that reconciles children's interpreted experiences and emotional states. The social attributes ascribed to the child by others may greatly influence this process of reconciliation and result in a particular sense of ethnic identity. Research shows that children are aware of attitudes toward ethnic differences by the age of 4.

6. The cultural systems approach to education considers the organization of a society, specifically the roles and status assigned to cultural groups, to be a major determinant of educational underachievement. This approach suggests that people's values, perceptions, and social behavior are directly influenced by the social status of the cultural group to which they belong.

7. A voluntary minority group is a population whose members moved voluntarily to the host society. An involuntary minority group is a population whose members were involuntarily incorporated through various means that degrade their status.

8. Members of voluntary and involuntary minority groups may live in the same society and experience similar effects from discrimination and prejudice. Their responses may widely differ, however, depending on five aspects of the cultural model under which they operate: (a) a frame of reference for comparing present status and future possibilities; (b) a folk theory of how to succeed, especially through education; (c) a sense of collective identity; (d) a cultural frame of reference for judging appropriate behavior and affirming group membership and solidarity; and (e) an assessment of the extent to which one may trust members of the dominant group and the institutions they control. Children absorb these cultural models and bring them to bear in their schooling experiences.

9. A focus on ethnic studies alone is not sufficient for addressing the educational needs of culturally diverse students because it is too often based on stereotypes. Educators must instead adopt a broader sociocultural approach to language, culture, and education. They must understand the child, the family and community, the school, and the larger society as constituting an ecological system with interacting elements.

10. Ethnically diverse families have offered valuable suggestions for improving school/family/community partnerships. Among the elements that build such partnerships are the development of parenting, family-school communication, parental participation in school governance, family representation in the schools, and home support for teaching and learning.

11. The cultural arrangements of the school can affect student performance. Instructional strategies such as scaffolding that provide a bridge between home and school can allow culturally diverse children to make a successful transition to school. Tracking and ability grouping, on the other hand, perpetuate cultural barriers and make it more difficult for such students to succeed academically.

EXTENDING YOUR EXPERIENCE

1. Study the diagram in Figure 4.1. How might a culturally diverse child's self-concept change as he or she crosses the border between one culture and another? What, specifically, are the psychological costs of crossing a "nonneutral" border? Describe any such experience you may have had. What or whom did you confront while trying to negotiate this border? What, if anything, helped you build a bridge and make the transition?

2. With a small group of your classmates, review the concept of social ecology discussed in this chapter. Why will it be important for you as an educator to understand the environmental context—family, community, and peers—for each student in your classroom? With your group, develop a list of all the possible environmental factors that might affect a student's ability to achieve academically. Think of a male or female student at a particular grade level, and be as specific as you can.

3. Examine various media, such as newspapers, magazines, films, and television shows, for portrayals of ethnic images. Bring some of this evidence to class and compare it with material gathered by your classmates. With these data in mind, discuss the implications of research quoted in the chapter indicating that a child's awareness of and attitude toward his or her own ethnicity is formed by age 4.

4. Observe an ESL classroom. Note the teacher's positive strategies for building bridges across language and cultural boundaries and for providing scaffolding. Describe in writing the students' reactions to these strategies.

5. In your own words, explain the difference between a voluntary and an involuntary minority status. Read closely the descriptions given in Tables 4.1 through 4.5 and select a contrast between voluntary and involuntary minority status that you find particularly striking. How might this contrast in cultural experience influence a child's academic success?

RESOURCES FOR FURTHER STUDY

Anyon, J. (1997). *Ghetto schooling: A political economy of urban educational reform.* New York: Teachers College Press.

Anyon clearly establishes that the economic decline of the inner cities places schools and students in these areas at particular risk. In essence, the broader changes in the economic, social, and political fabric of the inner city create specific and significant challenges for schools. The culture of anger and hopelessness that develops as a result of this situation has to be addressed if urban schools are to succeed or even survive. Although she is optimistic about the future, Anyon paints a picture of inner-city schools that is not bright.

Mead, M. (1937). *Cooperation and competition among primitive people.* New York: McGraw.

This landmark collection of essays written by various authors and interpreted by Mead opened a new window on how research into different cultures should be analyzed and presented, and offers a framework useful for the collection, analysis, and theorization of cultures. Each article is strong and can stand on its own merits. The connecting thread of the book is Mead's point of view. She argues that to truly understand individual behavior, one must first recognize and understand the patterns by which members of a group pass on knowledge and culture to the individual. The subjects in the book are from distinct parts of the world yet share similarities.

Mirón, L. F. (1996). *The social construction of urban schooling: Situating the crisis.* Cresskill, NJ: Hampton Press.

This volume's focus on the urban "culture," its challenges and its influence on schools and students, addresses the complexities of living faced by many culturally diverse students. It addresses broader social issues and organizations with a concern for the educator. Education, the author argues, is but one of several nonfamilial influences on students. He reminds us of our quest for democracy and the particular role for education in this country's urban sector.

Ogbu, J. (1987b). Variability in minority school performance: A problem in search of an explanation. *Anthropology and Education Quarterly, 18*(4), 312–334.

Based on a comparative analysis, this article suggests that the school adjustment and academic performance of minority students are directly influenced by cultural differences they encounter outside the school. Minority students, it is argued, perceive economic and social opportunities for the future to be dismal. This view interferes with their schoolwork and consequently affects their academic performance. Ogbu provides a historical account based on educational anthropology. Such background strengthens the author's case that minority students perceive society differently than mainstream students and that such views affect their schooling.

Ogbu, J., & Matute-Bianchi, M. E. (1986). Understanding sociocultural factors: Knowledge, identity, and school adjustment. In Bilingual Education Office, California State Department of Education (Ed.), *Beyond language: Social and cultural factors in schooling language minority students.* Los Angeles: Evaluation, Dissemination, and Assessment Center, California State University (pp. 145–160).

The central theme of this work examines why minority students continually experience a disproportionate amount of school failure. Why do some minority groups do better than others? What historical and social forces affect the view of education held by some minority groups? Why do such failures persist? The authors present two cases to illustrate minority students' perceptions of the U.S. educational system and their consequent response to their educational opportunities and job outlook.

Soto, L. D. (1997). *Language, culture, and power: Bilingual families and the struggle for quality education.* Albany: State University of New York Press.

This volume provides a comprehensive case study of Puerto Rican family interaction with the schools. Developed from a set of interviews, the analysis of the struggles these non-English-speaking parents confront in promoting their children's educational needs is instructive to all educators. Of specific relevance is the discussion of parental perceptions of and expectations for their children and the schools that serve them. The parents' critical stance toward the educational system offers important although challenging insights for teachers.

Weis, L. (1988). *Class, race, and gender in American education.* Albany: State University of New York Press.

School experiences set the tone for how future citizens function in society. The expectations students have about school are influenced by their gender, race, and class. This book discusses, using in-depth ethnographic and statistical data, some of the most heated issues that are at the core of the educational system. It describes the traditional debate between the "culturalists" and the "structuralists," and elaborates on both to enrich and promote discussion between the two camps. The presentation of such different frameworks produces a book full of the tension created by a broad range of perspectives and goals.

LANGUAGE

AND

COMMUNICATION

CHAPTER 5

Focus Questions

▼ What variables must interact for communication to occur?

▼ What is metalinguistic awareness?

▼ How do children develop skills in phonology, vocabulary, grammar, and language pragmatics?

▼ What are bilingualism and second-language acquisition? What is code switching?

▼ How is language used as a social instrument, and what are two important sociocultural variables that may affect a child's motivation to learn a second language?

▼ What is a dialect, and how is classroom use of dialect problematical for students in U.S. schools?

▼ What are the issues surrounding the use of Black English?

"As the test of what the potter molds is in the furnace; so in his conversation is the test of a man. The fruit of a tree shows the care it has had; so too does a man's speech disclose the bent of his mind." —THE WISDOM OF BEN SIRA 27:4–7

Place yourself again in Mrs. Tanner's fifth-grade classroom. As we learned in Chapter 1, in the last few years she has begun to teach students who speak a variety of languages in their homes and communities: Spanish, Vietnamese, Russian, Hmong, Chinese, and Farsi. The challenge of effectively communicating—of making meaning—is quite robust in this classroom. Mrs. Tanner has realized that she must understand the cultural context of these students if she is to provide an effective environment for their communication. In essence, she must determine the way to communicate that will most help her reach the teaching and learning goals so integral to her classroom.

Teaching and learning do not begin when students walk into a classroom. On the contrary, these processes are omnipresent in children's worlds. This point is so important it cannot be overemphasized. If Mrs. Tanner and other teachers in the U.S. schools do not build on a child's foundation of previous and nonschool learning, then the role of the teacher and the school is merely corrective. At worst the schools would be trying to subtract the learning experiences a child gains outside of school. As the previous chapters have shown, adding to a child's learning experiences is an objective that is much more conducive to the educational success of culturally diverse students. This chapter will establish a firm basis for the worthiness of this objective by focusing on the communicative aspects of human development as they relate to teaching and learning.

The Nature of Communication

Throughout the ages, politicians, theologians, philosophers, poets, playwrights, comedians, teachers, and social scientists have all relied in their own distinctive ways on the power of the spoken word to convey meaning. Recent interest in **communication** has broadened to a consideration of both verbal and nonverbal systems that enable humans to encode meaning and transmit it to others with some assurance of accurate reception.

Interaction of Variables

Scholars who study **language** characterize it as a complex interaction of many variables, including the verbal signal itself, the one who sends the signal, how and in what environment the signal is sent, the one who receives the signal, and previous experiences the sender and receiver may have had with similar signals.

Let's look at an example of communication in progress. To a naive observer, the interaction between a parent and a young child may seem simple and relatively devoid of meaning. Lots of silly sounds, exaggerated facial expression—what kind of "meaning" could they possibly convey? Upon closer examination, however, this scenario of communication proves to be quite rich and meaningful. An infant's cooing, crying, giggling, and other sounds prepare the parent to receive a signal and interpret its meaning. Anyone who has been around babies understands the difference between "an anger cry" and "a pain cry." Parents learn to decipher what an infant is feeling by paying attention to subtle changes in the sound of the cry. This is communication. The infant can be said to influence the reaction of the parents by sending these signals.

Later, as the growing child learns specifically articulated sounds and combinations of sounds, it seems as if a systematic, rule-governed set of communicative symbols is emerging almost magically. What was once for the infant a simple and idiosyncratic vocabulary, with limited grammatical arrangement, becomes in a matter of a few years an unbelievably large vocabulary with varied syntactical constructions. This is even the case for children who were born with speech or hearing impairments. These children develop alternative, but just as systematic, forms of nonverbal communication.

Making Meaning in School

A naive observer in Mrs. Tanner's classroom may likely note a series of seemingly disconnected communicative acts. In reality, these chunks of communication are so central that they may almost be overlooked. In the course of a day, Mrs. Tanner asks many questions, reads stories, explains science experiments, gives assignments, provides oral and written feedback, and engages in dozens of one-on-one interactions with students. Each time, a complex set of verbal, written, and/or nonverbal transactions is called upon to enhance meaning making—or, in other words, to institute teaching and learning. It is the role of teachers to communicate with students and the role of students to communicate with teachers. Most classroom activity in the U.S. schools is founded on this one principle. At the very root of our teaching and learning activity is the understanding that communication must be a prerequisite.

The Development of Language

Becoming
Aware of
Language

Learning to communicate may be a child's most impressive accomplishment. Language is a complex set of systems—phonology, vocabulary, grammar, and pragmatics and discourse rules—and each of these systems has its own rules. We shall examine these domains of communication more closely below. Each one is acquired relatively unconsciously by children in the course of use. Each also at some point emerges into consciousness and becomes a topic of conversation for children or a focus for play and problem-solving. Bringing the various domains of communication into conscious awareness is one of the important achievements of schooling. Becoming aware of distinct communicative systems is a necessary development if people are to understand important aspects of their own culture and the culture of others. Being consciously aware of how we use communication, a process called **metalinguistic awareness,** is the foundation of distinguishing diversity within the communicative activities going on around us all the time.

Phonology

Knowing a formal communicative system—a language—involves speaking and understanding words. Those words are made up of specific sounds, called syllables, which are the basic units for language production.

Phonology is the study of speech sounds. Much research has been devoted to the development of speech in humans. When infants exposed to English language environments are five to eight months old, they start producing spoken syllables ("ba," "ma," "ga") in the course of their babbling. Open syllables such as "ba" and "ma" are relatively easy to pronounce and thus form the basis for many "baby talk" words (e.g., "mama," "booboo," "peepee"). Words that contain closed syllables (those with a consonant at the end) are harder to pronounce, especially if quite different consonants need to be articulated within one syllable. Thus, young English-speaking children often say "goggie" for "doggie" or "guck" for "truck," because they are not yet able to put such different sounds as /g/ and /d/ or /t/ into one syllable.

Stages of
Development

Earlier we saw that the United States is home to over one hundred distinct language groups besides English, as well as a variety of dialects. Children exposed to these various languages proceed through similar stages of complex phonological development. Their learning process differs from that of English learners only in the phonological distinctiveness of the language they are learning. For example, Spanish-language learners progress through a distinct process of developmental acquisition marked by early acquisition of vowel sounds (Gonzalez, 1991). In contrast, English learners focus early on consonant sounds.

Children's pronunciation of words comes increasingly to resemble adult pronunciation around the ages of 3 to 5 years old. However, very young children still do not think of the sounds they are producing in the same ways that adults do. Young children find it difficult to produce rhymes or to segment particular sounds—for example, to say "meat" without the /m/ sound or without the /t/ sound. The reason for this is that when we speak, the articulation of each sound overlaps the articulation of those before and after it. Recognizing an abstract segment of sound such as *m* or *t* requires considerable sophistication in language ability and knowledge about how the phonological system of a language works. Such metalinguistic awareness develops as children grow older.

Rhyming Activities

Three-year-olds can be taught to identify the initial syllables in words fairly consistently. The ability to segment final syllables or to understand the internal structure of words with consonant clusters comes much later. Four-year-olds can judge with very high accuracy whether words rhyme, and many can also produce rhymes. Many educational activities for young children depend extensively on this rhyming ability. Both children and adults enjoy this metalinguistic activity of rhyming. Preschool children can also distinguish accents and may even incorporate the mimicking of dialect into their play.

Vocabulary

After a rather slow start, a child's knowledge of vocabulary grows very rapidly during the preschool period. **Vocabulary** is the sum of words understood and used by an individual in any language group. Children typically acquire their first word at about one year of age. Acquisition of the first 50 words may take several months. Thereafter the process of word acquisition proceeds so blindingly fast that it is impossible to keep accurate records. It has been estimated that children acquire six to ten new words a day between the ages of 2 and 6. Such rapid vocabulary acquisition relies on the child's use of very powerful strategies for guessing what words mean, on his or her considerable willingness to take chances in using new words, and on lots of help from adults and other children in providing information about words and their meanings.

Speed of Word Acquisition

It is important to recognize that the words a child acquires fall into various categories. Words learned early tend to be names for important people ("mama," "papa," "nana") or concrete objects ("socks," "spoon," "bed," "teddy," "cookie," "bottle"); expressions for important social functions ("hi," "bye-bye"); forms of requests ("wanna," "mommy," "mine"); and ways of directing attention ("there," "that," "what that?"). A bit later children begin to acquire verbs that refer to concrete actions: "eat,"

Categories of Words

"sleep," "read," "sing." As they progress through the preschool and elementary school period, though, children increasingly come to use verbs that refer to complex and private cognitive or communicative activities ("think," "wonder," "dream," "tell," "disagree," "deny"); nouns that refer to abstract, superordinate, or affective entities ("thought," "argument," "animal," "furniture," "sadness," "glee"); and other words that have roles in structuring discourse ("because," "but," "however") or representing one's perspective on matters ("hopefully," "doubtfully," "despairingly"). For avid readers in languages with a written tradition (English, Chinese, Japanese, and Spanish, for example), the process of word acquisition continues well into adulthood. In highly oral cultures (Navaho, Zuñi, and Hmong, for example), this same process of vocabulary acquisition continues as adolescents and adults encounter complex historical, religious, and personal accounts.

It is crucial in talking about vocabulary to acknowledge that children not only acquire new words as they get older but also expand their understanding of words they know. Thus, a Spanish-speaking child might first learn and understand a word like *padrinos* (godparents) in a relatively restricted context, such as the reliable giver of gifts at each birthday. It could take a child several years to learn exactly how *niño* relates to *padrino* (godfather) and *madrina* (godmother), and precisely what sorts of characteristics can be attributed to each term outside of gift-giving. In many cultures these individuals play critical roles for children over a lifetime. This is one reason why standard multiple-choice assessments of vocabulary knowledge cannot assess very accurately the full depth of children's vocabulary knowledge.

At some point during the school years children come to think, wonder, and talk about words themselves and their meanings.

Words as Symbols

As development of metalinguistic awareness continues to expand, children become able to distinguish between a big word ("building") and a word referring to a big thing ("building"). They come to understand that words are arbitrary symbols whose forms have no intrinsic connection to their meanings. Regardless of the language or languages to which they are exposed, all children achieve this truly significant understanding of the symbolic nature of language.

Grammar

Grammar is the system of rules implicit in a language that allows words to be arranged with some regularity of structure.

Rules for Interpreting

Grammar does not necessarily refer to prescriptive grammar ("Don't say 'he don't' or 'I ain't'"). More broadly, it refers to the system of rules by virtue of which we know whether words are nouns or verbs ("the hit" versus "he hit"). Grammar allows English speakers to decide which word specifies the subject, object, and indirect object of a sentence ("John gave Mary an apple") and French and Spanish speakers to distinguish the gender of a noun.

As soon as children put two words together, they begin to demonstrate what they are learning about the rules of grammar in their native language. Children learning English, for instance, show awareness of word order, or **syntax,** as an important feature of the grammatical system. In English, the sentence pattern subject-verb-object is so common that developing the ability to comprehend and use constructions that deviate from this pattern (passives, such as "The lion was bitten by the flea"; coordinations, such as "I want this and you want that"; and relative clauses, such as "The dog bit the cat that chased the rat") is a lengthy process for children that lasts well into the preschool years. In Spanish, gender and number (e.g., *la muchacha* [the girl] and *los muchachos* [the boys]) are distinct grammatical features. In Chinese, phonological emphasis—the spoken stress on words—marks the grammar in the language.

From normal communicative interactions with adults, children typically acquire the rules of grammar in their native language with little difficulty. Children also normally develop a metalinguistic capacity, displayed when they comment spontaneously on grammatical correctness or respond easily to questions about sentences being "right" or "wrong." Nonetheless, it is hard even for school-age children to attend more seriously to grammatical correctness than to meaning. They are likely to accept as "okay" a sentence such as "The boys is jumping in the lake" and to reject a perfectly grammatical but anomalous sentence such as "Ice cream tastes yucky."

Pragmatics and Discourse Rules

Knowing words, how to pronounce them, what they mean, and how to put them into sentences is only a small part of learning to communicate. Each of these skills depends greatly on the language or languages that are available in the child's environment.

Children must also learn how to use language appropriately—how to communicate effectively and to be responsive to the needs of listeners. These skills are closely tied to the child's culture. The term **language pragmatics** refers not only to the rules of the language itself but also to generally accepted notions about appropriate and effective language use. This latter category contains an enormous array of phenomena that are largely cultural in nature. Thus, rules such as "Don't talk with your mouth full" fall under pragmatics, as do rules for politeness that range from saying "please" to avoiding discussion of delicate topics.

Metalinguistic awareness in the domain of pragmatics tends to emerge first in rules for politeness, perhaps because parents initiate many transactions with children that are explicitly pragmatic: "What's the magic word?" or "Don't interrupt, I'm talking on the phone." Young children often violate pragmatic rules that have to do with giving their listeners enough information, but by the age of 4 or so they do understand clearly that some adults are likely to need more explanation if names of friends or toys are introduced. Unlike grammar, which is mostly acquired by the time children enter school, pragmatic skills, particularly those associated with understanding how to adjust one's language for different audiences, continue to develop throughout the school years.

Pragmatics for Conversation. Most of the oral communication young children experience involves face-to-face conversation with familiar people. Children of preschool age talk with their parents about events in their own and in others' daily lives, such as doing chores, eating, getting dressed, going for walks, and so on. They talk about experiences they have shared with others. As they get older, they increasingly come to talk about unshared events (what happened yesterday or what will happen tomorrow).

Teachers should realize that children do not often realize when they need to supply more information in conversation. Teachers who are fortunate enough to be informed about the general topic are usually more likely to be able to ask questions that fill in missing information. Those who are not so informed must be willing to draw the child out while interpreting and co-constructing missing information. It is easy to see how, if teacher and student do not share similar experiences or similar cultures, their face-to-face communication can be diminished. The concept of conversation and the pragmatic instructions for how it should be carried out are very much culturally determined. In large and authoritarian families (e.g., Mexican American, Appalachian, and American Indian families), children's conversations with adults are usually brief and abrupt. Children learn to listen and to speak very judiciously. A teacher who does not understand this context may mistakenly suspect that such a student is shy or language-delayed.

Pragmatics for Literacy. As children move through school, they become more familiar with written communication. Written language can differ from oral language not only in purpose but also in terms of the intended audience and the relationship between the speaker or writer and the audience. Written and oral language also tend to assign responsibility for effective com-

| Responsibility
| for Clarity

munication differently. For instance, writers must anticipate the needs of their readers and thus supply or clarify information to avoid confusing them. A speaker, on the other hand, may be directly questioned by the audience if something is not clear. The basic pragmatics for literacy are classically demonstrated in the typical newspaper editorial. The task of the essayist is to make a point clearly and completely and in the process to provide the audience with any background information necessary to understand the point on first reading.

Many types of oral language use pragmatics similar to those of the editorial—public lectures, for example, or telephone conversations with strangers. And some written forms of expression approximate oral communication in their private, personal, or ambiguous nature—diaries or journals, for example, or poetry. The pragmatic rules governing the sort of effective conversational exchange that the typical preschooler has mastered are only a first step toward the pragmatics of literacy and must be acquired through much oral classroom discourse.

Pragmatics for Different Discourse Situations. As suggested earlier, one important dimension distinguishing the pragmatics of different types of communication is the extent of audience collaboration. Can you expect your listeners to participate actively (asking questions, chiming in with agreements or supportive statements, proposing interpretations and conclusions)? If you can expect such listener involvement, then you do not need to make extensive preparations to ensure that your message is clear.

Expected audience participation is an element of discourse pragmatics that varies across cultures for both oral and written communication. For example, Hawaiian and Athabaskan children have been described as active audience participants, often interrupting enthusiastically when listening to stories (Boggs & Watson-Gegeo, 1991; Scollon & Scollon, 1981). In contrast, in mainstream

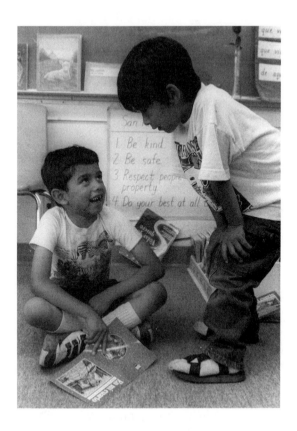

U.S. culture the storyteller has full responsibility for plot development and performance, and the audience is supposed to be silent until the end. Japanese novelists tend to demand a considerable amount of work from their readers, rarely providing the tidy, wrapped-up conclusion to the plot often expected by Western readers. In the United States, teenage girls from working-class backgrounds discuss serious topics by sharing comments with other audience members, who audibly echo or even anticipate the speaker's points. Girls from middle-class backgrounds, on the other hand, tend to take long and uninterrupted turns producing what in effect are brief oral editorials on the subject under discussion. Discourse in which responsibility is shared with the audience and discourse in which responsibility rests with the speaker are equally challenging communication skills for children to learn. Practice in the latter skill, in U.S. schools, usually focuses on the types of writing that children are expected to do.

The pragmatics of various discourse forms also differ concerning the degree to which background knowledge can be assumed to be shared with the audience. Consider the difference between recounting a harrowing experience to a friend and remembering it with someone who went through it with you. The first account requires considerably more attention to detail and clarity about the participants as well as the order and description of the events. These demands are played out linguistically by reduced use of pronouns (saying a name instead of "she" or "he"), more elaborated use of grammar ("We lost the paddles, and because of that we went over the falls"), and more explicit background and foreground detail.

An additional dimension of pragmatic complexity is added when the discourse form requires the speaker or writer to presume that background knowledge is not shared when in fact it is. This situation emerges in classroom discourse when teachers ask "known-answer" test questions. (Keep in mind that teachers are among the few individuals who ask questions to which they know the answers!) It is also at work when, at sharing time, children are expected to describe objects that they are holding and that the whole class can obviously see.

Classroom Discourse

Giving definitions for common words is a task that taps children's ability to understand that shared knowledge and context must be ignored in such a situation. When asked, "What is a clock?" children who assume shared knowledge might point at a clock or say something like, "They are like watches, but bigger." Children who are sophisticated in the pragmatics of school discourse, however, tend to avoid responses like these that presume shared knowledge and to respond instead with an answer such as, "A clock is a machine that tells time" (Snow, 1991).

Understand the Listener

For children to master pragmatics, they must be able to understand both the listener's perspective and the range of expectations the listener might hold. As members of a culture, we all acquire culture-specific expectations as to how interpersonal relationships should be marked linguistically and how information should be packaged for easy communication. Children in the United States have to grasp these culture-specific expectations and move beyond them as they learn to interact in new settings and with different people.

A fundamental challenge for everyone, child or adult, is to understand other people's perspectives and expectations. Part of addressing this challenge is acknowledging that individuals whose cultures are different often have different rules for language use. The specific challenge for any educator is to adapt to diverse communicative needs and expectations in the classroom. This is no easy task. But it is a task that recognizes the crucial importance of effective communication. If it is left undone, the role of the teacher in enhancing the teaching and learning enterprise is substantially compromised.

Bilingualism and Second-Language Acquisition

Let's now contrast what we've learned about the typical pattern of language development among children who speak one language with that of children who speak more than one language. In this section we shall examine how bilingualism and second-language acquisition relate to schooling contexts. In the next section we shall focus on the use of dialect in a schooling context. In the rest of this chapter we shall address issues of teaching and learning as they relate to research and theory developed over the last three decades. We shall see that studies of children's linguistic, cognitive, and social development have dramatically reshaped our view of language variation, multilingualism, and cultural "difference."

As the revealing demographic information cited in Chapter 1 indicates, bilingualism and second-language learning are fast becoming common elements in U.S. classrooms. How are these two attributes of language development defined? **Bilingualism,** which is the ability to speak two languages with equal fluency, occurs when children are exposed to two languages during their early years, usually before they are 5. (By contrast, monolingual children are exposed to only one language during these years.) **Second-language acquisition** is a process of language development whereby a child acquires first one language and then is exposed to and required to learn a second language.

Research Focus

Compared to the amount of research focusing on monolingual development, little systematic investigation has been available regarding children who are simultaneously acquiring more than one language during the early part of their lives. Research on this subject, particularly in terms of schooling contexts, has centered independently on three areas of language acquisition of young, multilingual populations:

1. *Linguistic:* The developmental nature of phonology (word sounds), morphology (word formation), and syntax (word order) (Bialystok & Hakuta, 1994; García & Gonzalez, 1984)
2. *Cognitive:* Related cognitive aspects of language acquisition (Cummins, 1979; García & McLaughlin, 1995)
3. *Social and communicative:* The social context of language development and its effect on language pragmatics (Hakuta, 1986; Zentella, 1997)

We will now review this research and highlight similarities and differences in underlying theoretical concepts. We will also relate these research findings to important schooling issues.

Patterns of Language Development and Cognitive Aspects

It does seem clear, from evidence in many societies throughout the world, that a child can learn more than one linguistic form. For example, Sorenson (1967) describes the acquisition of three to four languages by young children who live in the northwest region of the Amazon River. The Tukano tribal language serves as the lingua franca (common language of the region), but some twenty-five clearly distinguishable linguistic groups also continue to exist in the region. **Multilingualism** has also been reported within the European community (Baetens Beardsmore, 1982; Skutnabb-Kangas, 1979) and among school-age children in the United States (Skrabanek, 1970; Veltman, 1988; Waggoner, 1984).

Spanish-English Bilingualism

Research into bilingual development in U.S. children, and into Spanish-English language acquisition in particular, yields some common findings. Young children aged 2 to 4 do acquire complex morphological, phonological, and syntactic skills for both Spanish and English without any evidence of negative linguistic effects (García, 1983a; Padilla & Liebman, 1975; Valdés, 1996). Children also exhibit a significant ability to produce well-formed and communicative mixed-language utterances, a process referred to as **code switching** (García, 1983a; Huerta, 1977; Padilla & Liebman, 1975). On the topic of code switching, Padilla and Liebman (1975) report:

> The appropriate use of both languages in mixed utterances was evident; that is, correct word order was preserved. For example, there were no occurrences of "raining esta" or "a es baby" [inappropriate grammatical combinations of Spanish and English], but there was evidence for such utterances as "esta raining" and "es a baby" [appropriate grammatical combinations of the two languages]. There was also an absence of the redundance of unnecessary words which might tend to confuse meaning. (p. 51)

These researchers found that learning two languages simultaneously did not prevent children from understanding more abstract language rules such as those for correct word order or syntax.

Code Switching in Development

García, Maez, and Gonzalez (1979), in a study of Spanish-English bilingual children between the ages of 4 and 6 throughout the United States, found regional differences in the relative frequency of code switching. Spanish-English bilingual children from Texas, Arizona, Colorado, and New Mexico showed a higher incidence of switched-language utterances than did such children from California or Illinois, especially at prekindergarten levels. These findings suggest that some children may very well pass through an intermediate developmental stage in which the two languages can merge, before they move to the development of two independent language systems. Research indicates that code switching is a highly expected and normal developmental phenomenon in children exposed to multiple languages. It is not to be taken as evidence of a language disability or "confusion."

The mistakes language learners make have provided researchers with guideposts in understanding the strategies and processes employed during second-language acquisition (Corder, 1967). Dulay and Burt (1974b) studied the errors in the natural speech of 179 children between the ages of 5 and 8 (including a sample of Chicano children in California) who were learning English as a second language. They classified errors as related either to first language (interference errors) or to normal language development (developmental errors). Their analysis indicated that only 4.7 percent of the children's errors could be attributed to first-language interference, whereas 87.1 percent of the errors were similar to those made by children learning English as a first language.

Creative Construction

Dulay and Burt (1974b) postulated that a universal "creative construction process" accounts for second-language acquisition. They proposed that the process was creative because no one had modeled the hundreds of types of sentences that children produce when acquiring a second language. The authors suggested that innate mechanisms caused children to use certain strategies to organize linguistic input. They did not claim that they could define the specific nature of the innate mechanisms. They did claim, however, that these mechanisms have certain definable characteristics that cause children to use a limited set of hypotheses to deal with the knowledge they are acquiring. The strategies parallel those identified for first-language acquisition.

Unconscious vs. Conscious Learning

Krashen (1981a, 1985) has argued that this process of creative construction is fundamental to second-language acquisition. His thinking is based on two hypotheses about how bilingual children learn language. His "natural order" hypothesis indicates that the acquisition of grammatical structures by the second-language learner proceeds in a predictable, "natural" order independent of first-language experiences and/or proficiency. Such acquisition occurs unconsciously, without the learner needing to be concerned with recognizing or using structural rules. Krashen's "monitor" hypothesis suggests that a second language can be learned consciously, however, when the learner has achieved a significant knowledge of structural rules and has the time to apply those rules in a second-language learning situation. The "monitor" hypothesis extends Dulay and Burt's (1974a) concept of creative construction. Krashen concludes, however, that the conscious learning of a second language is not as efficient or functional as a natural acquisition.

Other research has documented a distinct relationship between first-language and second-language acquisition. Ervin-Tripp (1974) conducted a study of 31 English-speaking children between the ages of 4 and 9 who were attending French schools in Geneva. She found that the errors these children made in French, their second language, were a result of their application of the same strategies that they had used in acquiring a first language. Ervin-Tripp described the application of three of these strategies:

1. Overgeneralization
2. Production simplification
3. Loss of sentence medial items (items in the middle of sentences)

In overgeneralization, the American children acquiring French applied the subject-verb-object strategy of English to all French sentences and thus systematically misunderstood French passives. In production simplification, the children resisted using two appropriate French forms if they felt that they both had the same meaning. Finally, pronouns in the middle of French sentences were less often imitated than initial or final pronouns. Ervin-Tripp believed that interference errors occurred only when the second-language learner was forced to generate sentences about semantically difficult material or unfamiliar concepts in the culture of the new language.

Segments of Speech

Through rote memorization, children acquire segments of speech called prefabricated patterns (Hakuta, 1974). Examples of these prefabricated patterns are various renditions of the English verb "to be" (such as "I am," "you are," "he is") and the segments "do you" and "how to" as embedded in questions. These patterns are very useful in communication. Children use them readily without understanding their structure but knowing which particular situations call for which patterns in order to communicate in the target language.

Wong-Fillmore (1976) spent a year observing five Spanish-speaking Chicano children acquiring English naturally, and she noticed the same phenomenon of acquiring segments of speech. The first thing the children did in order to figure out what was being said was to observe the relationship between certain expressions and their situational contexts. They inferred the meaning of certain words, which they began to use as formulaic expressions. (They acquired and used these expressions as analyzed wholes.) The formulaic expressions became the raw material the children used to figure out the structure of the language. Wong-Fillmore provided two examples of how children use first-language acquisition strategies to begin to analyze these expressions: (1) children notice how parts of expressions used by others vary in accordance with changes in the speech situation in which they occur; and (2) children notice which parts of the formulaic expressions are like other utterances in the speech of others. As the children figured out which formulas in their speech could be varied, they were able to "free" the constituents they contained and use them in productive speech.

Children acquiring a second language may depend initially on transfer from the first language and on imitation and rote memorization of the second language. In more practical terms, the less interaction a second-language learner has with native speakers, the more likely it is that transfer from the first language to the second language will occur. As the second language is acquired, many of the strategies that children use to acquire this language seem to be the same as those used in first-language acquisition.

Role of Natural Conversations

Current research suggests that natural communication situations must be provided for second-language acquisition to occur. Regardless of the different emphases of the theories discussed above, recent theoretical propositions regarding second-language acquisition suggest that through natural conversations the learner receives the necessary input and structures that promote second-language acquisition (August & Hakuta, 1997; Bialystok & Hakuta, 1994).

Recent findings also recognize that the characteristics and circumstances of a particular child can and do influence the rate and quality of second-language development as well as maintenance or loss of the first language (Hakuta & August, 1997). One such characteristic is the child's attitude toward the two languages. For example, Hakuta and D'Andrea (1992) examined the relationship between English and Spanish proficiency and the language attitudes of Mexican American high school students. They reported that attitudes toward English were *not* related to English-language proficiency, while attitudes toward Spanish were indeed related to continued development in that language. This finding strongly suggests that, at least in this population of U.S. bilinguals, a positive or negative attitude toward English is not important for development of English language skills: in other words, you learn English whether you like it or not. But a positive attitude toward Spanish does directly influ-

Importance of Attitude

ence the child's continued development of that language and ultimate proficiency in it.

Individual characteristics are not always as important as we might suspect, however. For instance, the age at which an individual learns a second language has always been identified as a key factor in language acquisition. The common belief is that young children can learn a second language faster and more efficiently than older children and adults. Unfortunately, there is little evidence to support this idea, except for the fact that younger children will have less of an accent in the second language. Although there seems to be a critical age for primary language development, the existence of a similar period for a second language remains a myth (Bialystok & Hakuta, 1994). This suggests that adults are just as capable of learning a second language as young children. Keep in mind, however, that learning a second language may not be easy for everyone: many individual differences other than age *do* matter. Also remember that young children are less likely to be able to communicate their difficulties than adults.

To summarize, the research findings with regard to patterns in language acquisition suggest three things:

1. The acquisition of one or two languages seems to follow similar developmental processes. Language learners utilize a consistent set of cognitive hypotheses along with previous experiences with language.
2. The acquisition of more than one language may result in an intermediate phase of language convergence, called code switching, that incorporates the attributes of several languages.
3. The acquisition of two languages does not hamper the acquisition of either language, although individual differences in second-language acquisition can be traced to a variety of factors (August & Hakuta, 1997; García, 1983a; Hakuta, 1986).

Age Factor— A Myth?

Effects on Language Pragmatics

As noted, language is a critical social repertoire, a set of skills that enables children to function in a world of social interactions. The discourse component of any social interaction most often determines the general quality of that interaction. In this, it carries special significance for the culturally and linguistically diverse student. Social tasks that include a language choice are loaded for children who are learning the language as they use it. Most children acquire the ability to use linguistic codes differen-

Language as a Social Instrument

tially, according to the social attributes of the specific speaking context. Children who are culturally and linguistically diverse face the added task of multiple code differentiation. Implicit in this discussion is the general notion that languages must be not only mastered in terms of phonology, vocabulary, and grammar, but also used as social instruments.

Important sociocultural variables contribute to a child's motivation to communicate in the target language. One of these is the learner's attitude toward members of the cultural group whose language he or she is learning. Gardner and Lambert (1972) found that the positive attitude of English-speaking Canadians toward French-speaking Canadians led to their high integrative motivation to learn French. Ramirez (1985) reported a series of studies that investigated the relationship between Chinese, Japanese, and Chicano students' achievement in English and their attitude toward English speakers as a group. Positive attitudes toward the culture of the target language corresponded to higher language proficiency.

Relationship Between Cultures

The individual language learner's attitude toward the target culture is not the only important variable. Second-language acquisition is also influenced by the relationship between the two cultures. Schumann (1976) hypothesized that the greater the social distance between the two cultures, the greater the difficulty the second-language learner will have in learning the target language. Conversely, the smaller the social distance, the less difficulty the language learner will have. **Social distance** is determined in part by the relative status of the cultures. For example, two cultures that are politically, culturally, and technically equal in status have less social distance than two cultures whose relationship is characterized by the dominance of one and the subordination of the other. In addition, there is less social distance if the cultures have attributes that mesh well together.

Necessary Social Skills

Once a child is motivated to learn a second language, he or she needs certain social skills in order to establish and maintain contact with speakers of the target language. Wong-Fillmore (1976) and Wong-Fillmore and Valadez (1985) suggest that individual differences in social skills among children influence the rate of their second-language acquisition. Second-language learners who seem most successful use three specific social strategies:

1. Join a group and act as if you understand what is going on even if you do not. The learner must initiate interactions and pretend to know what is going on. As a result, he or she will be included in the conversations and activities.

2. Give the impression with a few well-chosen words that you can speak the language. The child must be willing to use whatever facility with the target language he or she has. As a result, other children will keep trying to communicate.
3. Count on your friends for help. The acquisition of language depends on the participation of both the learner and someone who already speaks the language—the friend. Friends can help in several ways, for example, by showing faith in the learner's ability to master the language and by including the learner in their activities. They also can provide the learner with natural linguistic input that he or she can understand.

Seliger (1977) has also demonstrated that high-input generators (children who solicit help with the language) are the most successful second-language learners. High-input generators place themselves in situations that expose them to the target language and are willing to use it for communication. They therefore receive the necessary input as well as the opportunity for practice. Following this general rule, most teachers of foreign languages recommend extended visits to a country in which a language learner will be maximally exposed to and required to participate in normal social interactions with native speakers of the language.

Another focus of research into pragmatics has been to investigate ways in which language is used and the rules that govern discourse. Phillips's (1972) research at Warm Springs Indian Reservation, now a classic study of discourse rule differentiation between school and nonschool settings, compared the conditions for speech use in the American Indian community and in the government school. She identified basic distinctions in **participant structures,** which are rules that govern who speaks when. American Indian students were reluctant to speak up when called on in class. Phillips attributed this reluctance to differences in the ways in which authority is exercised in the Indian community and the minimal role of verbalization in the teaching styles practiced within Indian families. She compared the students' lack of verbal responsiveness in teacher-directed situations with their different participation in peer-learning situations, which are more culturally congruent. Boggs (1972) addressed a similar reluctance among native Hawaiian children to respond to direct questioning by teachers. He documented the low frequency of adult questioning directed at a specific child in native Hawaiian homes. However, Boggs found that when students were invited to participate in the classroom in ways that were culturally congruent, utilizing peer-related discussions, they did, in fact, produce long narratives.

Different Ways of Using Language

Heath's (1983) study of ways of talking in middle-class white and working-class African American families in a southern community extended this line of research. Heath suggests that children of working-class African American families were reluctant to answer their teachers' questions because of differences in communicative patterns: working-class African American parents rarely used the "known-answer" question. Heath (1986) later explored "ways with words" within Asian and Latino communities, searching for similar clues to the discontinuities between language use at home and at school. She introduced the concept of the oral genre as a type of organizing unit into which smaller segments of language fit.

Oral genres, such as stories, accounts, and recounts, exist among all linguistic communities. However, their frequency varies among groups, as does the kind of language associated with each. In her research analysis, Heath posited that discrepancies between sociolinguistic conventions are the primary source of misunderstanding between children from language minority families and their mainstream teachers. She argued that the discontinuity between home and school languages (such as Spanish versus English, or Black English versus standard English) is not as disconcerting and detrimental as is the discontinuity between ways of using language in the home and at school. This finding addresses Dolson's (1984) report that children from homes in which the first language is used achieve better academically than those from homes where the parents and older siblings try to use English. When limited-English-proficient (LEP) parents and siblings insist on using their weaker language for communication at home, children may be exposed to a far more restricted array of genres.

Nonverbal Patterns

In a similar mode, Nine Curt (1991) identified areas of pragmatics that can cause particular confusion for Puerto Rican students: personal space, eye contact, touching, and body movements. Nine Curt reported on a study that found a high rate of retention of Puerto Rican gestures among students born and raised on the mainland. This work indicated that students may be retaining more of the nonverbal than the verbal patterns of their parents' native Spanish. Nine Curt's observations about Puerto Rican culture have been further summarized by Irujo (1988), who details research documenting the cultural variations in eye contact and gaze behavior among African Americans and white North Americans, Arabs, Latin Americans, Southern Europeans, East Asians, Greeks, and Northern Europeans.

García (1983b) reports on an investigation of mother-child interaction. Spanish and English were used by children and adults (the children's mothers) in three contexts: (1) preschool instruction periods; (2) preschool free-play periods; and (3) the home.

Language Choice

Descriptions of these interactions pointed out that children, in particular, were consistently "choosing" to initiate an interaction in either Spanish or English as a function of the language the mother was using to initiate the interaction. A closer qualitative examination suggested that almost 90 percent of mother-child interactions were initiated by the mother, most often in Spanish (i.e., mothers most often did not allow children to initiate). For those small number of instances in which children did initiate discourse, the topic determined language choice. That is, what the child spoke about was highly correlated with the language he or she chose to use.

The richest data on how bilingual children initiate interactions come from child-child interactions. While investigating the use of Spanish and English among first-graders, Genishi (1981) concluded that the general language initiation rule for these students was "Speak to the listener in your best language." Her analysis suggests that when speaking with others, these children first made a language choice based on the history of their previous language use with their fellow students. Zentella (1981) agrees that bilingual students make these decisions. However, she found another discourse rule operating: "You can speak to me in either English or Spanish." Although Genishi's (1981) and Zentella's (1981) discourse rules differ, each observation suggests that bilingual students employ their social and language-use history to construct guidelines for discourse initiation. These studies also indicate that particular sociolinguistic environments lead bilingual students to be aware of language choice when initiating discourse.

While there is much encouraging research that addresses the awareness of classroom discourse, it is not appropriate to conclude that all is well in those classrooms that serve culturally and linguistically diverse students. The one feature of the learning environments studied in detail by Ramirez and Merino (1990) and Ramirez, Yuen, Ramey, and Pasta (1991) was the quality of teacher and student language, whether in English or Spanish, in

Passive Language Environment

several language minority education programs. From analyses of tape recordings of classroom interaction, these researchers concluded that teachers in all programs offer a passive language environment, which limits student opportunities to produce language and develop more complex language and thinking skills. This finding parallels similar results for "regular" classrooms (Cazden, 1988), but it is likely that language use should be a

BECOMING A RESPONSIVE TEACHER

Real-Life Practices That Enhance Literacy Development

In October of his first year of school a third-grade Hmong child, Se, carefully copies into his journal a few lines of "The Good Morning Song" from the sentence strips his teacher keeps in a pocket chart. The room is filled with other print sources that he could have chosen to copy. The teacher has allowed the children to draw or write on whatever topic they wish. When Se's teacher asks him to tell her about what he's written, he only smiles, for he is not ready to speak in English except for occasional one-word answers, most often given in chorus with other students.

This teacher knows she's doing the right thing by immersing her children in print. She's familiar with the work of researchers, such as Brian Campbourne, who have pointed out that children learning English as a second language (ESL) may rely on environmental print as a writing source for their stories or journal entries for a longer period of time than do native-English speaking children. Sometimes ESL children, like young native speakers of English, copy print but don't refer to it when they talk to their teachers about their stories; later, however, they may use their copied words to generate a meaningful message or story. But all children, both ESL and native speakers of English, need a print-enriched classroom.

This teacher has also just begun to allow her students to exercise choice about the topics in their journals and stories. Like many other teachers, she thought that her ESL students, with their very limited knowledge of English, needed topics, frames, or sentences to copy. She and others did not think that their ESL students could go through all the stages of the writing process. But as the teachers at her school have raised their expectations about the language and literacy development their ESL students are capable of, they are finding that these students not only meet those standards but push them upward.

In a primary grade classroom, the student teacher asks the ESL children about the kinds of birds that they know. She makes a list of their answers, and asks them to listen and look for more kinds of birds to add to the list as she reads them the book *Where's the Green Parrot?* The book's repetitive structure allows children to predict what will happen next and to "read" the story aloud with their teacher.

This student teacher knows the crucial role of linking ESL children's background knowledge and personal experience to the beginning of any literacy event. She also knows that when she does this, she makes it possible for even those children with little English proficiency to construct meaning with her and with their peers as if they were more proficient in English. Lessons centered on the students' experiences become even more critical

BECOMING A RESPONSIVE TEACHER *Cont.*

when the children are asked to construct meaning in their second language.

This reminds us of how much ESL lessons have changed in terms of materials. We used to think that we needed boxes of special vocabulary- and grammar-controlled materials, with the accompanying dittos. Now those are nowhere to be found at this school. Instead, books—whole books, not excerpts—flood the rooms. Rather than buying basal readers and workbooks, the principal allots each teacher money to purchase trade books, the same children's books that are sold in bookstores. The students have access to attractive, whole books and poems. These sources help ESL students construct meaning by giving them the multiple cues that only authentic children's texts can, such as pictures, complete story grammars, and natural language patterns.

The single journal entry at the end of October for Yelena, a fourth-grade Russian child, shows at least four spelling strategies: (1) she has memorized a stock of English words and spells them correctly; (2) she spells an English word using her knowledge of the Russian sound system; (3) she produces a few invented spellings using her fledgling knowledge of the English sound- symbol system; and (4) she writes the last word of her entry in Russian.

Instead of correcting Yelena's "errors" in the entry, the teacher marvels at the obvious growth in her writing fluency during the past two months, as she has developed strategies for communicating her message. The teacher realizes that Yelena is showing successive approximations in her journal entries that indicate that she is using more and more conventional writing forms.

This attitude toward "errors" represents another recent shift in the ESL field. As ESL teachers, we were first taught to immediately correct children's mistakes, lest they develop bad language habits. Through the work of Stephen Krashen and many other researchers, we have come to know, as Yelena's teacher knows, that "errors" are wonderful examples of development—they are the successive approximations our students use as they become English proficient.

At a high-school Working Group on Language and Culture, a teacher examined data on immigrant students' school participation and achievement, and found that 25 percent left school after the ninth grade. To address the students' needs and reduce their dropout rate, the group planned and lobbied for funding for an ESL literacy program in which a small number of teachers would work with a small group of students to develop curricula, engage in intensive individual coaching, and track students' achievement. Thus, what

BECING A RESPONSIVE TEACHER *Cont.*

had began as one's teacher observation led to the development of a theoretically sound, clearly articulated, and practical program.

Most afternoons children in a combined second- and third-grade classroom may choose to participate in an array of learning centers: dramatic play, art, writing, or math. The talk one hears at these centers—in Hmong, Vietnamese, Spanish, Chinese, and sometimes English, as children from different language groups interact—is rich, rapid, and incessant.

The teacher has purposely organized her classroom so that the students are actively engaged in talking and learning. She knows that recent research indicates that limited-English-proficient children show greater growth in English when they are not in a traditional teacher-directed lesson. As the children are involved with the various classroom learning centers, the teacher circulates, talking with children and noting their language use in anecdotal records that she will add to their portfolios. She knows that these longitudinal records of observations and interactions give her much more information about her students' language development than any formal language proficiency test could provide.

The teacher comments: "It is true that setting up these conditions for students calls for a dramatic shift away from the curriculum offered them in the past. It essentially calls for a new view of students, of their learning, and of teachers' roles in facilitating that learning. But it also seems to me that teachers and students at this school start with the understanding that there are no barriers to optimizing instruction for students, except perhaps the ones we construct."

▼ Meeting the Challenge

1. Visit a bookstore that has a large collection of children's literature. Spend some time browsing the shelves. Do these books take into account the diverse backgrounds of children in the United States? Note down the author, title, and publisher of the five most interesting books you discover. Bring your notes to class and compile a master list.

BECOMING A RESPONSIVE TEACHER *Cont.*

2. Experiment with "story time" with your classmates. Bring a children's book written at any grade level to class and read it aloud. When you are a reader, remember to speak clearly and distinctly and to consider your audience. As an audience member while others read aloud, remain attentive to your responses to the story and the reader. During class discussion after all the stories, comment on your experience as a reader and as a listener.

3. What do you think of the concept of "errors" described above—that they are to be considered as examples of development rather than as mistakes to be corrected? What is your attitude toward your own errors? toward errors made by others? Using one example from a past schooling experience, describe the role error played in your learning process, either positive or negative. Did other people respond to this error in any particular way? If so, explain how.

4. Visit two elementary school classrooms, one that is all English-speaking and one that has a significant number of non-English-speaking students (e.g., an ESL classroom). In each classroom, observe the frequency and quality of social communication, both teacher-student and student-student. Note the structure of each classroom and the opportunities for language acquisition, such as environmental print, reading aloud, and writing. Record some of the interactions that you find significant and explain why they are or are not supportive of literacy development.

higher priority in classrooms that have many language minority students. Ramirez, Yuen, Ramey, and Pasta (1991) concluded:

> Direct observations reveal that teachers do most of the talking in classrooms, making about twice as many utterances as do students. Students produce language only when they are working directly with a teacher, and then only in response to teacher initiations. Of major concern is that in over half of the interactions that teachers have with students, students do not produce any language, as they are only listening or responding with non-verbal gestures or actions. Of equal concern is that when students do respond, typically they provide only simple information recall statements. Rather than being provided with the opportunity to generate original statements, students are asked to provide simple discrete close-ended or patterned (i.e., expected) responses. This pattern of teacher-student interaction not only limits a student's opportunity to create and manipulate language freely, but also limits the student's ability to engage in more complex learning (i.e., higher order thinking skills). (p. 8)

In order to develop a comprehensive understanding of culturally and linguistically diverse students, we must therefore take into consideration more than the students' linguistic attributes.

Social Context for Language

We must also consider their complex and active communicative environment. Recent data tentatively suggest that social context in and outside of classrooms will determine the specific social language rules for each language and the roles assigned to each language. In turn, these specific rules for social language use can inhibit or enhance communicative development in classrooms. It is the responsibility of any educator to understand these phenomena and organize classroom activities that enhance functional and effective communication both among students and between themselves and their students.

Use of Dialects

Along with the multiple languages in use in our society, a great many dialects also exist. A **dialect** is a regional variation of language characterized by distinct grammar, vocabulary, and pronunciation. Between speakers of the same language, different dialects are usually mutually intelligible, whereas different languages are mutually unintelligible. However, the dialects of some languages are so different that their speakers cannot understand each other. The Chinese language, for example, has two major dialects, Mandarin and Cantonese, which are mutually unintelligible. In contrast, Norwegian and Swedish, which are considered different languages, are mutually intelligible to speakers of each language.

Dialects of English

The English language consists of American, British, Australian, and Canadian dialects. Canadian English is more similar to American English than to British English. Each of these dialects has its own further variations. For instance, in American English there are southern, midland, northern, Boston, Appalachian, Cajun, Black, and Hawaiian dialects (Gleason, 1988). Dialects share most linguistic features with the language on which they are based, but they differ from each other primarily according to the frequency of certain usages. For example, speakers of the Boston dialect pronounce the terminal *r* of words less frequently than do speakers of other American English dialects. To a non-Bostonian, "car" in the Boston dialect may sound like "cah."

While language is associated with a specific national origin or geographic location, dialects tend to be associated with characteristics of the speaker, such as race, gender, age, social class, and geographic region of origin. Only when people change their status or role with respect to these important characteristics do they find it necessary to acquire a new dialect (e.g., in the United States, people who move to the South may acquire a southern dialect). As Harrison (1985) points out, languages are not fixed and isolated entities but rather are collections of repertoires that have appropriate occasions for use depending on the setting, topic, and social status of the respective speakers and listeners. In most cultures, not all dialects are considered appropriate for all occasions. Because of this, some speakers never have any need to learn more than one dialect in a single language, while others will need to learn many dialects or languages.

Standard and Nonstandard English

U.S. schooling practices presuppose that standard English is a vital tool for success in the United States and recognizes its increasing prominence as an international language. **Standard English** is the version of English that has the grammar, vocabulary, and pronunciation considered appropriate for most occasions of public discourse and for written communication. It is the "standard" in that its rules for grammar, vocabulary, and pronunciation are taken to be authoritative. Most dialects are "nonstandard," meaning that their rules for sentence structure, word usage, and phonology vary from those of standard English. Negative attitudes about speech start with the belief that some dialects are linguistically inferior to the standard version of the language. Until quite recently in the United States, any variation from standard English spoken by children was viewed as a limited and debilitating educational drawback. However, linguistic research (Labov, 1972a) indicates that language variation is a

BECOMING A RESPONSIVE TEACHER

Learning by Talking

A crucial aspect of nurturing culturally diverse students is to provide an environment in which they feel safe and comfortable speaking aloud, and in which differences of outlook and opinion can be aired and appreciated. One way to achieve this end is to reconfigure class discussion time so that most discussion takes place among the students. This is in contrast to the traditional classroom, where discussion is typically in the form of a teacher-student interaction. In this alternative model, the adult intervenes only as necessary to guide, stimulate, and facilitate student discussions, and to support the development of correct concepts. Students no longer direct most of their comments to the teacher, and the teacher steps in only selectively.

Let's look at how this process can work. The first step in developing discussion that teaches effectively is to get all of the students talking about the topic of, for example, a science lesson, in pairs or small groups—expressing opinions or beliefs in an unstructured manner, or simply raising questions. Next, the teacher should help the students to listen to others, using the three r's: *recognize* someone else's desire to speak, *respect* that person's thought or opinion, and *restate* what has been said to show that you understand. Students should learn that skilled communicators are able to anticipate and address other points of view. Good communicators are also aware that paying careful attention to someone else's view is an important prerequisite to developing a counterargument.

While engaging in speaking and listening, students will also develop thinking skills. They will enhance their ability to:

▼ Evaluate and substantiate opinions by giving reliable sources and using logical arguments and evidence.

▼ Become critical consumers of information, developing the view that not everything that is published or is stated by an "expert" is necessarily the ultimate truth.

▼ Think analytically, finding ways to elaborate their own ideas and explanations and to be attuned to the complex considerations and tradeoffs between different points of view.

▼ Recognize that there is no right or wrong side in many debates.

BECOMING A RESPONSIVE TEACHER *Cont.*

By working with this model, the teacher brings the whole class together from time to time to introduce and clarify important science concepts and to foster development of the thinking skills listed above. In addition, she or he has the class participate in monthly or bimonthly "dilemma discussions" on complex scientific and environmental issues, such as whether oil spills should be cleaned up or allowed to disperse naturally. Also, there can be personally relevant discussions in which students make predictions for their own lives based on what they are learning about the topic.

▼ Meeting the Challenge

1. Select an elementary or high school grade level and develop a series of possible topics on which to base a "learning by talking" curriculum. Keep in mind the diversity of backgrounds that will be represented in your classroom and the different learning issues that will be relevant to your students' grade level. Be sure to build into your plan the opportunity for students to shift the focus or to develop their own topics for discussion.
2. Create some guidelines for language use in your "learning by talking" classroom. Who will get to talk and for how long? How will speakers be recognized? Is interruption permitted? What will your role be? Devise a way to allow your students to have input into this decision-making so they will feel comfortable abiding by the guidelines.
3. When you next spend some time with friends, take a step back and observe the language pragmatics operating. What are the rules everyone seems to be following? What can be said or not said, and how are tone of voice and body language used? What happens when someone breaks a rule? How long does it usually take a newcomer to catch on to the rules? What if he or she is unable to master the pragmatics?

natural reflection of cultural and community differences. People's attitudes toward languages, and particularly dialects, stem from the social class structure. If some dialects of English are more highly regarded than others, this reflects a socially constructed hierarchy that makes deviations from these dialects seem "unnatural, incorrect and inferior" (Thornton, 1981).

Black English

Black English, also referred to as *Black English Vernacular* or *Ebonics,* is the most studied nonstandard American English dialect. It has its roots in African Creole and English but has distinct syntactic, phonological, semantic, and vocabulary rules. Labov (1972b) estimated that 80 percent of the black population in the United States speaks Black English; he noted that some Puerto Ricans in New York City speak Black English as well as Puerto Rican Spanish. More recent estimates suggest that 60 to 70 percent of the U.S. black population speaks Black English (Lucas, 1987; Wiley, 1996).

The terms *dialect* and *language* are sufficiently unclear to cause much confusion among educators who serve linguistically diverse students. These terms are not even well defined by linguists, although they have learned to live with their ambiguities. In understanding these terms, it helps to recall that everyone grows up speaking a language. If there are noticeable variations in the way the language is spoken by different individuals, we might conclude that they speak different dialects.

Confusing Terminology

Often there is no clear-cut way of distinguishing among different dialects. There are certain criteria, usually based on historical relationships within the language, that are used to make such determinations, but these distinctions are quite arbitrary and depend on the existence of good historical records and sometimes on formal analyses of the written language. Particularly for the spoken languages of today, much arbitrariness enters into decisions about whether the forms of English used by Appalachian miners, New York City children, and New Orleans hairdressers are distinct dialects. The decision-making process is neither precise nor scientific.

Social and Political Aspects of Dialects

Complicating the problem of identifying dialects are social and political factors. Typically, one dialect comes to be the preferred means of communication in formal institutions such as school, churches, and businesses. According to Wolfram (1993a), this preferred dialect can come to be known as the standard "language" of society, with all other dialects then perceived as failing the test of being a language. Each dialect may have its own well-defined linguistic structures that operate effectively and efficiently in well-

Figure 5.1 ▼ **Linguistic Society of America:
Resolution on Ebonics**

Whereas there has been a great deal of discussion in the media and among the American public about the 18 December 1996 decision of the Oakland School Board to recognize the language variety spoken by many African American students and to take it into account in teaching Standard English, the Linguistic Society of America [LSA], as a society of scholars engaged in the scientific study of language, hereby resolves to make it known that:

(a) The variety known as "Ebonics, " "African American Vernacular English" (AAVE), and "Vernacular Black English" and by other names is systematic and rule-governed like all natural speech varieties. In fact, all human linguistic systems—spoken, signed, and written—are fundamentally regular. The systematic and expressive nature of the grammar and pronunciation patterns of the African American vernacular has been established by numerous scientific studies over the past thirty years. Characterizations of Ebonics as "slang," "mutant," "lazy," " defective," " ungrammatical," or "broken English" are incorrect and demeaning.

(b) The distinction between "languages" and "dialects" is usually made more on social and political grounds than on purely linguistic ones. For example, different varieties of Chinese are popularly regarded as "dialects," though their speakers cannot understand each other, but speakers of Swedish and Norwegian, which are regarded as separate "languages," generally understand each other. What is important from a linguistic and educational point of view is not whether (AAVE) is called a "language," or a "dialect," but rather that its systematicity be recognized.

(c) As affirmed in the LSA Statement of Language Rights (June 1996), there are individual and group benefits to maintaining vernacular speech varieties and there are scientific and human advantages to linguistic diversity. For those living in the United States there are also benefits in acquiring Standard English, and resources should be made available to all who aspire to mastery of Standard English. The Oakland School Board's commitment to helping students master Standard English is commendable.

(d) There is evidence from Sweden, the United States, and other countries that speakers of other varieties can be aided in their learning of the standard variety by pedagogical approaches which recognize the legitimacy of the other varieties of a language. From this perspective, the Oakland School Board's decision to recognize the vernacular of African American students in teaching them Standard English is linguistically and pedagogically sound.

Chicago, Illinois
January, 1997

"Linguistic Society of America Resolution on Ebonics." January 1997. Reprinted by permission of the Linguistic Society of America.

recognized circumstances; yet each may still be seen as being inferior to the standard. In fact, the standard dialect does not have a higher linguistic status, only a higher social and political status. A common myth is that the standard is pure while dialects are full of errors. Recently, various individuals and organizations in the United States have attempted to correct this misconception as it applies to Black English, as the document in Figure 5.1 shows.

In the classroom and out, the dialect speaker will confront social attitudes toward dialects other than standard English. For some, the variation in usage may be based on pronunciation and

Dialect in School

vocabulary (e.g., the Boston dialect). For others, it may also involve syntactic changes (e.g., Black English). A student's use of language may influence his or her chances for success in the classroom and may have important social consequences. Rating children's personality and competence from their dialect alone is both inaccurate and unfair, yet it happens over and over. Williams (1970; cited in Dwyer, 1991) asked teachers to rate the voices of black, white, and Mexican American children. The voices of children with nonstandard speech were rated as less competent rather than socially different from the children with a more standard dialect. Cherry (1981) found that teachers were much more supportive, in terms of allowing requests and supplying information, to students who used the standard dialect.

Judgments Based on Dialect

Harrison (1985) concludes that a dialect can affect the initial judgment about how smart a child is likely to be, how well he or she will fare as a learner, how he or she is grouped for instruction, and how his or her contributions to class will be treated. This judgment, in turn, may affect the child's (1) attitude about herself or himself as a student, (2) willingness to participate in class, and (3) expectations for the results of participation. A child's competence is not easily predicted from dialect, but as Edwards (1981) found, it is more probable that teachers who expect problems with children who speak a dialect will treat those children differently, thereby creating a self-fulfilling prophecy.

Consider the example of an African American student who almost missed her opportunity to be class valedictorian at a high school in Northern California because of her Mississippi dialect. On the basis of her language, she was initially judged as not being capable of handling college-preparatory courses despite her straight-A record (California Tomorrow, 1997). She was able to overcome this initial assessment and did graduate as the valedictorian only after her parents convinced her teachers to allow her to take the college-preparatory classes. Dialect was similarly perceived as an educational liability for Chicano students in the same high school who spoke a dialect identified as "Calo" or "Spanglish," a mix of Spanish and English that has historical roots in the interaction of English- and Spanish-speaking communities in the Southwest (García, 1993).

Imagine what happens when a student who comes to school with the ability to use five present tenses (as an Ebonics speaker does) or to create meaning by switching from one language to another (as a Calo speaker does) must confront a language that is in some ways less expressive yet is more highly valued by the institution. The school's negative view of the student's language can be taken as a personal rebuke. In such situations, language problems are especially likely to develop when students are ridiculed for applying the grammatically consistent rules of their own language. The student who never manages to impress the teacher with "I be good" or "estoy leyendo" is more than likely to withdraw from conversation and ultimately fail to thrive in the classroom. For many educators, the effect can be too easily mistaken for the cause (Wolfram, 1993b).

Learning to Adjust Dialect

Research on code switching does indicate that children learn to use a more standard dialect in the classroom as they grow older. Destefano (1972) recorded the classroom and nonschool speech of black children between 8 and 11 years old. Their classroom speech appeared to be more formal or careful and to contain a greater frequency of standard features than their nonschool speech. Furthermore, it was reported that in a repetition task, first-graders who spoke Black English responded in standard English 56 percent of the time. It appears that even the younger children already knew most of the standard forms and were learning to use them in the appropriate contexts. A study conducted by Melmed (1971) revealed that black third-graders used standard English 70 percent of the time in school-related tasks.

Lucas (1987) refers to a study of instructional discourse that describes dialect features in predominantly black classrooms in Washington, D.C. The study reports a developmental progression in the use of dialect from kindergarten through fourth grade to sixth grade. Children in kindergarten are still in the process of learning which situations are appropriate or inappropriate for dialect. By fourth or sixth grade, the learning process is practically complete. Group interviews showed dialect awareness mostly in the fourth and sixth grades.

The Study of Dialect

With regard to the instructional use of dialect and its effects on academic outcomes, few data are presently available. Wolfram (1986; as cited in Dwyer, 1991) proposed that it is possible to introduce students to dialect as a type of language study in its own right. He suggested that the study of dialect would teach an understanding of language variation along with a deeper appreciation of the richness of American dialects. Moreover, he concluded that there is no evidence to suggest that Black English, as a dialect for school-age children, negatively affects academic achievement.

Conclusion

Humans seek meaning and understanding in every encounter. As educators, we seek to enhance understanding by introducing instructional environments that address our students' desires to

Table 5.1 Instructional Strategies for Helping Students Become More Effective Communicators

	INSTRUCTIONAL STRATEGIES	
Issue/Goal	**Topics for Class Discussion**	**Class Demonstrations**
Oral communication	Unique functions and appropriate uses of oral communication	Techniques for identifying appropriate uses of oral communication in specific situations
Audience analysis	The role of audience analysis in speech preparation	Techniques for identifying audience characteristics (i.e., motivations, needs, lifestyle objectives) to maximize communication with a specific audience
Language choices	Types, functions, and limitations of language use	Methods to analyze and use effective types of nonverbal communication
Nonverbal communication	The role and limitations of nonverbal communication in face-to-face oral interactions	How to use the most effective language choices for specific audiences
Vocal characteristics and articulation	The role and variables of vocal presentation, including social reactions to different types of vocal presentation	Techniques to enhance the articulation process, particularly in terms of social meanings conveyed to and from others (i.e., standard versus subculture pronunciation usage)
Delivery and style	The range of speaking styles (e.g., formal, conversational) and varied reactions to speaking styles	How to match delivery style to a specific circumstance or social setting
Organization	Audience need for patterned, systematic presentation of information and how organization affects audience perception and comprehension	Techniques to select most effective organizational pattern
Speaker credibility or ethos	The factors that affect a speaker's credibility and image with an audience	Selection of linguistic choices and nonverbal behavior that enhance speaker credibility
Logical and emotional appeals	How logic and emotional appeals can influence the audience	Methods to anticipate audience reactions to specific logical and emotional appeals
Speaking situation	Opportunities and constraints associated with specific types of speaking situations (e.g., interpersonal, intercultural, international)	How to adapt to unique communication requirements of a particular type of speaking situation

Table 5.1	Instructional Strategies for Helping Students Become More Effective Communicators *(cont.)*	
	INSTRUCTIONAL STRATEGIES	
Issue/Goal	**Topics for Class Discussion**	**Class Demonstrations**
Oral message construction	Characteristics of effective oral messages (i.e., characteristics that distinguish an oral message from a written message)	How best to construct oral messages
Feedback	The interaction between speaker and audience and how to monitor what is conveyed to and understood by listeners	Methods to monitor how effectively speakers achieve their objectives with an audience

make meaning. The environments we create must be structured around the multidimensional aspects of the communicative act and each participant's diverse set of cultural devices for making meaning. Table 5.1 presents a noninclusive set of strategies for educators to use to enhance communication in the classroom. They are offered here as specific practical suggestions that follow directly from the concepts presented in this chapter. Hopefully they will be a start toward the development of more specific guidelines for constructing effective instructional environments.

The research base and the understandings it has generated clearly show that our students come in many linguistic shapes and forms. We are always faced with the question of how to treat such variation in the classroom. This same research base suggests that educators cannot and should not legislate or regulate the use of language, particularly in the home and in the community. Variation is a phenomenon of the social roots of language and will persist because it feeds into whole sets of alternative identities, purposes, and cultures that speakers find rewarding and valuable. In the classroom, students' language variations should be perceived as linguistic capital that can be utilized to achieve the goals of the schooling process—one of which is to teach a common standard of English. With such an additive response to language variation, we are building upon the language the children already have to help them acquire the language and the subject matter they need to succeed in school. Language or dialect bashing has no place in a responsive classroom.

SUMMARY OF MAJOR IDEAS

1. Communication consists of both verbal and nonverbal systems that enable humans to encode meaning and transmit it to others. Language is a complex interaction of many variables, including the verbal signal, the signal sender, the manner and context in which the signal is sent, the signal receiver, and previous experiences the sender and the receiver may have had with similar signals. Children begin to communicate in infancy and in a matter of a few years develop skills in vocabulary and grammar. Communication is at the core of all teaching and learning activities.

2. Metalinguistic awareness is the conscious awareness of how one uses language. Schooling experiences that increase children's metalinguistic awareness can develop their understanding of their own culture and the cultures of others.

3. Phonology is the study of speech sounds. Infants exposed to environments in which English is spoken begin to produce speech sounds at 5 to 8 months of age. Children in all language groups proceed through similar stages of language development. Spanish-language learners acquire vowel sounds early, and English-language learners focus on consonant sounds early.

4. Vocabulary is the sum of words understood and used by an individual in any language group. Children typically acquire their first word at about age 1 and then gain vocabulary rapidly between the ages of 2 and 6.

5. Grammar is the system of rules implicit in a language that allows words to be arranged with some regularity of structure. From normal communicative interactions with adults, children typically acquire the rules of grammar in their native language with little difficulty.

6. Language pragmatics refers not only to the rules of a language but also to cultural notions about what is considered appropriate and effective use of the language. Children's knowledge of language pragmatics continues to develop throughout the school years. Among the most important skills in language pragmatics are the ability to be responsive to the needs of listeners and to adjust one's use of language for different audiences.

7. Children must learn the rules of language pragmatics for conversation, for written language, and for different discourse situations. The rules for discourse can vary widely across cultures. School discourse also has its own specific rules.

8. Bilingualism and second-language acquisition are becoming more common among students in U.S. schools. Bilingualism is the ability to speak two languages with equal fluency. Second-language acquisition is a process of language development whereby a child first acquires one language and then is exposed to and required to learn a second language.

9. Research into bilingualism indicates that children between the ages of 2 and 4 can acquire skills in both Spanish and English without any evidence of negative linguistic effect. Bilingual children also exhibit code switching as a normal state of language development. Code switching is the production of mixed-language utterances.

10. Research into second-language acquisition indicates that children use cognitive strategies they learned while acquiring their first language to acquire the second. They also rely on rote memorization and exposure to conversation with native speakers of the second language. Individual factors such as motivation are especially important in determining a student's rate of development and proficiency in a second language.

11. Language skills enable children to function and grow in a world of social interactions. Sociocultural variables that can affect an individual's motivation to learn a second language are the learner's attitude toward native speakers of the language and the degree of social distance between the two cultures the languages represent. Second-language learners need social skills in order to successfully acquire the target language.

12. Second-language learners must acquire the discourse rules of the target language along with the language itself. Research shows that it is not so much the use of different languages as a discrepancy in language use between the home and the school that constitutes the primary source of confusion for language minority students. The passive language environment of many classrooms may provide linguistically diverse students with only limited opportunities to produce language and to develop more complex language and thinking skills.

13. Dialect is a regional variation of language characterized by distinct grammar, vocabulary, and pronunciation. The dialect American English itself has a number of regional dialects. Students who speak a dialect, such as Black English, may encounter negative judgments about their ability from those who mistakenly believe that dialect is linguistically inferior to standard English. Such attitudes can negatively affect a stu-

dent's self-esteem, willingness to participate in class, and educational expectations. Research shows, however, that children who speak a dialect learn to adjust their speech and switch to more standard usage in school-based contexts.

EXTENDING YOUR EXPERIENCE

1. Interview the parent of a child under the age of 3. What has he or she discovered firsthand about language development from interacting daily with this child? Formulate your interview questions around the concepts discussed in the text: phonology, vocabulary, grammar, pragmatics, and metalinguistic awareness.

2. Review the text sections on language pragmatics and sociolinguistic conventions. Make a list of social communication rules for language use you have noticed in your general public interactions with others. Have you ever unintentionally violated such a rule? If so, describe that experience. Now think about the varied communication settings and types of audiences you encounter in a typical day (home, work, school, and so on.) List some of the rules for language pragmatics that operate in each of those settings. Do the rules vary depending on setting and audience? If so, why?

3. For this activity you will need a television and a VCR. With a group of your classmates, select and view a foreign film you have not seen before. Block off the lower portion of the television screen, where the subtitles appear, and try to follow the events in the film. Note your strategies for interpreting meaning and your feelings as you try to understand what is going on. Does your ability to "read" nonverbal communication help at all? Stop the film intermittently and compare notes. What do other group members think and feel? Prepare a report of your group experience for the whole class.

4. Informally survey your classmates in all your current courses and find out how many are bilingual. How many have acquired a second language (English or other)? Ask them to describe their schooling experiences as speakers of more than one language and record their comments, honoring those who wish to remain anonymous.

5. This chapter describes a good deal of research into language development and use. Why is it important for teachers to attend to the questions asked by educational researchers and to

understand their findings? Why is it important for teachers to understand the issues raised by educational theorists?

6. As you learned in this chapter, a child's motivation to learn a second language depends on three things: the child's social skills, the child's attitude toward the second language culture, and the social distance between the two language cultures. Create some teaching strategies for positively addressing these influences on motivations.

RESOURCES FOR FURTHER STUDY

Bialystok, E., & Hakuta, K. (1994). *In other words: The science and psychology of second-language acquisition.* New York: Basic Books.

Extending the important earlier work of Hakuta (1986), this volume brings together issues of the theory and research of language development and second-language acquisition. This discussion is interwoven with an examination of topics related to the education of second-language learners. Bialystok and Hakuta develop an important psycholinguistic base for understanding language development, second-language acquisition, and schooling.

García, E. (1983). *Bilingualism in early childhood.* Albuquerque: University of New Mexico Press.

This research focuses on the language children between three and five years old use when communicating with their mothers. The findings support the notion that there are differences in language acquisition in early childhood. Using statistical measures, home observations, and recordings of subjects, the author concludes that no significant differences in English were detected in monolingual and bilingual students and that bilingual students used different speech patterns at home.

Gleason, J. B. (1988). *The development of language.* Columbus, OH: Merrill.

This book is a collaborative effort targeted primarily at college students. The chapters present various topics and are written by individuals familiar with language theory, research, and practice. Models and theoretical perspectives are also offered. The book provides an insightful perspective on how language development occurs and what forces and issues foster it.

Hakuta, K. (1986). *Mirror of language: The debate on bilingualism.* New York: Basic Books.

This book offers a detailed overview of how bilingual skills are developed and argues for the need to move beyond simplistic research into bilingualism. The overall aim of the book is to dispel myths and misconceptions about bilingualism. It presents pressing issues that will be at the center of bilingual education in the future.

Heath, S. B. (1986). Sociocultural contexts of language development. In California Department of Education, *Beyond language: Social and cultural factors in schooling language minority students* (pp. 143–186). Los Angeles: Evaluation, Dissemination, and Assessment Center, California State University.

This chapter places the issue of native- and second-language acquisition at the forefront of educational reform. Using California as an example, the author argues that academic success has to do more with how students use the language they know than with the particular language they know. Educators can help students by involving them in a range of oral and written exercises. In order for educators to unlock new venues of academic delivery, such encouragement must take into account not only the students' language but also their past and present experiences.

Ramirez, J. D., Yuen, S. D., Ramey, D. R., & Pasta, D. J. (1991). *Final report: Longitudinal study of structured English immersion strategy, early-exit, and late-exit transitional bilingual education programs for language-minority children* (Vols. 1–2, No. 300-87-0156). San Mateo, CA: Aguirre International.

This extensive report was prepared for the U.S. Department of Education using three different U.S. models for the education of language minority students: structured English immersion and early- and late-exit bilingual programs. The overall results suggest that there are no significant differences between the three approaches. The factors that influence language acquisition and development have more to do with teacher qualification and parental involvement than the time spent learning the language. Without question, the author concludes, bilingual programs might not be proper for all language minority students, and more effective and structured means should be utilized to educate those students.

Zentella, A. C. (1997). *Growing up bilingual: Puerto Rican children in New York.* Norwood, NJ: Ablex Publishing Corp.

This is the author's most recent contribution to the understanding of multiple-language development in children. This documentation of bilingual children's interaction in their families, neighborhoods, and schools provides a detailed picture of how they live, learn, and communicate in diverse cultures and settings. Although its focus is on the language of the bilingual, the broader emphasis is on the multiple roles and relationships that shape that language, particularly for Puerto Rican children in New York City.

LANGUAGE,

CULTURE, AND

COGNITION

CHAPTER 6

Focus Questions

▼ What is sociocultural theory, and how does it provide a framework for approaching the education of culturally diverse students?

▼ How does children's language development relate to their development of higher-order thinking skills?

▼ What does the general trend in research suggest about the use of intelligence tests?

▼ What is instructional discourse, and how can it be used to develop students' ability to think and to communicate?

▼ What part does writing play in a child's symbolic repertoire?

"It is not the voice which commands the story, it is the ear."

—CICERO

As the quotation above suggests—and in some contradiction to ideas presented in the preceding chapter—it is the listener, the receiver of communication, who is the significant player in the communicative act. In its broadest sense, the "ear" represents the intellectual and social attributes of the receiver of communication. Listeners use their language skills, sociocultural background and experiences, and thinking abilities during the process of communication.

How and what the listener attends to represents all of the processes going on in the listener's mind. We saw in Chapter 3 that for humans the process of making meaning is a constructive act. Human cognition, the mental processes we use to acquire knowledge, is complex and multidimensional. Recent developments in cognitive science have shown that the mind includes both "structural" and "representational" aspects (Cole, 1996; Donald, 1991). Over the ages humans have evolved new systems of representation—not just new information but new ways of thinking. The mind is our storehouse of symbolic reference. It is a library of symbols that are distinctly assembled by our inherited mental "structures" and are also specifically ordered as "representations" of our own personal set of experiences.

Let's look at how this description of the mind as both structural and representational might apply to an educational situation. A new teacher (or a new student, for that matter) encountering the first day of school has prepared herself or himself for the encounter. He or she has called on previous experiences with formal education, on informal family and nonschool experiences in teaching and learning, and on expectations for social interaction and approaches to problem-solving. In short, a variety of experiences recorded and ordered in the "library" of the teacher's or the student's mind are mobilized to prepare for the classroom encounter: How should I behave toward others in the classroom? What language and tone of voice should I use to make my messages understood? What do I want to accomplish? All participants in education call on their own mental libraries to gather their present understandings of the classroom and related experiences and apply them to new classroom experiences.

But what, really, do we mean when we say the mind is like a library? Compared to the entire world, a library is very small. In the form of books, though, a large part of the world can be represented in that library. This is also true of the human mind: it is physically tiny but can contain representations of anything in the world. The mind is also shaped by what representations of the world are put in it and how those representations are organized (should we put nonfiction on the first floor or on the tenth floor?).

The represented world within our minds is determined both by the mental structures we have inherited and by our own personal experiences and how we tend to order these experiences mentally. Our inherited mental structures are the intellectual faculties that allow us to think and to think in many different ways—by means of formal argument, systematic categorization, induction, deduction, verification, differentiation, quantification, idealization, theoretical synthesis, and so on. But we do not think in a vacuum. We think in a context of our experience, and the world represented in our minds is shaped by that experience. There is an interaction between thinking processes and cultural experiences. We may all possess the thinking skills listed above, but if our experiences and mental representations of those experiences differ, the results of our thinking will differ. Herein is the basis for recognizing that diversity in experience leads to diversity in thinking. In day-to-day living and in the classroom, the workings of the human mind and the representations of culture are inseparable.

This chapter begins by discussing a theoretical framework for understanding the interaction of language, culture, and cognition as it relates to education. We then examine the problematical notion of "intelligence" and intelligence testing and consider research indicating that multilingualism may be an advantage in cognitive development. In the second half of the chapter we describe elements of teaching that may be particularly effective with culturally diverse students.

The Role of Culture in Cognition

Variables Affecting Learning

Early theories of teaching and learning focused on the individual learner and were influenced most directly by findings in the field of psychology. Within the last twenty to thirty years, however, scholars trained in such fields as anthropology, sociology, cognitive science, and sociolinguistics have begun to look into the question of how thinking processes and cultural experiences interact in schooling situations. The extent of fit or mismatch between home and school cultures provides a dynamic understanding of a wide variety of variables that affect student learning. Researchers in developmental and educational psychology are now devoting increased attention to the social context of learning and to the role of family, peer group, and community in children's school achievement.

During the last decade, many educational theorists have become interested in **sociocultural theory,** an international intellectual movement that brings together the disciplines of psychology, semiotics, education, sociology, and anthropology in what are often referred to as constructivist views of teaching and learning (see Chapter 3). This movement draws on work done by the Russian theorists L. S. Vygotsky and Mikhail Bakhtin, and relates it to the thought of earlier theoreticians and philosophers of education such as William James, John Dewey, C. S. Pierce, and Jean Piaget. The aim is to find a unified way of understanding issues of language, cognition, culture, human development, and teaching and learning. The following sections explore several aspects of this line of thought.

Constructivism and Cognition

As we learned in Chapter 3, constructivism assumes that all knowledge is constructed, using either innate cognitive structures or cognitive structures that are themselves the products of the continued construction of knowledge (Cole, 1996; Davis, Maher, & Noddings, 1990; Noddings, 1973). According to Noddings (1996) constructivists generally agree that:

1. All knowledge is constructed.
2. Certain cognitive structures are activated in the process of the construction of knowledge.
3. Cognitive structures themselves are under continual development.
4. Purposive activity brings about the transformation of existing cognitive structures.
5. The environment presses the organism to adapt.

According to this approach, learning can best be described as requiring the construction of knowledge, not the passive reception of new information. More directly, Vygotsky (1956) has provided a conceptual constructivist theory that identifies the developmental level of a child by what the child can do unassisted. Moreover, what the child can do *with* assistance is called

The Function of Teaching

the **zone of proximal development (ZPD).** It is within this zone that teaching is important. According to Vygotsky (1956), effective teaching "awakens and rouses to life those functions which are in the stage of maturing, which lie in the zone of proximal development" (p. 278). Teaching, in a constructivist view, is assisted performance, and learning is performance achieved through assistance.

The importance of sociocultural theory and constructivism for education is their proposal that individual learning and social interaction are inextricably connected. Sociocultural theorists and constructivists argue that the psychology of the individual learner is deeply shaped by social interaction—in essence, that both student and teacher are engaged in the process of con-

Learning and Social Interaction

structing their minds through social activity. In this view, knowledge is not a given set of fixed ideas that are passed from teacher to student. Rather, knowledge is created in the interaction between teacher and student. Higher-order mental processes, the tendency to look at things in certain ways, and values themselves are produced by shared activity and dialogue (Bakhurst, 1990; D'Andrade, 1995; Rogoff, 1990).

To sociocultural theorists our social lives, often considered to be the major products of culture, are also the major ingredients of cognition. Social experience is inseparable from thought. Moment by moment we construct reality. That process of construction, and the understanding it generates, depends on our previous understandings and social experiences.

The focus of sociocultural theory holds particular import for education, partly because education has been a major interest of many of its founding writers, but mostly because educational practice and theory are particularly needful of a unifying theory of teaching and learning. Educators of culturally diverse students will find this theoretical framework helpful because it conceives of learning as an interaction between individual learners and an

The Embedding Context

embedding context. That embedding context may be as immediate as the social environment of the classroom or as indirect as the traditions and institutions that constitute the history of education. Both contexts and many more come into play whenever teachers and students interact. Important contexts for teaching and learning include (1) close, detailed instruction of individual learners; (2) concern for the social organization of classrooms; and (3) a consideration of the cultural attributes of teachers, students, and peers. These contexts interweave, and we can follow their strands to gain a new understanding of the relationship between language, culture, and cognition (Cole, 1995).

Language and Culture as Tools of Thought

How do language and culture relate to cognitive development? Recall that human cognition—how and what we know—is a process of mental representation shaped by experience and the structural aspects of our minds. According to Vygotsky, language acquisition is the momentous occasion when internal mental representation and external reality converge. For him, "external reality" is first and foremost cultural: through the development of language in interpersonal experiences, children begin to construct meaning. In this view, language functions significantly as a tool of thought. As Hamers and Blanc (1989) stated:

> The shared representations and scripts which are basic to language proficiency arise in the interaction between the child and the significant others around him. The representations the child will construct are highly dependent on the shared social representations in his environment. The child will internalize those language functions that are valorized and used with him; it is through the socialization process that he becomes cognizant of functions and representations. (p. 100)

Mental Frameworks

Thus, as children develop their ability to use language, they absorb more and more understanding of social situations and improve their thinking skills. This in turn allows them to learn how to control their own actions and thoughts. It is through a culturally bound and socially mediated process of language development that children construct mental frameworks (or **schema**) for perceiving the world around them. If language is a tool of thought, it follows that as children develop more complex thinking skills, the mental representations through which language and culture embody the child's world play a significant role.

If, as Vygotsky proposed, a child's cognitive schema for operating in the world are culturally bound, what are the effects of trying to learn in an environment where the culture of the classroom differs from the culture of the home? Culturally diverse students face the challenge of either accommodating their existing schema or constructing new schema. When the educational focus is on transitioning culturally diverse students to a mainstream culture rather than building on what they already know, the students are forced to change in order to meet the needs of the classroom. As Duquette (1991) concludes:

> Children need to be understood and to express themselves (in the same positive light experienced by other children) in their own first language, home context and culture. Their minority background brings out the limitations not of the children but of the professionals who are asked to respond to those needs. (p. 98)

Negation of Cognitive Tools

Language minority students face a far greater challenge. It is through a child's first language that he or she creates mechanisms for functioning in and perceiving the world. If the culture of the classroom negates a child's first language and accompanying representations of the child's world, it is thus negating the tools the child has used to construct a basic cognitive framework.

In a discussion of Vygotsky's theory, Diaz and Klinger (1991) outline how language as a tool of thought has major consequences for a child's cognitive development. As language skills develop, a child's cognitive processes become more independent from the directly perceived environment. Through the use of language, children can organize and reconstruct their perceptions in terms of their own goals and intentions. Language development allows the child to act reflectively according to a plan rather than merely on impulse. As their language abilities mature, children can ultimately gain control over their own cognitive processes.

From the perspective of sociocultural theory, cognitive development is reflected by the increasing ability to use language in abstract ways. If the relationship between language and cognitive development operates as Vygotsky and later theorists claim, educational practices that ignore or negatively regard a student's native language and culture could quite possibly have adverse effects on the student's cognitive development. If a student's first language and culture are used only as a means to learn English and mainstream school culture and not to build on previous experiences and representations, then the student's cognitive development could be hindered or interrupted.

A Foundation for Language Proficiency

To further understand the link between language and cognition, various investigators have made the distinction between contextualized and decontextualized language. **Contextualized language** conveys meaning using physical cues such as gestures, intonation, and other concrete representations characteristic of face-to-face communication.

Abstract Linguistic Cues

Decontextualized language relies on more abstract linguistic and cognitive cues that are independent of the communicative context (Duquette, 1991). An example of decontextualized language is a reading assignment in science class. Such an assignment requires the student to construct meaning from a written context only. There is no opportunity to observe a physical demonstration of new concepts or to ask questions of others.

As students progress in school, they are increasingly required to use language in an abstract, decontextualized way (reading and writing as opposed to only listening and speaking). Proficiency in decontextualized language is considered to be most indicative of future academic success. In an extensive review of different research, Cummins (1991) shows that a high level of literacy (a decontextualized skill) in the first language is more closely related to development of literacy in the second language than is social communicative competence (a contextualized skill) in the second language. Cummins argues that it takes students much longer to develop decontextualized language and cognitive skills than to develop face-to-face, contextualized language skills. He further states that removing students too soon from educational programs that utilize their native language will lead to their future academic failure (Cummins, 1989). In essence, children use native-language abilities as a tool to construct higher-order thinking processes. Limiting their opportunities to learn in their first language will limit their cognitive growth and related academic achievement.

Learning in the First Language

Because they focus primarily on the oral acquisition of English, current policy and practice regarding the education of culturally and linguistically diverse students are overly simplistic. Such an approach does not take into consideration the complex interweaving of students' cultural, linguistic, and cognitive development. In their study of the possible effects of language on cognitive development, Hakuta, Diaz, and Ferdman (1986) recognize the importance of acknowledging these three major strands in children's development and addressing them in our schools. They conclude that most of the variance in cognitive growth directly relates to the way in which society affects and manipulates cognitive capacities. Therefore, cultural and contextual sensitivity theories that examine the social and cultural aspects of cognitive development will best serve diverse students.

An Assessment of Intelligence Testing

Over the last five to seven decades, the educational establishment has been guided by theories that consider the concept of intelligence to be the central factor in learning. **Intelligence** is generally defined as the ability of an individual's mind to perceive, organize, remember, and utilize symbolic information. To its credit, this idea of intelligence attempts to explain (albeit somewhat ambiguously) the relationship between the physical aspects of the brain and the human ability to reason and to symbolize. To its discredit, this concept depends extensively on the notion of biological determination (that is, we "inherit" our in-

Concept of Intelligence

telligence) and on the assumption that an individual's intelligence can be validly and reliably assessed through a simple set of test items.

Historically, culturally diverse children have been negatively affected by this enduring definition of intelligence (García, 1983b). Careful examination of the testing literature has revealed several problems in using the results of intelligence tests to understand the cognitive development of culturally diverse students. Personal, social, and cultural differences among students typically are not accounted for in **psychometrics,** which is the measurement of psychological attributes. Intelligence tests in particular have not adequately assessed the "intelligence" of culturally diverse populations because of language discrepancies, inappropriate test content, and failure to consider diversity in the development of test-scoring strategies. Inherent in this discussion of intelligence testing is the message that explanations of the human mind that rely on the concept of intelligence and on intelligence testing have been educationally misinformed.

Problems with Intelligence Tests

The use of intelligence tests with culturally diverse students and adults has generated much interest because of differences in scores found between this population and normative groups. As early as 1924, Sheldon compared the intelligence of 100 "white" and 100 "Mexican" children of the same age and same school environment by administering the Cole-Vicent group intelligence test and then the Stanford-Binet individual intelligence test. Sheldon's results were as follows:

Hypothesis of Mental Inferiority

1. The average Mexican child was below the normal development of the average white child by 14 months.
2. In a group comparison, Mexican children had approximately 85 percent of the scored intelligence of their white counterparts.
3. By combining several studies, Sheldon found that Mexican children scored lower than American, English, Hebrew, and Chinese children but higher than American Indian, Slavic, Italian, and Negro children.
4. As chronological age increased, differences in mental age became greater. Sheldon concluded that the average mental age of the Mexican group seemed to have reached its maximum at nine years.

These indicators of lower mental ability among Mexicans seemed to be supported by further research. In 1932, Manuel and Hughes administered the Goodenough Intelligence Test to 440 Mexican and 396 non-Mexican children from the San Antonio public schools. Based on an age and grade comparison, the Mexican children scored in the retarded stage.

The educational hypothesis that Mexicans were mentally inferior began to crumble, however, with such research as the work by Garth, Elson, and Morton (1936). These researchers tested 445 Mexican children between the ages of 8 and 16 on the Pintner Non-Language Intelligence Test and the Otis Classification Test. Their aim was to obtain a reliable nonverbal test to ascertain the influence of language and education. Results showed the Mexican children to be inferior to white American children in verbal tests across age and grade. However, on the nonverbal test, their scores were about equal to those of white Americans. The authors suggested that the verbal test could be unfair to the Mexican children.

Nonverbal Versus Verbal Tests

Despite evidence to the contrary, the hypothesis that some populations were mentally inferior to others continued to prevail. In the 1940s, Altus reported research findings related to racial and bilingual group differences within U.S. Army populations. In an initial study Altus (1945) examined racial and bilingual group differences in trainees' classification (discharged as inept or kept in the Army) and in mean aptitude test scores. The Wechsler Mental Ability Scale (WMAS) was used to test American Indians, Mexicans, Filipinos, Chinese bilinguals, whites, and Negroes. The results showed that the bilingual groups scored lower than the monolingual groups on all WMAS subtests. In a subsequent study Altus (1948) addressed the issue of group differences in intelligence and the type of test administered. The subject populations used in the study were "Anglos, Negroes, Mexicans, and Indians, who had been classified as illiterate when entering the army." The findings indicated that in the verbal subtest, the "Anglo" and "Negro" had higher scores than the "Mexican" and "Indian." However, there were no differences on the nonverbal subtests. Importantly, these data suggested that group inferiority or superiority was in part a consequence of the test used.

Intelligence as Predetermined

Through the subsequent decades, questions of how to assess and interpret individual differences in human intellectual abilities have persisted (for a historical overview, see Laosa, 1978). It has often been assumed that intelligence is an innate dimension of personal capacity and that it increases at a relatively fixed rate to a level that was predetermined at birth. These notions of fixed intelligence and predetermined potential clearly can have adverse effects on education, employment, and occupational policies and practices, since they encourage neglect of intellectual development. The argument is often made that because intelligence is predetermined, no amount of cultivation can significantly increase it (Laosa, 1978, 1984). Such thinking led Hernstein and Murray (1994) to the following conclusion:

> The lesson of this chapter is that large proportions of the people who
> exhibit the behaviors and problems that dominate the nation's social
> policy agenda have limited cognitive ability. Often they are near the
> definition for mental retardation. . . . When the nation seeks to lower
> unemployment or lower the crime rate or induce welfare mothers to
> get jobs, the solutions must be judged by their effectiveness with
> the people most likely to exhibit the problem: the least intelligent
> people. (p. 386)

There is no disagreement over the fact that there are differences in the scores of intelligence tests across ethnic groups. It is also generally agreed that differences among individuals *within* groups reflect both genetic and environmental influences. However, the disagreements arise over the relative importance of these two factors and the degree and changeability of inherited intellectual characteristics.

Effect of Vocabulary

Can ethnic differences in intelligence test scores be explained by something other than genetics? Laosa (1995) says they can. To illustrate, he considers the acquisition of vocabulary, which is a major component of widely used tests of intelligence. According to Laosa, the differences in ethnic groups' opportunities to learn the particular vocabulary employed in intelligence tests are sufficient to explain the ethnic variations in test scores, with no need for genetic analyses. In fact, for group differences to be correctly measured, "it would seem imperative that . . . we provide . . . equally detailed data on 'EIPQ,' an Environmental Intelligence Producing Quotient" (Campbell & Frey, 1970, pp. 456–457). In other words, it is only when we can assess an individual's "opportunity to learn" the material included on an intelligence test that we can properly interpret the meaning of that person's test score.

Social Class and Intelligence Tests

In another significant study, Christian and Livermore (1970) compared the effects of social class and ethnic origin on intelligence test scores. They divided the group of subjects into two categories: those with middle-class status and those with lower-class status. The results indicated that social class was a more important factor than ethnic origin in "intelligence" differences among children. With this information, important cautions about test bias began to emerge.

BECOMING A RESPONSIVE TEACHER

How Two Students Developed through Collaborative Learning

The Weaker Student: Valuing Not Knowing. Amiri entered school situations expecting failure. He could be heard saying over and over, "Boy, am I stupid," as he struggled through academic tasks. He assumed he was unable to do whatever was asked of him on his own and therefore sought a great deal of help from both teachers and peers. He did not appear to believe that he had anything of importance to contribute to others, nor that his participation in activities or discussions was valued. He often engaged in disruptive, attention-seeking activities or just "spaced out." His behavior was consistent with a belief that intelligence is something you are born with, that he hadn't been given much, and that no amount of effort would change that fact.

Some teachers who had worked with Amiri held a different view of his abilities; they thought he was more able than he himself believed, yet they found themselves at a loss to change his outward behaviors, his low social status in the class, or his apparent poor self-image. But all this began to change when computers were introduced to the classroom. In Amiri's words:

> See, really, when I first started off on computer—it was O.K. because we got to play games. And then I got a little bit serious about it . . . serious about it around April. At first I didn't really . . . I was like the dull one . . . really. I didn't know what was going on.

By the end of the school year, Amiri's school experience was very different from the one he had been used to. He had become an "expert," and the information he had acquired during the previous several months of research was valued by teachers and peers alike. The very expressions of uncertainty that had once marked him as unsuccessful in school were valued in this new environment. Repeated participation in reciprocal teaching groups and large group discussions provided Amiri with ample opportunities for guided practice in new social behaviors, in ways to enter group discussion, and in more successful learning strategies.

Amiri's developing confidence and increasing skills were evidenced by his growing eagerness to participate in large group discussions as well as in the quality of the questions he posed. This extract from a class discussion demonstrates his new thoughtfulness:

BECOMING A RESPONSIVE TEACHER *Cont.*

Paulette: The bamboo grove is real shady and the pandas is black and white so they sort of blend in.

Amiri: Why is it that the pandas eat all of the bamboo if they need to be protected? . . . Why would they eat all their, their camouflage?

This previously unsuccessful student came to be appreciated—by others and by himself—for qualities of his mind that his learning environment had enhanced and made visible. Amiri and other students like him found that their willingness to say, "I don't know," born of much real-world experience of not knowing, was actually valued here. And, as he reflected at the end of the year, learning was both possible and enjoyable to him: "I'm not going to drop this. . . . I have a lot to learn."

The Stronger Student: Learning to Reflect. Wilson scored in the 98th percentile on standardized tests of achievement in both reading and mathematics. He read voraciously, learned facts quickly, and performed school-related tasks with ease. He was articulate and confident. But Wilson rarely listened to others, did not work well in groups, and preferred finding things out on his own. He most often was heard making declarative statements or directing the activities of his peers. He was sure his way was best, and resisted suggestions by others to the contrary. Despite Wilson's high test scores, his inability to reflect interfered with his capacity to be a flexible and responsive learner.

As might be expected, it was difficult for Wilson to participate in a project emphasizing collaborative activity. Would a successful student like Wilson find such a project sufficiently challenging, or would the slower rate of his peers hold him back and frustrate him?

As it turned out, while working with a group, Wilson continued to develop skills and expertise in numerous areas. He learned to listen and to share his knowledge with others, and he began to engage in more flexible and reflective thinking. He also became more open to learning from his peers. In the following segment, Wilson is analyzing the changes in his own thinking and the classroom experiences that stimulated those changes. Later, for the first time, he is seeking clarification of new data rather than holding rigidly to his original point of view:

At first I thought I agreed with Stuart [that pandas are fat because they are indolent] except it really takes a lot of exertion to climb trees. It does. They must burn their en-

BECOMING A RESPONSIVE TEACHER *Cont.*

ergy climbing, because remember, we saw them in that laser disc . . . how the panda was climbing trees to get to the bamboo.

I'm sort of getting two pictures. First you're saying there's plenty of bamboo, and they sit around and munch it all day, and then you say that their bamboo is dying off. Can you sort of set me straight?

▼ Meeting the Challenge

1. Describe your reactions as you read the above stories of Amiri and Wilson. Were you surprised by either of these outcomes? Does the underlying teaching approach alluded to here seem to be "transmitting" or "facilitating"?
2. Do you feel you are more like Amiri or Wilson as a learner? Devise strategies for broadening the role of social interaction in your own learning process.
3. Observe a class and record two phenomena: (a) the number of times the teacher responds to the way a child learns; and (b) the number of times the teacher responds to what a child learns. Describe a teacher response that seemed to be particularly effective for some student.

Test Bias

Recent review of the use of intelligence tests with culturally and linguistically diverse populations has pinpointed several serious concerns (Figueroa & Garcia, 1994). First, the language of the test can bias the results, promoting lower scores for non-English-speaking populations. Second, social class is highly correlated with test performance, which calls into question any conclusions about intelligence and ethnic background. Third, the content of the tests is biased toward mainstream U.S. culture.

It seems appropriate to conclude that differences in test performance may be an artifact of the tests themselves or of other linguistic, psychological, or social factors as yet imperfectly defined. Intelligence tests and the concept of intelligence that underlies them have done and continue to do an educational disservice to culturally diverse students. The limitations of these educational "tools" should be recognized, and educators should be extremely cautious when using them to generalize about students.

Multilingualism and Cognitive Development

In the preceding chapter, we looked into some of the research that has explored bilingualism and second-language acquisition from the perspective of language development. A separate but significant research approach to the understanding of multilingualism and its effects has focused on the cognitive (intellectual) attributes of the student. Past correlational studies indicating a negative relationship between childhood bilingualism and performance on standardized tests of intelligence made it tempting to link bilingualism to "depressed" intelligence, and this negative conclusion characterized much early work (Darcy, 1953). Because of the many methodological problems in studies investigating this type of relationship, any conclusions about multilingualism and intellectual functioning (as measured by standardized individual or group intelligence tests) are extremely tentative in nature (Darcy, 1963; Diaz, 1983).

Mental Flexibility

In one of the first investigations of German-English bilingual acquisition, Leopold (1939) reported a general cognitive plasticity for his young bilingual daughter. He suggested that linguistic flexibility (in the form of bilingualism) was related to a number of nonlinguistic cognitive tasks such as categorization, verbal signal discrimination, and creativity. Peal and Lambert (1962) summarized their work with French-English bilinguals and English monolinguals by suggesting that the intellectual experience of acquiring two languages contributed to advantageous mental flexibility, superior concept formation, and a generally diversified set of mental abilities.

More recent research (Feldman & Shen, 1971) reports differential responding between Chicano Spanish-English bilinguals and English monolinguals across three separate tasks reflecting Piagetian-like problem-solving and metalinguistic awareness. Results indicated significantly increased cognitive flexibility for Chicano bilinguals. Other studies have compared matched bilinguals (Afrikaans-English) and monolinguals (either Afrikaans or English) on metalinguistic tasks requiring separation of word sounds and word meanings. Comparison of scores on these tasks indicated that bilingual speakers concentrated more on attaching meaning to words rather than to sounds. Ben-Zeev's (1977) work with Hebrew-English bilingual children also comments on the metalinguistic abilities of these children. Subjects in these studies showed superiority in symbol substitution and verbal transformational tasks. As Ben-Zeev (1977) summarizes, "two strategies characterized by thinking patterns of the bilingual in relation to verbal material . . . [are] readiness to impute structure and readiness to reorganize" (p. 1017).

Even more recent research, specifically with Chicano bilingual students (Kessler & Quinn, 1987), supplies additional empirical support for the emerging understanding that, all things being equal, bilingual children outperform monolingual children on specific measures of cognitive and metalinguistic awareness.

Greater Metalinguistic Awareness

Kessler and Quinn (1987) engaged bilingual and monolingual children in a variety of symbolic categorization tasks that required their attention to abstract features of concrete objects (for example, the relative size of toy blocks). Chicano Spanish-English bilinguals from low socioeconomic backgrounds outperformed English monolinguals from both high and low socioeconomic backgrounds on these tasks. Such findings are particularly significant given the criticism by McNab (1979) that many bilingual "cognitive advantage" studies utilized only subjects from high socioeconomic backgrounds and from non-U.S. minority populations. It is important to note that findings of metalinguistic advantage have also been reported for Puerto Rican students from low socioeconomic backgrounds as well (Galambos & Hakuta, 1988).

Theoretical attempts to link multilingualism with cognitive attributes have begun to emerge. To identify more specifically the relationship between cognition and bilingualism, Cummins (1979, 1981, 1984b) has proposed that children who do achieve balanced proficiency in two languages may be cognitively "advantaged," whereas those who do not achieve balanced proficiency in two languages may be cognitively "disadvantaged." Interestingly, Diaz (1985) has proposed an alternative hypothesis and supportive data that suggest that the cognitive "flexibility" of the multilingual is at its maximum during the early stages of multilingual development, before balanced proficiency is attained.

As yet, it is not quite clear how bilingualism or multilingualism directly influences cognitive development. Is it always an advantage? Can it be a disadvantage? Is early (and balanced) proficiency advantageous, and is late (and unbalanced) proficiency disadvantageous? These questions are not yet answerable (August & Hakuta, 1997; García, 1991b; Hakuta, 1986). What we do know is that multilingual children have been found to score higher on specific Piagetian, metalinguistic, concept formation, and creative cognitive tasks. Gone are the old myths that multilingualism is an intellectual and psychological liability.

Two Aspects of Effective Teaching in Culturally Diverse Classrooms

Goals of Education

Since the time of Socrates, educators and philosophers have argued for a kind of teaching that does more than impart knowledge and teach skills. Knowledge and skills are important enough, the argument goes, but true education and real teaching involve far more. They involve, fundamentally, helping students understand, appreciate, and grapple with important ideas while developing a depth of understanding in a wide range of issues.

Teaching aimed at these important goals is presently most notable for its absence from U.S. classrooms. Goodlad (1984), for example, reports that

> a great deal of what goes on in the classroom is like painting-by-numbers—filling in the colors called for by numbers on the page. . . . [Teachers] ask specific questions calling essentially for students to fill in the blanks: "What is the capital city of Canada?" "What are the principal exports of Japan?" Students rarely turn things around by asking questions. Nor do teachers often give students a chance to romp with an open-ended question such as "What are your views on the quality of television?" (p. 108)

If this portrait is accurate for mainstream American classrooms, it is even more accurate for classrooms in which the students are linguistically and culturally diverse and of low-income backgrounds. Because of the perception that these students fundamentally require drill, review, and redundancy in order to progress academically (Brophy & Good, 1986), their learning opportunities are likely to be excessively weighted toward low-level skills and fact-oriented rather than concept-oriented instruction. As important as skills and knowledge undoubtedly are, no less important are more cognitively demanding learning opportunities that promote, as the philosopher and educator Mortimer Adler (1982) has written, the "enlarged understanding of ideas and values" (p. 23).

With Adler's notion of such an "enlarged understanding" as a goal of education, in the rest of this chapter we shall attempt to consolidate the more theoretical issues of language, culture, and cognition addressed earlier. It is impossible to delineate all the interlocking pieces of this puzzle in this small space. We can make some headway, though. We will examine two recently researched areas that have attended to instructional delivery (the language and discourse of instruction) and the development of literacy. The selection of these two particular areas is not a random one. The basis of enhanced academic productivity for culturally diverse students lies in the manner in which their communicative and cognitive development is organized instructionally in oral and literacy activities (Tharp & Gallimore, 1991). In essence, the way these endeavors are handled in the classroom is highly significant for the student of interest in this book.

Basis for Enhanced Achievement

Instructional Discourse

In classrooms throughout the world, but particularly in the United States, daily teaching events are structured around teacher-student dialogues. In one study (García, 1992a), we recorded the following dialogue in a kindergarten classroom with the teacher leading a lesson for several children:

Teacher: Okay, Maria, let's see what we can figure out about the shapes of these blocks.

María: This one's yellow.

Teacher: Sí, yellow is a color, but can you tell me what shape this block is?

María: Todos son amarillos. [They are all yellow.]

Teacher: Sí, but we want to talk about shape. Tú sabes cómo? [You know how?]

María [holding up a triangle]: This one, this one, this one, es amarillo [is yellow].

These sorts of instructional interactions occur repeatedly every day in classrooms. Typically, the teacher asks a question or, as in the preceding example, requests a student response. The student then replies (as for María, not always the way the teacher would prefer). Finally, the teacher evaluates the child's response and may request further elaboration.

Effective **instructional discourse** (as reported by García, 1992a) and the use of **instructional conversation** (as reported by Tharp & Gallimore, 1988, 1989, 1991) have been demonstrated as highly relevant to the broader linguistic, cognitive, and academic development of linguistically and culturally diverse children. On the one hand, such conversations are an instructional strategy in that they are designed to promote learning. Yet they are structured to take advantage of natural and spontaneous interactions, free from the didactic characteristics normally associated with formal teaching. Such interactions are interesting and engaging. They center on an idea or a concept. They have a focus that might shift as the discussion evolves but remains discernible throughout. They allow a high level of participation without undue domination by any one individual, particularly the teacher. Students engage in extended discussions—interactions—with the teacher and among themselves.

Spontaneous Interaction

In instructional discourse, teachers and students are responsive to what others say, so that each statement or contribution builds upon, challenges, or extends a previous one. Topics are picked up, developed, and elaborated. Strategically, the teacher (or discussion leader) presents provocative ideas or experiences and then questions, prods, challenges, coaxes—or keeps quiet. He or she clarifies and instructs when necessary but does so efficiently, without wasting time or words. The teacher assures that the discussion proceeds at an appropriate pace, neither too fast to prohibit the development of ideas nor too slow to lose momentum and interest. The teacher knows when to bear down and draw out a student's ideas and when to ease up, allowing thought and reflection to occur. Perhaps most important, the teacher manages to keep everyone engaged in a substantive and extended interaction, weaving each individual participant's comments into a larger tapestry of talking and thinking.

Teacher's Role in Discourse

Such discourse is in many ways similar to interactions that take place outside school between children and adults (e.g., Ochs, Taylor, Rudolph, & Smith, 1989; Rogoff, 1990). These interactions appear to be very important for children's learning and cognitive development in general. For example, Rogoff (1990) notes that middle-class adults tailor their responses to children, "focusing their attention, and expanding and improving the children's contributions." Although not designed to teach in a formal sense, these tailored responses, Rogoff concludes, "appear to support children's advancing linguistic, thinking, and communicative skills" (p. 157).

Elements of Good Classroom Discourse. Moving beyond such general descriptions, what characterizes good classroom discourse? What are its constituent elements? What must teachers know and do in order to implement successfully these types of learning interactions with their students? Working in a low-income, language minority school in California (García, 1989) and building upon earlier work in Hawaii (e.g., Au, 1979; Tharp & Gallimore, 1988), recent research teams comprised of teachers and researchers have attempted to address these questions (see Goldenberg & Gallimore, 1990, 1991b; Goldenberg & Patthey-Chavez, 1991). What has gradually emerged is a more precise description of instructional discourse. As developed by Goldenberg (1992), Table 6.1 compares direct instruction with instructional conversation.

Although these comparisons in no way represent definitive or comprehensive descriptions of direct instruction and instructional discourse, they suggest important distinctions between these two teaching approaches. They are based on very different assumptions about teaching and learning. **Direct instruction** assumes that the teacher acts as a "transmitter," imparting knowledge to the student through modeling and step-by-step instructions. Instructional conversation, on the other hand, views the teacher as more of a "facilitator," building upon the student's existing knowledge. The two approaches imply different roles for the teacher. Instructional conversation emphasizes the teacher's role in facilitating and guiding student learning through extended verbal interactions, rather than emphasizing the direct delivery of instruction (Goldenberg, 1992, pp. 5–6).

The use of instructional conversation (IC) as a strategy in diverse classrooms is receiving more and more attention. Dalton and Sison (1995) have provided a fruitful analysis of this strategy in middle-school mathematics classrooms. Their work demonstrates how IC can be used to engage students in learning cognitively loaded concepts in geometry. IC always begins with interactions that address individual experiences regarding such concepts, without specifically or directly "teaching" them. This helps establish a "comfort zone" for further elaborations that extend beyond the personal experiences. This type of beginning allows all students to participate and develops a scaffold for structuring later conversations related to the instructional theme. It offers the teacher access to students' prior knowledge, including their linguistic and conceptual development.

IC and the "Comfort Zone"

Table 6.1	Characteristics of Direct Instruction and Instructional Conversation	
DIRECT INSTRUCTION	**INSTRUCTIONAL CONVERSATION**
Teacher models	Teacher facilitates
Exact, specific answers; skill directed	Draw from prior or background knowledge
Easier to evaluate	Many different ideas encouraged
Step-by-step systematic instruction	Build on information provided by students
Teacher centered	More student involvement
Guided and independent practice following instruction	Establish common foundation of understanding
No extensive discussion	Extensive discussion
Goal is mastery after each step	Fewer black-and-white responses
Check for understanding	Guided understanding

Source: Clarell Goldenberg, *Instructional conversations and their classroom application: Education practice report #2.* National Center for Research on Cultural Diversity and Second Language Learning, University of California, Santa Cruz. Copyright © 1992. Used with permission.

For example, a teacher who set out to teach the concepts of circumference and diameter began with a discussion of broader issues of space and objects in space, building on the students' knowledge base that was mostly generated by recent motion pictures or TV series. That discussion about space travel and planets, which was conducted in a conversational mode, led into talk about measuring the size of a planet and eventually to the concepts of circumference and diameter:

Teacher: How do you measure a planet?

Edgar: You can't measure a planet.

Teacher: You can't?

Daniel: Yeah.

Teacher: [to Edgar] No?

Luis: Yes you can?

Daniel: You can.

Teacher: How can you?

Luis: You can draw a circle.

Teacher: You can draw a circle? Is that the way to measure a planet?

Luis: Yeah.

Teacher: Explain to me what you mean by that?

Luis: You draw a circle and then you fold it like that?

Teacher: Uh-huh.

Luis: And you make a line in the middle. (Dalton & Sison, 1995, p. 9)

As this very informal conversation shows, IC strategy builds on the existing knowledge of the students, allows the students to engage the teacher and each other in an active way, and therefore leads to the parallel development of language and cognitive/academic content of relevance to the formal educational process.

As the preceding discussion suggests, a primary issue in determining the educational needs of linguistically and culturally diverse children is understanding instructional interaction. Children from different linguistic cultures will use language in ways that reflect their different social environments. As we saw in Chapter 5, an investigation of mother-child interaction in preschool instruction and free-play periods as well as the home showed that the mothers of bilingual children, and not the children themselves, generally initiated interactions, and that this was generally done in Spanish. On those few occasions when the children initiated discourse, their decision of what language to use was based on the topic (García, 1983a).

Elements of a Larger Understanding

A comprehensive understanding of instructional interaction must therefore take into consideration the linguistic and cognitive attributes of that interaction. It must consider the child's surrounding environment. Recent data tentatively suggest that social context will determine:

1. The specific linguistic and metalinguistic information important for the development of each language
2. The specific rules for social use of each language
3. The roles assigned to each language (García, 1986).

Table 6.2 provides a more fully elaborated vision of instructional discourse in terms of its instructional and conversational elements.

Instructional Discourse for Diverse Students. Tikunoff (1983), in the report of the Significant Bilingual Instructional Features Study (SBIF), also addressed the issue of language use in language minority classrooms. The 58 classrooms observed in the study were located in six school sites throughout the United States, where a variety of non-English languages were spoken. All the classrooms were considered effective on the basis of two criteria: (1) they were nominated by members of four constitu-

Table 6.2   Elements of Elaborated Instructional Discourse

INSTRUCTIONAL ELEMENTS

1. Thematic focus.

   The teacher selects a theme or idea to serve as a starting point for focusing the discussion and has a general plan for how the theme will unfold, including how to "chuck" the text to permit optimal exploration of the theme.

2. Activation and use of background and relevant schemata.

   The teacher either "hooks into" or provides students with pertinent background knowledge and relevant schemata necessary for understanding a text. Background knowledge and schemata are then woven into the discussion that follows.

3. Direct teaching.

   When necessary, the teacher provides direct teaching of a skill or concept.

4. Promoting more complex language and expression.

   The teacher elicits more extended student contributions by using a variety of elicitation techniques—e.g., questions, restatements, pauses, and invitations to expand.

5. Promoting bases for statements or positions.

   The teacher promotes students' use of text, pictures, and reasoning to support an argument or position. Without overwhelming students, the teacher probes for the bases of students' statements—e.g., "how do you know?" "what makes you think that?" "show us where it says ____."

CONVERSATIONAL ELEMENTS

6. Fewer "known-answer" questions.

   Much of the discussion centers on questions and answers for which there might be more than one correct answer.

7. Responsivity to student contributions.

   While having an initial plan and maintaining the focus and coherence of the discussion, the teacher is also responsive to students' statements and the opportunities they provide.

8. Connected discourse.

   The discussion is characterized by multiple, interactive, connected turns; succeeding utterances build upon previous ones.

9. A challenging, but nonthreatening atmosphere.

   The teacher creates a "zone of proximal development," where a challenging atmosphere is balanced by a positive affective climate. The teacher is more collaborator than evaluator and creates an atmosphere that challenges students and allows them to negotiate and construct the meaning of text.

10. General participation, including self-selected turns.

    The teacher encourages general participation among students. The teacher does not hold exclusive right to determine who talks, and students are encouraged to volunteer or otherwise influence the selection of speaking turns.

Source: Clarell Goldenberg, *Instructional conversations and their classroom application: Education practice report #2.* National Center for Research on Cultural Diversity and Second Language Learning, University of California, Santa Cruz. Copyright © 1992. Used with permission.

encies (teachers, other school personnel, students, and parents), and (2) classroom teachers were found to produce rates of academic learning time (a measure of student engagement on academic tasks) as high as or higher than those reported in other research on effective teaching.

Unique Instructional Features

Instructional features found to be unique to the education of language minority students included the use of two languages, special activities for teaching a second language, and teaching practices that took advantage of students' cultural background. According to the SBIF report, English was used approximately 60 percent of the time. Either the student's native language or a combination of the native language and English was used the rest of the time, with the percentage of English increasing with grade level. An additional significant instructional feature was the particular way in which the two languages were combined. Teachers of limited-English-proficient (LEP) students mediated instruction by using the students' native language and English for instruction, alternating between the two languages whenever necessary to ensure clarity of instruction. Moreover,

Integrative Approach

Tikunoff (1983) reports that students learned the language of instruction when engaged in instructional tasks expressed in that language. This integrative approach to developing English-language skills during ongoing instruction in the regular classroom contrasts with the more traditional procedure of "pull-out," in which LEP students leave the regular instructional setting to receive ESL instruction.

Influence of Classroom Practices

A study performed by Wong-Fillmore, Ammon, McLaughlin, and Ammon (1985) provides a detailed analysis of the influence of classroom practices on the development of oral English in language minority students of Hispanic and Chinese background. In this study, 17 language minority classrooms (13 third grade and 4 fourth grade) served as sites. In these classrooms either the native language and English or only English were used during instruction. The researchers obtained specific measures of English-language production and comprehension over the academic year. In addition, classroom observations documented the character of teacher-student and student-student interaction as well as the organizational features of instruction. These authors reported a series of potentially significant observations:

1. Instructional practices that were related to English-language development depended on the student's initial level of English proficiency. Therefore, instructional practices such as high levels of teacher and peer interaction were more related to enhanced English development for nonproficient speakers of English.

2. The instructional variables that were significant for the students differed. Students of Chinese background seemed to do best under classroom conditions in which they received independent help on English-language learning and in classrooms in which the instructional style was characterized by teacher-directed instruction. Students of Hispanic background demonstrated enhanced oral English-language development under classroom conditions in which there were more opportunities to interact with English-speaking peers.

In addition, these researchers reported that growth in English-language production and comprehension was related to several attributes of student-teacher interaction. Classrooms in which teachers adjusted the language level of their interaction based on student feedback were more likely to produce overall gains in English-language proficiency. Allowing and encouraging student participation and calling attention to the structure of language while using it were also characterized as instructional features that enhanced language development.

Effective Instructional Styles

García (1989) examined instructional interaction for linguistically and culturally diverse students under conditions identified as academically successful. Previous research has suggested a potential mismatch between the culture of the home and the culture of the school (Ramirez & Castaneda, 1974). Similarly, research has indicated potential discrepancies in interactional styles (Ramirez & Castaneda, 1974; Zentella, 1981). Specifically, García (1990a) examined instructional discourse in "effective" Hispanic classrooms. The study observed and analyzed the instructional styles of "effective" kindergarten, third-grade, and fifth-grade teachers of academically successful Hispanic (bilingual and nonbilingual) students. The results indicated that:

1. Teachers tended to provide an instructional initiation often reported in the literature. They elicited student responses but did so at cognitive and linguistic levels of relatively lower order.
2. However, once a teacher initiated a lesson, students were allowed to take control of the specific lesson topic and were able to invite interaction from fellow students.

Figure 6.1 diagrams the type of instructional discourse identified in this study, or student-dominated discourse, as compared to teacher-dominated discourse.

Student-Student Interaction

The finding that teachers were clearly allowing student-student interaction in the child-reply component of instructional discourse was considered significant. That is, the teacher was

BECOMING A RESPONSIVE TEACHER

A Tapestry of Interaction

The 32 seventh graders sit in a large circle on the floor. The teacher, who is sitting on the floor with them, begins:

Teacher: What I would like you to do is to look around and call on people to add to what you've said—anything that you left out or that people remember that you haven't said yet. . . .

LaWanda: Is this a thinking lesson?

Teacher: Ah, yes! Exactly. What I'd like you to do is think about your own thinking. That's exactly right.

[LaWanda raises her hand.]

Teacher: Go ahead.

LaWanda [calling on another student]: Elayne, what things does elephants has that is common to otters? Elephants and otters are—what does, what do they have in common?

Elayne: They both get hunted.

LaWanda: And?

Juan: Oh, they both need a lot of space.

LaWanda: What about your animal? The panda and the wolfs?

Marcus: They both need a lot of space. . . .

LaWanda: Is there anything [else] they have in common?

Marcus: They're running out of food.

LaWanda: Their habitats are being destroyed?

Marcus: Yeah....

LaWanda: And the bear group. Is, is, why is your bear becoming extinct? Yolanda?

Yolanda: They kill them for their fur.

Robert: They're used as a food source in China.

LaWanda: I know, you said they're using them for a food source. People eat them, right?

Robert: Right.

BECOMING A RESPONSIVE TEACHER *Cont.*

Teacher [forgetting to raise her hand]: It sounds like we need to—[LaWanda frowns, doesn't respond. The adult teacher raises her hand.]

[LaWanda calls on the adult teacher formally.]

Teacher: How do you know something is an animal?

LaWanda: Let's start with Juan. What do you think an animal is?

Juan: A creature that roams the earth.

LaWanda: Valencia?

Valencia: Anything that's alive, and breathing. Like plants aren't really animals. They're alive and everything, but they're not really animals. They can't walk around or do anything. They just sit there.

LaWanda: How do you know something is an animal? Marcus?

Marcus: Anything like mammals, reptile, amphibians, fish, even a virus are animals.

LaWanda: Can you explain what a virus is?

Marcus: Actually, yes. But I'm sorry, a virus is not a living thing. But animals can be microscopic.

LaWanda: Darius?

Darius: . . . People are animals. Bugs, forest animals, every living thing is an animal. Plants are like animals. Every living thing is an animal . . . .

LaWanda: I have a question. You say almost everything is an animal. Why do you say that?

Kaylan: Not human beings.

Darius: Every human being is an animal.

LaWanda: Which way do you mean? 'Cause of behavior?

Darius: Because they're living things, and living things are animals.

Teacher: Let's think about this for a minute. It sounds like everybody would agree that all animals are living things. Turning that around, are all living things animals? What living things are not animals?

LaWanda: [to teacher] Did you raise your hand? [To Chakita, who

had gone to get a dictionary] Say it.

Chakita: [reading from dictionary] *Animal . . . any living being that can move about by itself, has sense organs, and does not make its own food as plants do.*

BECOMING A RESPONSIVE TEACHER *Cont.*

▼ Meeting the Challenge

1. Reflect on your own experience as a student in U.S. elementary and secondary school classrooms. Does it match the version of American education portrayed above? If not, how does it differ, and what is the significance of that difference? What are these students being encouraged to learn that you may not have been?

2. Is this transcript an example of instructional discourse or direct instruction? Point out moments of interaction that suggest one or the other. Use Tables 6.1 and 6.2 for reference.

3. As the teacher of a fourth-grade class, devise a list of open-ended questions for discussion (versus fill-in-the-blank or known-answer questions). You may select any content field, such as language arts, math, science, social studies, and so on.

4. Develop a writing activity to engage the students portrayed in the above transcript. Be sure to take into consideration the emphasis put on social interaction in this classroom.

Figure 6.1 ▼ **Lesson Discourse Styles**

much more inviting of a student's "call" for peer response once the instructional interaction was set in motion. This finding is particularly important considering what we know about linguistic and cognitive processes. García (1983b) and Goldenberg (1993) have suggested that discourse strategies that emphasize student-student interaction are important to enhanced linguistic development. Moreover, McClintock, Bayard, and McClintock (1983) and Kagan (1983a) have argued that schooling practices that focus on cooperative child-child instructional strategies are in line with social motives in some Mexican American families. Such a style of instructional discourse would be of linguistic and cultural benefit to Mexican American students.

Student Writing Development

Like oral language, writing is crucial in schooling endeavors. As in all other areas of meaning-making, children first attempt to manipulate written symbols during familiar, manageable activities. Children may continue just to write letters or to use cursive writing (e.g., when writing stories or extended texts in dramatic play), but attempt more precise encoding when writing smaller units, especially names (Ferreiro, 1988; Miramontes, Nadeau, & Commins, 1997). While such labeling can occur as part of dramatic play, naming is itself an activity of great interest to many young children and one in which they will invest considerable intellectual energy, especially if they are in the company of interested adults and peers.

Initially children's written names do not represent spoken words. Instead, they are letters that belong to certain people or things. That is, rather than trying to encode speech into graphics,

Naming

children typically make meaningful graphics about what they say (e.g., "This is my Mama's name") (Dyson, 1983). Just as speech helps to organize and elaborate on the meaning of early drawn objects, so too it aids the early writing of names. For children, in fact, names are types of objects; they belong to people and things (Ferreiro & Teberosky, 1982).

Many publications describe for teachers the "developmental stages of writing," which progress from child scribbles to invented spelling. It is important to remind ourselves that these sorts of observations about children's writing are based on attention to superficial manifestations of development, not to the complicated process of representation. There is no linear progression in cognitive development, or in the development of oral and written language. Development is linked in complex ways to the whole of children's symbolic repertoires. Its evolution involves shifts of function, symbolic form, and social give-and-take as children explore and gradually control new ways to organize and represent their world and to interact with other people about that world.

Symbolic Repertoires

Putting writing in its symbolic place—seeing its emergence within the student's total symbolic repertoire—suggests, first, that in the early years children need many opportunities to use the arts freely: to draw, play, dance, and sing. For young children, the most accessible media are those that most directly capture the movements of their own bodies, the sounds of their own voices, and the images made by their own hands, as lines, curves, and colors take form on paper. This teaching strategy requires a knowledge base of the child's language and culture.

First-grade teacher Karen Gallas (1991) describes an instructional unit on insects and their life cycles, beautifully detailing how drawing, painting, music, movement, drama, poetry, and storytelling, "separately and together, became part of [the children's] total repertoire as learners" (p. 42). In a classroom in which cultural, social, and language barriers might have kept children apart, use of the arts allowed individuals many avenues for learning, expression, and communication. Some children sketched insects, focusing on visual details, while others dramatized the life cycle of an insect, using their bodies to capture the changing shapes of life. Still others drew grass as seen from the perspective of an insect. New intelligences, in Gardner's (1985) sense, were visible as children forged new understandings through colorful images and felt movements, understandings that will surely enrich each child's later experience with print as a reader and a writer.

The curious world and the students themselves should be the center of the curriculum, not the "steps" in writing or reading.

Literacy as a Tool

Indeed, making literacy the center of the curriculum may prevent reading and writing from becoming the dynamic, colorful intellectual and social tools they should be. Teachers must help connect print with the liveliness of students' use of other symbolic forms. In a series of books on her own classroom life with children, Paley (e.g., 1981, 1986) has illustrated how elementary students can collaboratively transform themes in their own lives into dictated texts, elaborated texts, and dramas. For many students, dictated words did not sufficiently represent the action, and they needed to share the action through media of their own voices and movements. Transforming their own texts into dramas allows students and teachers opportunities to find words for unarticulated ideas and previously unknown cultural representation of those ideas.

Importance of Reflection

Children's interweaving of language, culture, and thinking does pose developmental challenges, as eventually children must differentiate and gain control over the unique interactive powers of these domains. Therefore, it is important to talk to students about their expressive efforts and in this way to help them reflect upon their development. Indeed, many educators consider spending such reflective moments with a student discussing his or her ways of talking, playing, and writing to be an important means of supporting the student's development. What aspects of a student's imagined world are in the pictures? the print? in dramatized action? Which are still unarticulated, waiting for an interested other to help give them shape? At the same time, students must be allowed to remain in charge of their own intentions (Genishi & Dyson, 1984). Children feel no compulsion to put into written words the meanings they express through acting and talking. Their differentiation and control of these varied media are a gradual developmental process, one we nurture but cannot force.

Control of Written Symbols

In summary, the complexity of development is linked to the whole of children's symbolic repertoire. Unlike oral language, written language involves the use of a deliberately controlled system of symbols to mediate activity. An adult or an older student writing a letter is substituting written communication for the opportunity to speak in person to another individual. A student, however, who says she is pretending to write a letter may not be using written language to mediate her activity. To use Halliday's (1973) terms, the student may be showing an awareness of the interactional function of literacy, but the letter is fulfilling an imaginary as much as an interactional function. For some students whose native language is not written, such an act is quite revolutionary. It is more prop than mediator. To understand truly how development occurs, it would be necessary to understand how the child attempts to write the letter, the role of letter-writing in the child's social activity, the role of other media in the accomplishment of the letter-writing, and how the child's interaction with other people and with other media changes over time, as writing is transformed from primarily a prop to a mediator.

Both to understand and to foster written language development, we must view that development within the particularities of children's social lives. Indeed, we as adult writers may turn to media that seem to fit most comfortably the initial contours of our ideas before struggling to craft those ideas within the linear confines of print: we may draw, map, make gestures in the air, or even scrawl conversational language across a page. Written language emerges most strongly when it is firmly embedded within the supportive symbolic sea of gestures, pictures, and talk—that is, put simply, when it is embedded in our cultures.

Conclusion

This chapter has attempted to highlight theory and related educational practices that provide a broad understanding of issues of importance to the schooling of diverse student populations: language, culture, and cognition. As indicated, the knowledge base in this area continues to expand, and it is in no way to be considered comprehensive as yet. Also, it would be an error to conclude that the data and theory that have emerged have been used as a primary basis in determining the educational treatment of these students. Too often, the education of these students has been determined instead by "political" variables (Hakuta & García, 1989). However, we can identify possible program and policy implications derived from research and theory highlighted by the foregoing discussion and by other previous reviews, such as August and García (1988); August and Hakuta (1997); Cazden (1988); Goldenberg and Gallimore (1991a); Hakuta (1986); Hakuta and García (1989); Hakuta and Snow (1986); Tharp (1989); Tharp and Gallimore (1988); and Wong-Fillmore and Valadez (1985). This research suggests that:

1. One major goal regarding the education of culturally diverse students should be the development of the full repertoire of language, literacy, and cognitive skills.
2. For non-English speakers, time spent learning the native language is not time lost in developing cognitive and academic skills. Children can become cognitively competent best by

building on previous language and cultural experiences and representations.

3. There is no cognitive cost to the development of multilingualism in children. Very possibly, bilingualism enhances children's thinking skills.

4. Education programs should be flexible enough to adjust to individual and cultural differences among children, particularly in the development of expected cognitive literacy domains.

We have seen that the linguistic, cognitive, and social character of the child develop simultaneously and that linguistic, cognitive, and social development are interrelated. Cognitive factors may act to influence linguistic and social development. Linguistic development (the ability to operate within the structural and pragmatic aspects of languages) may in turn act to influence social and potential cognitive functioning. The development of social competence directly influences the acquisition of linguistic and cognitive repertoires.

Figure 6.2 presents a model of the interactions among language, cognition, and culture as children develop. This interactive model is not meant to provide a definitive description of human development but simply to reflect the integrated nature of linguistic, social, and cognitive factors in learning. Changes in each of these domains may be attributed to changes in other domains, and in turn may further alter the character of the individual child. This and other similar conceptualizations of integrated development should guide our instructional efforts for all children, but they are particularly important as a foundation for enhancing the cognitive development of our diverse student populations.

Figure 6.2 ▼ **A General Integrative Model of Language, Cognition, and Culture**

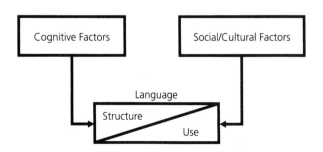

SUMMARY OF MAJOR IDEAS

1. The human mind is a library of symbols shaped by inherited mental structures and by representations of the world that come from our own individual experiences. The cognitive processes by which we acquire knowledge develop in conjunction with language background and sociocultural factors. To be effective, teaching and learning practices must consider the interactions of language, culture, and cognition.

2. Sociocultural theory is an international intellectual movement that draws on ideas from psychology, semiotics, education, sociology, and anthropology in what has been called a constructivist perspective. Recent work in this area seeks a unified way of understanding language, cognition, culture, human development, teaching, and learning. Proponents of this theoretical perspective claim that the psychology of the individual learner is deeply shaped by social activity and that knowledge is always constructed in a social context. In this view, learning occurs in an interaction between individuals and an embedding context.

3. Because children use language in a sociocultural context to construct meaning, language and culture function as significant tools for cognitive development. Children whose language and culture do not match those of the schools are usually forced to adjust their schema (their mental frameworks for understanding the world) or to construct new schema. Such negation of a child's language and culture also negates the child's cognitive tools and can seriously hinder cognitive development.

4. Contextualized language relies on more abstract linguistic and cognitive cues. Proficiency in the use of decontextualized language takes longer to achieve and is usually considered indicative of academic success. Limiting opportunities for children to learn in their first language may prevent them from developing the proficiency in decontextualized language required for academic achievement and for literacy.

5. Intelligence is generally defined as the ability of an individual's mind to acquire and apply knowledge. The traditional notion of intelligence presumes that it is an inherited intellectual capacity that can be measured by a test. Research into test bias over the past few decades has identified serious concerns about using intelligence tests to determine the intellectual capacity of culturally diverse students.

6. Research indicates that bilingual language ability may correlate with increased cognitive flexibility and metalinguistic awareness in children. Multilingualism should no longer be considered a cognitive and psychological liability in educational settings.

7. Effective teaching in culturally diverse classrooms involves organizing oral and literacy activities that develop students' communicative and cognitive abilities. Instructional discourse, or instructional conversation, is a teaching strategy that emphasizes discussion in the classroom. Compared to the didactic character of most formal teaching, it is structured to take advantage of natural and spontaneous interactions between teacher and students and among students.

8. In direct instruction as an approach to teaching and learning, the teacher transmits knowledge to students through modeling and step-by-step instructions. In instructional conversation, the teacher acts as a facilitator, building on students' existing knowledge and guiding learning.

9. Children from different language cultures will use language in ways that reflect their different social environments. Research indicates that effective instruction of language minority students includes the use of two languages in the classroom, special activities for teaching a second language, and teaching practices that take advantage of students' cultural backgrounds. Discourse strategies that emphasize student-student interactions, rather than solely teacher-student interactions, may also enhance linguistic development.

10. As for oral language, student development in the use of written language is likewise tied to language and sociocultural factors. Unlike oral language, however, using written language requires children to control a highly abstract system of symbols. To help children develop literacy as a social and intellectual tool, teachers must connect the student's use of print with other, more concrete symbolic forms such as physical movement and oral language.

EXTENDING YOUR EXPERIENCE

1. Describe the approaches used by a teacher who is a "transmitter" and a teacher who is a "facilitator," and explain how these approaches differ. Have you had both types of teachers

in your student career? Select two teachers who adopted contrasting approaches and describe your experience as a learner with each one. Remember to consider "teachers" you may have had outside the formal school environment, such music or art instructors and sports coaches.

2. As this chapter points out, sociocultural theorists argue that knowledge is not a fixed set of ideas passed from teacher to student but is created in the social interaction between teacher and student. What do you make of this claim? Do you agree or disagree? Note down the reasons for your position and discuss them in class.

3. Interview a psychology professor on your campus or a few friends who are majoring in psychology. Ask them to define the term "cognition" for you and to explain what they have learned about this concept. Then ask them to do the same with the term "intelligence." Only after you have recorded all their comments, refer to a dictionary or encyclopedia and note the definitions given there. Report the results of your investigation to your classmates.

4. This chapter quotes research showing that children use their ability in their first language as a tool in learning how to think. What are the implications of this research for the education of language minority students, whose first language is not English?

5. What do you consider to be the goals of education? List at least three and be prepared to discuss them in class.

6. What patterns of social interaction do you expect to encounter in your own educational experiences? Think back over your past and present classroom experiences as a learner. Would you characterize your interactions as mainly teacher-student or student-student? Has this pattern of interaction shaped how and what you learn? in what way?

RESOURCES FOR FURTHER STUDY

Collier, V. (1995). Acquiring a second language for school. In National Clearinghouse for Bilingual Education (Ed.), *Directions in Language and Education*, 1(4). [on-line]. Available: National Clearinghouse for Bilingual Education, Washington, DC, at http://www.ncbe.gwu.edu/.

This article details ongoing research related to the complexities associated with second-language acquisition in education contexts.

The author elaborates on the thesis that the acquisition of a second language in schools is not merely a linguistic enterprise. Instead, it involves cognitive "loads" that are related to content learning in science, mathematics, and so on. With this form of second-language acquisition, students need extended periods of time as well as structural experiences in order to achieve a high level of proficiency.

Diaz, R. M., & Klinger, C. (1991). Towards an explanatory model of the interaction between bilingualism and cognitive development. In E. Bialystok (Ed.), *Language processing in bilingual children* (pp. 140–185). New York: Cambridge University Press.

This article is part of a volume that reports research into basic processes in language acquisition and use for bilingual students. The aim of the book is to describe the acquisition and development of a second language and to explain how such processes affect language awareness. In particular, the authors revisit the old issue of the impact bilingualism has on intelligence. Ultimately they conclude that in order to substantiate the relationship, more detailed research needs to be done. The theoretical foundation for this essay is directly associated with Vygotsky's work, with a minor twist.

Duquette, G. (1991). Cultural processing and minority language children with needs and special needs. In G. Duquette & L. Malave (Eds.), *Language, culture, and cognition* (pp. 115–135). Philadelphia: Multilingual Matters.

This publication is a collection of recent research findings on topics that have generated more discussion of bilingualism and multiculturalism. Presenting an array of perspectives, the work lacks in-depth discussion of any single topic but does provide up-and-coming concepts and instructional approaches in the education of language minority students. Seventeen chapters are divided into three areas that deal with the cognitive process, the nature and role of language in culture, and aspects of teaching and learning. Taken together, all of these essays critically analyze and interpret how bilinguals acquire knowledge and develop academically.

Kagan, S. (1983). Social orientation among Mexican-American children: A challenge to traditional classroom structures. In E. García (Ed.), *The Mexican-American child* (pp. 163–182). Tempe: Arizona State University.

The competitive atmosphere that Mexican American students face in American schools runs contradictory to these students' cooperative nature. Such opposition has detrimental effects on most children who cannot understand the differences between the comfortable home and the competitive institution. Kagan offers some disheartening figures to argue that the educational system is set up to fail Mexican American students. To counter such a record, Kagan discusses how Mexican American students can succeed when their classroom experiences fall within their cultural boundaries.

Tharp, R., & Gallimore, R. (1988). *Rousing minds to life: Teaching, learning, and schooling in social context.* Cambridge: Cambridge University Press.

This book is considered a new and important contribution to the arena of multicultural education. It offers an improved model to advance the teaching and learning process. Using Vygotsky's theory, the authors present a series of educational concepts and discuss their impact and development in everyday interaction. One chapter examines the theory of teaching and the development of skills to improve teaching. The book centers mainly on the Kamehameha Elementary Education Program (KEEP) and explains how theory and practice developed this project into an exemplary model. It emphasizes the importance of education to society and stresses that the connection between theory and practice must be strengthened to ensure that future generations of students receive the best education possible.

Additional information can also be found on the following World Wide Web sites:

http://www.ncbe.gwu.edu

Funded by the U.S. Department of Education, Office of Bilingual Education and Minority Language Affairs (http://www.ed.gov/offices/OBEMLA), and operated by The George Washington University Graduate School of Education and Human Development, Center for the Study of Language and Education, in Washington, DC, this Web site brings together research and practice in an organized and accessible manner. It is a clearinghouse of information specific to research, classroom instruction, student assessment, teacher training, program development, and grant applications. The NCBE (National Clearinghouse for Bilingual Education) Web site also offers an online library that contains over 300 full-length articles, reports, guides, and other documents on topics related to school reform, student diversity, language, parental and family involvement, and instruction. Supplementing this information are resources that are available from teachers and administrators, such as lesson plans and discussions regarding practices. The Web site serves as a link to other Web sites that would also be helpful in your search.

http://www.stolaf.edu/network/iecc

Intercultural E-Mail Classroom Connections (IECC), for students in K–12 and college.

THE

EDUCATIONAL

RESPONSE

W hereas Parts One and Two of this book focused on the context and roots of diversity in American schools, Part Three centers on the practical side of teaching and learning.

Chapter 7 addresses the current system of professional preparation and assessment, outlines recent changes in teacher preparation programs, and traces the dimensions that define what it is to be an "effective teacher." In addition to discussing school reform, Chapter 8 offers an in-depth examination of "effective" schools and instructional practices, including specific case studies. Chapter 9 begins with this author's account of his own schooling, using it to introduce a discussion of school improvement, especially middle school and high school efforts in literacy, mathematics, and English language development.

THE EFFECTIVE

TEACHER:

PREPARATION,

ASSESSMENT, AND

CHARACTERISTICS

CHAPTER 7

Focus Questions

▼ How are teachers of culturally and linguistically diverse students currently prepared in the United States, and what institutions are responsible for assessing their competence?

▼ What are the patterns in state credentialing available for teachers of bilingual education and English as a second language?

▼ How have teacher preparation programs changed recently?

▼ What are some of the competencies, roles, and responsibilities of effective teachers of language minority students?

▼ How has the connoisseur model been implemented in at least one local school district to further the professional development of inservice teachers?

▼ What types knowledge, skill, disposition, and affect characterize effective teachers?

▼ How can schools and classrooms adopt useful strategies to serve culturally and linguistically diverse students effectively?

"You are the giver of a lifelong gift. An impulse; an enduring tool; a prolific engine called learning. The infectious transfer of enthusiasm."

—F. X. TRUJILLO

A typical teacher, looking at the students in the classroom, sees a picture much different from the classroom of her or his childhood. Today one in three children nationwide is from an ethnic or racial minority group, one in seven speaks a language other than English at home, and one in 15 was born outside the United States. The linguistic and cultural diversity of America's school population has increased dramatically during the past decade, and it is expected to increase even more in the future. The concept of "minority" group will soon become obsolete, because no group will be in a majority status.

Educating children from immigrant and ethnic minority group families is a major concern of school systems across the country. Please remember that for many of these children, American education is not a successful experience. While one-tenth of non-Hispanic white students leave school without a diploma, one-fourth of African Americans, one-third of Hispanics, one-half of Native Americans, and two-thirds of immigrant students drop out of school.

Confronted with this dismal reality, teachers, administrators, and parents urge each other to do something different—change teaching methods, adopt new curricula, allocate more funding. Such actions might be needed, but they all will be meaningless unless we begin to think differently about these students. In order to educate them, we must first educate ourselves about who they are and what they need to succeed. Thinking differently involves viewing these students in new ways that may contradict conventional notions.

As this country and the world shrink communicatively, economically, and culturally, our diversity becomes more visible and harder to hide. But it always has been and always will be there. Our schools will need to address it more than they have in the past, and of specific importance will be how our teachers, administrators, and parents help us address it successfully. Please recall that at the core of this success are two pivotal values for any professional serving a growing culturally diverse population:

To honor diversity is to honor the social complexity in which we live—to give integrity to the individual and to where he or she comes from.

To unify is absolutely necessary, but to insist upon it without embracing diversity is to destroy that which will allow us to unite—individual and collective dignity.

This chapter discusses effective teachers. We assume that who does the teaching is of major importance regardless of the educational model being implemented. We will extend our understanding of this basic idea by cautiously but directly addressing the development, assessment, and specific attributes of "effective" teachers who serve diverse student populations. We will look closely at credentialing policies and analyze their political and empirical underpinnings. We will also examine the attributes of effective principals, to see how these school leaders help establish a fruitful setting for teaching and learning. The overall purpose of this chapter is to suggest ways of enhancing the education of culturally diverse students by focusing on the educational professionals who serve them every day.

The Current System of Professional Preparation and Assessment

Professional preparation and assessment of teachers who serve culturally diverse students are problematic, complex, and cumbersome processes. It is an area ripe for criticism. A variety of programmatic efforts have been developed in response to the growing number of culturally diverse students in the U.S. schools, but it has become evident that professional preparation, particularly for teachers, has not kept pace with the demand for educational personnel who are specifically trained to implement these new programs. The following discussion provides an overview of the preparation and credentialing of educators and builds a foundation for understanding the relevant issues.

Teachers Are Professionals   In our society, teaching is considered a profession. A **profession** is characterized by two general features (Friedson, 1986): (1) acquisition of knowledge obtained through formal education endeavors; and (2) an orientation toward serving the needs of the public, with particular emphasis on an ethical, altruistic concern for the client. Practices for preparing and judging the competence of professionals have always been embedded in a local time and place, in line with generally accepted concepts and purposes—the profession's Zeitgeist. Thus, educational endeavors and assessments of professional educators, usually called teaching credentials, develop in concert with the general intellectual and ethical climate and needs of the time (McGahie, 1991).

Our present concerns about teaching credentials are derived from the ethical considerations of our time and the pressing need to prepare competent teachers to serve diverse student populations. As it stands, the training and assessment of educators are functions performed by the states or by professional societies, or by some combination of these institutions. Typically, the focus is on assessing either (1) the individual as a preprofessional (usually through an examination such as the National Teaching Exam) before allowing him or her to enter the profession or (2) the professional institutions and programs that produce teaching professionals (the National Council of American Teacher Educators [NCATE] Reviews are an example of such a review by an association, and the California Commission on Teaching Credentialing Program Reviews are an example of state-authorized reviews). In some cases, both individual and program reviews are required.

Types of Assessment

Professional Credentialing of Teachers

It is important to note that professional preparation for teachers of linguistically and culturally diverse students is a relatively new enterprise. Not until the mid-1960s did substantial educational initiatives exist in this specialized arena, and not until 1974 did the U.S. Congress authorize resources for institutions of higher education to use in teacher education (August & García, 1988). The recent nature of this innovation, much like similar developments in the field of special education, has spawned many new programs in teacher preparation that are still struggling to establish themselves alongside long-standing programs in elementary and secondary education. These new programs tend to have a more complicated content with a more multidisciplinary perspective. Such teacher preparation programs must be concerned not only with subject matter and pedagogy but also much more directly with language, culture, and instructional practices.

Need for Bilingual Teachers

The 1980–1982 Teachers Language Skills Survey identified the need for 100,000 bilingual teachers in the U.S. schools. This figure was based on the number of schools in which limited-English-proficient students from one language background were sufficiently concentrated to make bilingual programs feasible. Compare this finding with reality: in 1982, there were an estimated 27,000 to 32,000 bilingual teachers, which means 68,000 to 73,000 more were needed. A total of 168 institutions of higher education graduate approximately 2,000 to 2,600 trained bilingual teachers each year, which means the shortage will continue for some time. Furthermore, the Teachers Language Skills Survey reported that of 103,000 teachers assigned to teach English as a Second Language (ESL), only 40 percent had received any preparation in the methods of doing so. It is estimated that at least 350,000 teachers currently need such specialized preparation (O'Malley, 1981; Waggoner, 1984). Most unfortunately, the preparation of credentialed teachers of language minority students proceeds at a snail's pace. In 1994, the U.S. General Accounting Office (U.S. G.A.O., 1994) estimated a shortage nationally of some 175,000 teachers. Yet over 3 million children in the United States coming to their first day of school are from homes in which English is not the primary language. As is the case for the preparation and credentialing of "regular" teachers, the credentialing of teachers whose main function is the education of linguistically and culturally diverse students is quite variable.

Availability of Credentials

Twenty-five states and territories presently offer no professional credentialing for teachers of culturally diverse students. Half of the country does not produce a specific teaching credential, even though 20 percent of U.S. students might require such specially prepared teachers. It is not coincidental that those states least affected as yet by increases in the population of language minority students are in this group. Keep in mind that all states require some type of certification of teaching professionals in the public schools.

California, Florida, Illinois, New York, New Jersey, and Texas are home to almost two-thirds of this nation's language minority students. In these states, teacher credentialing in bilingual education, language development, and ESL or in some other related area is available. Four of these six states now mandate professional credentialing (California, Illinois, New Jersey, and Texas).

Uneven Progress

Therefore, in states that are greatly affected by growing numbers of language minority students, concern for professional teaching standards is developing, but the progress has been uneven. Valencia (1991) has suggested that because of the segregation of language minority students, particularly Chicano students in the Southwest, state school systems often do not feel the full impact of these students. Chicano students, for example, tend to be concentrated in a few school districts within the state, and even though their academic presence is felt strongly by these individual districts, this same pressure is not exerted statewide.

Even for those 25 states that either mandate or permit credentialing for teachers of culturally and linguistically diverse students, the present modes of assessment are highly problematic. As we saw in Chapter 1, present methods of professional assessment can be criticized in several ways (McGahie, 1991; Shimberg, 1983; Sternberg & Wagner, 1986):

1. Professional competence evaluations usually address only a narrow range of practice situations.
2. Professional competence evaluations are biased toward assessing formally acquired knowledge, rather than what the teacher can do in a classroom.
3. Almost no attention is given to the "disposition," "affective," and "commitment" domains of teacher behavior, which have been identified as being as significant as content knowledge and practice skills (Pease-Alvarez, Espinoza, & García, 1991).

We also saw that professional assessment instruments are subject to severe violations of reliability and validity (Berk, 1986; Feldt & Brennan, 1989).

Connoisseur Model

In Chapter 1 we also introduced the concept of assessment by "connoisseur." According to McGahie (1991), teacher assessment operates within the connoisseur model of professional assessment, which presumes that (1) not all professional practices can be quantified, (2) a professional problem or question may have more than one answer, and (3) practicing teachers are the most effective evaluators of teachers in training. As the need for more teachers who can effectively serve diverse student populations grows, the need to develop and assess the competence of these professionals will be of critical importance.

Recommended Competencies for Teachers of Linguistically Diverse Students

Methods of assessment aside, what skills should teachers of linguistically and culturally students have? All teacher preparation programs must identify as the desired goal of their efforts some set of performance competencies imparted to teachers. The literature abounds with numerous listings of such competencies (Collier, 1985; National Association of Bilingual Education, 1992; National Board of Professional Teaching Standards, 1996). The most recent and most detailed is presented by Chu and Levy (1988). Their list of competencies is derived from a review of federally and nonfederally supported teacher preparation programs presently operating within U.S. universities. It focuses on some 34 intercultural competencies, no small number, that serve as a foundation for the success of a well-prepared teacher of linguistically diverse students. These competencies cover the instructor's knowledge in three areas: educational theory, social trends, and classroom strategies.

Lists of Competencies

The most widely distributed list of teacher competencies to be used for credentialing was developed and published in 1984 by the National Association of State Directors of Teacher Education and Certification (NASDTEC). That list, presented in an abbreviated format in Table 7.1, resulted from combining previous competency lists developed by the Center for Applied Linguistics in 1974 and the Teachers of English to Speakers of Other Languages Association in 1975. Although not as comprehensive as the Chu and Levy (1988) list, it has served as a cornerstone of teacher preparation programs and credentialing analysis in the United States.

State Handbook

Recently, states and school districts have begun to articulate the expected roles and responsibilities of teachers of language minority students. One such effort is the handbook of the New Jersey State Board of Education (1991), which is summarized below.

Role of Bilingual Teachers. According to the New Jersey State Board of Education (1991), the bilingual teacher should:

▼ Help identify limited English proficient students
▼ Communicate with other teachers in planning for the teaching of bilingual programs that meet the needs of eligible students
▼ Communicate with ESL and other teachers in planning for the bilingual program students in ESL and special subject areas

Table 7.1 NASDTEC Certification Standards: Competencies Required for Teachers of Language Minority Students*

IN BILINGUAL/MULTICULTURAL EDUCATION (B/M ED)	POSSIBLE UNIVERSITY OFFERINGS
1. Proficiency in L1 and L2 for effective teaching	Foreign language and English department courses
2. Knowledge of history and cultures of L1 and L2 speakers	Cross-cultural studies, multicultural education (ME), history and civilization, literature, ethnic studies
3. Historical, philosophical, and legal bases for B/M ED and related research	Foundations of Bilingual Education (BE) (or introduction to BE)
4. Organizational models for programs and classrooms in B/M ED	Foundations of BE
5. L2 methods of teaching (including ESL methodology)	Methods of teaching a second language
6. Communication with students, parents, and others in culturally and linguistically different communities	Cross-cultural studies, ME, school/community relations
7. Differences between L1 and L2; language and dialect differences across geographic regions, ethnic groups, social levels	Sociolinguistics, bilingualism

IN ENGLISH FOR SPEAKERS OF OTHER LANGUAGES	POSSIBLE UNIVERSITY OFFERINGS
1. Nature of language, language varieties, structure of English language	General linguistics; English phonology, morphology, and syntax
2. Demonstrated proficiency in spoken and written English	English department courses
3. Demonstrated proficiency in a second language	Foreign language courses
4. L1 and L2 acquisition process	Language acquisition
5. Effects of sociocultural variables on language learning	Language acquisition, ME, cross-cultural studies, sociolinguistics
6. Language assessment, program development, implementation, and evaluation	Language assessment, program development, and evaluation

*Supplemental to the standards required for *all* teachers.
Source: National Association of State Directors of Teacher Education and Certification, 1984.

▼ Provide input in areas covered by pupil personnel services
▼ Apply current research findings regarding the education of children from diverse cultural and linguistic backgrounds
▼ Develop language proficiency in the native language of the students enrolled in the program and in English
▼ Have knowledge of techniques, strategies, and materials that aid teaching in the two languages

▼ Structure the use of the two languages to systematically make the transition from the native language to English
▼ Select activities and materials for classroom use which indicate an understanding of the developmental level of the students
▼ Help students to identify similarities and differences for successful interaction in a cross-cultural setting
▼ Provide experiences that encourage positive student self-concept
▼ Promote and understand the supportive role and responsibilities of parents/guardians and explain the bilingual program to them.

Role of ESL Teachers. The handbook of the New Jersey State Board of Education (1991) states that the ESL teacher should:

▼ Help identify limited English proficient students
▼ Participate with administrators in designing an ESL program that meets the needs of eligible students
▼ Communicate with other teachers in planning for the teaching of the ESL student in the bilingual or English-only classroom
▼ Demonstrate awareness of current trends in ESL and bilingual education
▼ Demonstrate proficiency in English commensurate with the role of a language model
▼ Use English as the principal medium of instruction in the areas of pronunciation, listening, comprehension, speaking, structure, reading, and writing
▼ Select activities and materials for ESL use that indicate an understanding of the language proficiency level of the students
▼ Express interest in and have an understanding of the native culture of the students
▼ Provide experiences that encourage positive student self-concept
▼ Promote and understand the supportive role and responsibilities of parents/guardians and explain the ESL program to them.

Preparing teachers of culturally and linguistically diverse students remains an innovative process. Assessment and credentialing of these teachers are new areas of research inquiry. We have no time-tested methods and specific educational results to direct us. The connoisseur model, however, holds great promise.

Changes in Teacher Preparation Programs

Leighton, Hightower, and Wrigley (1993) provide a well-articulated overview of teacher preparation programs for individuals with a particular interest in serving linguistically and culturally diverse students. In general, many of these programs are still in the development stages. None has the mature position or the national visibility that comes with long-standing status (Delpit, 1995; Grant & Secada, 1990; Ladson-Billings, 1994). Most programs designed for training teachers of culturally and linguistically diverse students are built around research findings that point to effective instructional strategies. Few of the people running these programs have thoroughly analyzed their own training efforts (August & Hakuta, 1997). Almost all these programs of teacher preparation, however, do address the issues of content integration, knowledge construction, prejudice reduction, equity, and empowerment of the school community (Banks, 1993b; Ladson-Billings, 1994).

Developing Programs

Factors to Address

According to Delpit (1995), five factors must be addressed in preparing teachers of culturally and linguistically diverse students:

1. Issues of power enacted in the classroom.
2. Codes or rules for participating in power.
3. Realization that the rules of power are those of the individuals in power.
4. Clarification of the rules of power to those who do not have power.
5. Recognition that those in power are the least aware of power and that those without power are most aware of it.

Simply put, if teachers continue to be prepared as they were in the past, the power will remain in exactly the same places, which very likely will mean that the status quo will be maintained and that culturally and linguistically diverse students will suffer the consequences.

Shift to Site-Based Training

Because of the need for changes in the way teachers of culturally and linguistically diverse students are prepared, the recent trend has been to withdraw many of the training activities from the standard "college of education" framework, in which a prospective teacher typically takes theory courses from professors and then does supervised teaching at a school site. Instead, the new programs have moved a greater proportion of teacher preparation to the school site itself (Leighton, Russo, & Hightower, 1993; Milk, Mercado, & Sapiens, 1992). For example, Calderón (1994) reports on a large-scale effort to train teachers in bilingual settings. Professors teach in the school in which the student teachers are working, so that the student teachers receive most of their own instruction at the school site. The professors attempt to make direct connections between daily classroom activity and the conceptual understandings that are usually discussed in formal teacher preparation courses. Similarly, the Latino Teacher Education Project (Genzuk & Hentschke, 1992) has developed a school-based program to train paraeducators, individuals from the school community who are initially hired as instructional aides. In Los Angeles, this program is an example of the "grow-your-own" philosophy. Besides allowing members of the target community to move from the status of nonprofessional instructor to professional teacher, the program preserves and makes use of their expertise in the local cultures and languages. It also promotes stability in the local teaching force.

Training at the School Site

Similarly, local school districts have implemented extensive professional development programs for existing teachers to increase the linguistic expertise of their teaching personnel. One such program, in Denver, exemplifies such professional development activity. This urban district, which serves a diverse population of Hispanic, African American, and Southeast Asian students, determined that its needs could be partially met by the professional development of its existing teaching staff. The plan had several key features:

Denver Inservice Program

1. The program developers believed that teachers needed both theoretical grounding and opportunities to apply theory practically in instructional settings.
2. External consultants with expertise would work collaboratively with a cadre of local teachers over an extended period (four to six years).
3. A local group of teachers demonstrating enhanced expertise would provide mentor support to their colleagues.
4. Development of new mentor groups at individual school sites would ensure the systematic augmentation of expertise throughout the district.

The school district also developed its own credentialing requirements, since state requirements were not responsive to the local needs. Over 500 district teachers participated in this preparation from the mid-1980s through the late 1980s. Significant gains in service delivery to Denver's growing population of diverse stu-

Results of Denver Program

dents have been documented. A corps of 100 mentor teachers, specifically available to train their colleagues, provides formal preparation experiences, classroom demonstrations, local site networking, and curricular leadership. These experts, or connoisseurs, also evaluate new teaching professionals.

Similarly, in California local school districts can now implement their own "intern" teacher education programs using an institution of higher education as a partner. This training initiative places the focus on the school district, rather than on the institution of higher education. Like the Denver program and the movement toward site-based training of student teachers, the California intern programs offer a way of blending theoretical learning and direct teaching experience.

Local Expertise

What was born out of great necessity in Denver may give us insight into the appropriate development of teaching professionals. First, in the examples we have been looking at, professional development takes on a localized flavor that reflects the diversity of students and programs in the school district. Second, a corps of expert teachers, who can serve in an evaluative capacity, develops over time. Local knowledge of educational needs is cultivated in experts who in turn evaluate the professional expertise of their colleagues.

Benefits of Teacher Support

Significantly, professional development also relates to teacher burnout. **Burnout** is physical or emotional exhaustion, most often caused by a great deal of stress experienced over a long period of time. It is particularly apparent in teachers whose major responsibility is serving highly diverse student populations (Calderón, 1991). Recent studies have made it very clear that ongoing support, particularly through the first few years of teaching, is crucial to instructors. Calderón (1991) has displayed these data in graphic form. Figures 7.1 and 7.2 portray the cycles of teacher engagement with the profession, with and without the presence of ongoing support in the form of professional development. As the figures show, all teachers experience anticipation, disillusionment, reenergizing, and periods of reflection. But only those with ongoing professional development support experience substantive growth without "termination," that is, withdrawal from the profession.

The alternative form of teacher preparation and district-level professional development, credentialing, and support that took shape in Denver was born of immediate needs that could not be met through more typical teacher preparation pathways or state credentialing standards. It demonstrates a useful and highly responsive solution to a problem many school districts face with respect to serving culturally and linguistically diverse student populations. This alternative form of local preparation, ongoing

Figure 7.1 ▼ **Self-Reported Efficacy in First Year of Teaching, for Teachers Without Support System**

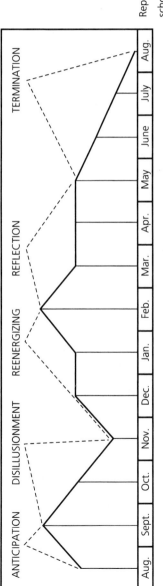

Reported each month of the school year.

------- Veteran Teacher

——— First-year Teacher

Figure 7.2 ▼ **Self-Reported Efficacy in First Year of Teaching, for Teachers with Support System**

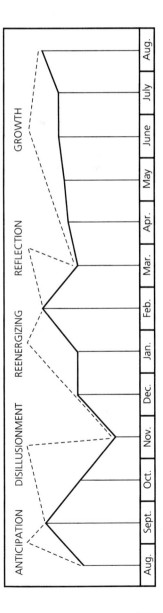

support, and credentialing could be appropriate for enhancing the effectiveness of most educational professionals. Specifically, though, it is worthy of particular attention to the field at a time when effective teachers are needed more than ever.

Characteristics of Effective Teachers of Culturally and Linguistically Diverse Students

Chapter 1 described research reports that have attempted to identify the qualities of effective teachers who serve culturally diverse student populations (Dwyer, 1991; Villegas, 1991; Villegas et al., 1995). This research emphasis is related to the broader interest in identifying "exemplary" characteristics for teachers in general (Reynolds & Elias, 1991). To go beyond these generalizations, we shall explore the research that has attempted to document empirically the attributes of "good" teachers. The studies are few, but they begin to provide a set of standards that may be useful in preparing and evaluating teachers of culturally diverse students. The purpose of this discussion is not to suggest that all "good" teachers must be like the ones described here. Instead, we shall examine this information in order to see if we may use it to better understand the needs of students.

Tikunoff (1983), in his analysis of the Significant Bilingual Instructional Features (SBIF) study, reports commonalties in the "exemplary" teacher's response to classroom organization and instruction. As we saw in Chapter 6, the 58 teachers observed in this study represented six sites and spoke a variety of non-English languages (Spanish, Chinese, Vietnamese, Hmong, Navaho, and Hopi). All classes were considered "effective" on two criteria: (1) teachers were nominated by other teachers and school personnel, students, and parents; and (2) their teaching behaviors produced rates of academic learning time as high as or higher than rates reported in other research on effective teaching.

Attributes of Effective Teachers

An initial set of instructional features identified as characteristic of effective teachers of diverse student populations pertains to the organization and delivery of instruction:

1. Successful teachers specify both task outcomes and what students must do to accomplish tasks. In addition, teachers communicate high expectations for students in terms of learning and a sense of efficacy in terms of their own ability to teach.
2. Successful teachers of diverse students, not unlike effective teachers in general, use "active teaching" behaviors found to be related to increased student performance on academic tests of achievement in reading and mathematics. These

teaching behaviors include (a) communicating clearly when giving directions, specifying tasks, and presenting new information; (b) obtaining and maintaining students' engagement in instructional tasks by pacing instruction appropriately, promoting involvement, and communicating their expectations for students' success in completing tasks; (c) monitoring students' progress; and (d) providing immediate feedback whenever required regarding students' success.

3. Successful teachers of limited-English-proficient (LEP) students mediate instruction for them by using the students' native language and English for instruction, alternating between the two languages whenever necessary to ensure clarity of instruction. Although they use this type of language switching, these teachers do not translate directly from one language to another.

Recent research (García, 1992b; Villegas, 1991) has focused on teachers who were consistently identified at the level of the school site and the district as "effective." In these classrooms, approximately 50 to 70 percent of the students were non-English-speakers, and the remaining English-speaking students represented several ethnic groups. For the purpose of discussion, we can divide the findings of these studies of teacher attributes into four distinct but interlocking domains: (1) knowledge, (2) skills, (3) disposition, and (4) affect.

Knowledge

Effective teachers held the prerequisite state teacher credentials and had graduated from programs with specific emphasis on multicultural and/or bilingual education. They had an average of 7.1 years of experience as teachers of culturally diverse students.

Experienced Teachers These were not novice teachers. They reported that they routinely participated in staff development efforts, either taking courses or attending workshops on teaching techniques they wanted to implement in their classrooms. Some of the workshops were sponsored by the school or district and were mandatory. These teachers also participated in courses that they sought out and financed on their own, some related to language development and others related to pedagogy and curriculum.

These teachers were knowledgeable and articulate with regard to the instructional philosophies that guided them. They communicated these philosophies coherently in their interviews.

Coherent Teaching Philosophy They never hesitated to explain why they were using a specific instructional technique and usually couched these explanations in terms of how they saw their role with regard to teaching and how students learn. Principals and parents also commented on the ability of these teachers to communicate the rationales for their instructional techniques. One principal commented, "She's always able to defend her work with her students. When I first came here, I didn't agree with all that she was doing, and sometimes I still do not agree. But she always helps me understand why she is doing what she is doing. I respect her for that. She is not a 'recipe teacher'" (García, 1992a:134).

One parent commented about her child's journal writing: "I didn't understand why she was letting _____ make all these spelling mistakes. It annoyed me. During the teacher-parent conference, she showed me the progress _____ was making. His spelling was getting better without taking a spelling test every week. I was surprised. She knows what she's doing" (Pease-Alvarez et al., 1991:356). A parent concerned about his daughter's lack of English competency indicated:

> Me explicó que aprendiendo en español le va a ayudar a mi hija hablar mejor el inglés. Dice bien, porque mi hijo que vino conmigo de México, hablando y escribiendo en español, aprendió el inglés muy facil. [She explained that my daughter's learning of Spanish would help her learn English. She was right, because my son knew more Spanish when he came to the U.S. and he learned English easily.] (García, 1992a:133)

Moreover, these teachers seemed to be quite competent in the content areas. For example, the upper elementary teachers who were instructing students in fractions had a solid and confident understanding of fractions. They did not seem to be only "one step ahead of the students."

Skills

Despite their differing perspectives, the teachers demonstrated specific instructional skills. Bilingual teachers used English and Spanish in highly communicative ways, speaking to students with varying degrees of Spanish and English proficiency in a communicative style requiring significant language switching. Direct translation from one language to another was a rarity, but utilization of language switching in contexts that required it was common.

Variations existed among these exemplary teachers, of course, but each had developed a particular set of instructional skills which, they indicated, led to their own effectiveness:

1. *Teachers had adopted an experimental stance toward instruction.* Along with many of their colleagues, these exemplary teachers had abandoned a strictly skills-oriented approach to instruction. To varying degrees they organized instruction in their classes so that children focused first on what was meaningful to them. Teachers in the early grades used an approach to reading instruction that treated specific skills in the context of extended pieces of text (e.g., an entire book, passage, or paragraph). They initiated shared reading experiences by reading to and with children from an enlarged book, pointing to each word as they read. Because most of these books relied on a recurring pattern (e.g., a repeating syntactical construction, rhyming words, repetitions), children who could not read words in isolation were able to predict words and entire constructions when participating in choral reading activities. With time, teachers encouraged students to focus on individual words, sound-letter correspondences, and syntactic constructions. The teacher also encouraged children to rely on other cueing systems as they predicted and confirmed what they had read as a group or individually.

Focus on the Meaningful

These teachers utilized a thematic curriculum. Science and social studies themes were often integrated across a variety of subject areas. Once a theme was determined, usually in consultation with students, the teachers planned instruction around a series of activities that focused on that theme. For example, a unit on dinosaurs included reading books about dinosaurs, categorizing and graphing different kinds of dinosaurs, visiting a museum that featured dinosaur exhibits, writing stories or poems about a favorite dinosaur, and speculating on the events that led to the dinosaurs' disappearance. In another example, a student in a third-grade classroom suggested that the theme address "the stuff in the field that makes my little brother sick" (García, 1992b:137). The teacher then developed a four-week unit that engaged students in understanding pesticide use, which is a relevant topic for the children of migrant farmworkers.

Thematic Curriculum

Despite the use of instructional strategies that depart from traditional skills-based approaches to curriculum and instruction, these teachers did sometimes structure learning around individual skills or discrete components. It was not uncommon for a teacher to form an ad hoc group of students needing special help with particular academic skills. Interestingly, the teachers reported that they devoted a week or two toward preparing students for standardized tests. During this time they taught skills that would be tested, and administered practice tests. One teacher related, "I don't like testing. But we have to do it. I teach my kids how to mark the bubbles and I make sure that they take their time. We practice test-taking" (García, 1992:131).

BECOMING A RESPONSIVE TEACHER

A Successful Practitioner in Math

Kay Toliver's math program has been celebrated—and for good reason. She teaches at Harlem Tech Middle School—15% AfroAmerican, 85% Hispanic, and located in a poor New York City neighborhood. Yet her teaching strategies exemplify those recently recommended by the National Council of Teachers of Mathematics.

Toliver, who is not a textbook fan, makes math interdisciplinary. Her students constantly hypothesize and engage in hands-on activities. In one activity, they constructed two paper bridges, one made of quadrilaterals and the other of triangles, and found that the triangle was better suited as a building block. Toliver's students also create and illustrate math problems based on their own lives. For example; "There are two fire escapes on the outside of the building. If one is rusted and opens twice as slowly as the other, which opens in 7.4 seconds, how long will it take the rusted one to open?"

Toliver prefers authentic assessment methods to conventional testing. Her students have been asked to form a pentagon from any combination of six pattern-block pieces which included a square, an equilateral triangle, a rectangle, a trapezoid, a parallelogram, and a rhombus. They then had to determine the sum of the interior angles of the pentagon and explain how they arrived at their answer.

Not surprisingly, many of Toliver's students have gone on to prestigious schools, such as the Bronx High School of Science, and to college and vocational schools.

Source: David Hill, "Overnight sensation," *Teacher Magazine,* March 1993, pp. 23–27.

▼ Meeting the Challenge

1. Develop two interdisciplinary math activities, one for an elementary-level classroom and one for a secondary-level classroom. Assume that your students are culturally and linguistically diverse. Include a collaborative aspect.
2. Contact the National Council of Teachers of Mathematics by letter, telephone, or internet (http://www.nctm.org/). Ask a representative of the organization how you might view the material referred to above regarding the strategies the council recommends for teaching math. Share any information with your classmates.

2. *Teachers provided opportunities for active learning.* A good portion of class time was organized around a series of learning activities that children pursued either independently or with others. During science and math, children worked in small groups doing a variety of hands-on activities designed to support their understanding of a particular concept (e.g., classification, estimation, place value) or subject (e.g., oceanography, dinosaurs).

Each teacher's commitment to active learning was revealed by the consistent use of a studio or workshop format for literacy instruction. Instead of teaching students about reading and writing, teachers organized their program so that students actively **Learning by** read and wrote. Real reading and writing took place in the context of a literature-based reading program and during regularly scheduled times when students wrote in their journals on topics of their own choosing, with teachers reliably responding to their entries. There was also time for students to engage in writer's workshop, during which they generated their own topics and wrote, revised, edited, and published their finished writings for a larger audience. Like published authors, they shared their writing with others and often received input that helped them revise and improve upon what they had written. For example, one teacher commented, "These kids produce their own reading material and they take it home to share it with their parents. It's real good stuff. I help a little, but it's the kids that help each other the most" (Pease-Alvarez et al., 1991:351).

3. *Teachers encouraged collaborative and cooperative interactions among students.* These teachers organized instruction so that students spent time working together on a wide range of instructional activities. Primary-grade teachers structured their day so **Student Col-** that students worked on group and individual activities (e.g., **laboration** graphing, journal writing, science projects) in small, heterogeneous groups. Students who worked in small groups on their own art project, journal, or experiment did not necessarily interact with other members of their group. Teachers explained that students, particularly those who did not share the same dominant language, often ignored one another during these kinds of group activities. They felt that cross-cultural interactions were much more likely to take place when students were obliged to work together to complete a single task. Middle-grade teachers followed this same collaborative approach.

Disposition

A person's **disposition** is his or her usual temperament and frame of mind. We can describe the following attributes of effective teachers as constituting disposition because no other cate-

Personal Commitment

gory seems relevant. The individual characteristics of these teachers explain their success as professionals. For instance, they were highly dedicated. They reported working very hard, getting to school first and being the last to leave, working weekends, and sometimes feeling completely overworked. They reported spending close to $2,000 of their own resources to modify the classroom and obtain the materials their students needed. They indicated that they saw themselves as "creative," "resourceful," "committed," "energetic," "persistent," and "collaborative." They sought assistance from their colleagues and were ready to provide as much assistance as they received.

Although these teachers felt that they were effective, they were not complacent. They reported that they continued to change their instructional practices and in some cases their in-

Change

structional philosophies over the years. These teachers reported undergoing great change in their approach to learning and instruction—of having "shifted paradigms." For example, teachers who once advocated skills-based and authoritarian modes of instruction such as DISTAR (a prescriptive reading program) were now considering and experimenting with child-centered approaches. Teachers felt that they enjoyed a certain degree of autonomy in their school. They felt free to implement change. In recent years, when they have wanted to institute a new classroom approach, they have presented a carefully thought-out rationale and eventually enlisted the principal's support.

The changes these teachers were involved in affected other classrooms as well as their own. With other teachers, they have worked to eliminate ability grouping across subject areas. They were involved in individual and group efforts to improve the quality of education at the school and district level. In short, these teachers were highly committed to improving themselves and the services to students in general.

Above all, they were highly confident, and even a bit "cocky" regarding their instructional abilities, as the following comments indicate:

"I have changed my own view on how students learn—we need to understand learning does not occur in bits and pieces. Why do teachers still insist on teaching that way?"

"I know what I am doing is good for kids. Some of my colleagues say I work too hard—I say they do not work hard enough. Not that they are lazy, they just don't seem to understand how important it is to do this job right."

"I know my kids are doing well, all of them. I would rather keep them with me all day than send them to someone who is supposed to help them in their 'special' needs but doesn't help them at all" (García, 1992a; Pease-Alvarez et al., 1991).

Affect

The term **affect** is used in psychology to refer to people's feelings and emotions as distinguished from their thoughts and actions. The emotional energy these teachers bring to their work contributes to their effectiveness. These teachers felt strongly that classroom practices that reflect the cultural and linguistic background of minority students are important ways of enhancing student self-esteem. They recognized that part of their job was to provide the kind of cultural and linguistic validation that is missing in the larger society, which more often deprecates minority cultures and languages. According to teachers working with Latino students, learning Spanish and learning about Latino culture benefits Anglo-American students as well as Latino students. In their eyes, people who learn a second language tend to be more sensitive to other cultures. Like other teachers, these teachers felt that multicultural awareness enriched their students' lives.

These teachers had high expectations for all their students:

High Expectations

"No 'pobrecito' [poor child] syndrome here—I want all my students to learn and I know they can learn even though they may come from very poor families and may live under 'tough' conditions. I can have them do their homework here and I can even get them a tutor—an older student—if they need it. I understand that their parents may not be able to help them at home. That's no excuse for them not learning." (García, 1992a:133)

In many respects, these teachers portrayed themselves as being quite demanding, taking no excuses from students for not accomplishing assigned work and willing to be "tough" on those students who were "messing around."

Most significant was the teachers' affinity for their students:

"These students are like my very own children."

"I love these children like my own. I know that parents expect me to look after their kids and to let them know if they are in trouble."

"When I walk into that classroom I know we are a family and we're going to be together a whole year. . . . I try to emphasize first that we are a family here. . . . I tell my students, "you're like brothers and sisters" and some students even call me Mom or Tía [Aunt]. It's just like being at home here." (García, 1992a:133)

Each teacher spoke of the importance of strong and caring relationships among class members and particularly between the teacher and the students. They felt that this provided students with a safe environment that was conducive to learning.

Parent Trust

Parents also reported a similar feeling. They referred to the teachers in the interviews as extended family members—someone to be trusted, respected, and honored for service to their children. These teachers were often invited to *bautismos* (baptisms), *bodas* (weddings), *fiestas de cumpleaños* (birthday celebrations), soccer games, and family barbecues. And they attended such occasions, reporting that such participation was inherently rewarding and instructive with regard to their own personal and professional lives. Parents commented during interviews:

"La señorita _____, le tengo mucha confianza, quiero que mi niño la respete como a mí." [Ms. _____, I trust her, my son respects her as he does me.]

"Nunca se larga mi niña de ella, se porta como mi hermana, siempre le puedo hablar y me gusta mucho ayudarle." [My daughter stays close to her, she is like my sister, I can always talk to her and I like to help her.]

"I know my son is well cared for in her class, I never worry—she even calls me when he does something good." (García, 1992a:137)

In summary, the teachers who are considered effective for culturally and linguistically diverse students are highly experienced, not novices to teaching or to the instruction of these students. They are skilled in communication with students, parents, and administrative supervisors. They think about and communicate their own instructional philosophies. They work hard to understand the community, families, and students whom they serve, and they incorporate into the curriculum attributes of the local culture. They have adopted instructional methods that are student centered, collaborative, and process oriented—no "worksheet" curriculum was found. They are dedicated hard workers who collaborate with colleagues and continue to be involved in personal and professional growth activities. Most significantly, these teachers care deeply for and personally connect with their students. They are advocates: having "adopted" their students, they watch out for their students' welfare while at the same time challenging them with high expectations and refusing to accept the "pobrecito" syndrome.

Effective Teaching and Learning

As we learned in Chapter 3, there are certain elements of teaching practices that increase the likelihood that culturally and linguistically diverse students can be academically successful (see Table 3.1). We shall now explore particular key questions that can serve as starting points for developing useful strategies for teachers.

Effective Learning Environments

August and Hakuta (1997:171) provide a comprehensive review of schools and classrooms in which linguistically and culturally diverse populations achieve high academic performance. These settings have been found to share the following attributes:

▼ A supportive schoolwide climate
▼ School leadership
▼ A customized learning environment
▼ Articulation and coordination within and between schools
▼ Use of native language and culture in instruction
▼ A balanced curriculum that includes both basic and higher-order skills
▼ Explicit skills instruction
▼ Opportunities for student-directed instruction
▼ Use of instructional strategies that enhance understanding
▼ Opportunities for practice
▼ Systematic student assessment
▼ Staff development
▼ Home and parent involvement

The following section draws on these concepts in order to develop several key questions that we need to ask in examining schools' efforts.

The Key Questions

Student Engagement

We can begin with the core issue of student engagement in the classroom. The literature on language acquisition and effective instruction for language minority students indicates that students are much more likely to be engaged learners in environments in which the curriculum and teaching approaches build on the diversity of the students and teachers (Pease-Alvarez et al., 1991; Wong-Fillmore, 1991). Further, teachers should have a close connection to, or at least a familiarity with, the home communities of their students. This connection allows the teachers to develop practices that reflect the kinds of experiences on which the students can construct an understanding of complex ideas and new concepts (Pease-Alvarez et al., 1991). In addition, culturally and linguistically diverse students can experience engaged learning only when they have the time to interact with each other and with the adults in the school community. Such interactions improve the students' social and communication skills and create a "safe" environment in which to learn. Finally, assessments of the students' progress in learning various subjects, developing conceptual understandings, and acquiring particular skills need to be aligned with the established curricular and instructional goals. To be a true gauge of the quality of the learning environment, these assessments must involve all students. In other words, if linguistically and culturally diverse students are systematically left out of regular schoolwide or classroom assessments, the results of such efforts cannot begin to address all of the learning that goes on in a school—or, more importantly, the areas to which further attention should be devoted. With these elements in mind, we can pose our first key question:

How are language, culture, and student diversity incorporated into instruction, curriculum, and assessment practices?

Professional Development

Very closely related to the issue of engaged student learning is the matter of professional development. As noted, teachers and other professionals who work with students with diverse backgrounds are called upon to bring many skills, strategies, and insights into their classrooms. A concern arises with regard to how their teaching strategies are developed and shared within (and beyond) the learning environment. It is thus appropriate to ask:

What resources, experiences, and structures contribute to the professional development of the school community; and how are they related to student achievement?

Schoolwide Vision

In addition to concerning ourselves with teaching practices and the classroom environment as support mechanisms for academic success among culturally diverse students, we must also focus on practices that affect the entire school. These include the development of (1) a schoolwide vision that celebrates cultural diversity and that is aimed at optimizing the learning opportunities for all students (Pease-Alvarez et al., 1991); and (2) relationships and structural features of the school that facilitate active participation across all sectors of the school community, again with the goal of high academic performance. To further our understanding of these elements as they operate in schools with large populations of culturally and linguistically diverse students, it is also important to know:

> How are the school's visions and missions alive in each instructor's teaching and values, and how are they articulated for and to each teacher?

Power Relationships

Finally, with respect to the broader organizational context (Delpit, 1995; Ladson-Billings, 1994), the research suggests asking:

> How do power relationships in the educational and local community as well as in the larger society become embedded in the classroom? What prevailing norms and underlying beliefs shape the roles, expectations, and standards in classroom instruction?

The Principal's Role in Effective Schooling

"Exemplary" Administrators

Just as our earlier discussion focused on the effective teacher, this section will use similar data to analyze the administrative leadership of schools that have proved "effective" for linguistically and culturally diverse students (García, 1997). It is no small task to identify the "exemplary" principal, a process that involves interviewing and observing these individuals along with teachers and parents to obtain a more comprehensive perspective. It is not my intent to suggest that all "good" principals must be like the ones described here. Instead, I want to describe carefully the attributes of these individuals so that others may use this information to serve highly diverse constituencies more effectively.

The following discussion is based on data derived from selected elementary and middle school principals in eight schools in California and Arizona. All these principals had been consistently identified at the school and district level as "exemplary" professionals, and their schools had been recognized for serving linguistically and culturally diverse students effectively (for specific selection criteria, see García, 1997). Approximately 50 to 70 percent of their students were Spanish-dominant speakers; the remainder were dominant in English or another language (Vietnamese, Hmong, and/or Cantonese). The findings with regard to professional attributes were divided into two distinct but interlocking domains: integrity and affect.

Integrity

The principals in this study were all bilingual and biliterate in English and Spanish. They had the prerequisite state credentials and had graduated from specific administrative programs after serving as teachers for 3–4 years. They had an average of 4.1 years (range 1.4–8.1 years) of teaching experience in schools with bilingual or second-language educational interventions. Therefore, these were relatively inexperienced professionals, with limited background as either teachers or principals. Many had been thrust into administrative roles because they had worked with diverse student populations, even though that experience may not have been extensive. As one superintendent said of one of the principals, "We needed her to help us in that principalship. I had no other candidate who could better understand this community."

Aspects of Integrity

However, these principals were perceived as individuals with high integrity: honest, dedicated, hardworking, professional. They reported participating in professional development activities that they sought out and financed on their own, some related to Spanish-language development and others directly related to management, assessment, and educational practice.

Articulateness

These principals were quite knowledgeable and articulate with regard to the district and local school philosophy, missions, and goals, which they communicated quite coherently in their interviews. Teachers and parents also commented on the principals' abilities to deal effectively with the district office. One teacher commented, "He's always able to defend our work to the superintendent and the Board. I respect him for that." Speaking about the principal's reactions to her child's disciplinary problems, a parent remarked, "I can count on him defending my son. He is fair and will make sure _____ is not mistreated." On the basis of such relationships, the principals had achieved a high degree of autonomy and respect from district administrators, teachers, and parents. One school board member indicated, "Someone is in the driver's seat."

Despite such positive characteristics, these principals were not always aware of the teachers' philosophical or theoretical positions. Nor were they the intellectual leaders found among the principals described in other research on "effective schools."

Building Respect

Overall, however, these principals were able to build on their limited experience and professional knowledge to "construct" a respect from the parent, teaching, and educational community. This seemed to come from the perception that the principal was hardworking and sincere. The principals themselves reported working, on average, 55–60 hours per week, most of that time at the school.

These "effective" principals were also self-critical, never satisfied that they were doing enough. They never hesitated to ask themselves why the school was using specific curriculum or instructional techniques. They looked more to teaching colleagues than to other administrators for support, and they themselves organized and sustained support networks—but usually with teachers rather than other administrators.

Affect

Much like the teachers in their schools, these principals felt strongly that their school practices must reflect the cultural and linguistic background of the students. They reported that part of their job was to provide the kind of cultural and linguistic validation that was missing in the local community, where minority culture and language were deprecated. In their eyes, people who learned a second language tended to be more sensitive to other cultures. They felt that being bilingual and bicultural enriched their students' lives.

No Excuses

The principals also had high expectations for all their students. In many respects, just like the effective teachers described earlier, these professionals portrayed themselves as strict, unwilling to accept excuses from students and willing to be firm with students who were misbehaving.

Most significant were the feelings the principals had toward those they served: "I know that parents expect me to look after their kids and to let them know if they are in trouble," said one. Another noted, "Some students even call me *tio* [uncle]. It's just like being at home here." Each principal spoke of the importance

Caring Relationships

of strong and caring relationships among themselves and those they served. Almost all indicated an interest in remaining at the school, even though they expected that they might be asked to take an "easier" assignment. They also said that they "liked" the community and the parents.

Parents also reported similar feelings about the principals, referring to them as extended family members, people to be trusted, respected, and honored. The principals were often invited to soccer and baseball games and family get-togethers. And they attended such occasions, reporting that such participation was inherently rewarding and instructive both personally and professionally. Parents commented: "Al señor _____, le tengo mucha confianza, quiero que mi niño lo respete como a mí"; "I know my son is well cared for at school, I never worry—I want my son to respect him just as he respects me."

This discussion has focused on attributes of principals who are considered effective among linguistically and culturally diverse students. Much like the teachers in these effective schools, these individuals are highly committed, although not always experienced administratively. They are highly skilled in communicating with students, parents, and administrative supervisors. They are able to articulate their schools' goals clearly. They work hard to understand the community, families, and students they serve, and incorporate into the school aspects of the local culture. They collaborate with teacher colleagues and continue to be involved in personal and professional growth activities. Most significantly, these professionals care for the students they serve. They are their students' advocates; having "adopted" them, the principals both look out for them and challenge them.

Conclusion

It seems clear that culturally and linguistically diverse students— often referred to en masse as "at risk" students—can indeed be served effectively by schools and educational professionals. Schools must develop educational structures and processes that consider both the general attributes of effective schooling practices and the specific attributes of effective teachers (Carter & Chatfield, 1986; García, 1988, 1992a; Tikunoff, 1983). Although the training of such teachers is in a developmental period, and further clarifying research is needed, it is clearly not in its infancy. A serious body of literature that examines instructional practices and organization, and their effects, is emerging.

The preparation of teaching innovators is a challenge for university, federal, state, and local educational agencies. The needs are great, and the production of competent professionals has lagged. Teacher organizations, credentialing bodies, and universities have responded with a new array of competencies, guidelines, and professional evaluation tools. The most often utilized professional evaluation tool is the connoisseur model of professional assessment. Like other assessment methods, the connoisseur model is not yet sufficiently reliable or valid to use at a statewide level. It has been employed with some success, however, at the level of the individual school district, using locally derived credentials. This district-level credentialing process is an alternative worthy of serious consideration. The challenge for all those engaged in the preparation, assessment, and credentialing of linguistically and culturally diverse teachers is to consider the rapidly expanding research literature, to evaluate its implications critically, and to apply it in educational contexts with the help of locally developed connoisseurs.

SUMMARY OF MAJOR IDEAS

1. A profession is characterized by (a) acquisition of knowledge obtained through formal education and (b) an orientation toward serving the needs of the public, with an emphasis on ethical and altruistic concern for the client. The professional preparation of teachers has not kept pace with the educational needs of culturally and linguistically diverse students in the United States.

2. At present, educators are prepared and assessed by state agencies, by professional societies, or by both. Assessment may focus on the individual preservice teacher, through a test such as the National Teaching Exam, or on the programs that prepare teachers, though state or association reviews. The professional credentials that teachers are required to have reflect the general intellectual and ethical climate and needs of the time.

3. Not until 1974 did the U.S. Congress provide institutions of higher education with resources for use in preparing teachers of culturally and linguistically diverse children. The 1980–1982 Teachers Language Skills Survey estimated that whereas 100,000 trained bilingual teachers were needed in the U.S. schools, barely a third of this number were available. The survey also reported that only 40 percent of teachers assigned to teach English as a second language had been formally prepared to do so. In 1994, there was an estimated national shortage of some 175,000 teachers of language minority students.

4. As of 1991, 25 states and U.S. territories offered no professional credentialing for teachers of bilingual education or ESL. Less than one-third of the states required schools to provide services to limited-English-proficient students, even in such places as California, Florida, and New York, which are greatly affected by growing numbers of language minority students.

5. Present methods of professionally assessing teachers are limited and are often unreliable and invalid. The connoisseur method of assessment, by which experienced practitioners

evaluate the effectiveness of teachers in training, is not sufficiently developed for use on a statewide level.

6. Performance competencies expected for teachers of culturally and linguistically diverse students cover the instructor's knowledge of (a) educational theory, (b) social trends, and (c) classroom strategies. In 1984 the National Association of State Directors of Teacher Education and Certification (NASDTEC) developed a list of competencies to be used for certifying teachers of language minority students. Some states, such as New Jersey, have detailed the roles and responsibilities of these teachers in published handbooks.

7. Although teacher preparation programs for linguistically and culturally diverse students are still in the developmental stage, the recent trend has been to conduct most training at the school rather than a university or college. Other programs have encouraged members of the local community to be hired and trained as education professionals.

8. Inservice preparation is professional training for teachers who are already working in a classroom. The local school district in Denver developed an inservice program for teachers that was based on the connoisseur model. From the mid- to late 1980s, over 500 district teachers participated, and a corps of 100 mentor teachers was formed to meet future training needs and to evaluate new teaching professionals. Such a local emphasis permits schools to respond to the specific diversity present in the district.

9. All teachers experience anticipation, disillusionment, reenergizing, and periods of reflection. Burnout is exhaustion caused by stress experienced over a long period of time and is prevalent among teachers who serve highly diverse student populations. Burnout may cause even good teachers to leave the profession. Research shows that first-year teachers can resist the effects of burnout and experience substantive growth if they are provided with ongoing support in the form of professional development.

10. Effective teachers of diverse student populations organize and deliver instruction in a characteristic way. They specify task outcomes and communicate high expectations for students. They use "active teaching" behaviors. Effective teachers of LEP students switch back and forth between the students' first language and English without directly translating.

11. Effective teachers have also been found to have specific attributes in the domains of knowledge, skill, disposition, and affect. Disposition is a person's usual temperament and frame of mind, and affect is a person's feelings and emotions

as distinguished from thoughts and actions. These effective teachers were highly experienced and skilled at communicating with students, parents, and administrators. They used student-centered, collaborative, and process-oriented instructional methods. They were dedicated to their own personal and professional growth. They personally connected with and advocated for their students.

12. Effective principals, like effective teachers, are highly committed to the diverse students they serve. Although they are not always experienced administratively, they communicate well with students, parents, and administrative supervisors, and work hard to understand the community, families, and students they serve. Most importantly, they care deeply about their students.

EXTENDING YOUR EXPERIENCE

1. Effective teachers have a deep commitment to the educational enterprise. Ask yourself and two other colleagues (a new teacher and a seasoned teacher) the following questions: Why did you choose teaching as a profession? Why are you now a teacher? Will you remain in teaching for the next five years? Why or why not?

2. Write to or explore the Web site of the National Clearinghouse for Bilingual Education at the U.S. Department of Education. Find out what information and services they provide that would be of interest to teachers of culturally and linguistically diverse children. In particular, compile a list of inservice training available through state education departments or local school districts.

3. In your local school district, who are the educators who might be called on to serve as mentors, or connoisseurs, in a training and assessment program for teachers of culturally diverse students? How would you go about identifying these experts and learning what they do to provide their students with an effective education?

4. This chapter describes the characteristics of effective teachers of culturally and linguistically diverse students according to four areas: knowledge, skills, disposition, and affect. How would you rank these areas in terms of importance? Write each one as a heading on a sheet of paper and take an inventory of yourself. Can you identify your own strengths and weaknesses in these four areas?

5. Working with a group of your classmates, design a series of questions to be used to interview candidates for a teaching position in an elementary or secondary school with a large population of linguistically and culturally diverse students. Base your interview questions on the four areas of teacher characteristics discussed in the chapter.

6. Interview one or two elementary or secondary school teachers about their experience with burnout. Ask them to describe their specific experiences and to explain how they battled burnout. Share your findings with your classmates, respecting the teachers' anonymity, if necessary.

RESOURCES FOR FURTHER STUDY

Collier, J. P. (1985). University models for ESL and bilingual teacher training. In National Clearinghouse for Bilingual Education (Ed.), *Issues in English language development*. Rosslyn, VA: Editor.

This publication is a collection of papers presented at a national exchange entitled "Issues in English Language Development for Minority Language Education." This particular paper points to the great challenge faced by programs created to help language minority students. From the point of view of staff, most professionals in the field are new, inexperienced, and young. The task of educating all students sometimes is counterproductive due to the duplication of resources and the inability to effectively direct resources to needed areas. It is clear to the author that many interested and determined individuals are willing to face the challenge to provide a better education to language minority students.

Pease-Alvarez, C., Espinoza, P., & García, E. (1991). Effective instruction for language minority students: An early childhood case study. *Early Childhood Research Quarterly, 6*(3), 347–363.

The authors offer a descriptive analysis of two teachers in order to illustrate effective instructional perspectives and practices. Such effective practices are quoted from large-scale studies. The two teachers' experiences demonstrate how to educate language minority students. The teachers' personal, professional, and educational goals provide the reader with insight into how language and culture can become an integral part of the classroom along with innovative perspectives, effective instructional practices, and different philosophies.

Villegas, A. M. (1991). *Culturally responsive pedagogy for the 1990's and beyond*. Princeton: Educational Testing Service.

The author's main goal is to identify the most current and significant literature dealing with promising instructional practices for minority students. The document reviews the most current thinking on minority students. A number of authorities from different disciplinary perspectives, such as anthropology, sociology, linguistics, sociolinguistics, psychology, psycholinguistics, and curriculum and instruction, were invited to provide input.

EFFECTIVE

INSTRUCTION OF

LINGUISTICALLY

AND CULTURALLY

DIVERSE CHILDREN

CHAPTER 8

Focus Questions

▼ What are some of the characteristics of elementary schools and high schools that effectively serve culturally and linguistically diverse students?

▼ How radically must schools be transformed in order to educate all of our students?

▼ How will acknowledgment of linguistic, sociocultural, and cognitive factors in children's development bring about change in educational practices?

▼ What classroom strategies have been identified as effective for enabling language minority students to achieve academically?

"Knowledge is not something separate and self-sufficing, but it is involved in the process by which life is sustained and evolved." —JOHN DEWEY

It seems only appropriate to begin our discussion of effective instructional practices by addressing the above statement by one of this country's most renowned educators, John Dewey. Too often the greatest purpose of our schools is perceived to be the "dispensing" of knowledge. Dewey, however, reminds us that knowledge cannot be dispensed. It must be constructed, reconstructed, and located in our own individual ways of living. It is more a process than an entity, something that maintains us while at the same time transforming us.

Today's teachers face numerous challenges. To begin with, a teacher must interact with many students, each with unique learning biographies, interests, strengths, and experiences. Schools exist, at least in part, to provide an opportunity for students to encounter ways of knowing and doing that they would not likely meet out of school. Under these conditions, it seems essential that the teacher give careful thought and preparation—both material and intellectual—to the creation of instructional events. Dewey (1916) recommends instruction that engages the interest of students so that each is enabled to meet the challenges and make meaningful, on his or her own terms, the "educational" material available in that milieu. Only then can the school, the classroom, and the teacher "step back and follow the student's lead" (Dewey, 1916, p. 19).

As the U.S. population continues to diversify racially and ethnically, particularly among school-age children, the nature of schooling must reflect this significant demographic transformation. Schools today are being asked not simply to improve their functioning but to adapt to new populations, new societal expectations, and new intellectual and employment demands. Our next generation of young people, and ethnic and racial minority children in particular, will continue to be vulnerable if our schools do not successfully complete the required metamorphosis. The future lies in understanding how a diverse population, with many individuals at risk for underachievement, can attain social, educational, and employment competence. As always, the new ideas, the energy, and the resources for our society's future reside in our youth.

We have seen that educational vulnerability is a historical reality for culturally and linguistically diverse students in the United States. The phrase "culturally and linguistically diverse" is a relatively new educational term that does not fully portray the stunning diversity among the populations it labels. Recent educational leaders, such as the former U.S. Secretary of Education, Richard Riley, have concluded that populations identified as such have been perceived by the majority of society as linguistically, cognitively, socially, and educationally inferior (Riley, 1994). This perception gave rise to a variety of social and educational programs that attempted to eliminate these "inferior" characteristics (August & Hakuta, 1997). Meanwhile, linguistically and culturally diverse populations continue to struggle to attain educational success.

Recent educational research and associated instructional practices have revealed the nature of educational vulnerability as it relates to language, culture, and cognition. In the following section we shall review some of the theoretical underpinnings of new educational strategies. We then look at research into characteristics of effective schools and effective instructional practices. Particular emphasis is placed on how an instructionally responsive stance can lead to a more productive educational future for culturally diverse student populations.

A Theoretical Framework: Two Divergent Views

Before we examine effective schools and instructional practices, let's go back a few chapters and review the theoretical base available to us. Recall from Chapter 3 that at one end of the continuum of educational theory, educators argue that addressing the academic underachievement of linguistically and culturally diverse populations requires a deeper understanding of the interaction between a student's home and school cultures (Tharp, 1989). These theorists claim that educational failure can be explained by the "culture clash" between home and school. Alternatively, other theorists state that the academic failure of any student rests on the failure of instructional personnel to implement the principles of teaching and learning that we know "work."

In any sincere attempt to address the educational circumstances of students, these theoretical positions need not be in-

Both Theories Are Useful

compatible. In fact, both positions offer a more informed perspective on the effective and efficient education of all students. Making distinctions among theories is a necessary starting point in our discussion of instructional practices that might enhance education for historically unsuccessful student populations. The continued failure of past and present schooling practices to serve these students effectively is highly significant. The rest of this chapter describes the extent to which schools and schooling practices must change in order to reverse this failure.

Characteristics of Effective Schools

Within the last twenty-five years, researchers have compiled a considerable body of data on effective school practices. A review of the accumulated data identifies the following characteristics of effective schools (Purkey & Smith, 1985):

Administrative leadership: Effective principals are actively engaged in curriculum planning, staff development, and instructional issues.

Teacher expectations: Teachers maintain high achievement expectations for all students.

Emphasis on basic skills: There is a deliberate focus on reading, writing, math, and language arts.

School climate: An orderly, safe environment conducive to teaching and learning is maintained.

Regular feedback: Continual feedback on academic progress is provided to students and parents.

Variables in Schools

Edmonds (1979) contributed to the emerging picture of effective schools, particularly with regard to "minority" students. He identified two groups of variables—organizational and structural variables, and process variables—that together define the climate and culture of the school. Organizational and structural variables include:

School site management: School leadership and staff have considerable autonomy in determining the exact means by which they address the problem of increasing academic performance.

Instructional leadership: The principal initiates and maintains procedures for improving achievement.

Curriculum planning and organization: In elementary schools, the curriculum has a clear focus on the acquisition of basic skills. Instruction takes into consideration students' linguistic and cultural attributes across grade levels and throughout the entire curriculum.

Staff development: This variable is essential to change and consists of a schoolwide program closely related to the instructional program. This activity is crucial in schools serving language minority students.

Parent support and involvement: Support from parents is essential to the success of any educational program for language minority students.

Schoolwide recognition of academic success: Recognition of student achievement is reflected in the school's activities.

District support: Financial and administrative support is fundamental to change and to the maintenance of effective schools.

Edmonds (1979a) defined process variables as factors that sustain a productive school climate. He identified four process variables:

Collaborative planning and collegial relationships: Teachers and administrators work together to implement change.

A sense of community: A feeling of belonging contributes to reduced alienation and increased student achievement.

Clear goals and high expectations: These are commonly shared. A focus on those tasks deemed most important allows the school to direct its resources and shape its functioning toward the realization of goals.

Order and discipline: These help to maintain the seriousness and purpose with which the school approaches its task.

Carter and Chatfield (1986, p. 224) report similar attributes present in effective elementary schools serving Mexican American, African American, and Asian students in California. Their analyses suggest that processes, not structures, of pedagogy, administrative arrangements, and classroom organization are most closely linked to effectiveness. Carter and Chatfield describe an effective school for language minority students as a well-functioning total system producing a school social climate that promotes positive outcomes. They broke their analysis into two parts:

1. Specific characteristics crucial to the development of effective schooling and thus to a positive school climate, such as a safe and orderly school environment, and positive leadership, usually from the formal leaders (administrators, principals, and curriculum specialists). Also important was common agreement on a strong academic orientation—that is, clearly

stated academic goals, objectives, and plans—and well-functioning methods to monitor school input and student outcomes.

2. A positive school social climate that includes high staff expectations for children and the instructional program; a strong demand for academic performance; denial of the cultural-deprivation argument and the stereotypes that support it; high staff morale, consisting of strong internal support, consensus building, job satisfaction, feelings of personal efficacy, belief that the system works, a sense of ownership, well-defined roles and responsibilities, and practices that reflect the policy that resources are best expended on people rather than on educational software and hardware.

Much like Edmonds (1979) and Purkey and Smith (1985), Carter and Chatfield (1986) examined the attributes of schools that selectively promoted achievement of immigrant students. Table 8.1 identifies factors that will facilitate teaching and learning with respect to immigrant students

These findings correspond with those of other recent studies of the effectiveness of programs specifically designed for diverse populations. California Tomorrow (1995, p. 8), in a study of early childhood care in California, concluded that the following principles guided quality child care across a variety of settings that serve a growing community of linguistically and culturally diverse families:

1. Supporting the development of ethnic identity and nonracist attitudes among children.
2. Building on the cultures of families and promoting cross-cultural understanding among children.
3. Fostering the preservation of children's home language and encouraging bilingualism among all children.
4. Engaging in ongoing reflection and dialogue.

After reviewing the literature on multicultural early childhood education and interviewing experts in the field, Cohen and Pompa (1994) came to the same conclusion, noting that universal notions of "developmentally appropriate" approaches must be revised to recognize the more specific "culturally appropriate developmental" issues.

A state-mandated study of exemplary schools serving California's linguistically and culturally diverse students indicated that several key attributes were common in such settings. These key attributes included the following:

Table 8.1 Reconceptualizing of Responsive Schools for Immigrant Students	
RECONCEPTUALIZING OF LEARNERS AS . . .	**IMPLICATIONS FOR IMMIGRANT STUDENTS**
Active constructors of knowledge	• Supports and values learning through various means, thus acknowledging different styles. • Reduces reliance on language as the medium for learning. • Conflicts with the views of many other cultures, which hold that learners take in what teachers deliver. • May require more language use and cultural knowledge than some immigrants have attained.
Collaborators	• Promotes language use in the classroom. • Promotes cross-cultural learning and communication. • Is consistent with learning strategies in cultures with a collective orientation, which traditional U.S. competitive learning is not. • May require more language use and cultural knowledge than some immigrants have attained. • Requires cross-cultural sensitivity for all involved.
Decision makers	• Draws on strengths of students who play decision-making roles. • Conflicts with collective orientation in emphasizing individual will, action, and responsibility. • May conflict with adolescent roles in other cultures.
Communities	• Encourages everyone to learn about immigrant students and families in order to integrate them into the community. • Requires personalization of schooling.
Learner centered	• Encourages everyone to learn about immigrant students and families in order to design schooling with learners at the center. • Requires personalization of schooling.
Part of a larger situational and chronological context	• Encourages schools to find ways to engage immigrant families in schooling. • Brings together multiple providers of service and assistance for immigrant families. • May eventually lead schools to provide assistance for immigrant students as they move beyond high school into work and higher education.
Mediators between home culture and mainstream culture	• Makes information about U.S. culture and schooling accessible to immigrant students. • Shows immigrant students that their cultures and experiences are valued. • Gives immigrant students access to academic knowledge and abilities.

Source: Adapted from T. Lucas, *Into, Through, and Beyond Secondary School: Critical Transitions for Immigrant Youth.* Washington, D.C. and McHenry, IL: Center for Applied Linguistics and Delta Systems, 1997, pp. 58–59. Reprinted by permission from Tamara Lucas.

1. *Flexibility:* Adapting to the diversity of languages, mobility, and nonschool needs of these students and their families.
2. *Coordination:* Utilizing sometimes scarce and diverse resources, such as federal and state funds and local community organizations, in highly coordinated ways to achieve academic goals.
3. *Cultural validation:* Validating students' culture by incorporating materials and discussions that build on the linguistic and cultural aspects of the community.
4. *Shared vision:* Uniting the principal, staff, parents, and community behind a common, coherent sense of who the students are and what they hope to accomplish (Berman, 1992a).

Three more recent analyses of exemplary schools that serve high percentages of linguistically and culturally diverse students are worthy of mention. The first is a series of studies in five urban and suburban school districts in various regions of the United States that focused on the variables that determine whether students achieve academic success in a second language (Collier, 1995). These studies included some 42,000 students per school year over an 8- to 12-year period for each school district. Three key factors were reported as significant in producing academic success for students in the schools studied:

Key Factors

1. Complex cognitive instruction in the students' first language for as long as possible and in the second language for part of the school day.
2. Use of current approaches to teaching academic curriculum in both the primary language and secondary language through active discovery and cognitively complex learning.
3. Such changes in the sociocultural context of schooling as integrating English speakers, implementing additive bilingual instructional goals, and encouraging positive minority/majority relations (Thomas & Collier, 1995b).

Another recent set of studies focused on selected schools in which highly diverse and poor student populations demonstrated academic success. These schools were subjected to intensive site-by-site study in order to identify the attributes that related to the effectiveness of each school and those that were common to all (McLeod, 1996). Schools in Texas, Illinois, California, and Massachusetts were particularly successful in achieving high academic outcomes with a diverse set of students. They shared the following goals for ensuring high-quality teaching:

**Steps to
Promote
High-Quality
Teaching**

1. *Foster English acquisition and the development of mature literacy.* Schools utilized students' native-language abilities to develop literacy expertise that was then transferred to English literacy development at high levels.

2. *Deliver grade-level content.* Challenging academic work was introduced along with the goal of learning English. Teachers organized lessons to deliver grade-level instruction through a variety of native-language, ESL or **sheltered English,** activities—specifically designed academic instruction in English that maximizes nonverbal instructional communication, combining content with English-language learning goals.

3. *Organize instruction in innovative ways.* Examples of innovations included developing "schools-within-schools" to deal more responsively with the diverse language needs of the students; forming "families" of students who stayed together for major parts of a middle-school day; creating "continuum classes" in which teachers remained with their students for two to three years in order to become more familiar with and respond to their diversity; and continually grouping students more flexibly in order to accommodate their native- and second-language developmental differences.

4. *Protect and extend instructional time.* Schools utilize after-school programs, supportive computer-based instruction, and voluntary Saturday and summer schools to multiply the opportunities for students to learn. Not surprisingly, a majority of the students took advantage of these voluntary extensions. Care was taken, however, not to allow teachers' auxiliary responsibilities to erode the daily instructional time.

5. *Expand teachers' roles and responsibilities.* Teachers were given much greater roles in instructional and curricular decision-making in order to ensure cross-grade articulation and coordination. Teachers in these schools became full co-partners with the administrators. They devised more authentic writing, math, and related assessment tools that could inform instruction.

6. *Address students' social and emotional needs.* These schools were located in low-income neighborhoods and served poor families. Therefore, they adopted a proactive stance with regard to community issues. For example, in one school an after-school activity aimed at families, and particularly at issues of alcohol and drug abuse, family violence, health care, and related needs, brought the school staff together with social service agencies. Similar instances of family counseling and direct medical care were arranged at other sites.

7. *Involve parents in their children's education.* Some of these schools were magnet schools; parents had chosen to send

their children there. In such sites, parent involvement was part of the contract, and it included participating in school committees, assisting with school programs, helping on student field trips, and the like. In nonmagnet schools, parent outreach services were an integral part of the school operation. In all cases, regular communication in the various languages of the home occurred. Parent participation in governance of the school was a common attribute, although highly variable.

In a third recent analysis—a more intensive case study of two elementary schools and one middle school—Miramontes, Nadeau, and Commins (1997) detailed the development of exemplary school attributes, emphasizing the link between decision-making (who decides what and how instruction is implemented) and effective programs. Over a period of several years these schools, where as many as five languages were represented, earned local, state, and national recognition for their academic success with their extremely linguistically and culturally diverse student bodies. Table 8.2 lists the basic premises that Miramontes, Nadeau, and Commins identified as keys to the schools' effective programs.

Link to Decision-Making

Transforming Schools

The research described above offers a quick set of checklists for assessing what "good" schools should be like. Whereas these examinations are based on "what is," other educational reformers have pointed us in the direction of "what ought to be." For example, Berman (1992a, 1996) offers us a view that portrays the ideal schooling transformation, as outlined in Table 8.3.

In summary, effective instructional strategies recognize that learning is rooted in sharing expertise and experiences through multiple avenues of communication. They also recognize that any attempt to address the needs of linguistically and culturally diverse students in a deficit or "subtractive" mode is counterproductive. Instead, educators add to the rich core of cognitive, linguistic, academic, and cultural understanding and skills that these students bring with them. Each one of us can assist in the development of instructional practices that more fully explore the issues raised here.

The National School Reform Perspective

Policy Statements

Recent policy statements regarding the challenges of educating a linguistically and culturally diverse student population reinforce this charge to all of us working in the field. The National Council of Teachers of English and the International Reading Association

Table 8.2   Basic Premises of Effective School Reform

Premise 1. Active learning. Knowledge is best acquired when learners actively participate in meaningful activities that are constructive in nature and appropriate to their level of development.

Premise 2. The primary language foundation. The more comprehensive the use of the primary language, the greater the potential for linguistically diverse students to be academically successful. There are always ways to nurture the primary language regardless of school resources.

Premise 3. The quality of primary language use. There is a difference between a token use of the primary language in instruction and its full development as a foundation for thinking and learning.

Premise 4. Strategies for second-language development. Second-language development creates an added dimension to instructional decision-making. Instruction must reflect specific strategies designed to meet the needs of second-language learners.

Premise 5. Contexts for second-language development. Second-language instruction must be organized to provide students the time, experiences, and opportunities they need to fully develop language proficiency. This requires a range of social and academic contexts in which both language and content are emphasized.

Premise 6. First- and second-language environments. Bilingual academic proficiency requires that clear, distinct, and meaning enriched contexts for each language be created during instructional time.

Premise 7. Transitions and redesignations. Decisions regarding transition to formal second-language reading and redesignations that exit students from programs cannot be made arbitrarily.

Premise 8. Instructional assessment. Instructional assessment must be based on students' first- and second-language development, rather than on grade level or predetermined criteria. An appropriate assessment plan should address language and literacy development, as well as content knowledge.

Premise 9. Parents and community. Parents and community need to play a major role in the learning and schooling of their children.

Premise 10. Planning for cross-cultural interactions. Instruction must be organized to help students understand and respect themselves and their own culture as well as the cultures of the broader society. Planned cross-cultural interactions are an essential component of programs for all students.

Premise 11. Socio-cultural and political implications. Socio-cultural factors and political context must be considered in making decisions regarding every aspect of program planning.

Premise 12. Teachers as decision-makers. Teachers are decision makers. As part of a learning community they are all equally responsible for decisions regarding the instructional program for linguistically diverse students.

Reprinted by permission of the publisher from O. B. Miramontes, A. Nadeau, & N. L. Commins, *Restructuring Schools for Linguistic Diversity: Linking Decision Making to Effective Programs* (New York: Teachers College Press, © 1997 by Teachers College, Columbia University. All rights reserved.), pp. 37–38.

(1996, p. 3), in their enunciation of standards for English language arts, state:

Students develop an understanding of and respect for diversity in language use, patterns, and dialects across cultures, ethnic groups, geographic regions, and social roles.

Table 8.3 Schooling Transformation: What Is Versus What Ought to Be

CURRENT SYSTEM: School as Learning Environment	NEW SCHOOL DESIGN: School as Community of Learners
Passive. Instruction relies on teacher as dispenser of known knowledge and student as consumer and is based on abstract modes of learning.	**Engaged.** Instruction relies on guided inquiry and conversations with teacher as mentor providing assistance to enable students to perform authentic tasks that they could not otherwise do by themselves; teachers create multiple learning activities and "group" for diverse learning styles, and students engage in self-regulated performance activities with clear goals and measures of performance.
Age-based groups and tracking. Classes and students are grouped by "ability" and/or tracks at age levels.	**Developmental.** Students would be organized in (cognitive and affective) developmentally appropriate groupings, rather than age-specific grades, and classes would be heterogeneous within development groups; students would work in smaller, fluid groups within classes, and act as coaches as well as performers.
Abstract curriculum. Curriculum based on abstract categorizations and driven by college entry requirements and standardized tests.	**Thematic and integrated curriculum.** Curriculum designed by teachers and students together and based on themes and projects that relate to student experiences and interests.
Unclear and/or irrelevant standards. Standards largely defined by college course entry requirements and vary greatly and idiosyncratically for students.	**Performance-based standards and assessments.** Standards defined and redefined by the broader community with a focus on authentic outcomes and indicators.
Affectively neutral. Pseudo "business" environment, professionals charged with producing academic goals.	**Affectively engaged.** Professional "care" for the students, to celebrate and embrace them, and for the intellectual well-being of the institution.

Source: Paul Berman, *The Status of Bilingual Education in California.* Copyright © 1992. Used with permission.

Students whose first language is not English make use of their first language to develop competency in the English language arts and to develop understanding of content across the curriculum.

Celebrating our shared beliefs and traditions is not enough; we also need to honor that which is distinctive in the many groups that make up our nation.

The National Association for the Education of Young Children (1997, p. 12) echoes these same concerns in its position statement:

Early childhood educators can best help linguistically and culturally diverse children and their families by acknowledging and responding to the importance of the child's home language and culture. Administrative support for bilingualism as a goal is necessary within the educational setting. Educational practices should focus on educating children toward the "school culture" while preserving and respecting the diversity of the home language and culture that each child brings to the early learning setting.

Lastly, the U.S. Department of Education has issued a set of principles that are meant to guide states and local school districts as they consider systemic reform of practices and knowledge regarding the education of linguistically and culturally diverse students (see Table 8.4).

Through all these efforts, schools are being asked to transform themselves into institutions that actively engage learners in a diverse community. They must be cognizant of the fluidity of human development, focused on a thematically integrated curriculum, responsive to performance-based standards and assessments, and staffed with highly professional and caring personnel. Although this is a tall order, such an envisioned transformation drives home the point that the schools of the future will not only need to do a better job but will need to change radically.

Table 8.4   Guiding Principles

Principle #1. Limited English proficient students are held to the same high expectations of learning established for all students.

Principle #2. Limited English proficient students develop full productive and receptive proficiencies in English in the domains of listening, speaking, reading, and writing, consistent with expectations for all students.

Principle #3. Limited English proficient students reach challenging content and performance standards in all content areas, including reading and language arts, mathematics, social studies, science, the fine arts, health, and physical education, consistent with those for all students.

Principle #4. Limited English proficient students receive instruction that builds on their previous education and cognitive abilities and that reflects their language proficiency levels.

Principle #5. Limited English proficient students are evaluated with appropriate and valid assessments that are aligned with state and local standards and that take into account the language acquisition stages and cultural backgrounds of the students.

Principle #6. The academic success of limited English proficient students is a responsibility shared by all educators, the family, and the community.

Source: The George Washington University Center for Equity and Excellence in Education, *Promoting Excellence: Ensuring Academic Services for Limited English Proficient Students,* 1996, Arlington, VA: Evaluation Assistance Center East.

Effective Instructional Practices

Socialization

Instructional reform is a necessary element of radical change in our schools. Given the notion that schools, like families, directly or indirectly socialize children as much as they formally teach (Spindler, 1955), the development of academic competence may be related to academic socialization (Trueba, 1987). Recent ethnographic studies and case studies (Au & Jordan, 1981; Diaz, Moll, & Mehan, 1986; Duran, 1983; Erickson, 1987; Moll, 1988; Tharp & Gallimore, 1988; Trueba, 1988b) have reported a significant relationship between instruction that is congruent with a student's culture and that child's academic success.

Successful Techniques

For example, Gallimore and Tharp (1989) have carefully described the educational program developed for native Hawaiians. These programs utilize gender-relevant cooperative education procedures that match the gender roles in this population: boys and girls work together in small groups. Similar cooperative education structures are utilized effectively in Navaho classrooms: boys are grouped together and girls are grouped together (Tharp, 1989). Moll (1988) has also described successful cooperative techniques used with Hispanic students in southwestern U.S. schools. He concludes that such cooperative social structures directly "match" specific Hispanic family values and practices. Other sociolinguistic studies have shown that the language of the classroom—or academic discourse—is a highly specialized code that students need to learn and "is not simply a transparent medium through which the academic curriculum is transmitted" (Mehan, 1979, p. 124). From this perspective, schooling involves not only cognitive development and the acquisition of knowledge but socialization as well (Spindler, 1974, 1982).

Interaction of Factors

The understanding that cognitive development and socialization are paired leads to several important implications for the education of culturally and linguistically diverse children. Language and culture, and their accompanying values, are acquired in the home and community environment. Children come to school with some knowledge about language, how it works and how it is used, and learn higher-level cognitive and metalinguistic skills as they engage in socially meaningful activities. Children's development and learning are best understood as the interaction of linguistic, sociocultural, and cognitive factors.

These conclusions can be directly supported by recent research that documents instructionally effective practices with linguistically and culturally diverse students in selected schools around the United States (August & Hakuta, 1997; California Tomorrow, 1995 ; Carter & Chatfield, 1986; Cohen & Pompa, 1994 ; Faltis & Hudleson, 1997; Fashola, Slavin, Calderón, & Duran, 1997;

Lucas, Henze, & Donato, 1990; McLeod, 1996; Miramontes et al., 1997; Moll, 1988; Pease-Alvarez, Espinoza, & García, 1991; Rose, 1995; Tikunoff, 1983). These descriptive studies identified specific schools and classrooms that served linguistically and culturally diverse students well. Using the case study approach, the researchers looked at instructional practices in preschool, elementary school, and high school classrooms. They interviewed teachers, principals, parents, and students, and conducted specific classroom observations that assessed the dynamics of the instructional process. We shall now examine two of these studies: the SBIF study and the García and related studies.

The SBIF Study

In Chapter 7 we described the Significant Bilingual Instructional Features (SBIF) study performed by Tikunoff (1983) in order to identify attributes of exemplary teaching approaches. The SBIF findings can be divided into two parts: instructional features common to language minority and majority classrooms and instructional features unique to language minority classrooms. As we saw in Chapter 7, this study of 58 "effective" classrooms identified the following set of instructional features:

SBIF Findings

1. Task outcomes were clearly specified for students.
2. "Active teaching" behaviors were utilized extensively to (a) maintain students' engagement in tasks by pacing instruction appropriately and promoting involvement, (b) monitor students' progress, and (c) provide immediate feedback to students.

Effective instructional features specific to limited English proficient (LEP) students of Hispanic background included the use of two languages, special activities for teaching a second language, and instructional practices that took advantage of the students' culture.

Use of Language

The SBIF study reported that English was used approximately 60 percent of the time, and that the native language (L1) or a combination of L1 and the second language (L2) was used the rest of the time. The percentage of English used increased with grade level. The two languages were often combined in one of the following ways:

1. Instructors alternated between the students' native language and English whenever necessary to ensure clarity. They switched languages but rarely translated directly from one language to another.

BECOMING A RESPONSIVE TEACHER

An Effective Teacher's Reflections, in Her Own Voice

Cup of coffee in one hand and my journal in the other, I sit down to write my reflections. It is 7:30 a.m. and my bilingual first-grade class will start in half an hour. I flip to yesterday's page and recall how well our learning logs are going and how unsure I had been about their use. I also jot a short comment about how well Sammy is approximating in his phonetic guesses in reading and writing, something I also was not sure about just 24 hours ago. In fact, just eight years ago I was unsure about a lot of my teaching because of the paradigm shift that I was going through. That isn't true now because of the knowledge and practice I have acquired through professional reading, peer discussion groups, risk-taking, time, and reflection.

Today, April 2, 1993, I look around and I see a classroom filled with print: print that is chosen for its functional use; print that often reflects what we are currently learning and hope to learn; print that belongs to children in process of becoming literate community members. Today the children are immersed in a print-filled classroom that identifies our theme, dinosaurs. The brainstorm charts include the titles "What We Know" and "What We Want to Learn" about dinosaurs. One vocabulary chart in particular will be used to classify dinosaur words or put them in ABC order. In the book corner there is a minimum of 100 books, with at least 20 authored by the children. Lists around the room remind us of our schedules, what we need to order, or who will be visiting our classrooms. I stop and look at a chart that lists the books we have already read during our dinosaur theme. We also have noted whether they inform us with scientific facts or teach us about literature. The condition of immersion supports children's reading and writing as well as collections of their knowledge.

The student-centered feeling in my classroom comes from children bringing themselves and their world into our collaborative learning. Their language, background, experiences, and interests, what they know and what they want to learn, are continually shared. On the first day of school we shared what we wanted to learn in first grade and why. These themes then became the curriculum, and my role became one of orchestrating grade-level objectives, instructional strategies, and the content of the theme.

When my students write in interactive journals they highlight for me this condition of student-centeredness. They share their lives, what they know or are not sure about. Children write about the visit they had with their grandparents or what they hope Mommy will buy for them on Saturday or why the doctor can't help their little sister get better. I respond to each child about his or her written entry with both written and oral discourse. We read together my response and the child then responds orally to

BECOMING A RESPONSIVE TEACHER *Cont.*

my questions or comments. A student-centered condition reflects that children have ownership of their learning.

As an instructional strategy, interactive journals allow me to demonstrate literacy on a very individual basis. I demonstrate that oral language is meaningful, that written language uses a phonetic system and that what they write (initially strings of letters) is important to me. During interactive journal writing, I sit next to each child, and we read, write, speak, and listen to each other. Demonstration informs children as to how I do it and informs me as to how they do. Through thinking aloud during my demonstrations I try to communicate why and how they might make better approximations in their learning.

Approximation is a condition that allows children to take risks in all areas of literacy. I see approximations in their writing pieces that are in their learning logs, journal entries, and narrative first drafts. I hear approximations in their reading and their personal response to literature as well as in their oral discussions about their learning. These approximations include the quality of being close to as well as knowing what is almost exact. These approximations help to inform my instruction so that I am able to plan for optimal learning.

I have organized my classroom in four distinct areas. These areas call for children to actively participate in social organizations that promote specific types of engagement. The main area of the classroom places children in desks that are in foursomes, allowing children to actively participate in cooperative structures quickly. It also produces lots of talk. The discourse that is shared might be about the content of the theme or about constructing meaning from one language to another.

Near the front of the room is a small area where I teach to four small groups, one group each half hour. The active participation that occurs during this strategy comes in part from the nature of the text we use for literacy lessons: whole texts. This morning I will be teaching about sequencing within a wordless book strategy. Even the wordless book has a complete story to be told, and therefore it supports the students as they construct with me a written text to accompany the story in pictures. Another lesson I will teach today begins with a whole poem which the children learned through repeated choral reading. During this shared reading lesson I will focus on rhyming words and their smaller parts, called short vowels.

Wholeness is a condition that also lies within theme work and literature conversations. A theme cycle begins with the whole class sharing thematic knowledge, moving into smaller groups to share and gain specific information, and returning to the whole to share new learning and initiate a new theme cycle. Within a literature conversation, I or a student reads the whole

BECOMING A RESPONSIVE TEACHER *Cont.*

book, then in small groups or pairs we share personal connections as well as our thoughts on literature elements such as plot and setting.

Across the room, eight to ten children are able to sit around a long rectangular table and participate in the writing process. Children choose their own topics, share what they are writing, and ask for support in content and mechanics from each other at the writing table. Around the room there are centers that are organized by theme, ABC awareness, bilingual use, listening, and/or art. Two children work at each center in pairs. These pairs were created so that children could demonstrate to each other language, knowledge, social skills, and/or work habits. Active participation as a condition occurs more often when the condition of choice is also present.

Choice happens in my classroom individually and collaboratively. In both interactive journals and during the author's cycle children choose the topic, amount, genre and even language (Spanish or English) of their written work. During DEAR [Drop Everything and Read] Time, children choose what book or books they will read. In theme work they often choose what they will research and what group they will join. At the listening center children choose what form (such as story map, word web, or character profile) they will use to share their connections to the book with the rest of the class.

When children see the authentic purpose for the choices they are making they become more involved in their learning. The purpose must go beyond the classroom and beyond covering the skills of first grade. Again, the organization of my classroom supports children in real-life uses of language and literacy: children engage in talk in large groups, small groups (teacher-directed), groups of four (peer talk at the desk groups), and one-on-one (centers). The organization also helps them in the real-life task of selecting which kind of talk is most functional. If students choose to author a book about their younger brother and his adventures, they realize they will go through the same process that real authors do. The narrative text will call for teaching and learning opportunities but the authenticity lies in the sharing of the published book with an audience. Much of the written work that my children write is shared with others for response.

Response helps children to understand their work better through the reflections of others. These reflections assist children in their oral and written performance. In the Author's Chair phase of writing, my children read their first draft to an audience that understands that they are to listen for story line or informational facts. If students in the audience are unable to

BECOMING A RESPONSIVE TEACHER *Cont.*

construct meaning during Author's Chair, they need to ask the author for support and then assist him or her with words or ideas that support meaning. During editing, both peers and I will help with mechanics, such as spelling or punctuation. This type of response helps to create the condition of community.

The community of co-learners that my students and I belong to has common interests and commitment to working together. I often find this condition hard to describe but it is one you can feel and observe in a very short time. What is often mentioned by visitors to our classroom is the ownership that the children have of their classroom, how they participate in its management, and their interest in sharing their community with others.

As I sit here and complete my reflections, I am surprised that I have not mentioned the condition called expectations. In fact, this condition is the one I bring to my classroom and can be the most important one for my children. It is also the one condition that teachers control through what they believe their children are able to do. Can all the children learn to read and write in my classroom? Yes, and so they will. Once, a long time ago, I expected that only one group of children in my classroom would read at grade level, that another group would almost achieve that level, and that the third group would just get through one small book. Expectations or lack of expectations are often influenced by social and economic factors that we note about our children (such as being poor, having no books at home, or no one to help at home). Our lack of understanding of the linguistic or cultural diversity that our children bring to our classrooms also influences the expectations that we set for our children. This condition is also of interest because my peers set expectations for themselves, as I do each school year. I have never failed to meet the expectations I have set for myself and would guess that very few others have failed to meet theirs. Yet, I often hear about how expectations had to be lowered so that students could feel successful in learning. Holding high expectations for all learners not only calls for trust in the learner but also for creating conditions for optimal learning in every classroom.

It's 7:55 a.m., my coffee is cold, and the children will arrive in five minutes. As I look through my written reflections, I wonder what my colleagues think about these conditions creating optimal learning for all children?

Source: Erminda García, Alianza School, Watsonville, CA. Used by permission of the author.

BECOMING A RESPONSIVE TEACHER *Cont.*

▼ Meeting the Challenge

1. According to this teacher, what are the conditions that create optimal learning for all children? Identify as many as you can, using the teacher's own wording.
2. If you could sit and talk with this teacher for a while, what questions would you ask? Describe what you think would be your areas of agreement or disagreement regarding the methods and goals of education.
3. Experiment with interactive journal writing in class. Go back through this book and select a topic that you still have questions about. Write a page or two of reflection as a journal entry. Now exchange journals with a classmate, write a response, and exchange journals once again.

2. Students developed English language skills during ongoing instruction in the regular classroom rather than in a separate ESL classroom.

Language Switching

Of interest is the finding that bilingual instruction was characterized by the use of both the native language and English in classroom interactions. This language switching seemed to directly assist in clarifying instructional discourse. However, Wong-Fillmore and Valadez (1985) have suggested that language switching may be detrimental to second-language acquisition if too much translation is encouraged. In a study of a concurrent bilingual instructional model, Milk (1986) reports that a nontranslation concurrent approach yielded functional language-switching discourse patterns similar to those found for separation instructional models. Students in the study followed a language choice rule ("Speak to the speaker in the language in which you are addressed") in a discourse situation that included 47.5 percent Spanish use and 57.5 percent English use. Such data suggest further that instructional discourse should concentrate on clarity, and that clarity can be enhanced through the use of the students' native language.

The SBIF study also reports that incorporating aspects of the LEP students' home culture can promote engagement in instructional tasks and contribute to a feeling of trust between children and their teachers. The SBIF researchers found three ways in which home and community culture was incorporated into classroom life: (1) cultural referents in both verbal and nonverbal forms were used to communicate instructional and institutional demands, (2) instruction was organized to build upon rules of discourse from the home culture, and (3) values and norms of the home culture were respected equally with those of the school.

The García and Related Studies

In recent research on Mexican American elementary school children, García (1988, 1991d, 1997) reported several related instructional strategies utilized in "effective" schools. Students at these schools, which were nominated for the study by teachers of language minority students, scored at or above the national average on standardized measures of academic achievement in Spanish and/or English. This research characterized instruction in the effective classrooms as follows:

1. Students were instructed primarily in small groups, and academic-related discourse was encouraged between students

throughout the day. Teachers rarely utilized large-group instruction or more individualized (e.g., mimeographed worksheets) instructional activities. The most common activity across classes involved small groups of students working on assigned academic tasks with intermittent assistance by the teacher.

2. Teachers tended to initiate instruction in a way often reported in the literature (Mehan, 1979; Morine-Dershimer, 1985) and to elicit student responses at relatively lower cognitive and linguistic levels. They then allowed students to control the discourse and to invite participation from peers. These invited interactions often occurred at higher cognitive and linguistic levels.

Of particular relevance are intensive case studies of elementary and middle schools (Heath & Mangiola, 1991; Freeman & Freeman, 1997; García, 1988, 1992a; García & Stein, 1996; Henderson & Landesman, 1992; Miramontes et al., 1997; Moll, 1988; Pease-Alvarez & García, 1991; Secada, 1996). The results of these studies are summarized below according to several instructional categories that were empirically relevant. Much like the attributes of effective teaching discussed in Chapter 7, the attributes described are not to be construed as necessary for the effective instruction of linguistically and culturally diverse students. Instead, they are offered as an example of how instructional environments can be structured to serve diversity.

High Levels of Communication. In the classrooms studied, functional communication between teacher and students and among fellow students was emphasized more than might be expected in a regular classroom. Teachers were constantly checking with students to verify the clarity of assignments and the students' roles in those assignments. Classrooms were characterized by a high, sometimes even noisy, level of communication that stressed student collaboration on small-group projects organized around learning centers. This organization minimized individualized work tasks, such as worksheet exercises, and provided a very informal, familylike social setting in which the teacher either worked with a small group of students (never larger than eight and at times as small as one) or traveled about the room assisting individuals or small groups of students as they worked on their projects. Large-group instruction was rare, and was usually confined to start-up activities in the morning.

| Informal
| Setting

Integrated and Thematic Curriculum. Significantly, the instruction of basic skills and academic content was consistently organized around thematic units. In the majority of classrooms studied, the students actually selected the themes in consultation with the teacher, either through direct voting or some related negotiation process. The teacher's responsibility was to ensure that the instruction revolving around the chosen themes covered the school district's content- and skill-related goals and objectives for that grade level.

Benefits of Theme Approach

The theme approach allowed teachers to integrate academic content with the development of basic skills. The major thrust in these classrooms was the appropriation of knowledge centered on chosen themes, with the understanding that students would necessarily develop basic skills as a means to appropriate this knowledge. Students became "experts" in thematic domains while also acquiring the requisite academic skills. Henderson and Landesman (1992) provide an excellent example of this approach as used by middle-school mathematics teachers, who worked closely with their colleagues in language arts, science, and social studies to construct thematic lessons across these disciplines.

Interactive Cross-Age Tutoring. A common occurrence in exemplary classrooms was the use of older students as tutors for younger students (August & Hakuta, 1997; Heath & Mangiola, 1991). These student tutors usually were able to communicate in the younger students' native language, even if the teacher

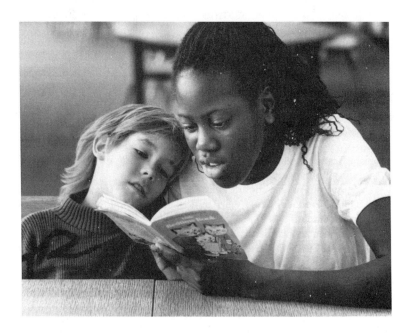

INTERACTIVE JOURNALS: An Example of Responsive Pedagogy

In *Interactive Journals,* students write about what is important to them. They share their life stories and their burning interests. In return, teachers are able to say to their students through their oral and written responses. "What goes on in your life is important to me." *Interactive Journal* writing also promotes the development of written conventions through written demonstration by teachers as they respond to the student's entries. Furthermore, the emphasis on the message (and not the mechanics) encourages students to take more risks with their writing topics and skills (in the language they chose). *Interactive Journals* in which students write and teachers respond on a daily basis create a developmental record of writing progress (Flores & García, 1984; García, 1996).

Recommended Procedures:

1. The *Interactive Journals* procedure has at least three basic parts: (a) the student draws and writes; (b) a teacher/paraprofessional/parent volunteer or peer responds with a written question about the student's entry; and (c) the student answers the question either orally or in written form.

2. Before beginning this instructional strategy, it is helpful to demonstrate the three basic parts of the interaction. In a large format such as an overhead transparency or a chart, write the date, brainstorm a topic out loud, draw, and then vocalize the words as you write your entry. Then, if possible, ask another teacher or parent to write a written question to your entry. Finally, orally respond to the question.

3. Ask students to follow the same procedures that you have demonstrated. As they finish their entries, students bring them to a teacher for a response in the form of a question. Students in turn orally or in written form answer the teacher's question.

   For emergent readers and writers: When students bring you a journal entry that you cannot read (i.e., it is scribbled or in letter string form), simply ask them to "read" it to you. As you respond with a written question, be sure and vocalize as you write so that the students can understand the question and respond to you.

   For independent readers and writers: Experiment with buddy journals. Pair students up with a buddy (either randomly or by allowing students to suggest their top choices for a writing partner with you making the final decision), and ask them to write to each other. Teachers occasionally collect and respond to the journals to provide both a model of writing and to monitor students' progress.

INTERACTIVE JOURNALS: An Example of Responsive Pedagogy (*cont.*)

Reminders:

▼ Students, not teachers, choose topics for [the language and] journal entries.

▼ Students receive a response each time they write.

▼ During journal time, teachers write in their own journals and ask a student to respond.

Adapted from Barbara Flores and Erminda García, "A Collaborative Learning and Teaching Experience Using Journal Writing," *NABE: The Journal for the National Association for Bilingual Education*, vol. 8, no. 2 (Winter 1984). Reprinted by permission of the National Association of Bilingual Education.

Students Tutoring

could not do so. Literacy experiences—working with students in reading and analyzing a story, assisting them with the writing process, and participating in interactive journals—were among the more typical activities of the tutors, although specific math and science tutoring also took place. This interactive cross-age tutoring had the benefits of providing more instructional assistance for the teacher, allowing for the use and development of more first- and second-language lesson activities in small groups with native speakers, and supplementing the academic experiences of the student tutors.

Collaborative Learning. Reported analyses of instructional events in literacy and math, along with analyses of actual literacy products (dialogue journals, learning logs, writing workshop publications, etc.) and math products (learning logs, homework, surveys, etc.), indicate that teachers in Latino language minority classrooms organized instruction in such a way that students were required to interact with each other utilizing collaborative

Student Discourse

learning techniques. It was during student-student interactions that most linguistic discourse of a higher cognitive order was observed (García, 1988, 1992a). Students asked each other hard questions and challenged each other's answers more readily than they did in interactions with the teacher. Moreover, students were more likely to seek assistance from other students and were successful in obtaining it. Specific techniques, such as "think-pair-share," "four corners," and "heads together," which have been well articulated by Kagan (1993), were commonly utilized.

Language and Literacy. In classes with Spanish speakers, lower-grade teachers used both Spanish and English as the language of instruction, whereas upper-grade teachers utilized mostly

English. However, students were allowed to use either language. With regard to the literacy development of Spanish-speaking students, observations revealed the following:

▼ Students progressed systematically from writing in the native language in the early grades to writing in English in the later grades.
▼ Students' writing in English emerged at or above their grade level of writing in Spanish.
▼ Students' writing in English was highly conventional, contained few spelling or grammatical errors, and showed systematic use of invented spelling.
▼ Students made the transformation from Spanish to English themselves, without any pressure from the teacher to do so.

Freeman and Freeman (1997) have provided a detailed analysis of native-language reading processes, particularly in Spanish, that is relevant to all literacy programs with an initial focus on the student's native language. They have developed a very useful checklist for assessing effective reading instruction (see Table 8.5). Too often, students are moved from native-language reading into English reading without attention to the level of their reading effectiveness in their native language. The "reading cost" to students in such circumstances can be severe, since they are not able to transfer their instructional gains in reading from one language to the other.

"Reading Cost"

Table 8.5 Checklist for Effective Reading Instruction

1. Do students value themselves as readers and do they value reading?
2. Do teachers read frequently to students for a wide variety of genres?
3. Do students see teachers engaged in reading for pleasure as well as for information?
4. Do students have a wide variety of reading materials to choose from and time to read?
5. Do students make good choices and read a variety of genres for authentic purposes?
6. Do students regard reading as meaning making at all times?
7. Are students efficient readers? That is, do they make a balanced use of all three cueing systems?
8. Are students efficient readers? That is, do they make a minimal use of cues to construct meaning?
9. Do students have opportunities to talk about what they have read, making connections between the reading and their own experiences?
10. Do students revise their individual understandings of texts in response to the comments of classmates?
11. Is there evidence that students' writing is influenced by what they read?
12. Are students provided with appropriate strategy lessons if they experience difficulties in their reading?

Reprinted by permission of Yvonne S. Freeman and David E. Freeman. *Teaching Reading and Writing in Spanish in the Bilingual Classroom* (Heinemann, A division of Elsevier, Inc., Portsmouth, NH, 1997).

Table 8.6 Sheltered English Techniques in the Mainstream Classroom

1. **Increase wait time.**

   Give your students time to think and process the information before you rush in with answers. A student may know the answers, but need a little more processing time in order to say it in English.

2. **Respond to the message.**

   If a student has the answer correct and you can understand it, don't correct his or her grammar. The exact word and correct grammatical response will develop with time, especially with young children. Instead, repeat his or her answer, putting it into standard English, and let the student know that you are pleased with his or her response.

3. **Simplify your language.**

   Speak directly to the student, emphasizing important nouns and verbs, and using as few extra words as possible. Repetition and speaking louder doesn't help; rephrasing, accompanied by body language, does.

4. **Don't force reticent students to speak.**

   Instead, give the student an opportunity to demonstrate his or her comprehension and knowledge through body actions, drawing pictures, manipulating objects, or pointing.

5. **Demonstrate; use manipulatives.**

   Whenever possible, accompany your message with gestures, pictures, and objects that help get the meaning across. Use a variety of different pictures or objects for the same idea. Give an immediate context for new words.

6. **Make use of all senses.**

   Give students a chance to touch things, to listen to sounds, even to smell and taste when possible. Talk about the words that describe these senses as the student physically experiences something. Write new words as well as say them.

7. **Pair or group students with native speakers.**

   Much of a child's language learning comes from interacting with his/her peers. Give your students tasks to complete that require interaction of each member of the group, but arrange it so that the student has linguistically easier tasks. Utilize cooperative learning techniques in a student-centered classroom.

8. **Adapt the materials.**

   Don't "water down" the content. Rather, make the concepts more accessible and comprehensible by adding pictures, charts, maps, time-lines, and diagrams, in addition to simplifying the language.

9. **Increase your knowledge.**

   Learn as much as you can about the language and culture of your students. Go to movies, read books, look at pictures of the countries. Keep the similarities and differences in mind and then check your knowledge by asking your students whether they agree with your impressions. Learn as much of the student's language as you can; even a few words help. Widen your own world view; think of alternate ways to reach the goals you have for your class.

10. **Build on the student's prior knowledge.**

    Find out as much as you can about how and what a student learned in his or her country. Then try to make a connection between the ideas and concepts you are teaching and the student's previous knowledge or previous way of being taught. Encourage the students to point out differences and connect similarities.

11. **Support the student's home language and culture; bring it into the classroom.**

    Your goal should be to encourage the students to keep their home languages as they also acquire English. Many children in this world grow up speaking more than one language; it's an advantage. Let students help bring about a multicultural perspective to the subjects you are teaching. Students

(continued)

Table 8.6 Sheltered English Techniques in the Mainstream
            Classroom (cont.)

might be able to bring in pictures, poems, dances, proverbs, or games. They might be able to demonstrate a new way to do a math problem or bring in a map that shows a different perspective than that given in your history or geography book. Encourage students to bring these items in as a part of the subject you are teaching, not just as a separate activity. Do whatever you can to help your fluent English-speaking students see all students as knowledgeable persons from a respected culture.

Source: P. Sullivan, *ESL in Context* (Newbury Park, CA: Corwin Press: 1992). Used with permission.

Sullivan (1992) and Becijos (1997) have identified a set of important instructional adaptations of importance to teachers who serve linguistically and culturally diverse students in mainstream classrooms. Table 8.6 provides several techniques of sheltered English.

Making Instruction Understandable

Strategies that assist in making instruction more understandable include: (1) simplifying but not artificially restricting language structures (using shorter sentences, unambiguous terminology, etc.), (2) contextualizing both oral and written texts with pictures, charts, diagrams, and realia, (3) providing for repeated access to ideas and vocabulary, and (4) creating interactive structures that allow for both comprehension and the need to act on and talk about content (Becijos, 1997). The key is not to depend solely on lecture (words) and text to provide meaning. Instead, a mix of drawings, visuals, demonstrations, and collaborative interaction should be woven into the lesson. Meaning-based lessons that are designed to maximize comprehensibility can serve a wide range of language-learning needs. They are helpful instructional methods for all students but are particularly useful to second-language learners. With such an approach, the focus is not on learning English but on learning content *and* English.

For example, Ms. Otero, who uses a sheltered English technique, arrives at class with her lecture notes. She also brings a box full of equipment, including many bowls, a small hot plate, and a bag of ice cubes. Ms. Otero writes "Three States of Matter: Solid, Liquid, Gas" on the board. Underneath each word she adds a drawing to represent the concept and illustrate its molecular structure. As Ms. Otero lectures, she melts ice and then boils water, and under the respective drawings on the board she writes "ice," "water," and "steam." She also assigns students a portion of the text to read. Rather than answering the questions in the text, they work in pairs to write their own comprehension questions about the passage to ask their peers. As students begin to read the text, Ms. Otero sits down with a group of four beginning ESL students to review the main ideas and prepare them to participate in the next day's lesson. She also shows them that they are to copy the drawings of the three molecular structures into their science journals and add labels.

Growing Practice Support for a Responsive Pedagogy

A Research Base

To illustrate some of the points made in this chapter, we can look at a series of classroom and school "snapshots." These are based on reports from research and demonstration programs, most of which were funded by the U.S. Department of Education. The snapshots come directly from specific reports, from site visits, and from the *Directory of Two-Way Bilingual Programs in the United States* (Christian & Whitcher, 1995). These snapshots provide a picture of a developing empirical base that supports a new vision of educational programming for a linguistically and culturally diverse population (García & Stein, 1996).

Three Unusual "R's"

▶ **Watsonville, California.** In Erminda García's third-grade classroom at Alianza School in Watsonville, California, students are asked at the very outset of the academic year to consider the thematic study of the "Three R's: Resourcefulness, Responsibility, and Respectfulness." In essence, they are asked to study how they can become resourceful, responsible, and respectful in relationship to each other and to what they have to accomplish in their classroom. In this regard, the languages of the students (Spanish and English) are immediately identified as resources, and the children articulate the ways in which these and other resources (parents, family, books, computers, etc.) can be used to enhance their academic pursuits. This discussion, coupled with the question "What do we want to learn?," helps the students see both where they need to go academically and what resources are available to get them there.

To promote the sharing of students' language resources, Ms. García organizes the desks so that the children face each other in groups of four. Even in whole-group instruction, children are paired for interactive discussion. Students select from Spanish and English resources, often using one another for assistance in choosing those materials. The knowledge they acquire is displayed in published works, in brainstorming charts, and in posted student products; examples of learning are always put on display in whatever language that learning was accomplished. Students also keep individual learning logs and participate in daily interactive journal communication with selected peers using their language of choice—sometimes their native English or Spanish, and other times their second language. Similarly, learning logs and dialogue journals are shared with parents and other family members.

In such circumstances, students and parents are asked to share each other's language resources and related expertise. This approach emphasizes using language as a learning tool rather than learning a language. Although the latter is achieved through the former, language continues to be viewed as a *resource* for learning.

▶**Chicago.** Sixth-graders in Chicago's Interamerican Magnet School, a K–8 school where all instruction is in both Spanish and English, cluster in small groups for a Writer's Workshop. The teacher asks them to write sentences using these words: "unintelligibly," "committee," "prop," "rambunctious," "intention," "loyalist," "instinctively," "elaborated," "defiantly," and "daintily." Students discuss the assignment among themselves and write sentences in their journals in either Spanish or English. Then a first-grade class enters, and the younger students pair up with the older ones; each pair has an English- and a Spanish-speaker. The older students read stories they have written to the younger ones. The first-graders have an endless supply of questions, and really push the sixth-graders to explain and elaborate on what they have written. In the last part of the class, the teachers ask the students to focus on what they like and dislike about the stories.

Pairing Older and Younger Students

The sixth-grade teacher has thus created a learning environment that is distinct from that of the traditional classroom. Here students assume responsibility for their learning, serve as resources for one another, get feedback on their work from an audience, and engage in teaching younger children. This level of interaction did not happen by accident; at this school the pedagogical approaches have been designed to support students' active participation in their own learning process.

Use of Themes

The teachers often develop their curriculum around themes that are drawn from the culture of the Americas. For example, the fourth-grade teachers developed a social studies unit on Mayan civilization. As part of this unit, classes visited the Field Museum in Chicago to see an exhibit on Mayan culture, architecture, and religion. Teachers used this theme to integrate the studies across curriculum areas. In social studies, students explored the geographic spread of the Mayan civilization as well as its religious and cultural traditions. In science, they studied Mayan agriculture and architecture. In language arts, students wrote about the Mayans. Using such thematic instruction allows students to see the natural connections among traditional disciplines. At the same time, linking those themes to cultures allows students to learn about their own backgrounds and those of their fellow students.

▶ **Los Angeles.** Korean- and English-speaking kindergarten children in Los Angeles's Denker School concentrate on language-rich arts and design activities. The classroom talking fits the task at hand. Four students at one instructional center make posters of city scenes and cutouts and pasted models of houses, cars, buildings, streets, parks, and schools for an upcoming parent conference. On this day, everything, including all the talk, is in Korean. The English speakers have learned some Korean vocabulary and struggle to put these words into sentences; their Korean-speaking friends help them out.

| Using Korean

After 20 minutes or so, each group changes tables and takes up the next task. The tasks are cumulative; as the children move from site to site, they add to what others have already done at the site. One group now takes up Korean letters and words to spell out the days of the week and the calendar for the month of February on a poster. Another builds intricate mobiles and other room decorations. Students at a third table read large-print storybooks with the teacher. These books focus on school and neighborhood themes that correspond with the themes of the instructional centers. The children begin the reading, with each one taking a page. The teacher becomes involved only rarely, to keep the children on track and to answer questions. An instructional assistant and several parent volunteers help at some of the instructional centers. Groups of parents meet on evenings and weekends to learn either English or Korean as a second language.

These children are strongly devoted to their tasks. They rarely get distracted. They move from table to table when the time to switch tasks arrives, and they are truly engaged in their activities. The project director tells of recently talking to some of the Korean children who had no idea that Korean is a minority language in the United States: they had assumed it was of equal importance to English, because the students at their school speak both languages.

▶ **Milwaukee.** Milwaukee's Fratney Elementary School has gone a step further than the Denker School: the whole school is conducted in Spanish and English. One day all subjects are taught in Spanish; the next day everything is in English. Half of the stu-

**A School
in Two
Languages**

dents are from English-speaking backgrounds, and half are from Spanish-speaking backgrounds. They serve as peer coaches and tutors to one another; the languages have equal status in the learning enterprise. However, the languages are not mixed. The students are truly immersed; they have to rely on their inner strength, their memory, and each other. Thus they actually produce the languages, rather than merely absorbing them. Each month a schoolwide theme emerges that has a classroom focus, and it is tied to field trips, hall displays, assemblies, library exhibits, mapping exercises, and interviews with community members (Wood, 1992).

**Activity
Centers**

▶**Arlington, Virginia.** Upon entering Key Elementary School in Arlington, Virginia, you feel the pulse of the learning process. Clusters of classes are located in a pod matrix. In this arrangement, students can move easily back and forth from learning centers in the classroom to activity centers in the oval-shaped pods that encircle the classroom clusters. On a Spanish day, you hear only Spanish; on an English day, only English. As the learning is going on, the students are adding to their home experience, not deleting it. They are being encouraged to communicate with their parents and grandparents, not to ignore them or put them down for being immigrants.

**A Two-Way
Program**

▶**San Clemente, California.** Parents and grandparents turn out in significant numbers during parents' night at the Las Palmas Elementary School's two-way program in San Clemente, California. More than 80 percent of the Spanish- and English-speaking parents of the kindergarten and first-grade students attend. In some cases, divorced or separated parents are both present. Most of the questions the parents ask the teachers and the principal are concerned with trying to ensure that a similar two-way program will be available when their children move on to middle school. One mother reports that her child already feels in command of English and Spanish and wants to know about the possibility of studying a third language, maybe Chinese.

The parents break into discussion groups in their native languages and begin a few curricular exercises with the teachers that help explain how content is taught in the classroom. Discussion topics include how to strengthen their children's homework and study habits and particularly how the school and parents can work together as closely as possible. In addition, some of the English-speaking parents are learning Spanish, while many of the Spanish-speakers are in ESL classes. At the end of the evening, all the parents regroup and plan future activities, and they all promise to keep coming to the bimonthly meetings.

▶ **Dearborn, Michigan.** Arab parents and community members in Dearborn, Michigan, attest to their satisfaction with the Arabic-English bilingualism in the local public schools. Several parents say that they had sent their children to private Arabic-language evening or weekend schools, but were not seeing their children develop full proficiency. They preferred the school program because it taught students to grasp both Arabic and English. Some of the parents were longtime Michigan residents whose children spoke English as their first language. They were extremely happy that their children could now communicate with relatives, visit the parents' home country, master Arabic as a future career enhancer, and participate more fully in community and religious services. They talked about outreach programs to the newest arrivals: students from Iraq and Yemen. They worked with the school system's outreach workers to make the newcomers feel welcome and to deal with issues like the chaperoning of female students and the wearing of native dress.

Parent Satisfaction

▶ **Artesia, California.** The Elliot School in Artesia, California, uses a series of devices to assess the literacy, numeracy, and other content skills of its students. About a third of these students are Portuguese LEP students whose parents or grandparents immigrated from the Azore Islands following devastating earthquakes in the late 1950s. Although performance-based assessment is the norm in this school, student achievement is described in other ways in its Portuguese-English two-way program. The students' reading performance, for example, is assessed along a continuum ranging from "emerging reader" to "expert leader." Even the term "emerging reader" gives a positive connotation to the direction of learning. A "native leader report card," on which comments about various types of student performance can be written, has also been developed so that parents can become fully involved in their children's learning. In addition, the school has recently been able to obtain a steady supply of literature from Portugal. At times in the past, the school had to buy Spanish books and manually insert Portuguese spellings.

Unique Assessment Measures

BECOMING A RESPONSIVE TEACHER

A Letter Home

The following letter was written by a student in a new program integrating linguistically and culturally diverse students with the general school population:

Dear Mom and Dad,

Please read all of the theme assignments for the last two quarters in my portfolio. The folder should be set up so that the pieces for the "Coming of Age in the '90s" theme are on the left, and the assignments for the "Gangs" theme are on the right. I would like you to read the writing for the activities I have done about these themes.

When you read my folder, I am asking that you take the time to answer, in a letter back to me, a few questions:

1. What assignment in my portfolio tells you the most about my schoolwork?
2. What do you see as strengths in my writing?
3. What do you see as the areas that need improvement?
4. What suggestions do you have that might aid my growth as a student?

Thank you very much for investing your time in my theme portfolio.

    Sincerely,

▼ Meeting the Challenge

1. In addition to the letter response requested above, what other activities might increase parental involvement in children's education?
2. Explain why it is important for parents to understand the challenges their children face in school.

Conclusion

The research described in this chapter addresses several significant practical questions about effective academic environments for linguistically and culturally diverse students:

1. *Did native language instruction play a role in providing effective instruction?* The schools in these studies considered instruction in the student's native language a key component of academic success in the early grades (K–3).
2. *Was there one best curriculum?* No common curriculum was identified in these studies. However, a well-trained instructional staff that is capable of implementing an integrated, student-centered curriculum in which literacy is pervasive in all aspects of instruction was consistently observed across grade levels. Basal readers were utilized sparingly and usually only as resource material.
3. *What instructional strategies were effective?* Teachers consistently organized instruction so as to ensure collaborative learning in small, heterogeneous groups. Group academic activities required a high degree of student-student interaction. Individual instructional activity was limited, as was individual competition as an ingredient of classroom motivation.
4. *Who were the major players in effective schooling?* School administrators and parents played important roles, but teachers were the key. They gained the confidence of their peers and supervisors. They worked to organize instruction, create new instructional environments, assess effectiveness, and advocate for their students. They were proud of their students but consistently demanding. They rejected any notion of academic, linguistic, cultural, or intellectual inferiority in their students.

These features of effective classrooms for linguistically and culturally diverse students support, above all, need for the establishment of an interactive, student-centered learning context. In other words, effective instructional staff recognize that academic learning has its roots in processes of social interaction. The practices identified here as effective have also been affirmed by recent educational intervention research aimed at restructuring education for these students (August & Hakuta, 1997). The convergence of findings from this new empirical research generates the following set of specific guidelines:

▼ Any curriculum, including one for diverse children, must address all categories of learning goals (cognitive and academic, advanced as well as basic). We should not lower our expectations for these students; they, too, need to be intellectually challenged.

▼ The more linguistically and culturally diverse the children, the more closely teachers must relate academic content to the children's own environment and experience.

▼ The more diverse the children, the more integrated the curriculum should be. That is, multiple content areas (e.g., math, science, social studies) and language learning activities should all be centered around a single theme. Children should have opportunities to study a topic in depth and to apply a variety of skills acquired in home, community, and school contexts.

▼ The more diverse the children, the greater the need for active rather than passive endeavors, particularly informal social activities such as group projects, in which students are allowed flexibility in their participation with the teacher and other students.

▼ The more diverse the children, the more important it is to offer them opportunities to apply what they are learning in a meaningful context. Curriculum can be made meaningful in a number of creative ways. Science and math skills can be effectively applied, for example, through hands-on, interactive activities that allow students to explore issues of significance in their lives, such as an investigation of the quality of the local water supply.

In conclusion, recent research indicates that schools can effectively serve linguistically and culturally diverse students. These students can achieve academically at levels at or above the national norm. Instructional strategies that serve them best acknowledge, respect, and build upon the language and culture of their home. Teachers play the most critical role in students' academic success, and students become important partners with teachers in the teaching and learning enterprise. Although much more research is required, we are not without a knowledge base that can make a difference.

SUMMARY OF MAJOR IDEAS

1. As American educator John Dewey claimed, knowledge is not a thing to be dispensed but a process of construction and reconstruction that allows us to live and to grow. Schooling practices in the United States must begin to reflect this understanding of knowledge and to adapt to new populations of students and new societal expectations. If not, the educational vulnerability of culturally diverse students, with their accompanying loss in employment competence, will continue.

2. Some theorists claim that educational failure can be explained by a "clash" between the student's home and school cultures. Others claim that academic underachievement is

caused by educators' failure to use principles of teaching and learning that have been proved to be effective with students. Both these theoretical perspectives are useful in identifying instructional practices that might enhance education for culturally diverse students.

3. Research indicates that effective schools focus on making improvements according to the following organizational and structural variables: autonomy in school-site management, instructional leadership from the principal, curriculum that considers students' cultural and linguistic attributes, staff development, parent support and involvement, recognition of student success, and district support. Effective schools also attend to the following process variables: flexibility, collaborative planning and collegial relationships, validation of the students' cultures, a sense of community, clear goals and high expectations, and order and discipline.

4. Case studies show that schools that effectively serve a diverse student population promote literacy, deliver grade-level content, organize instruction innovatively, protect and extend instructional time, expand teachers' roles and responsibilities, address students' social and emotional needs, and involve parents in their children's education.

5. Proponents of education reform claim that U.S. schools generally encourage passive learning, age-based groupings and tracking, abstract curriculum, unclear and irrelevant standards, and neutral affect. These reformers state that schools must be transformed to constitute a community of learners that emphasizes active engagement, developmentally appropriate heterogeneous groupings, thematic and integrated curriculum, performance-based standards and assessments, and care for students.

6. For children, development and learning occur as a result of interactions among linguistic, sociocultural, and cognitive factors. Effective instruction of diverse student populations is additive rather than subtractive; that is, it recognizes the importance of adding to the rich cultural understandings and skills these students bring with them.

7. Research into instructional practices has shown that high levels of communication between teacher and students can be especially effective, as can the use of a thematic curriculum and collaborative, small-group instruction. Students who work together in small groups tend to participate in linguistic discourse of a higher cognitive order. LEP students are more successful if both the native language and English are used for instruction. Sheltered English, or specifically designed academic instruction in English that combines content with the learning of English, has proved to be especially productive.

8. Recent research has provided an increasing body of empirical evidence that supports the new vision of a pedagogy that is responsive to the needs of culturally and linguistically diverse students and their families.

EXTENDING YOUR EXPERIENCE

1. Much of the research cited in this text indicates that culturally and linguistically diverse children learn higher-level cognitive skills best in a social context—by talking and writing, reading and listening. What do these findings imply for the way classrooms are organized? for the role of teachers?
2. Explain the difference between active and passive learning activities. Give an example of a passive learning task typical of a traditional, teacher-centered classroom, and then describe a way to transform it into an active, student-centered activity.
3. Plan an integrated curriculum for a school of linguistically and culturally diverse children. Together with a few of your classmates, decide on the grade levels and demographic make-up of your students. Each one of you could design a single facet of the curriculum and then, acting as a collaborative team of teachers, assemble these facets into a whole. Specify the learning materials you will use, such as books, music, physical objects, resource people, and so on. Remember the importance of student-student interaction, and try to apply some of the research findings discussed throughout this text. Present your curriculum plan to the class.
4. Create a class book titled "Why Teach?" Ask each member of your class to contribute a single sheet of paper on which he or she personally answers this question, in writing or in any other graphic form. Make sure your classmates use black ink, so their contributions are legible for duplicating. Bind enough copies for everyone in class, including your instructor, and distribute them.

RESOURCES FOR FURTHER STUDY

Carter, T. P., & Chatfield, M. L. (1986). Effective bilingual schools: Implications for policy and practice. *American Journal of Education*, 95(1), 200–234.

The authors describe the relationship between bilingual programs and effective schools. They argue that all students, including LEP students, can succeed in an academic environment that is always striving to improve learning. This approach must be planned, organized, and sustained, and the guidelines for improvement must be part of the school's structure in order to be effective. Actions that promote support across departments, including bilingual programs, produce high levels of student achievement.

Purkey, S. C., & Smith, M. S. (1983). Effective schools: A review. *Elementary School Journal, 83,* 52–78.

This article presents an extensive review of literature and case studies that focus on ways of making schools more effective. The authors offer a series of characteristics to use to improve the learning environment and make it more conducive to knowledge transmission. Schools, they argue, are not solitary entities but rather an integral part of a social system with diverse cultures. For change to occur, educators must reexamine institutions and priorities to provide the best education possible for all students. Additional questions and issues are raised to further the discussion of promoting effective schools.

Slavin, R., Karweit, N., & Madden, N. (1989). *Effective programs for students at risk.* Needham Heights, MA: Allyn and Bacon.

This volume reviews a large amount of research on effective programs for students at risk for school failure. The conclusion centers around two themes: (1) the type of program offered and (2) the prevention methods used to avoid implementing remedial programs for those students who are failing. The authors argue that there should be school programs and curriculum to help students catch up or improve their academic standing. Major changes are needed to enable the educational system to offer at-risk students a chance to succeed. Fundamental changes in the organization of schools, curriculum, and delivery of knowledge must be initiated to ensure that all students receive a good education.

Tharp, R. G. (1989). Psychocultural variables and k constants: Effects on teaching and learning in schools. *American Psychologist, 44,* 349–359.

The literate and cognitive activities in schooling are deeply connected to the psychocultural teachings and learning processes developed in the student's home and community. Psychocultural variables are also responsible for the sharp differences in school achievement shown by members of different cultural groups. All cultures bring different variables to the academic field, and schools must not only recognize but also embrace these variables to promote diversity and academic growth. The author offers some recommendations as to how schools can adapt and how the environment of the classroom may be improved. The author also suggests research questions that must be answered to advance school reform.

EDUCATIONAL

APPROACHES

AT THE MIDDLE

AND SECONDARY

SCHOOL LEVEL

CHAPTER 9

Focus Questions

▼ What special challenges do middle and high schools face in attempting to serve diverse populations?

▼ What types of instructional strategies for serving diverse students might these schools implement?

▼ What organizational issues are important to consider in efforts to serve underachieving adolescents?

▼ How can Specially Designed Academic Instruction in English (SDAIE) be helpful to a responsive teacher?

"For students, dropping out forecloses a lifetime of opportunities—and makes it far more likely that our children will be less successful academically." —U.S. Department of Education, 1998

Both my own experience and recent research indicate that students like me—those who do not fit into the "typical American" model—are at particular risk at the secondary level (Lucas, 1997; Olsen, 1997; Romo & Falbo, 1996). For that reason I will devote this chapter to detailed discussion of the schooling of culturally diverse adolescents. I'd like to begin with an account of some of my own experiences as a youngster and as an adult. This very personal case study will set the stage for examination of some important research on educational practices at the middle school and secondary level.

Then and Now: A Personal Rendition of What Works

It is a very common phenomenon: I always know the question is coming when I address an audience regarding the research on effective educational intervention for linguistically and culturally diverse students. It usually comes from a "nonminority" individual, but not always. The negative implication of the question is one that we are all aware of—the "yes, but" attitude. It's as if the person had not been listening, but instead had been thinking up a way to counter the point he or she believed the speaker was making.

A Typical Question

The question goes something like this: "Yes, but how do you account for your own academic success? You are Latino, from a large and poor family, you did not speak English, and yet here you are, a product of a system you have strongly suggested must change to meet the needs of individuals just like you." Sometimes the question is accompanied by the description of a relative's experience, usually the questioner's grandfather or grandmother, who came to this country in poverty, did not speak English, and has left a legacy of economic and educational success among his or her progeny.

This is a difficult situation for me, because it requires me to think of my own grandfather, father, mother, sisters, brothers, cousins, nephews, and nieces, and to think about the unforgivable lack of educational opportunity that they experienced. It makes me feel as if someone is using my academic success to point the "blame" for the absence of others' achievement at each of my family members and collectively at my entire family and similar families. Imbedded in this question is the predominate American perspective that the individual is master of his or her destiny. Success is accordingly attributable to individual characteristics, particularly native intelligence, talent, and motivation. Should I then not see this question as applauding my own individual intelligence, talent, and motivation? Not at all. Instead, it reflects a superficial understanding of academic success in this country generally and for our culturally diverse students specifically.

Understanding Academic Success

My first reaction each time the question is asked is to attribute my success to "luck." How else *could* I react? In a family that included brothers and sisters and 60 or so cousins (one of my aunts had 18 children, including 3 sets of twins), I am the only one to have graduated from college. Five attended a college (4 of these attended a community college), but none except myself ever graduated. In fact, more than 60 percent of the family cohort never graduated from high school, with many never finishing the tenth grade.

All the members of the cohort were born, like our parents and grandparents, in the southwestern and western United States. We all attended schools in these areas, some public and some private. Was I so smart and so motivated and so different from the rest of my family that I have succeeded where they failed? Absolutely not. I have brothers, sisters, and cousins who I know are "smarter" than I am. I grew up with these individuals, saw them articulate and solve complex intellectual problems, and watched them succeed in challenging circumstances. I saw firsthand the high motivation, hard work, goal-setting, analysis, and "stick-to-it-iveness" that are often associated with success in any endeavor. In short, I am about as talented as the rest of my family cohort—I'm not even in the upper 10 percent in terms of native physical or intellectual talent. Nor am I more motivated or more hardworking than most of them. Was I just lucky? Luck is but one legitimate explanation for my success. I would like to think that more than luck was responsible.

The Foundation of Family

The roots of my success began in a family that valued education. My father, a poor and humble man who taught himself to read by using the Spanish Bible (remind you of Abraham Lincoln?), said to all of us, *"La educación nunca te la pueden quitar"* (No one can take away what you have learned). This was a profound insight from a family head of household who had been asked to move his family when he couldn't pay the rent, had lost much of what he owned during the Great Depression, and had worked primarily as a farm laborer in situations that were for the most part completely out of his control—sometimes there was work and sometimes there wasn't. He understood, as did my mother, aunts, and uncles, that it was what we learned—our education—that was the key to our future economic and social well-being. That fact was unquestionable. My father and mother made certain we all attended that first day of school at the age of six (I remember arriving with my Big Chief tablet and pencil in hand) and gave us the *consejo* (advice), *"Portate bien"* (Behave yourself and make us proud).

For me and the rest of my family, this belief in education was a very sound foundation. It was not, however, what would be called an academic foundation. My parents did not read to me; in fact, my mother never learned to read and write at all. I did not have the opportunity to "see the world." We had no vacations, no travel, no museum visits, and only limited access to the mass media (we had a radio that worked sporadically but was never fixed since there was no Spanish-language programming). My playmates, for the most part, were my many cousins, and each of us was socialized in the same linguistic and cultural environment until we went to school. Even after we went to school, our social and economic dependence on the family minimized our interactions with other students and their families. We were insulated, but we were safe and secure. We knew who our friends were, and we knew where to go for help—to our nuclear and extended family. But even under such safe and nurturing circumstances, most children in my family did not succeed educationally.

What was important about this upbringing, then, was not the specific roots of educational preparation but instead the broader understanding that education was crucial, that hard work was important, and that respect for adults who could show you the way, particularly our own elders and schoolteachers, was natural. My uncles were wonderful storytellers who could weave wonderful lessons about life from their own experiences, handed-down proverbs (*dichos* or *consejos*), and religious teachings. As young children we gathered around these individuals as they shared these tales among themselves, knowing fully well that we were all listening. It never seemed like a directed lesson in life, ethics, or the literacy of the oral tradition, but we all learned a great deal. In addition, we learned by watching and doing. When you are poor, every able hand is a resource; we all had chores from the earliest age I can remember. We were told to "watch, then do." We were never provided a verbal or written description of our assigned tasks. And we were never rewarded socially or economically for accomplishing those tasks. The clear expectation was that you would do those things assigned to you, work hard while doing them, and understand that you would do them well or do them again. All this would seem to have set the stage for being a good student.

My "luck" for academic success came from several important factors. I was one of the youngest in this family of 60 or so offspring of my parents and their brothers and sisters. The critical barrier that my older family members confronted was the absence of their language and culture in the schools they attended. When we all went to school, we met the English-speaking world in its harshest terms. My brothers and sisters lost their names— "Ciprinita," for example, became "Elsie," because the teacher could not pronounce her name—and could not engage in an English curriculum or for the most part communicate with the teachers, people we were told repeatedly to trust implicitly for their wisdom and roles as mentors. I recall very clearly that my previous learning opportunities, in a language and culture rich with learning and teaching opportunities, were not even considered in my schooling. My older brothers, sister, and cousins came to the conclusion that school was not for them, even when our family elders continued to insist that they do well in school.

Language and Culture Barriers

It was the younger members of our family—such as me—who succeeded, to some extent, in such an environment. Very directly, we benefited from the experience of our older brothers and sisters, who had learned enough English in school to help us master rudimentary skills in that second language. We younger family members thus arrived at school bilingual in Spanish and English; we could communicate with the teacher and engage the curriculum. Before you conclude that English-language ability was the critical variable in my success, however, allow me to remind you that my own brothers' and sisters' children were either bilingual or predominantly English-speaking when they entered school, and yet their educational success has not been significantly different than that of their parents. It is much more than English that has accounted for my success.

The Importance of Teachers

For me, the key to access was a critical set of teachers—teachers who recognized my talents but challenged me to meet even higher standards. Most teachers did not expect much of me. I was quiet and spoke enough English to get by, but was not articulate in the language. It was also obvious that I was poor and came from a background of "educational disadvantage." Although it may seem that all of this should have signaled to educators that I might need more assistance than the average student, instead it appeared to tell them that they should expect *less* than what they expected of the average student and *substantially less* than they expected of their "good" students. And I obliged them in my elementary and junior high school years by meeting their expectations perfectly. I learned not to work too hard in my studies, to get by, and like many of my Latino peers, to look elsewhere for opportunities to achieve—in sports, in gangs, in jobs, but not in school. But several teachers and coaches would prove to be the exception among my teachers. They were truly my "lucky charms."

My Spanish teacher in junior high school wondered why I took her class since I spoke Spanish fluently, but she never seemed to worry about it. I easily earned C's in her class without even opening the book or doing any homework. I do recall my English-speaking classmates recognizing me as a resource and asking my help, which made me feel good. At the time, this was probably the only positive feeling I had had in school, except in sports. It was not that I had negative feelings toward school—I just didn't have many positive feelings.

In sports, as in my Spanish class, I did have some successes, thanks to my brothers and cousins, who had me playing basketball and baseball at an early age. In school, my forte was sports. I could run, jump, shoot baskets, and hit home runs with the best of them. My shyness, quietness, and Spanish-dominant background were not liabilities here. Coaches and students alike recognized my talents—I was captain of my junior high basketball team. I worked hard and met the high expectations of the coaches and the competition. Sports was a place for me to achieve, to be respected, and to be appreciated.

This was not the experience of many of my Spanish-speaking or bilingual friends. For them, school was "a real drag." For them, defending our turf and making money (usually illegally) led to the formation of and participation in gangs. Of my Latino sixth-grade classmates, who numbered about 50, I can count on my fingers those who graduated from high school. Twice as many, mostly males, had serious brushes with the law, serving time in *la reforma* (reform school) and prison. Most left school prior to high school to assist their large families financially or started their own families early. When I visit my hometown, I often run into them and ask about them, their families, and our school colleagues. Most are surviving well, but none report positive educational experiences for themselves or their offspring. Education in general is still highly regarded, but schooling success is the exception, not the rule.

My athletic achievement continued in high school, thanks to a demanding baseball coach who expected to field the state championship team each year and who searched for, recognized, and developed the talent he needed. He was demanding and nurturing at the same time, going out of his way to respect both individuality and team performance. He looked after his players as if they were his own children. He cared about me—possibly because I could help him achieve his goals, but he cared about me nonetheless. He made sure I attended a community college on a baseball scholarship. That was my partial ticket to a higher education.

Motivation for Success

The other part of that ticket came from similarly dedicated educators. My tenth-grade Spanish teacher seemed very strange to me at first. I was in the class for an easy grade. Why wouldn't she cooperate? Instead she made it very clear that because I already knew most of what she would be teaching my classmates, her expectations for me, should I choose to remain in her course, were going to be much higher. "You have a gift," she said. "I had to work very hard to speak a language that I love but that comes so naturally and easily for you, a language you almost refuse to respect—I want you to use that gift." Thus I read *Don Xijote* while I helped my classmates with *"Buenos dias. ¿Como estas?"* In addition, this teacher made it very clear that to participate in high school sports, I had to have a C average, and that she was willing to fail me if I didn't meet her high standards. I later learned she was in close communication with my basketball and baseball coaches and my geometry and English teachers, all of whom went out of their way to remind me that I needed to stay academically eligible for sports. It was a conspiracy that led me to my first academic achievement and feelings of academic worth. My study habits improved, my participation in class improved, and my grades improved.

My academic success thus started with someone who cared, who saw the resources that I brought with me and was determined to make me use them to take me further, or in my mother's words, "to provide the wings of an eagle." My eleventh-grade Spanish teacher kept the pressure on me, and soon academic success became its own reward. Access to that success opened new worlds, created new visions and goals, and offered me resources that were not available to many of my family members.

I graduated in the top 15 percent of my high school class and went on to the local community college on a baseball scholarship that paid for tuition and books (I lived at home and worked part-time). My interest in mathematics at the community college led to some good grades and an especially solid relationship with a professor who encouraged me to move on to a four-year institution. Another professor at the four-year school in turn urged me to go to graduate school, something my parents, other family members, and I didn't even know existed as a professional opportunity.

Having received some excellent counseling and summer research experience as an undergraduate, I decided I was deeply interested in psychology and particularly in the development of young children. I was fascinated to learn that children acquire as much knowledge in their first five years as they will in the remainder of their lives. Moreover, I had a younger brother who, I learned in college, had Down Syndrome. While we were growing up and I was responsible for his care as our family worked in the fields, I could not understand why he just never "learned" like I did and why he didn't enjoy the same games I did. I thus can trace my initial interest in psychology to a personal need to understand my brother, who had been institutionalized at the age of eight because a social worker and a court of law determined that my aging mother and father could not "handle" him. Poverty, I learned, has its legal and personal consequences. These were the days when institutionalization was an answer to such a situation, long before the time of special education and the Individuals with Disabilities Education Act. (Years later, with the help of my family and my own professional understanding of the psychology of mental disabilities, my brother was removed from the institution. He now lives in a group home, working to earn his own living.)

Professional Responsibilities

These personal circumstances and educational opportunities led me to enroll in a graduate program in human development, where professors and other students encouraged me to take on the responsibilities of research, scholarship, and teaching. Thanks to the consciousness created in the early days of affirmative action, and specifically an affirmative action program at the University of Utah, I was recruited to my first academic position. There I began the slow but sure academic socialization process, procuring extramural support for conducting and publishing my research, teaching undergraduates, preparing graduate professionals, and in general moving up the academic ladder.

As I gradually attained senior status, I gained a double-sided opportunity and responsibility: to *do things right*—that is, to ensure that my research and teaching and those of my colleagues are of the highest integrity, and that they promote an important domain of intellectual inquiry—and to *do the right thing*—to ensure that our work engages us in the crucial theoretical, empirical, and professional preparation pursuits that foster equity and excellence in education for all learners.

As you might conclude, it was neither all good luck nor individual talent nor motivation that allowed me to achieve educationally; nor was it all bad luck and lack of talent and motivation that led many of my family and friends to fail educationally. It was a strong family infrastructure, combined with school personnel who saw the potential and resources in me and who adapted their pedagogy, curriculum, and expectations to address my own circumstances—along with, of course, a little bit of luck—that enabled me to succeed.

As educators, we can't do much about luck, and we can only remotely influence family infrastructure. But we can adapt our pedagogy, curriculum, and expectations so that *all* students can in fact succeed educationally. The remainder of this chapter focuses on educational endeavors that demonstrate the reality of this conclusion. We will examine how the components that helped me are leading to academic success for millions of other students like me. Some of these programs are ones that I have had the honor to study personally, while others I have only admired from a distance. All make it evident that students like me need not experience academic failure.

The Genesis of Project Theme

It was right after the release of our "effective schools" research (García, 1991c) that a local middle school principal issued the following public challenge: "Well, that's all very interesting. But I'm not sure we can *change* our school. We are not doing well and we want to do better. How do we change? Maybe you ought to come out and help us to become an 'effective' school rather than studying those that have already attained their goal."

I couldn't answer his question, but how could I refuse his challenge? Here was a principal who had an interest in developing effective schooling for a highly linguistically and culturally diverse student population, and he was giving me an opportunity to answer that important question of how one moves from ineffective schooling to effective schooling. Of course we called a meeting immediately to discuss this!

First Steps in an Intervention

And our activities soon went beyond the stage of meetings. The principal, Carlos García, now a superintendent of a large and diverse school district, invited me and a group of my university colleagues to his school to speak to the teachers. On the day of our visit, an announcement was read over the public address system: "Dr. Gene García and a group of his colleagues will be in the library after school today to discuss a possible intervention at this school based on his research." I learned later that the principal had also put notices in the mailboxes of the 30 or so teachers. Mr. García could not attend the meeting because a student crisis had arisen, but some 9 teachers joined us in the library. I lectured to the group a bit about the research we had done, and we discussed the possibilities of working in the school. Two teachers, after politely indicating their lack of interest, left. The remaining group decided to meet one more time to consider our offer. These teachers also said they would ask around to see if other teachers were interested in joining us. About two weeks later I held another meeting that was attended by 8 teachers, 6 from the first group and 2 new recruits. (Unfortunately Mr. García again had a scheduling conflict and could not be present.) At this meeting, we decided to give our proposed intervention a try. We named it Project Theme.

Project Theme: Principles and Strategies

Our team of eight teachers, four university faculty members, and two graduate students agreed that Project Theme would be guided by a number of principles, which our review of the literature had demonstrated to be effective in promoting literacy, mathematics learning, and English-language development for linguistically and culturally diverse students. Some of our principles were the same ones listed in the Conclusion for Chapter 8 (see pages 323–324). In addition, we noted the following:

▼ The more diverse the students, the more likely it is that excessive practice and drill that focus only on skill development will endanger their willingness to use those skills.

▼ In general, the more the curriculum emphasizes *performance goals*, rather than *learning goals* of relevance to the students, the more likely it is that they will distance themselves from the school. Performance goals rely on pressure to get the right answer, whereas learning goals emphasize how much one can learn.

Intervention Strategies

Because Project Theme was ultimately concerned with students learning how to learn, particular significance was assigned to the following strategies, again drawn from effective schooling research. These strategies support the development of both basic skills and higher-order linguistic and cognitive processes, and they use linguistic, analytical, cognitive, and metacognitive processing to maximize academic learning:

Strategy 1: Use of thematic, integrated curriculum, so that academic objectives are achieved through content-integrated instruction.

Strategy 2: Emphasis on small-group activities incorporating heterogeneous language grouping and peer tutoring, and emphasizing higher-order linguistic and cognitive processes (in which learning proceeds from the concrete to the presentational to the symbolic).

Strategy 3: Emphasis on literacy activities, such as interactive journals, silent reading followed by small-group discussion, interactive literature study, individual- and group-authored literature, and mathematics logs.

Strategy 4: Use of cooperative learning strategies emphasizing the systematic participation of each student in processing curriculum materials.

Strategy 5: Documentation of interpersonal inequities related to gender differences among middle school students, with a focus on strategies that foster equal-status interactions and support effective learning in general.

The project reorganized the seventh-grade instructional environment of 110 students at the school. Specifically, an instructional intervention was implemented for two heterogeneous groups of approximately 30 students each. One group was made up of English-only (EO) and reclassified bilingual (Spanish and English) students. All the instruction for this group was conducted in English. The second group included EO and fluent-English-proficiency (FEP) students, along with higher-level LEP students who were already in transitional English reading or near that level. For this group the instruction was bilingual. In both groups, the students were with the same classmates in four of the school's six periods. During the other two periods they were integrated with students from the rest of the school for physical education and an elective.

Integrated Thematic Curriculum

The eight teachers worked with the university faculty to implement an interdisciplinary, collaborative curriculum for these two groups of theme students. The content-area subjects taught were reading, English, science, mathematics, and social studies (science was taught for one semester and social studies for the other). A comparison group was established, consisting of 48 students in the regular middle school program who were matched with the Project Theme group on measures of academic achievement. Students in the comparison group changed classes throughout the day; in their six nonintegrated content-area subjects, they experienced six different combinations of classmates.

Recall that the theme students were heterogeneously grouped in two strands, one bilingual and one English-only, in which they remained through math, reading, language arts, and social studies/science. Within the first week of school, Project Theme's instruction began using the Olympics as the first unit. With that theme as a springboard, the four content areas were taught. The teachers met in order to share their individual areas of curriculum focus and to integrate lessons across the curriculum.

Team Meetings

The teachers and the university faculty met weekly during lunch to update one another and to share pertinent information, such as needed resources and materials, student involvement, the theme's progress, assessment scheduling, classroom visitations, collective field trips, and parent meetings.

The overflow of business and actual instructional/collaborative planning time was handled during a monthly **release-time meeting.** The school staff and university faculty met to review teaching issues, share assessment data, solve problems, plan cross-content lessons, and basically expand on, in depth, the actual mechanics of the project.

The tasks of organizing the meetings and facilitating project business were handled by the project's half-time site coordinator, who also taught one of the classes in the two strands. It was the coordinator who maintained communication between the university and the school, planned field trips, scheduled substitutes, ordered materials, disseminated information, arranged instructional support, dealt with problems, and served as the project's contact person.

At the end of the project's second theme, the fine arts, a parents' potluck dinner with student presentations took place. This provided an opportunity to involve parents and further inform them about the project. The staff was available to explain Project

Theme's rationale and to answer questions. The students described their theme classes and shared completed projects.

Specific Activities of Project Theme

Implementing changes in instruction within the complexities of a school site is no small matter. The success of such a program requires the augmentation and reconstruction of various activities that already form the core of the school:

1. Professional development for teachers
2. Assessment practices
3. Enhancement of students' academic learning
4. Improvement of students' self-esteem

The project, in a very direct and highly collaborative mode, attempted to address each of these issues, as the following sections will explain.

Professional Development for Teachers. Project Theme addressed professional development in a number of ways:

Methods of Professional Development

▼ Project teachers participated in preservice and inservice training activities in LEP-effective instructional strategies, particularly those related to cooperative learning, peer tutoring, literacy as a sociopsycholinguistic phenomenon, and the cognitive foundations of literacy, mathematics, and science. This was accomplished at a week-long institute held at the university and in two preservice workshops.

▼ Project teachers met monthly to go over the implementation of instructional strategies.

▼ Project teachers observed each other's classrooms and discussed their observations.

Assessment Practices. Project Theme developed a strategy for assessment of students' progress as well as assessment of the program itself. The key assessment features included these:

▼ Theme students were pretested in September/October using the California Test of Basic Skills (CTBS) and the Spanish Assessment of Basic Education (SABE). Later in the academic year they were post-tested. The comparison group of 48 students was also pretested and post-tested.

Collaborating on Assessment

▼ Project teachers and research team members collaborated in the development and implementation of specific academic assessment strategies.

▼ Previous effective schooling measures were reviewed, assessed, and used to develop a specific assessment of the instructional character of the program.

▼ Members of the team participated in training relevant to assessment techniques, including student, parent, and teacher interview techniques. Then team members applied these techniques in interviews with students, parents, and teachers.

Enhancement of Students' Academic Learning. Specific steps were taken to enhance academic learning for all the students in the project:

Groups and Themes

▼ Theme students were placed in collaborative learning groups intended to maximize effective communication and learning. These groups were characterized by academic heterogeneity and by an orientation toward positive interdependence.

▼ Theme students participated in a core-integrated curriculum that promoted increased opportunities for language and literacy development and integrated content-related instruction. The integrated instruction was organized around the following themes: (1) the Olympics; (2) the fine arts (popular music, art, and fashion); (3) the ocean; (4) crime and nonviolence; (5) careers; (6) gender; (7) AIDS; and (8) ethnic identity. Students and teachers together selected these themes.

Improvement of Students' Self-Esteem. In addition to academic learning, the cultivation of students' self-esteem was considered vital to the success of the program, and Project Theme used the following strategies to foster good self-images among the students:

Building a Good Self-Image

▼ Theme students were recognized for both their individual achievements and their contributions to group products.

▼ Theme students worked in cooperative learning structures—particularly the "Tribes" process—to develop skills in leadership and cooperation.

▼ Theme students in cooperative groups discussed specific situational conflicts and utilized problem-solving skills to determine solutions.

▼ Teachers implemented programs that recognized student improvement and success across a range of abilities.

▼ Teachers integrated lessons that promoted understanding and appreciation of individual and cultural differences.

The Results of Project Theme

The pre- and post-testing, for both the Project Theme students and the comparison group, focused on the areas of language, reading, writing, and mathematics. In addition, survey and interview data regarding the students' academic self-concept and social identity were gathered. (Besides gathering the data when students were in middle school, researchers also conducted interviews at the end of the students' sophomore year in high school.) Moreover, parents were interviewed regarding their social identities and their perceptions of schooling. The results can be grouped in the following specific areas:

1. Academic achievement in language, reading, and writing
2. Ethnographic data on students' self-concepts
3. Social identity of students and parents
4. Math achievement, attitudes, and self-concepts
5. Long-term effects of the project

These five areas are discussed in detail in the following sections.

Academic Achievement in Language, Reading, and Writing

To examine the effects of the instructional intervention in the domains of language, reading, and writing, academic achievement measures in English and Spanish were obtained during the spring semester. For English-only and bilingual students in the theme group and the comparison group, six subtests of the English version of the CTBS along with seven subtests of the English version of the Language Assessment Scales Reading/Writing (LAS) were used. The CTBS subtests were (1) Vocabulary, (2) Language Mechanics, (3) Reading Comprehension, (4) Reading Total, (5) Language Expression, and (6) Language Expression Total. The LAS subtests included (1) Synonyms, (2) Fluency, (3) Antonyms, (4) Mechanics and Usage, (5) Reading for Information, (6) What's Happening, and (7) Let's Write. For LAS subtests 1–5, students were given multiple-choice items, while for subtests 6 and 7 they were required to write a description of a scene that was depicted, create a description of their own scene, or both. In addition, bilingual students were administered the vocabulary and reading subtests of the SABE.

Test Results
On each subtest, the English-only theme students received higher scores than the bilingual theme students. More important, however, the bilingual theme group did not differ signifi-

cantly from the English-only comparison group on any of the subtests. The students in the bilingual theme group had originally been identified by their need for further academic development. As noted earlier, the group included both English-dominant and Spanish-dominant students, and they were taught in bilingual classrooms. It was striking that this group did not differ in academic achievement from a group of English-only students in the regular curriculum.

In other respects, the theme groups consistently performed higher than their comparison counterparts. This was particularly true for bilingual students. On six of the seven Language Assessment Scale (LAS) subtests, bilingual theme students scored significantly higher than bilingual comparison students. Of particular interest were the significant differences found between these groups in the sixth and seventh subtests, which measure written-language ability. Moreover, on the two SABE subtests, the scores of the bilingual theme group were higher than those of the bilingual comparison group, though this difference was not statistically significant on the vocabulary subtest. Similarly, English-only theme students significantly outscored English-only comparison students on four of the six CTBS subtests (Vocabulary, Language Expression, Language Expression Total, and Reading Comprehension).

In summary, the results consistently show higher achievement among the theme students, for both the bilingual and the English-only groups.

Ethnographic Data on Students' Self-Concepts

Several themes related to students' self-concepts emerged from the participant classroom observations, student interviews, and teacher interviews. These themes may be categorized in the following four domains: (1) ethnic identity, (2) positive self-esteem, (3) future aspirations, and (4) academic strategies and perceptions about schooling. Let's examine each of these domains in turn.

Ethnic Identity. *Students of Mexican origin and Anglo origin did not use a wide range of ethnic labels when referring to themselves and other students.* When we asked students to identify the different types of students at the school in terms of specific ethnic labels commonly heard in the community, they usually used only a few terms: "Mexican," "Mexican American," and "American." Very few students were familiar with the term "Chicano." When asked what distinguished individuals within the generic category of "Mexican," they talked in terms of language ability, physical

Ethnic Labels

appearance, and country of birth. One Anglo girl discussed differences among Project Theme students in terms of those "who are bilingual and those who are straight." Most of the Mexican-origin students were familiar with other ethnic labels (e.g., "Cholo," "Pocho") but did not feel they applied to the Mexican-origin student population at the school. When asked to categorize themselves, students of Mexican origin most frequently chose "Mexican" or "Mexican American." The most commonly used ethnic labels for the Anglo students among both groups were "white," "American," and occasionally "Anglo."

Most of the Project Theme students stressed commonalities among people, especially among the groups in the school. They gave responses like, "It doesn't matter if you're Mexican or American; people are people." This is not to say that the students did not perceive differences among students at their school or even among categories of students. However, the distinguishing features they used did not necessarily reflect differences in ethnic identification. When asked to identify different groups in school, without any prompts for ethnicity, all but two students distinguished students in other ways (e.g., athletes versus nerds, popular versus not popular, good students versus bad students).

Positive Self-Esteem. *Students of Mexican descent exhibited a positive sense of self and expressed pride in their Mexican heritage.* In a variety of contexts, students expressed pride in being Mexican, giving examples of holidays and other special occasions when they felt particularly proud. At this point, we are not sure in what specific ways, if any, this ethnic pride was linked to a positive sense of self, to a particular ethnic label, to positive attitudes toward Spanish-English bilingualism, or to other social experiences in the school, family, and community.

**Ethnic
Self-Image**

We were particularly interested in finding out if any of the Mexican-descent students wanted to change places with any of the Anglo students in the class or in the school, especially those who were identified as being popular, attractive, and/or high academic achievers. However, very few of the Mexican American students we interviewed expressed any desire to switch places with anyone else, and in fact they were frequently surprised that such a question would even be asked. "Why would I want to do that?" was a typical response. "I like being me."

We also asked the students to identify which, if any, aspects of their physical appearance they would change. Here there were some important gender differences, especially among some of the darker-skinned Mexican American girls. While the boys, with several exceptions, did not identify any changes they would make in their physical appearance, many of the girls said they

---

ETHNIC IDENTITY: Who Am I?

We observed that a handful of students, girls in particular, appeared to exhibit a certain amount of tension in discussing specific ethnic labels carrying a negative connotation (e.g., "Cholo"), especially if these labels indicated behaviors that could be linked to ethnic identity. One girl in the bilingual theme group discussed how she had changed in the last year. She described how just a year before she had been an "angel," someone who did her homework regularly, listened to her mother, did what her older brother told her to do. "Now, my friends have changed me: I now dresses differently, don't do my school work, gets into fights with family members, things like that." She concluded that this was both "good" and "bad." It is "good" that she no longer allows her overbearing brother to boss her around, but "bad" that she talks back to her mother and that her work is lagging.

In many ways her description of herself contradicts with her grades and her teachers' perceptions of her as a student. By these standards, she appears to be one of the stronger students in the program.

---

would change the shape of their nose, remove freckles, and/or lighten the color of their hair or skin. This preliminary finding bears more careful scrutiny, especially as the girls mature and go on to high school. Furthermore, it will be important to explore in greater detail any relationship between elements of ethnic awareness—both positive and negative—and feelings of self-worth and confidence in one's appearance, especially among the Mexican-descent girls.

Future Aspirations. *All students, regardless of ethnicity, aspired to professional careers.* All the Project Theme students were interested in pursuing a profession. The survey data indicate that the most commonly chosen categories were law (45.7 percent), medicine (40.6 percent), and the arts (over 30 percent). When presented with a choice of careers, students often identified a range of possibilities that included professional as well as service-related jobs. For example, one student expressed interest in becoming a scientist, mechanic, doctor, waitress, photographer, and beautician.

Visions of the Future

Finishing high school and/or college was in everyone's future plans, and the students linked schooling to future success. The students believed that a college education was needed in order to get a "good" job, although they thought they could get an "adequate" job—such as mechanic or beautician—with a high school diploma. Moreover, everyone reported a similar attitude among their parents. With very few exceptions, all students said that their parents would be moderately to greatly upset if they quit

ASPIRATIONS: Who Will I Become?

Among the Mexican-descent students, there was no interest in becoming a farm-worker or cannery worker, the jobs that were commonly held by their parents. They were aware of the difficulties of these occupations, as revealed in the following comments:

"A mi no me gusta trabajar en el campo porque asi aprende uno como se cansan los padres para mantenernos y comprarnos lo que queremos."

"If I played professional football, I wouldn't have to work as hard as my parents. They sweat for hours working in the fields. I wouldn't like that."

school before high school graduation. Some talked about how their parents set forth their options in very realistic terms: working in the fields versus something better. For them, the "something better" meant an occupation that could be attained by staying in school and going on to college. The survey data revealed one distinction between Anglos and Mexican-descent students: Mexican-descent students were evenly divided in terms of planning to pursue two years of college and four years, while Anglo students overwhelmingly favored finishing four years of college.

This leads us to another point. Despite their aspirations, *students of Mexican descent lacked specific instrumental knowledge on how to prepare for the careers they wanted to pursue.* It was clear from our interviews that although these students knew that college was a prerequisite to many of the professions they were interested in, they did not have the specific knowledge about the types of postsecondary education that were available, the different cre-

CAREER OPTIONS: What About College?

Among those Mexican-origin students who did have some idea about the demands of a college education, its pursuit was seen as a potentially very difficult struggle. One girl identified the obstacles in her way: "getting pregnant and poor grades." Money was also frequently reported as a major barrier. As one girl noted, "You need lots of money to learn in college." This is not to say that these students think college is an impossible dream, but they do believe that it entails a great deal of hard work, above and beyond the rigors of the academic requirements. Several students explicitly stated that if they worked hard enough, they would make it to and through college, citing as examples the experiences of a cousin, aunt, older sibling, or close family friend.

dentials and opportunities each might offer, and the number of years required to complete particular levels of training. This is in marked contrast to many of the Anglo students we interviewed, who had a much clearer, although sometimes inaccurate, picture of the differences between a community college and a four-year institution. Most of the Anglo students understood the connection between higher-status occupations (e.g., teaching, nursing, architecture) and the need to complete at least four years of college. In contrast, many of the Mexican-descent students felt that a two-year education at the local community college would be sufficient to enter these occupations. One Mexican American girl said that to be a doctor, "You have to have five years of something before you can get out of the university." Very few of these students knew the names of colleges other than one or two of the local community colleges, and none knew where to obtain this information. Many assumed that this information would be presented to them at some later point in their education. During these discussions we became aware of the extent to which these students conceptualized the pursuit of a college education as something one sets out to acquire in much the same way that one purchases an expensive car or other concrete object. What is lacking in their comments is any substantive knowledge of the instrumental behaviors, attitudes, motivations, orientations, and scholastic achievements required.

The research also probed the students' beliefs about the role of bilingualism in their desired careers. *Students of Mexican descent felt that being bilingual and biliterate would contribute to their future success.* These students frequently expressed very positive attitudes about bilingual ability. They believed that knowing Spanish and English would benefit them in terms of future job opportunities. Frequently, students gave examples of specific work situations, possibly derived from their own experiences, in which a bilingual employee was able to assist a monolingual speaker. According to our survey data, the perception of this advantage was also held by half of the non-Mexican-descent students. On the whole, Mexican-descent students were eager to maintain or improve upon their Spanish-language skills by continuing to take classes in Spanish.

Academic Strategies and Perceptions About Schooling.
Doing homework and listening and behaving in class were the attributes students most often linked to success in school. When we asked students to describe how one becomes a good student, they responded in ways like these: "by doing my homework and listening in class"; "by paying attention to the teacher and doing all

the work"; "by not messing around and getting your work in on time." They felt that being quiet in class was also important.

Attributes of a Good Student

Given a choice among several attributes of a successful student, 50 percent of our sample ($N = 30$) felt that completing schoolwork was the most important attribute. When asked to identify a successful student in their class or describe someone they considered to be a good student, they invariably named or described someone who did his or her homework and was well-behaved. When we asked them how they thought they could improve their own academic performance, nearly all said that they should do their work, listen in class, and pay attention to the teacher.

Nevertheless, *the students were not challenged by their schoolwork.* In our interviews, as well as in many—but not all—of our observations of actual classroom sessions, students exhibited little enthusiasm or genuine engagement in their classes. Only 15 percent of the students felt that their schoolwork was too hard. Moreover, the majority wished that their classes were more interesting.

Social Identity of Students and Parents

Social identity is an intriguing and complex phenomenon. It is both a social *product*, emerging out of biological, social, and cultural influences, and a social *force*, emanating from the created social product to guide an individual's choices in behavior.

Identity research with people of Mexican descent has focused almost exclusively on ethnic identity, or the sense of oneself as a member of an ethnic group. However, while ethnic identity is undeniably significant, it is not the only critical dimension of one's social identity. Few studies have investigated such potentially important nonethnic dimensions of social identity as occupation, race, family, religion, and language. In one study that did examine this issue, adolescents living in inner-city Detroit chose to describe themselves by using a nonethnic label rather than an ethnic category.

In Project Theme we examined the social identities of the seventh graders and their parents by administering a measure of social identity that included race, class, family, and ethnicity. By comparing the differences and similarities in the social identification of parents and their offspring, we can form an empirical basis for how social identity, including ethnic identity, is transmitted from one generation to another.

Table 9.1 profiles the social, economic, and linguistic background of theme students and their parents. Note the difference in language choices between parents and students. With these

Table 9.1 Social, Economic, and Linguistic Background of Project Theme Students and Their Parents	
Mexican-descent students	87
Anglo students	23
Students language choice for interview	
Spanish	31
English	56
Parents' language choice for interview	
Spanish	77
English	23
Family income	
$2,000–$10,999	21%
$11,000–$24,999	53%
$25,000–$34,999	12%
$40,000 and above	14%
Parents' education level (average)	6.5 years
Parents' marital status	88% married

basic characteristics in mind, what would you expect to find in the survey data about social identities?

As it turns out, the data indicate both similarities and differences in the social identities of parents and their children. Both parents and children had a familial dimension (that includes gender) to their social identities (e.g., sibling, daughter/son, mother/father, wife/husband, *comadre/compadre*). For parents, there was a strong religious dimension (e.g., Catholic, Christian, religious person) that was not present in their offspring. As might be expected, while parents identified with their occupations (e.g., family bread-winner, farmworker), their children did not. The greatest divergence between parents and children was in the manifestation of their ethnicity. While the ethnic dimension of social identity for parents included such labels as "Mexican" and "Hispanic," for their children it included "Mexican American," "American of Mexican descent," "U.S. citizen," "Mexican," and "American." *Thus these adolescents had not yet formed a clear ethnic identity for themselves. Students of this age group are in the formative stages of the development of the identifiers that society uses for them and that they are likely to adopt for themselves later in their lives.*

Generational Differences

Math Achievement, Attitudes, and Self-Concepts

In our study we also addressed the general problem of under-achievement in mathematics among Hispanic students, as well as their underrepresentation in high school classes that are prerequisite to educational and occupational opportunities in science and technology. The multifaceted intervention involved thematic integration of mathematics content across the curriculum. This approach broadly engaged students in gathering, processing, representing, and communicating about quantitative concepts. Since traditional approaches to instruction for Hispanic students tend to emphasize computation more than meaning, we hypothesized that students exposed to such thematic instruction would perform better than comparison subjects on a test of mathematical concepts and applications. We expected no achievement differences in computational skills. The data supported both of these hypotheses.

Attitudes Toward Math

A secondary function of this aspect of the research was to obtain baseline data on attitudes toward mathematics in order to examine similarities and differences between the National Assessment of Educational Progress (NAEP) sample and our sample. Preliminary analysis of these data indicate that theme students expressed more positive feelings toward mathematics than either the white or the Hispanic students in the NAEP sample. To a greater extent than students in the NAEP sample, they also considered themselves to be good at mathematics and expected to work in an area requiring mathematics when they left school. The implications of such findings, when juxtaposed to the students' overall low performance in mathematics, were puzzling.

A final purpose of this research was to test for changes in motivational self-perceptions regarding mathematics through the academic year, and to examine the relationship of self-perceptions to instructional outcomes. Contrary to our earlier assumptions, females reported more positive math self-concept than males on these measures. The influence of self-perception variables on learning outcomes in mathematics was examined as well. Results indicate that the best predictor of math achievement was a positive math self-concept rather than a generally positive self-concept.

Long-Term Effects of the Project

Three years after we completed Project Theme, we conducted a follow-up study to measure the following variables among both the theme and the comparison students: (1) future aspirations, (2) academic performance as measured by course grades, and (3) perceptions of middle school. Data were obtained by means of a self-administered survey, which included the following questions:

What is your grade-point average?

Was your middle school a good institution?

Did you receive excellent grades in middle school?

Did you find the subjects in middle school to be very interesting?

Did middle school teachers help you develop interest?

Did middle school teachers help you plan for future goals?

Did middle school teachers like you?

Did you hate your middle school?

What are your future plans?

Do high school teachers help you plan for the future?

Do high school teachers like you?

Do you feel comfortable at your high school?

Do you get along well with other students in high school?

In the follow-up study the questionnaire was submitted to the former theme and comparison students enrolled at Watsonville High School who were able to attend the one-afternoon session near the end of the academic year. Thirty-eight students participated, 21 from the theme group and 17 from the comparison group. Students completing the survey were not told that its purpose was to assess the effects of any particular program.

Impact of Project Theme

The survey revealed that Project Theme had a significant effect on grades, with approximately 70 percent of the grades of the theme group being *above average* and about 75 percent of the grades of the comparison group being *below average*. Although this is a self-report indicator, we have some confidence in the finding because students were clear about the confidentiality of their responses. Also, 65 percent of the theme students thought of their middle school as a good institution, while only 40 percent of the comparison group reported such a perception. Moreover, 80 percent of the theme students described their middle school subjects as interesting, as opposed to 30 percent of the comparison students.

In addition, teachers were perceived by the theme students as providing greater inspiration. Some 85 percent of this group agreed that teachers helped them develop interest, versus only 47 percent of the comparison students. Also, 57 percent of the theme students indicated that teachers had helped them plan for the future, as opposed to 40 percent of the comparison students. The implementation of this project also created a significant difference in the students' future aspirations. About 85 percent of the theme students indicated a strong desire to go on to college, while only 69 percent of the comparison students expressed this desire.

In summary, the follow-up study indicated a consistent pattern of outcomes related to grades, perceptions of middle school, and future aspirations that dramatically favors the theme students.

The Conclusion of Research on Project Theme

Project Theme brought together middle school teachers with university faculty in a redesign of seventh-grade instructional organization. This redesign was based on recent empirical work that identified components of instruction and curriculum that proved to be effective with linguistically and culturally diverse students. It was also based on recent theoretical formulations that are of general relevance in enhancing academic learning.

Theme students were part of an educational experience that kept them together for the majority of their school day. This experience included participation in small, heterogeneously structured learning groups. Instruction focused on jointly determined themes that integrated reading, language arts, math, science, and social studies. The academic outcomes of these theme students were compared to a group of students who participated in the same school's typical seventh-grade organization: seven independently taught, homogeneously leveled classes with limited curriculum integration and a more traditional, whole-group instructional approach.

Lessons of Project Theme

The implementation of the project required extensive rethinking of the existing middle school organization by teachers, administrators, and participating university faculty. Moreover, the restructuring that took place required wide-ranging collaboration, especially by the teachers. These teachers reported that without the time the project allowed them to meet and plan, the program would not have been possible. In addition, they stated that the onsite coordinator played a key role in bringing them together and in ensuring that the specific objectives were always at the forefront of the project activity. Recall that the teachers had at least one release-time meeting each four to six weeks, and they also met on a weekly basis during lunch. The coordinator, who had the time to meet individually with teachers and university faculty, was a key resource person with regard to finding and developing theme-related curriculum material. In sum, the project could not have been implemented without the additional release time for teachers and the presence of an effective onsite coordinator.

The results of the project are clearly positive. That is, the data show consistently more positive academic outcomes for the theme students compared to those in the school's conventional program. Most notably, comparative analyses in reading comprehension, vocabulary, language mechanics, and language expression in English significantly favored the theme students. Similar results were found on Spanish measures.

Constraints of Project Theme

Although these empirical results are promising, we should identify two important constraints of the study. First, the study was a voluntary effort by a group of self-selected and particularly motivated teachers and university faculty. Second, we could not identify specific causal links between the intervention subcomponents and the dependent variables. For example, were the improvements on language and reading tests "caused" by the theme structure, by the cooperative learning methods, by the efforts to bolster students' self-concepts, by any other individual components of the program—or by all of these components in combination? For these reasons, among others, the results of the study are difficult to interpret in detail. It does seem appropriate, however, to conclude that the findings suggest a set of school and classroom restructuring alternatives that may provide enhanced educational success for a population of educationally vulnerable students. The teachers, parents, and students of Project Theme echo this conclusion.

Rethinking, Rebuilding, and Engaging Change at the High School Level

California is a microcosm of the peculiar state of affairs concerning the high school experiences of linguistically and culturally diverse students. A recent study of California high schools indicated that "California is generating 50,000–75,000 noncompleters (students who go to high school but never finish), just about the same number as students who become eligible for the University of California system" (Minicucci & Olsen, 1992). The number of Latinos graduating from high school in 1995 was reported to be 60,000, but only 2,000, less than 4 percent, actually found their way to the University of California. These figures are just one sign of the complicated and often neglected educational circumstances of minority high school students. Recently researchers, educators, and many others have begun to voice their concern about these California students, whose language and diversity should be viewed as an advantage for the future and not a liability for the present (Hurtado, Figueroa, & García, 1996).

Minicucci and Olsen (1992) direct our attention to four areas that directly affect the education of linguistically and culturally diverse and immigrant high school students, in California and elsewhere:

▼ Overt conflict, violence, and tension
▼ Status quo of separations (both social and institutional)
▼ Conflict students feel when caught between two worlds, and when a world around them requires assimilation for acceptance
▼ The ability of secondary schools to address these issues and design appropriate interventions

These recent findings undeniably require additional study. Lucas, Henze, and Donato (1990) provide a useful summary of research on the effective instruction of minority populations in general and of immigrant students in particular (see Table 9.2). This work has yielded conceptual understandings and empirical findings that could be included in a practical, multifaceted instructional plan to enhance the academic learning of such students at the high school level.

A substantive impediment to many students is tracking, a practice that directs students into low-, regular-, or high-achieving groups (Oakes, 1984a). Although tracking may begin as early as elementary school, it is most often initiated at the junior high school level. By high school, tracking is vividly established, and class assignments often are driven by perceptions (accurate or inaccurate) of the student's level of academic achievement. Once minority students are placed in a track identified as being for low achievers, their opportunities for academic success are significantly limited (Oakes, 1984a). Putting a student in a remedial class automatically increases his or her chances of being enrolled in another remedial class. Such a student receives a less effective education, because remedial courses do not expose students to a challenging curriculum. In most cases, in fact, the teachers assigned to remedial classrooms with low-income and linguistically diverse students are teachers who have no expertise in language acquisition and development and no particular cultural sensitivity. In other words, the students who are most in need of high-quality instruction and experienced teachers instead get the opposite (Finley, 1984; Haycock & Navarro, 1988).

Pitfalls of Tracking

As many researchers have pointed out, "most American high schools still have a long way to go to substantially improve the engagement and achievement of their students" (National Center of Effective Secondary Schools, 1991, p. 19). Yet in their efforts to "improve" the quality of education, high schools often

Table 9.2 Attributes of High Schools That Promote the Achievement of Language Minority Students

1. Value is placed on the students' languages and cultures by:
   - Treating students as individuals, not as members of a group
   - Learning about students' cultures
   - Learning students' languages
   - Hiring bilingual staff with cultural backgrounds similar to the students'
   - Encouraging students to develop their primary language skills
   - Allowing students to speak their primary languages
   - Offering advanced as well as lower division content courses in the students' primary languages
   - Instituting extracurricular activities that will attract language minority (LM) students

2. High expectations of language minority students are made concrete by:
   - Hiring minority staff in leadership positions to act as role models
   - Providing a special program to prepare LM students for college
   - Offering advanced and honors bilingual/sheltered English classes in the content areas
   - Making it possible for students to exit ESL programs quickly
   - Challenging students in class and providing guidance to help them meet the challenge
   - Providing counseling assistance (in the primary language if necessary) to help students apply to college and fill out scholarship and grant forms
   - Inviting college and minority graduates who are in college to speak
   - Working with parents to gain their support for students going to college
   - Recognizing students for doing well

3. School leaders make the education of language minority students a priority. These leaders:
   - Hold high expectations for LM students
   - Are knowledgeable of instructional and curricular approaches to teaching LM students and communicate this knowledge to staff
   - Take a strong leadership role in strengthening curriculum and instruction for all students, including LM students
   - Are often bilingual minority group members themselves
   - Hire teachers who are bilingual and/or trained in methods for teaching LM students

4. Staff development is explicitly designed to help teachers and staff serve language minority students more effectively. Schools and school districts:
   - Offer incentives and compensation so that the school staff will take advantage of available staff development programs
   - Provide staff development for teachers and other school staff in:
        effective instructional approaches to teaching LM students, e.g., cooperative learning methods, sheltered English, and reading and writing in the content areas
        principles of second language acquisition
        the cultural backgrounds and experiences of the students
        the languages of the students
        cross-cultural communication
        cross-cultural counseling

5. A variety of courses and programs for language minority students is offered.
   - Include courses in English as a second language and primary language instruction (both literacy and advanced placement) and bilingual and Sheltered English courses in content areas
   - Make sure that the course offerings for LM students do not limit their choices or place them in low level classes. Offer advanced as well as basic courses taught through bilingual and sheltered English methods
   - Keep class size small (20–25) in order to maximize interaction
   - Establish academic support programs that help LM students make the transition from ESL and bilingual classes to mainstream classes and prepare them to go to college

(continued)

Table 9.2 Attributes of High Schools That Promote the Achievement of Language Minority Students (*cont.*)

6. A counseling program gives special attention to language minority students through counselors who:
- Speak the students' languages and are of the same or similar cultural backgrounds
- Are informed about post-secondary educational opportunities for LM students
- Believe in, emphasize, and monitor the academic success of LM students

7. Parents of language minority students are encouraged to become involved in their children's education. Schools can provide and encourage:
- Staff who can speak the parents' languages
- On-campus ESL classes for parents
- Monthly parent nights
- Parent involvement with counselors in the planning of their children's course schedules
- Neighborhood meetings with school staff
- Early morning meetings with parents
- Telephone contacts to check on absent students

8. School staff members share a strong commitment to empowering language minority students through education. This commitment is made concrete through staff who:
- Give extra time to work with LM students
- Take part in a political process that challenges the status quo
- Request training of various sorts to help them become more effective
- Reach out to students in ways that go beyond their job requirements, for example, by sponsoring extra-curricular activities
- Participate in community activities in which they act as advocates for Latinos and other minorities

Source: Tamara Lucas, Rosemary Henze, and Ruben Donato, "Promoting the Success of Latino Language Minority Students: An Exploratory Study of Six High Schools," *Harvard Educational Review*, (60)3, (1990): 315–340. Copyright © 1990 by the President and Fellows of Harvard College. All rights reserved.

seem to forget the most vulnerable groups in their ranks. It is for the forgotten students that we must create robust academic programs with the flexibility to combine research, theory, and practice into an agenda of change. The following section describes one such effort at the high school level. Known as Project AVANCE, it took place in California, a state that, as we have seen, serves as an important microcosm of our nation's educational system.

Project AVANCE

Project AVANCE (the Spanish word for "advance") incorporated alternative instructional strategies that are demonstrably effective in advancing the linguistic minority student's literacy, mathematics, and English-language skills. Ultimately, AVANCE's aim was to promote "students learning how to learn." The project's specific instructional strategies included the following:

▼ Use of a thematic, integrated curriculum, with academic objectives that were achieved through content-integrated instruction

▼ Emphasis on small-group activities incorporating heterogeneous language grouping and peer tutoring, and emphasizing higher-order linguistic and cognitive processes (in which learning proceeds from the concrete to the representational to the symbolic)

▼ Emphasis on literacy activities such as interactive journals, silent reading followed by small-group discussion, interactive literature study, individual- and group-authored literature, and mathematics logs

▼ Use of cooperative learning strategies that emphasized the systematic participation of each student in processing curriculum materials

▼ Documentation of interpersonal inequities related to ethnic and gender differences and implementation of strategies to foster equity

These strategies were consistent with techniques that the California Department of Education (1990) had already identified for use in its high school curriculum frameworks:

1. *Language arts and reading:* Reading Situations, Anticipating the Reading, Reading Process, Initial Response, Discussion, Written Interpretation, Reflections on the Reading Experience
2. *Mathematics:* Free Response Questions, Mathematical Investigations, Portfolios
3. *Science:* Performance Tasks, Open-Ended Questions, Student Portfolios
4. *Social studies:* Portfolios of Student Work; Performance Assessment (including oral presentations, drama, debates, group collaborations, student-assessor dialogues, etc.); Writing Tasks; Integrated Assessment (incorporating more than one technique and interdisciplinary skills in a complex task that demands higher-order cognition)

Reorganizing the Structure of the School

Like many of the other projects discussed in this book, AVANCE was based on a good deal of theoretical work in language development and effective schooling. Such theoretical foundations often suggest that typically underserved students can succeed academically if instructional strategies that emphasize cooperative learning, student-generated themes, and close staff networking are woven into the existing academic framework of the institution with relatively minor changes. Yet modifications that on the surface seem quite simple or minor can be very difficult to fulfill, especially if they challenge "seldom-questioned regularities of school culture" (Oakes, 1992, p. 5). The AVANCE intervention was not immune to this problem. Let's examine the way AVANCE was set up.

The intervention at the high school was designed to benefit 60 students, who were divided into two heterogeneous groups of approximately 30 students each. Both groups were made up of English-only, reclassified bilingual (Spanish and English), and ESL students. Students were selected only if teachers, counselors, or classmates considered them to be "high-motivation" students.

Building the Framework

A team of seven teachers, one counselor, and university researchers worked collaboratively to plan and implement the curriculum. The content-area subjects were English, science, mathematics, and social science (world civics was taught for one semester and health studies for the other). The two groups of students were integrated with the rest of the student body for two periods: physical education and an elective class.

The comparison group was made up of 60 randomly selected students in the regular high school curriculum. As these students changed classes throughout the day, they experienced six combinations of classmates in six different, nonintegrated content areas.

An office at the high school was established where the team met weekly to discuss, share, update, and relate pertinent information. The agenda for the meeting included discussions on the theme's progress, classroom visitations, budget, meetings, and data collection. The organization of meetings and related onsite business was delegated to AVANCE's part-time coordinator, who also taught four classes. The coordinator's main responsibilities were to schedule meetings, order materials, arrange instructional support, and deal with any logistical problems.

Preparing Teachers

Project teachers participated in workshops specifically related to culturally and linguistically diverse children. These workshops, created by the National Center for Santa Cruz, included presentations by prominent researchers in the field who shared their research findings as well as demonstrations, classroom videos, and hands-on activities. Other preparatory events for the teachers included the following:

▼ The teachers and the school's principal visited the site of Project Theme to observe the classrooms and discuss the program with the instructors.

▼ Two leading educators conducted a workshop to address specific concerns and field questions about thematic teaching.

▼ Teachers planned a series of five monthly meetings to discuss and plan the curriculum and structure of the program.

▼ Teachers attended a three-day summer conference to share and plan their individual areas of curriculum focus within the overall program theme and to integrate lessons across the curriculum. Here they also chose "Community" as their first thematic unit, which they implemented in the first week of school.

▼ Students and teachers participated on a one-day tour and workshop on science and technology at UC Santa Cruz.

Outcomes of the AVANCE Intervention

To assess AVANCE's reforms, teachers were interviewed and classrooms observed. In one sense, teachers were the judges and jury regarding the program's effectiveness in challenging the traditional delivery of education. Often their evaluations brought to the fore dimensions that had never been discussed during the planning of the intervention.

Course Standards and Evaluation. Teachers in this study wanted at once to retain the standards required for students to enter college preparatory courses and to meet the needs of the students who were performing slightly below those academic levels. They discussed this issue extensively, considering both course content and student assessment. While the majority of the teachers used the student-centered content of AVANCE, one teacher at times felt a need to alter the content to allow the less academically prepared students to participate effectively. The teachers were, however, unwilling to "water down" the curriculum for any student, and they made their commitment to this principle eminently clear.

A major change occurred in the teachers' attitude toward performance-based—sometimes called authentic—assessment of the students' academic achievement. One teacher stated:

> "When you say, 'Evaluation,' I say, 'Grade.' I have what I hope to be a wide variety of activities. I evaluate their portfolio, their lab binder or lab notebook, exams, unit test, quiz, lab work, and their self-evaluation. I grade on a participate/not-participate basis. If I have an exam which is in English (all

exams are in English), I would allow students to do other things to make up for points they missed in the test."

This attitude carried over to the manner in which teachers viewed their own performance as teachers. As one person said, "Not only do I have to cover what I'm required and they'll be tested on, but I have to cover the themes." It was also apparent in the curriculum shift from strictly "book" academics to "everyday-life" academics:

> "[One way in which I changed the test reflects] what people do in real life. For example, in my ESL class on library skills I phrase all questions [like this]: 'What would be the first thing you would do if you were interested in electronics at the library?' The test [in this class] mimics a real-life process of being able to get a book."

One factor that was expected to have an impact on the AVANCE project was the scarcity of Spanish-language minority students who could meet the academic challenge in the way that the teachers required. Considering the current state of education, some teachers felt that AVANCE recruited and received students who were willing to face the academic rigors but were not fully prepared to deal with the academic consequences. In fact, the teachers generally agreed that their students with a strong knowledge of English benefited the most from the intervention because they could participate fully in an academic environment that was unlike a mainstream classroom. Despite this potential problem, an English teacher stated:

> "I would be willing to say that I would put my English I class against any other group at [this school] in the CORE pieces of work. Pick any other English teacher. Give a multiple-choice test. They'd do O.K. Those who have English will come out stronger."

During the program, teachers appeared enthusiastic about the manner in which academics could be used to communicate with parents. There was an air of optimism when teachers realized that their academic curriculum could also help to establish a dialogue among parents, students, and teachers.

Student-Generated Themes. A major challenge teachers encountered was the notion of allowing students to participate actively in defining the curriculum. The first challenge arose when teachers questioned how to forge a comprehensive academic partnership between teachers and students while simultaneously embracing the community. In other words, the issue was how to continue to deliver the mandated, districtwide curriculum effectively and weave into it the new theme-centered agenda. Particular attention was given to the composition of the student body: the students in this program, who were either members of groups with low socioeconomic status or recent immigrants, had been given the least amount of academic support and were perceived as unwilling to work academically. With initial hesitation, the teachers embraced the concept of allowing student input. Once the first theme had been selected, they welcomed the partnership. As one teacher put it,

> "Having student-generated themes formalized student input for curriculum [because] they create the theme, [and] we [teachers] let them imagine what they want to study. They write the curriculum at the start of the six-week unit. From assignment to assessment, they are more involved."

Student Input

The formation of this partnership became one of the more successful aspects of the program. It allowed students to nominate their top three interests as themes. These ideas were analyzed to determine which one was the most popular, best used available resources, and could be woven into the mandated curriculum. In some instances, themes were discussed and then expanded to cover a broader range of issues and provide more leeway to include the mandated curriculum.

One theme that required little expansion was "Gangs." The English teacher incorporated *Romeo and Juliet* into this unit. In mathematics, the curriculum centered on the number of Hispanics in prisons, and students drew the connections between Hispanics, gangs, and prison. In science, students studied gangs from the perspective of animal behavior, including social grouping and territoriality.

As the program progressed, teachers realized that the student-teacher partnership that had originally been envisioned as problematic and difficult to implement became one of the best means of promoting student participation, input, and academic responsibility.

Staff Networking. At the outset of AVANCE, teachers were made aware that they were free to inquire, suggest, or constructively criticize as the program moved forward. This unique opportunity to discuss students, curriculum, and decisions that affected their own academic environments gave the teachers a

Teacher Camaraderie

sense of professional growth and camaraderie. As one said, "I've gotten to know some of the teachers in the program very well. You don't really get to know people in other departments. It's affected us as teachers. *We* can share things in the future around campus."

In a traditional school organization, most teachers felt, the lack of opportunity to interact with teachers from other departments restricts the development of a collective consciousness. "An issue on the positive side," said one teacher about the project, "is that we've been able to communicate between the teachers on a daily or weekly basis. It's pretty evident if a student is not [himself or herself]. We work together on understanding some of that behavior."

Effective Strategies and Practices. A major aim of AVANCE was to implement effective instructional strategies that promoted an integrated curriculum and student interaction. The

Alternative Classroom Techniques

same English, math, and science content was included, but it was taught with a different approach. The new method required more hands-on activities, language-proficiency grouping, and gestures and drama, as these examples from teachers illustrate:

"[I] put notes on the board or the overhead; explaining or rephrasing of texts; doing symbols or pictures of concepts. I did more close activities; I tried to work in a tutorial second period."

"I use the same palette of tools [found in traditional classrooms but] . . . in different combinations . . . [such as] prior knowledge—saying, 'You are the content of the course,' telling them my job will change [the text] rather than looking at [the] text as school, looking at their experience as the source of knowledge."

Specially Designed Academic Instruction in English (SDAIE). Of particular significance for non-Spanish-speaking teachers in AVANCE was the use of Specially Designed Academic Instruction in English (SDAIE) techniques (Becijos, 1997). These strategies attempt to minimize the use of English as the primary mode of delivering content-based instruction while tapping the existing knowledge base of the students. By using SDAIE techniques, teachers can enable students to do the following:

BECOMING A RESPONSIVE TEACHER

Using Instructional Conversations for Content-Area Learning

As we saw in Chapter 6, it is common during the early phase of an instructional conversation (IC) for middle school teachers and students to converse about a broad range of topics, particularly individual experience and background knowledge. In this way, teachers develop a comfort zone that encourages all students to share. For language minority students, talking with peers and teacher means an opportunity to express language with native speakers of both the language of the home and the language of instruction. For teachers, student talk is a rich source of information about students' life experiences and funds of knowledge, a basis for relationship, and an occasion for authentic assessment. In conversation, student talk reveals students' language proficiency in the languages of home and of instruction.

In early IC conversation, what appears to be divergent—even desultory—discussion is important preparation for scaffolding later conversation to intended IC themes. The teacher used a photograph from a familiar television series, "Star Trek," as a stimulus for students to talk about space, a topic used in the regular class. In the conversation, students moved the topic to talk about stars.

> **Edgar:** They have like holes in them. Like . . . [he moves his hands in a curved motion]
>
> **Teacher:** They have like holes in the planet. "Holes in the planet," does anybody know what else we can call that ?
>
> **Edgar:** *Pozos.* [Holes.] [Another student, Concha, giggles.]
>
> **Edgar:** Shooting stars.
>
> **Teacher:** Shooting stars? Is that another name for the holes in the planet? Does anyone know what those . . .
>
> **Edgar:** Shooting stars are like stars, but they go shoo [hand gesture] really fast and when you see them, you can make a wish.

In this excerpt, the students participated comfortably in English, with one response in Spanish, giving the teacher a sense of their proficiency when conversing on a general topic. Following the direction of students' talk about stars, the teacher encouraged students' participation using prompts, restatements, and probes.

> **Luis:** The black hole.
>
> **Teacher:** Do you know what the black hole is? Can you explain that to everybody in the group?

BECOMING A RESPONSIVE TEACHER *Cont.*

Luis: It is a round thing, and it has a lot of stars.

Teacher: It is a round thing. [Turns and writes on board.] So you're saying that the black hole is something . . .

Concha: I don't really care.

Teacher: . . . that is round [Luis and Concha laugh] and it has, what else did you say?

Luis: Stars.

In this excerpt, the teacher pressed students to use language to express what they know, while ignoring an inappropriate response. Without interrupting the IC, she heard one student's attitude toward the topic. She and the other students modeled constructive social interaction that comprises appropriate IC talk. For students with little experience of conversation on an academic content topic, the ordinary conversational quality of early IC is familiar, attractive, and an occasion to model conversation conventions.

As the excerpts show, the students' conversation was at an everyday level and included an instance of Spanish-language use. The students used incomplete utterances and gestures to convey meaning. The teacher demonstrated prompting, questioning, and restating student utterances. In the following excerpt, the teacher continues to probe students' background knowledge about planets and draw every student into participation in the conversation.

Teacher: Yeah, and we also talked about some other characteristics. We talked about colors and sometimes some planets have rings around them, right?

Luis: Just Saturn has it, only Saturn? [He looks up at a poster.]

Teacher: I don't know, does only Saturn have a ring around it?

Daniel: Yeah.

Teacher [to Daniel]: Yeah?

Luis: They're all right there. Look. [Points up. Everyone is looking up at the wall poster.]

Edgar: Yeah, I think, huh?

Concha: Yeah, only Saturn.

Teacher [to Concha]: Only Saturn? [Concha nods.]

The teacher tracked the conversation by listing space- and math-related terms on a chart. The list became another visual aide for reviewing the course of conversation and for transitioning conversation to math topics—in this case, measurement.

BECOMING A RESPONSIVE TEACHER *Cont.*

Teacher: When we look up here, do we see any words, on our list that we made, that have to do with math?

Luis: Yeah.

Teacher: Like what?

Luis: Star Trek.

Concha: Saturn.

Teacher: Star Trek?

Luis: Like in the movies, like in . . . ?

Teacher: What does that have to do with math?

Luis: Mmm, on the machines, the computers that they have on the *Enterprise,* like they measure stuff.

Teacher: They measure stuff? With their computers, okay. Yeah, so the computers on a starship would help you measure, like measure what? What sort of things?

Luis: Planets.

Using Luis's speculation about measuring planets, the teacher hooked onto a mathematics topic. Luis's answer, "planets," was an opportunity to bridge the conversation to measurement.

The first IC yielded abundant information about students' language proficiency, content knowledge, and conversational skills. The majority of the students participated competently at a general or everyday level, while one, Concha, was extremely reticent. The teacher accepted all student responses nonjudgmentally, including inappropriate contributions, treating them as genuine attempts to contribute to the conversation.

BECOMING A RESPONSIVE TEACHER *Cont.*

▼ Meeting the Challenge

1. Instructional engagement is particularly important in moving older students from what they know or understand toward new concepts and understandings.

   A. Consider introducing a new scientific concept to students. How would you introduce the concept to ensure student engagement?

   B. Do the same for a mathematics or social science concept (the concept of "ego" in psychology or the "depression/recession" cycles in economics are always good ones).

2. In the dialogues below, where would you have responded differently as the teacher? Why?

3. Student engagement in the learning process does not always involve communicative acts. Think of some examples of student engagement like these. How can they be enlisted to help other forms of student engagement like the ones depicted below?

From "Enacting instructional conversations with Spanish-speaking students in middle school mathematics" by S. Dalton and J. Simon, p. 8–9. © 1995. Reprinted by permission of the National Center for Research on Cultural Diversity and Second Language Learning and the authors.

Benefits of SDAIE

1. Present their own abilities that do not depend only on English proficiency (for example, by making material representations or using pictures to portray a science concept).

2. Connect their real-world experiences to the subject under study (for example, by beginning with fiction the students have read in their primary language or analyzing biological phenomena present in their own lives).

3. Utilize their talents not normally interjected into academic content learning (for example, by incorporating music or drama into instruction).

4. Seek and receive support from their peers (for example, by working on group projects or community-based data-gathering).

5. Utilize diverse ways to focus on and attack the assigned material (for example, by using journals and learning logs, **quick-writes,** or graphic organizers).

6. Connect content-area material through thematic units (for example, by presenting an interdisciplinary organization of the material in a theme).

Table 9.3 outlines how SDAIE strategies can be used to engage students in reading texts.

Learning from Project AVANCE

Theory into Practice

Project AVANCE attempted to realize the vision of creating a program specifically to give linguistically and culturally diverse students access to the content curriculum in their high schools and to expand their language skills. Principles developed by researchers and theoretical frameworks of "what works" for Hispanic students were closely examined and translated into actual practice. The collaborative team wanted to learn not only new instructional skills but also the theoretical perspectives on which such "effective" skills could be developed. The team established guidelines for a "tailored" program capable of improving the academic and social opportunities of all the participating students. The lengthy team discussions touched on the social, educational, racial, psychological, and structural changes needed to serve these students effectively. Some of the most salient issues the team considered were as follows:

1. The recruitment of students who met the requirements established by the team (grades, self-esteem, etc.)

Table 9.3 SDAIE Techniques for Promoting Interactive Reading

Activities for Accessing a Text

1. Read portions aloud as an introduction.
2. Use guest speakers as classroom resources and to provide background experience.
3. Incorporate journal writing, quickwrites, or discussion about similar situations so that students can personally relate to the material.
4. Provide overviews and synopses for students; tell students they needn't understand every word of what they are going to read to still understand the main points.
5. Study vocabulary in context; students may keep vocabulary notebooks.
6. Provide background for students, such as information on the author, historical facts, or dates.
7. Use films, filmstrips, or recordings to evoke an interest in the material.
8. Use graphic organizers to help with vocabulary, upcoming concepts, or background information.

Activities for Addressing a Text

1. Explore text in depth; for example, study the implications of crucial quotations.
2. Use oral presentations; for example, present a scene from a literary work dramatically.
3. Let students take on the role of one of the characters or important figures from the text in written or oral work.
4. Have students keep reading logs to record quotations they like, to relate ideas to their own experience, and to make predictions.
5. Have students visualize the text artistically through illustrations, collages, charts, diagrams, time lines, and the like.
6. Establish collaborative groups for students to explore the work together.
7. Independently develop questions on the text to use in group or class discussion.
8. Evaluate the learning process and integrate it with students' prior knowledge.

Activities for Students to Select

1. Use parallel readings to illustrate common concepts and themes.
2. Create games or presentations relating to the reading.
3. Write and perform a play or reader's theater based on the reading.
4. Make connections to happenings in the news or in the students' lives.
5. Interview other students or adults relating to a topic introduced in the reading.
6. Research a topic of interest relating to the reading.
7. Write a letter, story, sequel, or poem on the topic of the reading.
8. Create a poster, mural, collage, or other artistic representations of the theme.
9. Relate the information to other content areas.
10. Use technology to represent the text; for example, create an audio- or videotape, or use the computer.

Source: Adapted from J. Becijos, *SDAIE: Strategies for Teachers of English Learners* (Bonita, CA: Torch Publications, 1997), p. 37.

2. The implementation of effective instructional methods to deliver a strong academic curriculum for students with limited English skills
3. Reliance on the suggestions provided by work conducted in elementary and junior high schools
4. The impact the program might have on the educational and social lives of the students
5. The positive and negative elements of the intervention

6. The most appropriate means of spending the limited financial resources the team received

The fact that the AVANCE team was able to conceptualize, create, and implement this project at a high school allows the researchers to offer various thoughts about its process and outcomes:

Lessons of AVANCE

1. With minimal administrative support, teachers can organize, create, and reorganize within a school's framework to improve the educational environment for students.
2. Allowing new teaching techniques and organizational methods into the classroom can enhance the learning of both teachers and students.
3. Educational change at the high school level must take into account volatile issues (for example, plans after high school and inter- and intragroup relations) that can affect the students on a daily basis.
4. Regardless of students' English-language knowledge, they will respond positively when they are academically challenged.
5. The means by which teachers meet to discuss their students must be significantly updated.
6. Hispanic students at the high school level must be provided with a challenging and integrated curriculum in order to optimize their opportunities to succeed in life.

Conclusion

This chapter has traveled a route from an individual assessment of "what works" for a student to a broader discussion of effectiveness issues and case studies that document effective instruction in middle school and high school. This route and the stops along the way provide detailed insights into the development and implementation of educational interventions in schools that serve diverse student bodies. These are instances that my own experiences and research suggest are valuable. Understanding the efforts described in this chapter will help us address the underachievement so often experienced by the diverse students in our middle and secondary schools.

It is important here to offer my thanks to the teachers, administrators, students, and parents at the sites in which these studies took place. Their contribution to our understanding of effective schooling for Hispanics has been significant. In particular, the teachers in these studies played a major role in making the educational programs work. I cannot say enough about their hard work, instructional skills, and personal commitment to serve as advocates for these students. It was as if the students were the teachers' own children. Such commitment to advocacy is very difficult to measure and quite impossible to teach. Yet, in each of the case studies in this chapter, such unflagging dedication of the teachers was present in major proportions. It reminds me, as it did my colleagues, that effective schooling is a social enterprise, conducted by individuals who care about one another, respect what they bring to the enterprise, and then go forward together. The ability to create such an enterprise is the key to the future success of educational professionals working with linguistically and culturally diverse students, families, and communities.

SUMMARY OF MAJOR IDEAS

1. Students who do not fit the "typical American" model are at particular risk at the secondary school level. However, they can achieve academic success if teachers are able and willing to adapt their pedagogy, curriculum, and expectations to the particular circumstances of such students.

2. Specific interventions such as Project Theme have been effective in promoting academic achievement in reading, language, writing, and mathematics among linguistically and culturally diverse students in middle school. Teachers' professional development and students' self-esteem and future aspirations are also enhanced by such programs.

3. Strategies that have been particularly effective in improving the academic learning of linguistically and culturally diverse students include the use of thematically integrated curriculum, heterogeneous small groups, literacy activities, cooperative learning, and interactions that foster equal status and support effective learning.

4. Language-minority high school students are an especially neglected population in terms of education. Research has identified the following attributes of high schools that promote the academic achievement of such students: placing value on their language and culture, having high expectations for such students, making their education a school pri-

ority, training staff to serve them more effectively, offering them a variety of courses and programs, developing a counseling program that gives special attention to their needs, involving parents in their education, and having staff who are strongly committed to empowering these students through education.

5. Tracking, or the practice of directing students into low-, regular-, or high-achieving groups, can be especially detrimental for minority students. Once such students enter a track designated for low achievers, their chances for academic success are significantly limited.

6. In order to serve the linguistically and culturally diverse students in our high schools, we need to create robust academic programs that combine research, theory, and practice in an agenda of change. AVANCE is one such program that has successfully incorporated alternative instructional strategies to advance the linguistic minority student's literacy, mathematics, and English-language skills.

7. A commitment to high academic standards for all students, a willingness to involve students in the process of curriculum definition, the establishment of an open network for staff communication, and the use of Specially Designed Academic Instruction in English (SDAIE) are some of the strategies that have proved most effective in projects such as AVANCE. Central to the success of such a program is a collaborative team that is willing and able to conceptualize, create, and implement its guidelines and goals.

EXTENDING YOUR EXPERIENCE

Your assignment is to assess in a critical and comprehensive manner the attributes of ethnic difference within two populations—*your family* and *one other minority group* residing in your area (e.g., African American, Hispanic, Native American, Asian, etc.). These projects will require clear consent from the informants involved and should include interviews, analysis, and a written report incorporating the following areas:

A. Description of informant (including yourself as informant)
   1. Age, sex, self-identified ethnicity
   2. Family attributes (over three generations)

(a) Work
(b) Education (with an emphasis on secondary schooling)
(c) Social status
B. Language history (over three generations)
C. Values (over three generations)
1. Work
2. Family
3. Education (with emphasis on secondary schooling)
4. Success/failure
D. Other cultural attributes

Examples: social attributes (competition, sharing, groupings, etc.), sex roles, rites of passage, etc. with particular emphasis on adolescence)
E. Future prospects for cultural maintenance/change

Share these reports with your colleagues so you can compare and contrast findings. Keep in mind that such sharing should maintain the highest levels of confidentiality regarding your informants. This suggested exercise should reveal in some detail the complexities over generations of "culture" and "culture change" that are particular to adolescence.

RESOURCES FOR FURTHER STUDY

Hawley, W. D., & Jackson, A. W. (Eds.) (1995). *Toward a common destiny.* San Francisco: Jossey-Bass.

This edited volume provides a comprehensive assessment of research on ethnic relations in the United States. Of particular interest are the issues of ethnic identity formation, group membership during adolescence, and the influence this identity has on school experiences. The book offers much more than a theoretical treatment of issues such as race, class, national identity, and group formation. The authors provide specific in-depth studies and analyses of direct importance to education.

Lucas, T. (1997). *Into, through, and beyond secondary schools: Critical transitions for immigrant youths.* New York: National Center for Restructuring Education, Schools, and Teaching, Teachers College, Columbia University.

Lucas provides a comprehensive overview of the immigrant experience in the United States and its relationship to schooling. Immigrant students' lives are best understood as a set of critical transitions: from one schooling system to another, from complex micro- and macro-societies to yet others. Focusing on secondary school transitions, this volume identifies four major attributes from recent research on immigrant students and highlights findings from excellent secondary schools. Specific examples are a major contribution of this volume.

Moya, S., & O'Malley, M. (1994). A portfolio assessment for ESL. *The Journal of Educational Issues of Language Minority Students, 13*, 13–36.

The authors define portfolio assessment, offer a rationale for using portfolios with LEP students, and summarize a model of portfolio implementation. This issue is especially important because alternative assessment is increasingly being used with both LEP and other students. Portfolio assessment is particularly appropriate for the evaluation of an LEP student's language development because it offers the flexibility to address and even offset the cultural and linguistic bias often found in standardized testing measures.

Olsen, L. (1997). *Made in America: Immigrant students in our public schools.* New York: The New Press.

This in-depth ethnographic study of a highly racially, economically, and linguistically diverse California high school takes the reader directly into the educational challenges of the urban setting. It pulls no punches in telling stories of students and teachers as they address these challenges. The author, who spent over two years in the school, offers insightful analyses of the multilayered perceptions, articulations, and actions of the individuals who inhabit it. In so doing, the volume serves as a sequel to an earlier influential study by Goodlad (1984). Both works show the changes American high schools have undergone in little more than a decade, chiefly as the result of a large influx of immigrant students. This author concludes that cultural relations will need substantial improvement if we are to enhance the secondary education of U.S. students.

Romo, H., & Falbo, T. (1996). *Latino high school graduation: Defying the odds.* Austin: University of Texas Press.

Paradoxically, while 35 percent of Latino students in the United States drop out of school, larger *absolute* numbers of Latino students are graduating from high school than ever before. Documenting the educational experience of 100 students in an Austin high school, the authors identify the various obstacles and support strategies that the students encounter, and offer the following recommendations for school reform: (1) put the learning of students first; (2) clarify scholastic standards; (3) eliminate programs that lead to student failure; (4) reward participation in schoolwork; (5) emphasize hard work; (6) make school accessible; and (7) create clear pathways to outcomes.

acculturation The process by which the members of a society are taught the elements of the society's culture.

act psychology A model for human cognitive processes that focuses on the assertion that the mental functions of perceiving, remembering, and organizing—ultimately knowing—are all acts of consumption.

affect A term used in psychology to refer to people's feelings and emotions as distinguished from their thoughts and actions.

Americanization *Assimilation* as it is practiced in the United States. See *assimilation.*

assimilation An approach to acculturation that seeks to merge small ethnically and linguistically diverse communities into a single dominant national institutional structure and culture.

bilingualism The ability to speak two languages with equal fluency.

Black English The most-studied non-standard American English dialect. Although its roots lie in African Creole and English, Black English has its own distinct syntactic, phonological, semantic, and vocuabulary rules.

burnout Physical or emotional exhaustion, most often caused by a great deal of stress experienced over a long period of time.

code switching The production of mixed language utterances.

cohort rates report A report, compiled over a given time period, that describes what happens to a single group of students.

communication A combination of verbal and nonverbal systems that enables humans to encode meaning and transmit it to others.

connoisseur model A method of teacher assessment that allows experienced and knowledgeable educators to train and judge other educators.

constructivist perspective The belief that, for humans, knowing is the result of continual building and rebuilding.

contextualized language Language that conveys meaning using physical cues such as gestures, intonation, and other concrete representations characteristic of face-to-face communication.

cultural capital The notion, grounded in an economic perspective, that knowledge and ideas are a means of symbolic wealth that can be used to gain access to or maintain the use of resources. Thus, a primary way of building cultural capital is through education.

cultural systems approach The approach to education that considers the organization of a society, specifically the roles and status assigned to cultural groups within it, to be a major determinant of educational underachievement. Also known as *institutional racism, perceived labor market explanation, secondary cultural systems theory,* and *structural inequality.*

culture A system of values, beliefs, notions about acceptable and unacceptable behavior, and other socially constructed ideas characteristic of a society of a subgroup within a society.

culture concept A term defined by Edward Tylor in 1871 as "that complex whole which includes knowledge, belief, art, law, morals, custom, and other capabilities and habits acquired by man as a member of society."

curriculum The area of schooling that addresses the content of instruction.

decontextualized language Language that relies on abstract linguistic and cognitive cues that are independent of the communicative context.

dialect A regional variation of language characterized by distinct grammar, vocabulary, and pronunciation.

direct instruction A teaching strategy wherein the teacher transmits knowledge to students through modeling and step-by-step instructions.

disposition An individual's usual temperament and frame of mind.

distributive model of culture A model that implies that each individual's portion of the culture differs in some ways from that of any other individual.

double immersion A program whose goal is to produce a student population that is bilingual and bicultural.

ecology The study of the relationships between an organism and it environment.

ethnic A general term used to refer to groups of people who are differentiated by race, religion, nationality, and/or region of origin.

ethnic images A term used to designate general beliefs that people have about the characteristics and attributes of a cultural group.

event rates report A report, compiled within a single year, that gives the percentage of students who left high school without finishing work toward a diploma.

grammar The system of rules implicit in a language that allows words to be arranged with some regularity of structure.

group-oriented concept of culture The use of attributes that are shared by all individuals in a group to define culture.

individual-oriented concept of culture The use of individual attributes to identify participants of a culture.

inservice preparation Professional training for teachers who are already working in a classroom.

institutional racism See *cultural systems approach.*

instructional conversation (IC) Conversation that allows the student to engage the teacher and other students in an active way, thus leading to the parallel development of language and cognitive/academic content of relevance to the formal education process.

instructional discourse A teaching strategy that emphasizes discussion in the classroom.

intelligence The ability of an individual's mind to acquire and apply knowledge.

language The use by human beings of voice sounds, written symbols, and hand signals to communicate thoughts and feelings. For the purposes of this text, *language* is a complex interaction of many variables, including: the verbal signal, the signal sender, the manner and context in which the signal is sent, the signal receiver, and previous experiences the sender and the receiver may have had with similar signals.

language minority student A student characterized by substantive participation in a non-English-speaking social environment, who has acquired the normal communicative abilities of that social environment and is exposed to an English-speaking environment on a regular basis only during the formal school process.

language pragmatics The rules of a language as well as cultural notions about what is considered appropriate and effective use of the language.

limited English proficient (LEP) student identified as nonproficient in English based on: (a) the use of a language other than English at home; (b) an English-language assessment by the school; and (c) low academic performance in English.

magnet school A school whose purpose is to attract a highly diverse set of students around a thematically designed curriculum that is multilingual and multicultural.

May 25 memorandum A memorandum, issued by the U.S. Department of Health, Education, and Welfare in

1970, which clarified the mandate of the 1964 Civil Rights Act with respect to non-English-speaking populations of students.

meta analysis A method of analyzing and summarizing large numbers of research studies.

metalinguistic awareness The conscious awareness of how one uses language.

minority A group that is subordinate to another dominant group and that is subject to a negative power relationship.

modal grade level The academic level considered normal for students of a particular age.

multicultural education A curriculum whose content educates students on the contribution of more than one culture.

multilingualism The ability to speak three or more languages with equal fluency.

participant-structured demand In education, the demands of instruction that are imposed on children by the organization of the learning environment itself.

participant structures In communication, the rules that govern who speaks when.

perceived labor market explanation See *cultural systems approach.*

personality The pattern of the character, behavioral, mental, and emotional traits of an individual. In education, the personality is a structure that reconciles a child's interpreted experiences with his or her emotional states.

phonology The study of speech sounds.

profession A job characterized by (1) the acquisition of knowledge obtained through formal education; and (2) an orientation toward serving the needs of the public, with an emphasis on ethical and altruistic concern for the client.

psychometrics The measurement of psychological attributes.

release-time meeting A meeting, usually three hours in length and scheduled during the school day, when teachers work collaboratively, often developing lessons together or observing each other. Substitute teachers are scheduled to teach classes during this time.

quickwrites A story or essay written by a student with a specific time frame. The writing is guided by a set of questions.

scaffolding An educational practice that provides support for children as they move between disparate home and school cultures.

schema A mental framework for perceiving the world.

secondary cultural systems theory See *cultural systems approach.*

second-language acquisition A process of language development whereby a child acquires first one language and then is exposed to and required to learn a second language.

sheltered English A varied set of instructional techniques that recognize that the student is not a primary speaker of English and that the teacher is not proficient in the student's primary language. These techniques maximize nonverbal instructional communication (e.g., the use of visual/demonstration strategies) that combine content (e.g., math, science, and social studies) and English-language-learning goals.

social distance The relationship between two cultures, determined in part by their relative status.

socialization The process through which prescriptions (ideas about what one should do) and prohibitions (ideas about what one should not do) are transmitted to members of the social group.

sociocultural theory An international intellectual movement that brings together the disciplines of psychology, semiotics, education, sociology, and anthropology.

standard English The version of English that has the grammar, vocabulary, and pronunciation considered appropriate for most occasions of public discourse and for written communication.

status rates report A report, compiled at any point in time, that gives the percentage of the population of a given age range who either have not finished high school or are not enrolled.

structural inequality theory See *cultural systems approach*.

syntax The feature of a grammatical system having to do with word order.

transitional bilingual education The program that provides language minority students of Spanish-speaking backgrounds with a transition from early-grade instruction with Spanish emphasis to later-grade instruction with English emphasis and eventually to English-only instruction.

vocabulary The sum of words understood and used by an individual in any language group.

zone of proximal development (ZPD) A term defined by Tharp and Gallimore (1988) as "the distance between the actual development level as determined by individual problem solving and the level of potential development as determined through problem solving under adult guidance or in collaboration with more capable peers" (p. 30).

REFERENCES

Abi-Nader, J. (1990a, April). *Helping minority high school students redefine their self-image through culturally sensitive instruction.* Paper presented at the annual meeting of the American Educational Research Association, Boston.

—— (1990b). A house for my mother: Motivating Hispanic high school students. *Anthropology and Education Quarterly, 21*(1), 41–58.

Adler, M. (1982). *The paideia proposal: An educational manifesto.* New York: Macmillan.

Allport, G. (1954). *The nature of prejudice.* Reading, MA: Addison-Wesley.

Altus, W. (1945). Racial and bilingual group differences in predictability on mean aptitude test scores in an Army special training center. *Psychological Bulletin, 42,* 310–320.

—— (1948). A note on group differences in intelligence and the type of test employed. *Journal of Consulting Psychology, 12,* 194–196.

Appleton, C. (1983). *Cultural pluralism in education: Theoretical foundations.* New York: Longman.

Au, K. (1979). Using the experience-text-relationship method with minority children. *Reading Teacher, 32,* 677–679.

Au, K., & Jordan, C. (1981). Teaching reading to Hawaiian children: Finding a culturally appropriate solution. In H. Trueba, G. Guthrie, & K. Au (Eds.), *Culture and the bilingual classroom: Studies in classroom ethnography* (pp. 139–152). Rowley, MA: Newbury House.

August, D., & Garcia, E. (1988). *Language minority education in the United States: Research, policy, and practice.* Chicago: Charles C. Thomas.

August, D., & Hakuta, K. (1997). *Improving schooling for language-minority children: A research agenda.* Washington, DC: National Research Council.

Baden, B., & Maehr, M. (1986). Conforming culture with culture: A perspective for designing schools for children of diverse sociocultural backgrounds. In R. Feldman (Ed.), *The social psychology of education* (pp. 289–309). Cambridge, MA: Harvard University Press.

Baetens Beardsmore, H. (1982). *Bilingualism: Basic principles.* Clevedon, England: Tieto.

Bakhurst, D. (1990). *Consciousness and revolution in Soviet philosophy: From the Bolsheviks to Evald Ilyenkov.* Cambridge, England: Cambridge University Press.

Banks, C. A., & Banks, J. (1995). Equity pedagogy: An essential component of multicultural education. *Theory into Practice, 34*(3), 152–158.

Banks, J. (1981). *Multiethnic education: Theory and practice.* Boston: Allyn and Bacon.

—— (1982). Educating minority youths: An inventory of current theory. *Education and Urban Society, 15*(1), 88–103.

—— (1984). *Teaching strategies for ethnic studies.* Boston: Allyn and Bacon.

—— (1993a). Multicultural education as an academic discipline: Goals for the 21st century. *Multicultural Education, 1*(3), 8–11.

—— (1993b). Multicultural education: Development, dimensions, and challenges. *Phi Delta Kappan, 75*(1), 22–28.

—— (1993c). The canon debate, knowledge construction, and multicultural education. *Educational Researcher, 22*(5), 4–14.

Banks, J., & Banks, C. A. (1995). *Handbook of research on multicultural education.* New York: Macmillan.

Beauf, J. (1977). Development of ethnic awareness in Native American children. *Developmental Psychology, 13,* 244–256.

Becijos, J. (1997). *SDAIE: Strategies for teachers of English learners.* Bonita, CA: Torch Publications.

Bell, D., Kasschau, P., & Zellman, G. (1976). *Delivering services to elderly members of minority groups: A critical review of the literature.* Santa Monica, CA: Rand.

Ben-Zeev, S. (1977). The influence of bilingualism on cognitive strategy and cognitive development. *Child Development, 48,* 1009–1018.

Berk, R. A. (1986). *Performance assessment: Methods and applications.* Baltimore: Johns Hopkins University Press.

Berman, P. (1992a). *Meeting the challenge of language diversity: An evaluation of California programs for pupils with limited proficiency in English.* Paper presented at a meeting of the American Educational Research Association.

—— (1992b). *The status of bilingual education in California.* Berkeley: Paul Berman and Associates.

—— (1996). *High performance learning communities: Proposal to the U.S. Department of Education.* Emeryville, CA: Research, Policy, and Practice Associates.

Bernstein, B. (1971). A sociolinguistic approach to socialization with some reference to educability. In B. Bernstein (Ed.), *Class, codes, and control: Theoretical studies towards a sociology of language* (pp. 146–171). London: Routledge and Kegan Paul.

Bialystok, E., & Hakuta, K. (1994). *In other words: The science and psychology of second-language acquisition.* New York: Basic Books.

Bilingual Education Act: Report together with minority views. H. Rep. No. 915, 90th Cong., 1st Sess. (1967) (Serial Set 12753-6).

Bilingual Education Act of 1967, Pub. L. No. 90-247, 20 Stat. 919 (1967).

Bilingual Education Act of 1974, Pub. L. No. 93-380, 88 Stat. 503 (1974).

Bilingual Education Act of 1978, Pub. L. No. 95-561, 92 Stat. 2268 (1978).

Bilingual Education Act of 1984, Pub. L. No. 98-511, 98 Stat. 2370 (1984).

Bloom, B. (1984). The search for methods of group instruction as effective as one-to-one tutoring. *Educational Leadership, 41*(8), 4–17.

Boggs, S. T. (1972). The meaning of questions and narratives to Hawaiian children. In C. Cazden, V. John, & D. Hymes (Eds.), *Functions of language in the classroom* (pp. 299–330). New York: Teachers College Press.

Boggs, S. T., & Watson-Gegeo, K. (1978). Interweaving routines: Strategies for encompassing a social situation. *Language in Society, 7*(3), 375–392.

Bok, D. (1990). *Universities and the future of America.* Durham, NC: Duke University Press.

Boykin, A. W. (1983). The academic performance of Afro-Americans. In J. T. Spence (Ed.), *Achievement and achievement motives: Psychological and sociological approaches* (pp. 321–372). San Francisco: W. H. Freeman and Co.

—— (1986). The triple quandary and the schooling of Afro-American children. In U. Neisser (Ed.), *The school achievement of minority children* (pp. 57–92). New York: New Perspectives.

Brophy, J., & Good, T. (1986). Teacher behavior and student achievement. In M. Wittrock (Ed.), *Handbook of research on teaching* (3rd ed., pp. 102–112). New York: Macmillan.

Brown v. Board of Education, 327 U.S. 483 (1954).

Calderón, M. (1991). Trainer of trainers: Professional development for diversity. In Office of Bilingual Education and Minority Language Affairs (Ed.), *Proceedings of the First National Research Symposium on Limited English Proficient Students* (pp. 24–42). Washington, DC: U.S. Department of Education.

—— (1994). *Cumulative reports: Vol. 1. Bilingual teachers' development within school learning communities: A synthesis of the staff development model. Vol. 2. The impact of the bilingual cooperative integrated reading and composition model on bilingual programs.* El Paso: Department of

Educational Leadership, University of Texas at El Paso.

California Commission on Teacher Credentialing. (1991). *Teacher credentialing in California: A special report.* Sacramento: Author.

California Department of Education. (1990). *High school curriculum frameworks.* Sacramento: Author.

——— (1997). *Language census report for California public schools, 1997.* Sacramento: Author.

California Tomorrow. (1995). *The unfinished journey: Restructuring schools in a diverse society.* San Francisco: Author.

——— (1996). *Looking in, looking out: Redefining child care and early education in a diverse society.* San Francisco: Author.

——— (1997, July). *The schools we need now: How parents, families, and communities can change schools.* San Francisco: Author.

Campbell, A., & Frey, G. (1970). *Methods in social science research.* New York: Appleton Books.

Carter, T. P., & Chatfield, M. L. (1986). Effective bilingual schools: Implications for policy and practice. *American Journal of Education, 95*(1), 200–234.

Castaneda v. Pickard, 648 F.2d 989 (5th Cir. 1981); 103 S.Ct. 3321 (1981).

Cazden, C. B. (1988). *Classroom discourse: The language of teaching and learning.* Portsmouth, NH: Heinemann Press.

Chavez, L. (1991). *Out of the barrio: Toward a new politics of Hispanic assimilation.* New York: Basic Books.

Cherry, L. J. (1981). Teacher-student interaction and teachers' expectations of students' communicative competence. In O. Garnica & M. King (Eds.), *Language, children, and society* (pp. 246–261). New York: Pergamon Press.

Christian, D., & Whitcher, A. (1995). *Directory of two-way bilingual programs in the United States* (rev. ed.). Santa Cruz: National Center for Research on Cultural Diversity and Second-Language Learning, University of California, Santa Cruz.

Christian, T., & Livermore, G. (1970). A comparison of Anglo-American and Spanish-American children on the WISC. *Journal of Social Psychology, 81,* 9–14.

Chu, H., & Levy, J. (1988). Multicultural skills for bilingual teachers. *NABE Journal, 12*(2), 17–36.

Civil Rights Act of 1964, Pub. L. No. 88-352, 70 Stats. 241 (1964).

Clahsen, H. (1988). Parameterized grammatical theory and language acquisition: A study of the acquisition of verb placement and inflection by children and adults. In S. Flynn & W. O'Neil (Eds.), *Linguistic theory in –second-language acquisition* (pp. 47–75). Dordrecht: Kluwer Academic Press.

Clark, K. B., & Clark, M. P. (1939). Segregation as a factor in the racial identification of Negro preschool children. *Journal of Experimental Education, 8,* 161–163.

Clark, R. M. (1983). *Family life and school achievement: Why poor black children succeed or fail.* Chicago: University of Chicago Press.

Clement, D., & Harding, J. (1978). Social distinctions and emergent student groups in a desegregated school. *Anthropology and Education Quarterly 9*(4), 272–283.

Cohen, N. E., & Pompa, D. (1994). *Multicultural perspectives on quality in early care and education: Culturally specific practices and universal outcomes* (Working Paper, Quality 2000, Advancing Early Care and Education). New Haven: Yale University.

Colangelo, N., Foxley, C. H., & Dustin, D. (Eds.). (1982). *The human relations experience.* Monterey, CA: Brooks/Cole.

Cole, M. (1996). *Cultural psychology: A once and future discipline.* Cambridge, MA: Belknap Press of Harvard University Press.

Cole, R. W. (1995). *Educating everybody's children: What research and practice say about improving achievement.* Alexandria, VA: Association for Supervision and Curriculum Development.

Coleman, J. S. (1963). *The adolescent society: The social life of the teenager and its impact on education.* New York: The Free Press.

The College Board and the Western Interstate Commission for Higher Education. (1991). *The road to college: Educational progress by race and ethnicity.* New York: The College Board.

Collier, J. P. (1985). University models for ESL and bilingual teacher training. In National Clearinghouse for Bilingual Education (Ed.), *Issues in English-language development* (pp. 26–36). Rosslyn, VA: Editor.

Collier, V. P. (1995). Acquiring a second language for school. *Directions in Language and Education, 1*(4), 1–9. [Online]. Available: National Clearinghouse for Bilingual Education, Washington, DC, at http://www.ncbe.gwu.edu/

Committee for Economic Development. (1991a). *Children in need. Investment strategies for the educationally disadvantaged: A statement by the Research and Policy Committee of the Committee for Economic Development.* New York: Author.

———— (1991b). *The unfinished agenda: A new vision for child development and education.* New York: Author.

Coons, J. E., Clune, W., III, & Sugarman, S. D. (1970). *Private wealth and public education.* Cambridge, MA: Harvard University Press.

Cooper, C. R., Baker, H., Polichar, D., & Welsh, M. (1991). *Ethnic perspectives on individuality and correctedness in adolescents' relationships with family and peers.* Paper presented at a meeting of the Society for Research in Adolescence, Alexandria, VA.

Corder, S. P. (1967). The significance of learners' errors. *International Review of Applied Linguistics in Language Teaching, 5*, 161–170.

Cuellar, J. B. (1980). A model of Chicano culture for bilingual education. In R. Padilla (Ed.), *Ethnoperspectives in bilingual research: Vol. 2. Theory in bilingual education* (pp. 81–97). Ypsilanti: Department of Foreign Languages and Bilingual Studies, Eastern Michigan University.

Cummins, J. (1979). Linguistic interdependence and the educational development of bilingual children. *Review of Educational Research, 19*, 222–251.

———— (1981). The role of primary language development in promoting educational success for language minority students. In California Department of Education, *Schooling and language minority students: A theoretical framework* (pp. 3–50). Los Angeles: Evaluation, Dissemination, and Assessment Center, California State University.

———— (1984a). *Bilingualism and special education.* San Diego: College Hill Press.

———— (1984b). Wanted, a theoretical framework for relating language proficiency to academic achievement among bilingual students. In C. Rivera (Ed.), *Language proficiency and academic achievement* (pp. 137–150). Clevedon, England: Multilingual Matters.

———— (1986). Empowering minority students: A framework for intervention. *Harvard Educational Review, 56*(1), 18–35.

———— (1989). *Empowering minority students.* Sacramento: California Association for Bilingual Education.

———— (1991). Interdependence of first- and second-language proficiency in bilingual children. In E. Bialystok (Ed.), *Language processing in bilingual children* (pp. 70–89). Cambridge, England: Cambridge University Press.

Dalton, S., & Sison, J. (1995). *Enacting instructional conversation with Spanish-speaking students in middle school* (Research Report No. 12). Santa Cruz: National Center for Research on Cultural Diversity and Second-Language Learning, University of California, Santa Cruz.

D'Andrade, R. (1995). *The development of cognitive anthropology.* New York: Cambridge University Press.

Darcy, N. T. (1953). A review of the literature of the effects of bilingualism upon the measurement of intelligence. *Journal of Genetic Psychology, 82,* 21–57.

——— (1963). Bilingualism and the measurement of intelligence: Review of a decade of research. *Journal of Genetic Psychology, 103,* 259–282.

Davis, R. B., Maher, C. A., & Noddings, N. (Eds.). (1990). *Constructivist views on the teaching and learning of mathematics.* Reston, VA: National Council of Teachers of Mathematics.

Delpit, L. (1995). *Other people's children: Cultural conflict in the classroom.* New York: New Press.

Destefano, J. (1972). Social variation in language: Implications for teaching reading to black ghetto children. In J. A. Figurel (Ed.), *Better reading in urban schools* (pp. 18–24). Newark, DE: International Reading Association.

Developmental Associates. (1984). *Final report: Descriptive study phase of the national longitudinal evaluation of the effectiveness of services for language minority limited English proficient students.* Arlington, VA: Author.

——— (1993). *Final report: Descriptive study phase of the national longitudinal evaluation of the effectiveness of services for language minority limited English proficient students.* Arlington, VA: Author.

Dewey, J. (1916). *Democracy and education: An introduction to the philosophy of education.* New York: Macmillan.

——— (1921). *Reconstruction and philosophy.* London: University of London Press.

Diaz, R. M. (1983). The impact of bilingualism on cognitive development. In E. W. Gordon (Ed.), *Review of research in education* (Vol. 10, pp. 23–54). Washington, DC: American Educational Research Association.

——— (1985). Bilingual cognitive development: Addressing these gaps in current research. *Child Development, 56,* 1376–1388.

Diaz, R. M., et al. (1991). The effects of bilingualism on preschoolers' private speech. *Early Childhood Research Quarterly, 6*(3), 377–395.

Diaz, R. M., & Klinger, C. (1991). Towards an exploratory model of the interaction between bilingualism and cognitive development. In E. Bialystok (Ed.), *Language processing in bilingual children* (pp. 140–185). New York: Cambridge University Press.

Diaz, S., Moll, L. C., & Mehan, H. (1986). Sociocultural resources in instruction: A context-specific approach. In Bilingual Education Office (Ed.), *Beyond language: Social and cultural factors in schooling language minority students* (pp. 197–230). Los Angeles: Evaluation, Dissemination, and Assessment Center, California State University.

Dolson, D. (1984). *The influence of various home bilingual environments on the academic achievement, language development, and psychosocial adjustment of fifth- and sixth-grade Hispanic students.* Unpublished doctoral dissertation, University of San Francisco.

Donald, M. (1991). *Origins of the modern mind: Three stages in the evolution of culture and cognition.* Cambridge, MA: Harvard University Press.

Dulay, H., & Burt, M. (1974a). A new perspective on the creative construction process in children. *Language Learning, 24,* 253–278.

——— (1974b). *Natural sequence in child second-language acquisition* (Working Papers on Bilingualism). Toronto: Ontario Institute for Studies in Education.

Duquette, G. (1991). Cultural processing and minority language children with needs and special needs. In G. Duquette & L. Malve (Eds.), *Language,* *culture, and cognition* (pp. 200–213). Philadelphia: Multilingual Matters.

Duran, R. (1983). *Hispanics' education and background: Predictors of college achievement.* New York: College Entrance Examination Board.

——— (1986). *Improving Hispanics' educational outcomes: Learning and instruction.* Unpublished manuscript, Graduate School of Education, University of California, Santa Barbara.

Dwyer, C. (1991). *Language, culture, and writing* (Working Paper No. 13). Berkeley: Center for the Study of Writing, University of California.

Dyson, A. H. (1983). The role of oral language in early writing processes. *Research in the Teaching of English, 17,* 1–30.

Eckert, P. (1989). *Jocks and burnouts: Social categories and identity in high school.* New York: Teachers College Press.

Eder, D. (1982). Difference in communication styles across ability groups. In L. C. Wilkinson (Ed.), *Communicating in the classroom* (pp. 245–263). New York: Academic Press.

Edmonds, R. (1979a). Effective schools for the urban poor. *Educational Leadership, 37,* 20–24.

——— (1979b). Some schools work and more can. Social Policy, 9(5), 28–32.

Education Amendment of 1978, Pub. L. No. 95-561, 92 Stat. 2143 (1978).

Edwards, J. (1981). *Ratings of black, white, and Acadian children's speech patterns.* Unpublished doctoral dissertation, Mount St. Vincent University, Halifax, Nova Scotia.

——— (1995). A commentary on discursive and cultural psychology. *Culture and Psychology, 1,* 55–65.

Elam, S. (1972). Acculturation and learning problems of Puerto Rican children. In F. Corradasco & E. Bucchini (Eds.), *The Puerto Rican community and its children on the mainland* (pp. 37–45). Metuchen, NJ: Scarecrow Press.

Elementary and Secondary Education Act of 1965, Title II, Pub. L. No. 89-10, Stat. 27 (1965).

Epstein, J. L. (1995). School/family/community partnerships: Caring for the children we share. *Phi Delta Kappan, 76*(9), 701–712.

Equal Educational Opportunities and Transportation Act of 1974, Pub. L. No. 93-830, Stat. 514 (1974).

Erickson, F. (1987). Transformation and school success: The politics and culture of educational achievement. *Anthropology and Education Quarterly, 18*(4), 335–355.

Ervin-Tripp, S. M. (1974). Is second-language learning like the first? *TESOL Quarterly, 8*(2), 111–127.

Faltis, C. J., & Hudleson, S. J. (1997). *Bilingual education in elementary and secondary school communities: Toward understanding and caring.* Boston: Allyn and Bacon.

Fashola, O. S., Slavin, R., Calderón, M., & Durán, R. (1997). *Effective programs for Latino students in elementary and middle schools* (Report No. 11). Baltimore: Center for Research on the Education of Students Placed at Risk.

Fasold, R. W. (1972). *Tense marking in Black English: A linguistic and social analysis* (Urban Language Series No. 8). Arlington, VA: Center for Applied Linguistics.

Feldman, C., & Shen, M. (1971). Some language-related cognitive advantages of bilingual five-year-olds. *Journal of Genetic Psychology, 118,* 235–244.

Feldt, L. S., & Brennan, R. C. (1989). Reliability. In R. L. Linn (Ed.), *Educational measurement* (3rd ed., pp. 105–146). New York: American Council on Education and Macmillan.

Fernandez, R., & Shu, G. (1988). School dropouts: New approaches to an enduring problem. *Education and Urban Society, 2*(4), 363–386.

Ferreiro, E. (1988, April). *Emergent literacy.* Paper presented at the annual convention of the American Educational Research Association, New Orleans.

Ferreiro, E., & Teberosky, A. (1982). *Literacy before schooling.* Exeter, NH: Heinemann.

Friere, P. (1970). *Pedagogy of the oppressed.* New York: Seabury Press.

Figueroa, R., & García, E. (1994). Issues in testing students from culturally and linguistically diverse backgrounds. *Multicultural Education, 2*(1), 10–24.

Finley, M. K. (1984). Teachers and tracking in a comprehensive high school. *Sociology of Education, 57*(4), 233–243.

Fishman, B. J., & Duffy, T. M. (1990). Classroom restructuring: What do teachers really need? *Educational Technology, Research, and Development, 40*(3), 95–111.

Fishman, J. A. (1990). What is reversing language shift (RLS) and how can it succeed? *Journal of Multilingual and Multicultural Development, 11*(1–2), 5–36.

Flores, B. M., & García, E. M. (1984). A collaborative learning and teaching experience using journal writing. *NABE: The Journal for the National Association for Bilingual Education, 8*(2), 67–83.

Fordham, S. (1988). Racelessness as a factor in black students' school success: Pragmatic strategy or pyrrhic victory? *Harvard Educational Review, 58*(1), 54–83.

Frase, M. (1989). *Dropout rates in the United States: 1988* (Analysis Report). Washington, DC: Superintendent of Documents, U.S. Government Printing Office.

Freeman, Y. S., & Freeman, D. E. (1997). *Teaching reading and writing in Spanish in the bilingual classroom.* Portsmouth, NH: Heinemann.

Friedson, E. (1986). *Professional powers.* Chicago: University of Chicago Press.

Galambos, S. J., & Hakuta, K. (1988). Subject-specific and task-specific characteristics of metalinguistic awareness in bilingual children. *Applied Psycholinguistics, 9,* 141–162.

Gallas, K. (1991). Arts as epistemology: Enabling children to know what they know. *Harvard Educational Review, 61,* 40–50.

Gallimore, R., et al. (1986). Self-regulation and interactive teaching: The effects of teaching conditions on teachers' cognitive activity. *Elementary School Journal, 86*(5), 613–631.

Gallimore, R., & Tharp, R. G. (1989). *Challenging cultural minds.* London: Cambridge University Press.

García, E. (1983a). *Bilingualism in early childhood.* Albuquerque: University of New Mexico Press.

——— (1983b). *The Mexican-American child: Language, cognition, and socialization.* Tempe: Arizona State University.

——— (1986). Bilingual development and the education of bilingual children during early childhood. *American Journal of Education, 95*(1), 96–121.

——— (1988). Effective schooling for language minority students. In National Clearinghouse for Bilingual Education (Ed.), *New focus* (pp. 49–62). Arlington, VA: Author.

——— (1989). Instructional discourse in "effective" Hispanic classrooms. In R. Jacobson & C. Faltis (Eds.), *Language distribution issues in bilingual schooling* (pp. 104–120). Clevedon, England: Multilingual Matters.

——— (1990a). Bilingualism and the academic performance of Mexican-American children: The evolving debate. *ERIC Digest.*

——— (1990b). Language minority litigation policy: The law of the land. In A. Barona & E. García (Eds.), *Children at risk* (pp. 53–64). Washington, DC: National Association of School Psychologists.

———(1991a). Attributes of effective language minority teachers: An empirical study. *Journal of Education, 173,* 130–141.

——— (1991b). Bilingualism, second-language acquisition in academic contexts. In A. Ambert (Ed.), *Bilingual education and English-as-a-second language: A research annual* (pp. 181–217). New York: Garland.

——— (1991c). *Characteristics of effective teachers for language minority students: A review* (Education Report No. 1). Santa Cruz: National Center for Research on Cultural Diversity and Second-Language Learning, University of California, Santa Cruz.

——— (1991d). *The education of linguistically and culturally diverse students: Effective instructional practices.* Santa Cruz: National Center for Research on Cultural Diversity and Second-Language Learning, University of California, Santa Cruz.

——— (1992a). Effective instruction for language minority students: The teacher. *Journal of Education, 173*(2), 130–141.

——— (1992b). Hispanic children: Theoretical, empirical, and related policy issues. *Educational Psychology Review, 4*(1), 69–93.

——— (1993). Language culture and education. In L. Darling-Hammond (Ed.), *Review of research in education* (pp. 51–98). Washington, DC: American Education Research Association.

——— (1995). Educating Mexican American students: Past treatments and recent developments in theory, research, policy, and practice. In J. Banks & C. A. Banks (Eds.), *Handbook on research on multicultural education* (pp. 372–384). New York: Macmillan.

——— (1996). Early childhood education reinvention and education policy: Addressing linguistic and cultural diversity. *Early Childhood Development and Care, 123*, 203–219.

——— (1997, March). The education of Hispanics in early childhood: Of roots and wings. *Young Children, 52*(3), 5–14.

García, E., & Gonzales, G. (1984). Spanish and Spanish-English development in the Hispanic child. In J. V. Martinez & R. H. Mendoza (Eds.), *Chicano psychology* (pp. 98–114). New York: Academic Press.

García, E., & Gonzalez, R. (1995). Issues in systemic reform for culturally and linguistically diverse students. *College Record, 96*(3), 418–431.

García, E., Maez, L., & Gonzalez, G. (1979). Language switching in *Mexican-American child: Language, cognition, and social development* (pp. 56–73). Tempe: Arizona State University.

García, E., & McLaughlin, B. (1995). *Meeting the challenges of linguistic and cultural diversity in early childhood.* New York: Teachers College Press.

García, E., & Stein, G. B. (1996). Multilingualism in U.S. schools: Treating language as a resource for instruction and parent involvement. *Early Childhood Development and Care, 127–128*, 141–155.

García, R. (1979). *Teaching in a pluralistic society.* New York: Harper and Row.

Gardner, H. (1985). *Frames of mind: The theory of multiple intelligences.* New York: Basic Books.

Gardner, R. C., & Lambert, E. (1972). *Attitudes and motivation in second-language learning.* Rowley, MA: Newbury House.

Garth, T., Elson, T., & Morton, M. (1936). The administration of non-language intelligence tests to Mexicans. *Journal of Abnormal and Social Psychology, 31*, 53–58.

Gay, G. (1975). Organizing and designing culturally pluralistic curriculum. *Educational Leadership, 33*, 176–183.

——— (1997). The relationship between multicultural and democratic education. *Social Studies, 88*(1), 5–11.

Geertz, F. (1973). *The interpretation of cultures: Selected essays.* New York: Basic Books.

Genishi, C. (1981). Code switching in Chicano six-year-olds. In R. Duran (Ed.), *Latino language and communicative behavior* (pp. 133–152). Norwood, NJ: Ablex.

Genishi, C., & Dyson, A. H. (1984). *Language assessment in the early years.* Norwood, NJ: Ablex.

Genzuk, M., & Hentschke, G. (1992). *Career pathways for practitioners: Progress report.* USC Latino Teacher Project. Los Angeles: University of California at Los Angeles.

George Washington University Center for Equity and Excellence in Education. (1996). *Promoting excellence: Ensuring academic success of limited English proficient students.* Arlington, VA: Evaluation Assistance Center East.

Gibson, M. A. (1987). The school performance of immigrant minorities: A comparative view. *Anthropology and Education Quarterly, 18*(4), 262–275.

—— (1995). Promoting additive acculturation in schools. *Multicultural Education, 3*(1), 10–12, 54.

Gibson, M. A., & Ogbu, J. (Eds.). (1991). *Minority status and schooling: A comparative study of immigrant and involuntary minorities.* New York: Garland.

Giroux, H. A., & McLaren, P. (1986). Teacher education and the politics of engagement: The case for democratic schooling. *Harvard Review, 56,* 213–238.

Gleason, J. B. (1988). *The development of language.* Columbus, OH: Merrill.

Goals 2000: Educate America Act, Pub. L. No. 103-227, 108 Stat. 125 (1994).

Goldenberg, C. (1992). *Instructional conversations and their classroom application* (Education Practice Report No. 2). Santa Cruz: National Center for Research on Cultural Diversity and Second-Language Learning, University of California, Santa Cruz.

—— (1993). Instructional conversations: Promoting comprehension through discussion. *Reading Teacher, 46*(4), 316–326.

Goldenberg, C., & Gallimore, R. (1990). *Meeting the language arts challenge for language-minority children: Teaching and learning in a new key* (Progress Report for 1989–90 to Presidential Grants for School Improvement Committee, University of California, Office of the President).

—— (1991a). Local knowledge, research knowledge, and educational change: A core study of early Spanish reading improvement. *Educational Researcher, 20*(8), 2–14.

—— (1991b). *Teaching and learning in a new key: The instructional conversation.* Paper presented at the annual meeting of the American Educational Research Association, Chicago.

Goldenberg, C., & Patthey-Chavez, G. (1991). *Discourse processes in instructional conversations: Interactions between teacher and transition students.* Manuscript submitted for publication.

Goldman, S., & Trueba, H. (Eds.). (1987). *Becoming literate in English as a second language: Advances in research and theory.* Norwood, NJ: Ablex.

Gollnick, D. M., & Chinn, P. C. (1986). *Multicultural education in a pluralistic society.* New York: Maxwell Macmillan International Press.

—— (1990). *Multicultural education in a pluralistic society* (3rd ed.). Columbus, OH: Merrill.

—— (1994). *Multicultural education in a pluralistic society* (4th ed.). New York: Maxwell Macmillan.

Gonzalez, G. (1990). *Chicano education in the segregation era: 1915–1945.* Philadelphia: The Balch Institute.

—— (1991). Spanish-language acquisition research among Mexican-American children. *Early Childhood Research Quarterly, 6,* 411–426.

—— (1994). *Labor and community: Mexican citrus worker villages in a southern California county, 1900–1950.* Urbana: University of Illinois Press.

Goodenough, W. H. (1981). *Culture, language, and society* (2nd ed.). Menlo Park, CA: Cummings Publishing Co.

Goodlad, J. (1984). *A place called school.* New York: McGraw-Hill.

Goodman, Y. (1980). The roots of literacy. In M. P. Douglass (Ed.), *Reading: A humanizing experience* (pp. 286–301). Claremont, CA: Claremont Graduate School.

Grant, C. A. (1977a). The mediator of culture: A teacher role revisited. *Journal of Research and Development in Education, 11* (1), 102–117.

——— (Ed.). (1977b). *Multicultural education: Commitments, issues, and applications.* Washington, DC: Association for Supervision and Curriculum Development.

——— (1991). Educational research and teacher training for successfully teaching LEP students. In Office of Bilingual Education and Minority Affairs (Ed.), *Proceedings of the Second National Research Symposium on Limited English Proficient Student Issues* (pp. 31–47). Washington, DC: U.S. Department of Education.

——— (1998). *Multicultural research, race, class, gender, and sexual orientation.* New York: Falmer Press.

Grant, C. A., & Secada, W. G. (1990). Preparing teachers for diversity. In W. R. Houston (Ed.), *Handbook of research on teacher education* (pp. 403–422). New York: Macmillan.

Grant, C. A., & Sleeter, C. (1987). An analysis of multicultural education in the United States. *Harvard Educational Review, 57,* 421–444.

——— (1988). Race, class, and gender and abandoned dreams. *Teachers College Record, 90*(1), 19–40.

Guerra, M. H. (1979). Bilingualism and biculturalism: Assets for Chicanos. In A. Trejo (Ed.), *The Chicanos: As we see ourselves* (pp. 129–136). Tucson: University of Arizona Press.

Hakuta, K. (1974). *A preliminary report on the development of grammatical morphemes in a Japanese girl learning English as a second language.* In The Ontario Institute for Studies in Education, *Working Papers in Bilingualism* (Vol. 3, pp. 294–316). Toronto: Author.

——— (1986). *Mirror of language: The debate on bilingualism.* New York: Basic Books.

Hakuta, K., & August, D. (Eds.). (1997). *Improving schooling for language-minority children: A research agenda.* Washington, DC: National Academy of Sciences—National Research Council, Board on Children, Youth, and Families.

Hakuta, K., & D'Andrea, D. (1992). Some properties of bilingual maintenance and loss in Mexican background high-school students. *Applied Linguistics, 13,* 72–99.

Hakuta, K., Diaz, R., & Ferdman, M. (1986). *Bilingualism and cognitive development: Three perspectives and methodological implications.* Los Angeles: CLEAR.

Hakuta, K., & García, E. (1989). Bilingualism and bilingual education. *American Psychologist, 44*(2), 374–379.

Hakuta, K., & Snow, C. (1986, January). *The role of research in policy decisions about bilingual education.* Washington, DC: Testimony before the U.S. House of Representatives, Education and Labor Committee.

Hall, N. (1987). *The emergence of literacy.* Portsmouth, NH: Heinemann Educational Books.

Halliday, M. A. K. (1973). *Explorations in the functions of language.* London: Edward Arnold.

Hamers, J. F., & Blanc, M. (1989). *Bilinguality and bilingualism.* New York: Cambridge University Press.

Harrison, J. (1985). Functions of language attitudes in school settings. *Language in Society, 22,* 1–21.

Hawley, W. D., & Jackson, A. W. (1995). *Toward a common destiny.* San Francisco: Jossey-Bass.

Haycock, K., & Navarro, M. S. (1988). *Unfinished business: Fulfilling our children's promise. A report from the Achievement Council.* Oakland, CA: Achievement Council.

Heath, S. B. (1981). Towards an ethnohistory of writing in American education. In M. Farr-Whitman (Ed.), *Variation in writing: Functional and linguistic cultural differences* (Vol. 1, pp. 225–246). Hillsdale, NJ: Lawrence Erlbaum.

——— (1982). Questioning at school and at home: A comparative study. In G. D. Spindler (Ed.), *Doing the ethnography of schooling: Educational anthropology in action* (pp. 102–131). New York: Holt, Rinehart and Winston.

——— (1983). *Ways with words: Language, life, and work in communities and classrooms.* Cambridge, England: Cambridge University Press.

——— (1986). Sociocultural contexts of language development. In Bilingual Education Office, *Beyond language: Social and cultural factors in schooling language minority students* (pp. 143–186). Los Angeles: Evaluation, Dissemination, and Assessment Center, California State University.

Heath, S. B., & Mangiola, L. (1991). *Children of promise: Literate activity in linguistically and culturally diverse classrooms* (NEA School Restructuring Series). Washington, DC: National Education Association.

Henderson, R. W., & Landesman, E. M. (1992). *Mathematics and middle school students of Mexican descent: The effects of thematically integrated instruction* (Research Report No. 5). Santa Cruz: National Center for Research on Cultural Diversity and Second-Language Learning, University of California, Santa Cruz.

Henze, R., Regan, K., Vanett, L., & Power, M. (1990). *An exploratory study of the effectiveness of the Lower Kuskokwin School District's bilingual program.* Paper prepared for the Lower Kuskokwin School District, Oakland, CA.

Herrnstein, R. J., & Murray, C. (1994). *The bell curve: Intelligence and class structure in American life.* New York: The Free Press.

Hetherington, E. M., & Parke, R. D. (Eds.). (1988). *Contemporary reading in child psychology* (3rd ed.). New York: McGraw-Hill.

Hoffman, D. M. (1988). Cross-cultural adaptation and learning: Iranians and Americans at school. In H. Trueba &

C. Delgado-Gaitan (Eds.), *School and society: Learning content through culture* (pp. 13–27). New York: Praeger Publishers.

Hopwood v. Texas, 78 F.3d 932 (5th Cir. Tex. 1996).

Huerta, A. (1977). The development of code switching in a young bilingual. *Working Papers in Sociolinguistics, 21,* 1–27.

Hurtado, A., Figueroa, R., & García, E. (Eds.). (1996). *Strategic interventions in education: Expanding the Latina/Latino pipeline.* Santa Cruz: University of California, Santa Cruz.

Hurtado, A., & Gurin, P. (1987). Ethnic identity and bilingualism attitudes. *Hispanic Journal of Behavioral Sciences, 9*(1), 1–18.

Irujo, S. (1988). An introduction to intercultural differences and similarities in nonverbal communication. In J. Wurzel (Ed.), *Toward multiculturalism* (pp. 72–89). Yarmouth, ME: Intercultural Press.

Jackman, M. R. (1973). Education and prejudice or education and response-set. *American Sociological Review, 38,* 327–339.

Jaynes, G. D., & Williams, R. M., Jr. (Eds.). (1989). *A common destiny: Blacks and American society.* Washington, DC: National Academy Press.

Jencks, C., Smith, M., Acland, H., Bane, M., Cohen, D., Gintis, H., Hynes, B., & Micelson, S. (1972). *Inequality: A reassessment of the effects of family and schooling in America.* New York: Basic Books.

Johnson, D., & Johnson, R. (1981). Effects of cooperative and individualistic learning experiences on interethnic interaction. *Journal of Educational Psychology 73*(3), 444–449.

Johnson, D. L., Teigen, K., & Davila, R. (1983). Anxiety and social restriction: A study of children in Mexico, Norway, and the United States. *Journal of Cross-Cultural Psychology, 14,* 439–454.

Joyce, B., Murphy, C., Showers, B., & Murphy, J. (1989). School renewal as cultural change. *Educational Leadership, 47*(3), 70–77.

Kagan, S. (1983a). Interpreting Chicano cooperativeness: Methodological and theoretical considerations. In J. L. Martinez & R. H. Mendoza (Eds.), *Chicano psychology* (2nd ed., pp. 289–333). Orlando, FL: Academic Press.

——— (1983b). Social orientation among Mexican-American children: A challenge to traditional classroom structures. In E. García (Ed.), *The Mexican-American child: Language, cognition, and social development* (pp. 75–89). Tempe: Arizona State University.

——— (1984). Interpreting Chicano cooperativeness: Methodological and theoretical considerations in Chicano psychology. In E. García (Ed.), *The Mexican-American child* (pp. 79–90). Tempe: Arizona State University.

——— (1986). Cooperative learning and sociocultural factors in schooling. In Bilingual Education Office, *Beyond language: Social and cultural factors in schooling language minority students* (pp. 146–191). Los Angeles: Evaluation, Dissemination, and Assessment Center, California State University.

——— (Ed.). (1993). *The essential functions of the early care and education system: Rationale and definition* (Working Paper, Quality 2000, Advancing Early Care and Education). New Haven: Yale University.

Kagan, S., Knight, G. P., Martinez, S., & Espinosa-Santana, P. (1981). Conflict resolution style among Mexican children: Examining urbanization and ecology effects. *Journal of Cross-Cultural Psychology, 12,* 222–232.

Kaufman, P., & Frase, M. J. (1990). *Dropout rates in the United States: 1989.* Washington, DC: National Center for Education Statistics.

Keefe, S. E. (1979, Summer). Urbanization, acculturation, and extended family ties: Mexican-Americans in cities. *American Ethnologist,* pp. 349–362.

Keefe, S. E., & Padilla, A. M. (1987). *Chicano ethnicity.* Albuquerque: University of New Mexico Press.

Keefe, S. E., Padilla, A. M., & Carlos, M. L. (1979a). *Mental health issues of significance in Mexican American families* (Hispanic Mental Health Working Papers). Los Angeles: University of California.

——— (1979b). The Mexican-American extended family as an emotional support system. *Human Organization, 38,* 144–152.

Kessler, C., & Quinn, M. E. (1985). Positive effects of bilingualism on science problem-solving abilities. In J. E. Alatis & J. J. Staczek (Eds.), *Perspectives on bilingual education* (pp. 289–296). Washington, DC: Georgetown University Press.

——— (1987). Language minority children's linguistic and cognitive creativity. *Journal of Multilingual and Multicultural Development, 8*(1), 173–185.

Knight, G. P., Bernal, M. E., & Carlos, G. (1988). Socialization and the development of cooperative, competitive, and individualistic behaviors among Mexican American children. In E. García, L. Moll, & A. Barona (Eds.), *The Mexican-American child: Language, cognition, and socialization* (Vol. 2, pp. 101–111). Tempe: Arizona State University.

Knight, G. P., & Kagan, S. (1977). Acculturation of prosocial and competitive behaviors among second- and third-generation Mexican American children. *Journal of Cross-Cultural Psychology, 8,* 273–284.

Kozol, J. (1991). *Savage inequalities: Children in America's schools.* New York: Crown.

Krashen, S. D. (1981a). Bilingual education and second language-acquisition theory. In California Department of Education (Ed.), *Schooling and language minority students: A theoretical framework* (pp. 3–50). Los Angeles: Evaluation, Dissemination, and Assessment Center, California State University.

———— (1981b). *Second-language acquisition and second-language learning.* New York: Pergamon Press.

———— (1985). *The input hypothesis: Issues and implications.* New York: Longman.

Kroeber, A. L., & Kluckhohn, D. (1963). *Culture: A critical review of concepts and definitions.* New York: Vintage Books.

Labov, W. (1972a). The logic of nonstandard English. In W. Labov (Ed.), *Language in the inner city: Studies in black English vernacular* (pp. 201–240). Philadelphia: University of Pennsylvania Press.

———— (1972b). *Sociolinguistic patterns.* Philadelphia: University of Pennsylvania Press.

Ladson-Billings, G. (1994). *The dreamkeepers: Successful teachers of African American children.* San Francisco: Jossey-Bass.

Laosa, L. (1978). Maternal teaching strategies in Chicano families of varied educational and socioeconomic levels. *Child Development, 49,* 1129–1135.

———— (1982). School, occupation, culture, and family: The impact of parental schooling on the parent-child relationship. *Journal of Educational Psychology, 74*(6), 791–827.

———— (1984). Ethnic, socioeconomic, and home language influences upon early performance on measures of abilities. *Journal of Educational Psychology, 76*(6), 1178–1198.

———— (1995). *Intelligence testing and social policy* (Research Report No. 95-32). Princeton: Educational Testing Service.

Larkin, R. W. (1979). *Suburban youth in cultural crisis.* New York: Oxford University Press.

Lau v. Nichols, 414 U.S. 563 (1974).

Lave, J. (1988). *Cognition in practice: Mind mathematics and culture in everyday life.*

Cambridge, England: Cambridge University Press.

Lee, L. C. (1991, Winter). The opening of the American mind: Educating leaders for a multicultural society. *Human Ecology Forum,* pp. 2–5.

Leighton, M. S., Hightower, A. M., & Wrigley, A. M. (1993). *Model strategies in bilingual education: Professional development.* Washington, DC: U.S. Department of Education.

Leighton, M. S., Russo, A. W., & Hightower, A. M. (1993). *Improving education for language minority student: Promising practices in professional development.* Unpublished paper, Policy Studies Associates, Washington, DC.

Leopold, W. F. (1939). *Speech development of a bilingual child: A linguist's record: Vol. 1. Vocabulary growth in the first two years.* Evanston, IL: Northwestern University Press.

Levin, H. M. (1986). *Educational reform for disadvantaged students: An emerging crisis.* Washington, DC: National Education Association.

Levin, I. (1988). *Accelerated schools for at-risk students* (CPRE Research Report Series RR-010). New Brunswick, NJ: Rutgers University Center for Policy Research in Education.

Lindholm, K., & Christiansen, A. (1990). *Directory of two-way bilingual programs.* Washington, DC: Center for Applied Linguisitics.

Lindholm, K. J., et al. (1979). Comprehension of relational concepts: Use of bilingual children to separate cognitive and linguistic factors. *Hispanic Journal of Behavioral Sciences, 1* (4), 327–343.

Lucas, T. (1987). *Black English discourse in urban contexts.* Unpublished doctoral dissertation, Georgetown University, Washington, DC.

———— (1997). *Into, through, and beyond secondary school: Critical transitions for immigrant youths.* Washington, DC, and McHenry, IL: Center for Applied Linguistics and Delta Systems.

Lucas, T., Henze, R., & Donato, R. (1990). Promoting the success of Latino language minority students: An exploratory study of six high schools. *Harvard Educational Review, 60*(3), 315–334.

Luria, A. R. (1928). The problem of the cultural development of the child. *Journal of Genetic Psychology, 35,* 493–506.

Manuel, H., & Hughes, L. (1932). The intelligence and drawing ability of young Mexican children. *Journal of Applied Psychology, 16,* 382–387.

Matute-Bianchi, E. (1986). Ethnic identities and patterns of school success and failure among Mexican-descent and Japanese-American students in a California high school: An ethnographic analysis. *American Journal of Education, 95*(1), 233–255.

———— (1990). *A report to the Santa Clara County School District: Hispanics in the schools.* Santa Clara, CA: Santa Clara County School District.

McAdoo, H. P., & McAdoo, J. L. (Eds.). (1985). *Black children: Social, educational, and parental environments.* Beverly Hills, CA: Sage.

McClintock, C. G. (1972). Social motivation: A set of propositions. *Behavioral Science, 17,* 438–454.

———— (1974). Development of social motives in Anglo-American and Mexican-American children. *Journal of Personality and Social Psychology, 29,* 348–354.

McClintock, E., Bayard, M. P., & McClintock, C. G. (1983). The socialization of prosocial orientations in Mexican American families. In E. García (Ed.), *The Mexican-American child: Language, cognition, and social development* (pp. 143–162). Tempe: Arizona State University.

McDermott, R. P. (1987). The exploration of minority school failure, again. *Anthropology and Education Quarterly, 18*(4), 361–364.

McGahie, W. C. (1991). Professional competence evaluation. *Educational Researcher, 20*(1), 3–9.

McLeod, B. (1996). *School reform and student diversity: Exemplary schooling for language minority students.* Washington, DC: Institute for the Study of Language and Education, George Washington University.

McNab, G. (1979). Cognition and bilingualism: A re-analysis of studies. *Linguistics, 17,* 231–255.

Mead, M. (1937). *Cooperation and competition among primitive people.* New York: McGraw.

———— (1939a). *Culture of the islander.* New York: Academic Press.

———— (1939b). Native languages as field-work tools. *American Anthropologist, 41,* 189–205.

Mehan, H. (1979). *Learning lessons: Social organizations in the classrooms.* Cambridge, MA: Harvard University Press.

———— (1987). Language and schooling. In G. Spindler & D. Spindler (Eds.), *Interpretive ethnography of education at home and abroad* (pp. 109–136). Hillsdale, NJ: Erlbaum.

Mehan, H., Villanueva, I., Hubbard, L., & Lintz, A. (1996). *Constructing school success: The consequences of untracking low-achieving students.* New York: Cambridge University Press.

Melmed, P. J. (1971). *Black English phonology: The question of reading interference.* Berkeley, CA: University of California.

Milk, R. D. (1986). The issue of language separation in bilingual methodology. In E. García & B. Flores (Eds.), *Language and literacy in bilingual education* (pp. 67–86). Tempe: Arizona State University.

Milk, R., Mercado, C., & Sapiens, A. (1992). *Re-thinking the education of teachers of language minority children: Developing reflective teachers for changing schools.* Washington, DC: National Clearinghouse for Bilingual Education.

Minicucci, C., & Olsen, L. (1992). *Programs for secondary limited English proficient students: A California study* (FOCUS No. 5, Occasional Papers in Bilingual Education). Washington, DC: National Clearinghouse for Bilingual Education.

Miramontes, O., Nadeau, A., & Commins, N. (1997). *Linguistic diversity and effective school reform: A process for decision making.* New York: Teachers College Press.

Mirón, L. F. (1996). *The social construction of urban schooling: Situating the crisis.* Cresskill, NJ: Hampton Press.

Moll, L. (1988). Educating Latino students. *Language Arts, 64,* 315–324.

Moll, L., & Diaz, S. (1983). Bilingual communication skills in classroom contexts. Final report. San Diego: Laboratory of Comparative Human Cognition, California University.

Montone, C. (1995). *Teaching linguistically and culturally diverse learners: Effective programs and practices.* Santa Cruz: National Center for Research on Cultural Diversity and Second-Language Learning, University of California, Santa Cruz.

Morine-Dershimer, G. (1985). *Talking, listening, and learning in elementary classrooms.* New York: Longman.

Moya, S., & O'Malley, M. (1994). A portfolio assessment of ESL. *Journal of Educational Issues on Language Minority Students, 13,* 13–36.

Nanda, S. (1990). *Cultural anthropology.* New York: D. Van Nostrand.

National Assessment of Educational Progress. (1990). *Literacy: Profiles of America's young adults.* Princeton: Educational Testing Service.

National Association of Bilingual Education. (1992). *Professional standards for the preparation of bilingual/multilingual teachers.* Washington, DC: Author.

National Association for the Education of Young Children. (1997). *Leadership in early age and education.* Washington, DC: Author.

National Board for Professional Teaching Standards. (1996). *Proposed: English as a new language standards.* Washington, DC: Author.

National Center for Children in Poverty. (1990). *Five million children: A statistical profile of our poorest young citizens.* New York: Columbia University.

———— (1995). *Five million children: A statistical profile of our poorest young citizens.* New York: Columbia University.

National Center for Educational Statistics. (1991). *The condition of education* (Vols. 1–2). Washington, DC: U.S. Department of Education.

———— (1995). *The condition of education.* Washington, DC: U.S. Department of Education.

———— (1996). *The condition of education* (Vols. 1–2). Washington, DC: U.S. Department of Education.

National Center of Effective Secondary Schools. (1991). *Annual report: Effective secondary schools.* Madison, WI: Author.

National Commission on Children. (1991). *Beyond rhetoric: A new American agenda for children and families. Final report of the National Commission on Children.* Washington, DC: Author.

National Commission on Excellence in Education. (1983). *A nation at risk: The imperative for education reform.* Washington, DC: U.S. Department of Education.

National Council of Teachers and International Reading Association. (1996). *Standards for the English language arts.* Urbana, IL, and Newark, DE: Authors.

National Research Council. (1993). *Losing generations: Adolescents in high-risk settings.* Washington, DC: National Academy Press.

New Jersey State Board of Education Handbook. (1991). *Guidelines for development of program plan and evaluation summary, bilingual/ESL programs and English-language services, fiscal year 1991.*

New Jersey State Department of Education.

Nieto, S. (1979). *Curriculum decision-making: The Puerto Rican family and the bilingual child.* Unpublished doctoral dissertation, University of Massachusetts, Amherst.

———— (1992). *Affirming diversity: The sociopolitical context of multicultural education.* New York: Longman.

Nine Curt, C. J. (1991). *Lost talent: The underparticipation of women, minorities, and disabled persons in science.* Santa Monica, CA: Rand.

Noddings, N. (1973). Comments on the wisdom of scientific inquiry on education. *Journal of Research in Science Teaching, 10*(3), 279.

———— (1996). Rethinking the benefits of the college-bound curriculum. *Phi Delta Kappan, 78*(4), 285–289.

Oakes, J. (1984a). *Keeping track.* New Haven: Yale University Press.

———— (1984b). *Nonverbal communication.* Cambridge, MA: Evaluation, Dissemination, and Assessment Center.

———— (1989). What educational indicators? The case for assessing the school context. *Educational Evaluation and Policy Analysis, 11*(2), 181–199.

———— (1990). *Multiplying inequalities: The effects of race, social class, and tracking on opportunities to learn mathematics and science.* Santa Monica, CA: Rand.

———— (1991). *Lost talent: The underparticipation of women, minorities, and disabled persons in science.* Santa Monica, CA: Rand.

———— (1992). Can tracking research inform practice? Technical, normative, and political considerations. *Educational Researcher, 21*(4), 12–21.

Ochs, E., Taylor, C., Rudolph, D., & Smith, R. C. (1989). *Narrative activity as a medium for theory-building.* Unpublished manuscript, University of Southern California.

Ogbu, J. (1982a). Cultural discontinuities and schooling. *Anthropology and Education Quarterly, 13*(4), 168–190.

———— (1982b). Socialization: A cultural ecological approach. In K. M. Borman (Ed.), *The social life of children in a changing society* (pp. 253–267). Hillsdale, NJ: Erlbaum.

———— (1983). Minority status and schooling in plural societies. *Comparative Education Review 27*(22), 168–190.

———— (1986). The consequences of the American caste system. In Ulric Neisser (Ed.), *The school achievement of minority children: New perspectives* (pp. 15–29). Hillsdale, NJ: Erlbaum.

———— (1987a). *Minority education and caste: The American system in cross-cultural perspective.* New York: Academic Press.

———— (1987b). Variability in minority school performance: A problem in search of an explanation. *Anthropology and Education Quarterly, 18*(4), 312–334.

———— (1992a). Adaptation to minority status and impact on school success. *Theory into Practice, 31*(4), 287–295.

———— (1992b). Understanding cultural differences and school learning. *Education Libraries, 16*(3), 7–11.

———— (1992c). Understanding cultural diversity and learning. *Educational Researcher, 21*(8), 5–14, 24.

Ogbu, J., & Matute-Bianchi, M. E. (1986). Understanding sociocultural factors: Knowledge, identity, and school adjustment. In Bilingual Education Office (Ed.), *Beyond language: Social and cultural factors in schooling language minority students* (pp. 73–142). Los Angeles: Evaluation, Dissemination, and Assessment Center, California State University.

Olsen, L. (1988). *Crossing the schoolhouse border: Immigrant students and the California public schools.* San Francisco: California Tomorrow Policy Research.

———— (1997). *Made in America: Immigrant students in our public schools.* New York: The New Press.

O'Malley, M. J. (1981). *Children's and services study: Language minority children with limited English proficiency in the*

United States. Rosslyn, VA: National Clearinghouse for Bilingual Education.

Ovando, C. J., & Collier, V. P. (1985). *Bilingual and ESL classrooms: Teaching in multicultural contexts.* New York: Mc-Graw-Hill.

Padilla, A. M., & Liebman, E. (1975). Language acquisition in the bilingual child. *The Bilingual Review/La Revista Bilingüe, 2,* 34–55.

Paley, V. (1981). *Wally's stories.* Cambridge, MA: Harvard University Press.

——— (1986). *Mollie is three: Growing up in school.* Chicago: University of Chicago Press.

Paul, B. (1965). Anthropological perspectives on medicine and public health. In James K. Skipper, Jr., & Robert C. Leonard (Eds.), *Social interaction and patient care* (pp. 187–124). Philadelphia: J. B. Lippincott.

Peal, E., & Lambert, W. E. (1962). The relation of bilingualism to intelligence. *Psychological Monographs: General and Applied, 76*(546), 1–23.

Pearl, A. (1991). Democratic education: Myth or reality? In R. Valencia (Ed.), *Chicano school failure and success* (pp. 101–118). New York: Falmer Press.

Pease-Alvarez, L., Espinoza, P., & García, E. (1991). Effective instruction for language minority students: An early childhood case study. *Early Childhood Research Quarterly, 6*(3), 347–363.

Pelto, P., & Pelto, G. H. (1975). Intracultural variation: Some theoretical issues. *American Ethnologist, 2*(1), 1–45.

Perry, J. (1975). Notes toward a multicultural curriculum. *English Journal, 64.*

Phelan, P., Davidson, A. L., & Cao, H. T. (1991). *Students' multiple worlds: Negotiating the boundaries of family, peer, and school cultures.* Stanford: Center for Research on the Context of Secondary Teaching.

Phillips, S. U. (1972). Participant structures and communication incompetence: Warm Springs children in community and classroom. In C. Cazden,

D. Hymes, & W. J. Johns (Eds.), *Function of language in the classroom* (pp. 161–189). New York: Teachers College Press.

——— (1983). *The invisible culture: Communication in classroom and community on the Warm Springs Indian reservation.* New York: Longman.

——— (1984). *The invisible culture.* New York: Longman.

Purkey, S. C., & Smith, M. S. (1983). Effective schools: A review. *Elementary School Journal, 83,* 52–78.

——— (1985). School reform: The district policy implications of the effective schools literature. *Elementary School Journal, 85*(3), 353–389.

Rambaut, R. (1997). *Immigrants in San Diego County.* New York: Russell Sage Foundation.

Ramirez, A. (1985). *Bilingualism through schooling.* Albany: State University of New York Press.

Ramirez, J. D., & Merino, B. J. (1990). Classroom talk in English immersion, early-exit, and late-exit transitional bilingual education programs. In R. Jacobson & C. Faltis (Eds.), *Language distribution issues in bilingual schooling* (pp. 61–103). Clevedon, England: Multilingual Matters.

Ramirez, J. D., Yuen, S. D., Ramey, D., & Billings, D. (1991). *Final report: Longitudinal study of structured English immersion strategy, early-exit, and late-exit bilingual education programs for language minority children* (Vols. 1–2, No. 300-87-0156). San Mateo, CA: Aguirre International.

Ramirez, J. D., Yuen, S. D., Ramey, D. R., & Pasta, D. J. (1991). *Final report: Longitudinal study of structured English immersion strategy, early-exit, and late-exit transitional bilingual education programs for language minority children.* San Mateo, CA: Aguirre International.

Ramirez, M., & Castaneda, A. (1974). *Cultural democracy, bi-cognitive development, and education.* New York: Academic Press.

Rand. (1994). *Educational achievement of generations: Executive summary.* Los Angeles: Author.

Reynolds, A., & Elias, P. (1991). *What is good teaching: A review of the literature.* Princeton: Educational Testing Service.

Riley, R. (1994). Systemic reform: The U.S. Department of Education agenda. *College Record, 96*(3), 5–21.

——— (1995). *Turning the corner: From a nation at risk to a nation with a future. Second annual address.* Washington, DC: U.S. Department of Education.

Rodriguez, C. E. (1989). *Puerto Ricans born in the U.S.A.* Winchester, MA: Unwin Hyman.

Rodriguez, R. (1982). *Hunger of memory.* New York: Bantam.

Rogoff, B. (1990). *Apprenticeship in thinking: Cognitive development in social context.* Oxford: Oxford University Press.

Romo, H., & Falbo, T. (1996). *Latino high school graduation: Defying the odds.* Austin: University of Texas Press.

Rose, M. (1989). *Lives on the boundary: The struggles and achievements of America's unprepared,* New York: The Free Press.

——— (1995). Calexico: Portrait of an educational community. *Teachers & Writers, 26*(5), 1–15.

——— (1996). *Possible lives: The promise of public education in America.* New York: Penguin Books.

Rosenshine, B. (1986). Synthesis of research on explicit teaching. *Educational Leadership, 43*(3), 60–69.

Rueda, R., & Mehan, H. (1987). Metacognition and passing. *Anthropology and Education Quarterly, 17*(3), 145–165.

Rumberger, R. W. (1995). Dropping out of middle school: A multilevel analysis of students and schools. *American Educational Research Journal, 32*(3), 583–625.

Rutter, M., Maughan, B., Mortimore, P., & Ouston, J. (1979). *Fifteen thousand hours: Secondary schools and their effects on children.* Cambridge, MA: Harvard University Press.

San Antonio Independent School District v. Rodriguez, 11 U.S. 1 (1973).

Sarason, S. B. (1990). *The predictable failure of educational reform: Can we change course before it's too late?* San Francisco: Jossey-Bass.

Schneider, S. G. (1976). *Revolution, reaction, or reform: The 1974 Bilingual Education Act.* New York: Las Americas.

Schuman, H., & Harding, J. (1964). Prejudice and the norm of rationality. *Sociometry, 27,* 353–371.

Schuman, H., Steeh, C., & Bobo, L. (1985). *Racial attitudes in America: Trends and interpretations.* Cambridge, England: Cambridge University Press.

Schumann, J. H. (1976). Affective factors and the problem of age in second-language acquisition. *Language Learning, 25,* 209–239.

Schwartz, T. (1978). Where is the culture? Personality as the distributive locus of culture. In G. Spindler (Ed.), *The making of psychological anthropology* (pp. 197–218). Berkeley: University of California Press.

Scollon, R., & Scollon, B. K. (1981). *Narrative literacy and face in interethnic communication.* Norwood, NJ: Ablex.

Scribner, S., & Cole, M. (1981). Unpackaging literacy. In M. Farr-Whiteman (Ed.), *Variation in writing: Functional and linguistic-cultural differences: Vol. 1. Writing: The nature, development, and teaching of written communications* (pp. 71–88). Hillsdale, NJ: Lawrence Erlbaum.

Secada, W. G. (1996). Urban students acquiring English and learning mathematics in the context of reform. *Urban Education, 30*(4), 422–448.

Seginer, R. (1989). *Adolescent sisters: The relationship between younger and older sisters among Israeli Arabs.* Paper presented at the meeting of the International Society for the Study of Behavioral Development, Jyvaskyla, Finland.

Seliger, H. W. (1977). Does practice make perfect? A study of international patterns and L2 competence. *Language Learning, 27*(2), 263–278.

Sharan, S. (1980). Cooperative learning in small groups: Recent methods and effects on achievement, attitudes, and ethnic relations. *Review of Education Research, 50*(2), 241–271.

Sheldon, W. (1924). The intelligence of Mexican children. *School and Society, 19,* 139–142.

Shimberg, B. (1983). What is competence? How can it be assessed? In M. R. Stern (Ed.), *Power and conflict in continuing professional education* (pp. 17–37). Belmont, CA: Wadsworth.

Skinner, B. F. (1957). *Verbal behavior.* Englewood Cliffs, NJ: Prentice-Hall.

Skrabanek, R. L. (1970). Language maintenance among Mexican Americans. *International Journal of Comparative Sociology, 11,* 272–282.

Skutnabb-Kangas, T. (1979). *Language in the process of cultural assimilation and structural incorporation of linguistic minorities.* Rosslyn, VA: National Clearinghouse for Bilingual Education.

Slavin, R. E. (1988). Cooperative learning and student achievement. In R. E. Slavin (Ed.), *School and classroom organization* (pp. 68–81). Hillsdale, NJ: Erlbaum.

——— (1989). The pet and the pendulum. Fadism in education and how to stop it. *Phi Delta Kappan, 70.*

Slavin, R. E., Karweit, N., & Madden, N. (1989). *Effective programs for students at risk.* Needham Heights, MA: Allyn and Bacon.

Sleeter, C. E., & Grant, C. A. (1987). An analysis on multicultural education in the U.S. *Harvard Educational Review, 57*(4).

Smith, J. P., & Edmonston, B. (Eds.). (1997). *The new Americans: Economic, demographic, and fiscal effects of immigration.* Washington, DC: National Academy Press.

Smith, M. S., & O'Day, J. (1990). *Systemic school reform: Politics of Education Association Yearbook* (pp. 223–267). New York: Falmer Press.

Smith, T. (1997). Lessons and questions: Excerpts from the 1996 Kurt Hahn Address. *Journal of Experiential Education, 20*(1), 22–26.

Smith, T. W. (1971). *Understanding reading.* New York: Holt, Rinehart and Winston.

——— (1990). *Ethnic images* (GSS Topical Report No. 19). Chicago: National Opinion Research Center, University of Chicago.

Smith, T. W., & Sheatsley, P. B. (1984). American attitudes towards race relations. *Public Opinion, 7,* 14–15, 50–53.

Snow, C. E. (1990). The development of definitional skill. *Journal of Child Language, 17*(3), 697–710.

——— (1991). The theoretical basis for relationships between language and literacy in development. *Journal of Research in Childhood Education, 6*(1), 5–10.

Solorzano, D. G. (1997a). Images and words that wound: Critical race theory, racial stereotyping, and teacher education. *Teacher Education Quarterly, 24*(3), 5–19.

——— (1997b). Theoretical formulation of minority underachievement. *Black Education, 17*(2), 261–275.

Sorenson, A. P. (1967). Multilingualism in the Northwest Amazon. *American Anthropologist, 69,* 67–68.

Soto, L. D. (1997). *Language, culture, and power: Bilingual families and the struggle for quality education.* Albany: State University of New York Press.

Spencer, D. (1988). Transitional bilingual education and the socialization of immigrants. *Harvard Educational Review, 58*(2), 133–153.

Spencer, M. B. (1988). Self-concept development. In D. T. Slaughter (Ed.), *Black children and poverty: A developmental perspective* (pp. 103–116). San Francisco: Jossey-Bass.

Spencer, M. B., & Horowitz, F. D. (1973). Effects of systematic social and token reinforcement on the modification of racial and color concept attitudes in black and in white preschool children. *Developmental Psychology, 9,* 246–254.

Spindler, G. (1955). *Anthropology and education.* Stanford: Stanford University Press.

———— (1974). *Education and cultural process: Toward an anthropology of education.* New York: Holt, Rinehart and Winston.

———— (1982). *Doing the ethnography of schooling: Educational anthropology in action.* New York: Holt, Rinehart and Winston.

———— (1987). *Education and cultural process: Anthropological approaches.* Prospect Heights, IL: Waveland Press.

Spindler, G., & Spindler, L. (1989). Instrumental competence, self-efficacy, linguistic minorities, and cultural therapy: A preliminary attempt at integration. *Anthropology and Education Quarterly, 20*(1), 36–50.

Spiro, M. E. (1951). Culture and personality: The natural history of a false dichotomy. *Psychiatry, 14,* 19–46.

Stanton-Salazar, R. (1997). A social capital framework for understanding the socialization of racial minority children and youths. *Harvard Educational Review, 67*(1), 1–40.

Sternberg, R. J., & Wagner, R. K. (Eds.). (1986). *Practical intelligence.* New York: Cambridge University Press.

Suarez-Orozco, M. M. (1985, May). *Opportunity, family dynamics, and school achievement: The sociocultural context of motivation among recent immigrants from Central America.* Paper presented at the University of California Symposium on Linguistics, Minorities, and Education, Tahoe City, CA.

———— (1987). Becoming somebody: Central American immigrants in U.S. inner-city schools. *Anthropology and Education Quarterly, 18,* 287–299.

Sue, S., & Okazaki, S. (1990). Asian-American educational achievements: A

phenomenon in search of an explanation. *American Psychologist, 45*(8), 913–920.

Sue, S., & Padilla, A. (1986). Ethnic minority issues in the United States: Challenges for the educational system. In Bilingual Education Office, *Beyond language: Social and cultural factors in schooling language minority students* (pp. 35–72). Los Angeles: Evaluation, Dissemination, and Assessment Center, California State University.

Sullivan, P. (1992). *ESL in context.* Newbury Park, CA: Corwin Press.

Suzuki, R. H. (1984). Curriculum transformation for multicultural education. *Education and Urban Society, 16*(133), 294–322.

Swain, M., & Lapkin, R. (1991). The influence of bilingualism on cognitive functioning. *Canadian Modern Language Review, 47,* 635–641.

Tajfel, H. (1978). *The social psychology of minorities.* London: Minority Rights Group.

Tharp, R. G. (1989). Psychocultural variables and *k* constants: Effects on teaching and learning in schools. *American Psychologist, 44,* 349–359.

———— (1991). Cultural diversity and treatment of children. *Journal of Consulting and Clinical Psychology, 59*(6), 799–812.

Tharp, R., & Gallimore, R. (1988). *Rousing minds to life: Teaching, learning, and schooling in social context.* Cambridge, England: Cambridge University Press.

———— (1989). *Challenging cultural minds.* London: Cambridge University Press.

———— (1991). *The instructional conversation: Teaching and learning in social activity* (Research Report No. 2). Santa Cruz: National Center for Research on Cultural Diversity and Second-Language Learning, University of California, Santa Cruz.

Thomas, S. V., & Park, B. (1921a). *Culture and personality* (2nd ed.). New York: Random House.

———— (1921b). *Culture of immigrants.* Cambridge, MA: Newcome Press.

Thomas, W. P., & Collier, V. P. (1995a). *A longitudinal analysis of programs serving language minority students.* Washington, DC: National Clearinghouse for Bilingual Education.

———— (1995b). *Language minority student achievement and program effectiveness. Research summary of ongoing study: Results as of September.*

Thornton, S. (1981). *The issue of dialect in academic achievement.* Unpublished doctoral dissertation, University of California, Berkeley.

Tikunoff, W. J. (1983). *Compatibility of the SBIF features with other research on instruction of LEP students* (SBIF-83-4.8/10). San Francisco: Far West Laboratory.

Trueba, H. T. (1987). *Success or failure? Learning and the language minority student.* Scranton, PA: Harper and Row.

———— (1988a). Peer socialization among minority students: A high school dropout prevention program. In H. Trueba & C. Delgado-Gaitan (Eds.), *Schools and society: Learning content through culture* (pp. 178–193). New York: Praeger.

———— (1988b). *Rethinking learning disabilities: Cultural knowledge in literacy acquisition.* Unpublished manuscript, Office for Research on Educational Equity, Graduate School of Education, University of California, Santa Barbara.

Trueba, H. T., Moll, L. C., Diaz, S., & Diaz, R. (1982). *Improving the functional writing of bilingual secondary students.* Washington, DC: National Institute of Education.

Trujillo, F. X. (1989). *The teacher.* Poem prepared for the celebration of the teacher, Sacramento, CA.

Ueda, R. (1987). *Avenues to adulthood: The origins of the high school and social mobility in an American suburb.* Cambridge, England: Cambridge University Press.

U.S. Bureau of the Census. (1970). *Historical statistics of the United States, colonial times to 1970.* Washington, DC: U.S. Government Printing Office.

———— (1975). *Historical statistics of the United States, colonial times to 1970.* Washington, DC: Author.

———— (1990). *Statistical abstract of the United States, 1991.* Washington, DC: Government Printing Office.

———— (1991). *Census of the population.* Washington, DC: U.S. Government Printing Office.

———— (1995). *Immigration report.* Washington, DC: U.S. Government Printing Office.

U.S. Department of Education. (1998). *No more excuses: Final report of the U.S. Department of Education Hispanic dropout project.* Washington, DC: Author.

U.S. General Accounting Office. (1987a). *Bilingual education policy and practice.* Washington, DC: Author.

———— (1987b, March). *Research evidence on bilingual education* (GAO/PEMD-87-12BR). Washington, DC: Author.

———— (1994). *Limited English proficiency: A growing and costly educational challenge facing many school districts* (GAO/HEHS-94-38). Washington, DC: Author.

U.S. Immigration and Naturalization Service. (1995). *Statistical yearbook of immigration and naturalization services.* Washington, DC: U.S. Government Printing Office.

United States v. Texas, 647 F.2d 69 (9th Cir. 1981).

Valdés, G. (1996). *Con respeto: Bridging the distances between culturally diverse families and schools. An ethnographic portrait.* New York: Teachers College Press.

Valencia, R. (1991). *Chicano school failure and success: Research and policy agendas for the 1990s.* New York: Falmer Press.

Valenzuela, A., & Dornbusch, S. M. (1994). Familism and social capital in the academic achievement of Mexican-origin and Anglo adolescents. *Social Science Quarterly, 75*(1), 18–36.

Valsiner, J. (1989). How can developmental psychology become "culture inclusive"? In J. **Valsiner** (Ed.), *Child development in cultural context* (pp. 1–8). Lewiston, NY: Hogrefe and Huber.

Varenne, H. (1982). Jocks and freaks: The symbolic structure of the expression of social interaction among American senior high school students. In G. Spindler (Ed.), *Doing the ethnography of schooling: Educational anthropology in action* (pp. 112–121). New York: Holt, Rinehart and Winston.

Veltman, C. (1988). *The future of the Spanish language in the United States.* New York: Hispanic Policy Project.

Villegas, A. M. (1991). *Culturally responsive pedagogy for the 1990's and beyond.* Princeton: Educational Testing Service.

Villegas, A. M. , Clewell, B. C., Anderson, B. T., Goertz, M. E., Joy, M. F., Bruschi, B. A., & Irvine, J. J. (1995). *Teaching for diversity: Models for expanding the supply of minority teachers.* Princeton: Educational Testing Service.

Vogt, L., Jordan, C., & Tharp, R. (1987). Explaining school failure, producing school success: Two cases. *Anthropology and Education Quarterly, 18*(4), 276–286.

Vygotsky, L. S. (1929). The problem of the cultural development of the child. *Journal of Genetic Psychology, 36,* 414–434.

——— (1956). *The genesis of higher psychological functions.* Moscow: Academy of Pedagogical Sciences.

——— (1981). The genesis of higher mental functions. In J. V. Wertsch (Ed.), *The concept of activity in Soviet psychology* (pp. 42–60). Armonk, NY: Plenum.

Waggoner, D. (1984). The need for bilingual education: Estimates from the 1980 census. *NABE Journal, 8,* 1–14.

——— (1991). *Language minority census newsletter.* Washington, DC:

Walberg, H. (1986a). Synthesis of research on teaching. In M. Wittrock (Ed.), *Handbook of research on teaching* (3rd ed., pp. 15–32). New York: Macmillan.

——— (1986b). What works in a nation still at risk. *Educational Leadership, 44*(1), 7–11.

Walker, C. L. (1987). Hispanic achievements: Old views and new perspectives. In H. Trueba (Ed.), *Success or Failure? Learning and the language minority student* (pp. 15–32). Cambridge, MA: Newbury House.

Wallace, A. F. C. (1970). *Culture and personality* (2nd ed.). New York: Random House.

Walsh, D. (1990, October 12). Minority students in Santa Clara County continue to deteriorate academically. *San Francisco Examiner,* p. B1-4.

Weinberg, M. (1990). *Racism in the United States: A comprehensive classified bibliography.* New York: Greenwood Press.

Weis, L. (Ed.). (1988). *Class, race, and gender in American education.* Albany: State University of New York Press.

Wertsch, J. V. (1985). *Vygotsky and the social formation of the mind.* Cambridge, MA: Harvard University Press.

Whiting, B. B., & Edwards, C. P. (1988). *Children of different worlds: The formation of social behavior.* Cambridge, MA: Harvard University Press.

Wiesner, T. S., Gallimore, R., & Jordan, C. (1988). Unpackaging cultural effects on classroom learning: Native Hawaiian peer assistance and child-generated activity. *Anthropology and Education Quarterly, 19*(4), 327–353.

Wigdor, A. K., & Garner, W. R. (Eds.). (1982). *Ability testing: Uses, consequences, and controversies: Part 1. Report of the committee.* Washington, DC: National Academy of Sciences–National Research Council, Assembly of Behavioral and Social Sciences.

Wiley, M. S. (1996). Environmental education in the school culture: A systemic approach. *Clearing, 94,* 25–27.

Wilson, W. J. (1987). *The truly disadvantaged: The inner city, the underclass, and public policy.* Chicago: University of Chicago Press.

Wolfram, W. (1993a). Ethical considerations in language awareness programs. *Issues in Applied Linguistics, 4*(2), 225–255.

—— (1993b). A proactive role for speech-language pathologists in sociolinguistic education. *Language, Speech, and Hearing Services in Schools, 24*(3), 181–185.

Wong-Fillmore, L. (1976). *The second time around: Cognitive and social strategies in second-language acquisition.* Unpublished doctoral dissertation, Stanford University.

—— (1991). When learning a second language means losing a first. *Early Childhood Research Quarterly, 6*(3), 323–346.

Wong-Fillmore, L., Ammon, P., McLaughlin, B., & Ammon, M. S. (1985). *Final report for learning English through bilingual instruction* (NIE Final Report No. 400-360-0030). Rosslyn, VA: National Clearinghouse for Bilingual Education.

Wong-Fillmore, L., & Valadez, C. (1985). Teaching bilingual learners. In M. S. Wittrock (Ed.), *Handbook on research on teaching* (3rd. ed., pp. 481–519). Washington, DC: American Educational Research Association.

Wood, C. J. (1992a). Culture, language, and child development. *Language and Education, 6*(2–4), 123–140.

—— (1992b). Fostering collaborative reading and writing experiences in mathematics. *Journal of Reading, 36*(2), 96–103.

—— (1992c). Toward more effective teacher evaluation: Lessons from naturalistic inquiry. *NASSP Bulletin, 76*(542), 52–59.

Zentella, A. C. (1981). *Ta bien* you could answer me *en cualquier idioma:* Puerto Rican code switching in bilingual classrooms. In R. Duran (Ed.), *Latino language and communicative behavior* (pp. 109–132). Norwood, NJ: Ablex.

—— (1997). *Growing up bilingual: Puerto Rican children in New York.*

INDEX

Cultures: building bridges between, 153–159; interaction of, 126–129
Curriculum: effective: attributes of, 85; characteristics of, 45; focus of multiculturalism on, 102
Customs, ethnic, and acculturation, 73–74

Data, value of, 54
Decision-making, and effective teaching, 298
Decontextualized language, definition of, 219
Demographic shifts in U.S., 6–7
Denver inservice program, 265–266
Department of Education, 48
Developmental Associates, 40, 41
Dewey, John, 290
Dialect: judgments based in, 202–203; *vs.* language, 200; learning to adjust, 203; use of, 196–200
Difference, attitudes toward, 127–128
Direct instruction, 232; characteristics of, 233
Directory of Two-Way Bilingual Programs in the United States, 317
Disabled students, and culture, 77
Discourse: good, elements of, 232–234; teacher's role in, 231–232. *See also* Conversation
Discourse rules, acquisition of, 177–179
Disposition of effective teachers, 273–274
Distributive model of culture, 72
Diversity: acceptance of, 65; addressing, in schools, 116, 244–245; among immigrants, 15–16; educational implications of, 149–153; and educational vulnerability, 23–31; importance of, 86; increase in, 256–257; measuring, 18–19; projected trends in, 19–20; respect for, 106
Dorsey, J. O., 71
Double immersion programs, 106
Dropout rates: among ethnic minorities, 23–24; comparative, 24–25; types of reports on, 24

Ebonics, 200–203
Ecology of family, 134–136

Economic background, and educational track, 162
Education: culture and, 69–70, 76–78; and distributive model of culture, 72; family preferences regarding, 150–151; goals of, 229–230; for immigrants in information age, 14–18; multicultural, 101–107; new contexts for, 62–67; social benefits of, 98–99
Educational achievement, low, costs of, 30–31
Educational approaches, historical survey of, 94–107
Educational funding policies, 27–30
Educational Summit (Charlottesville, 1990), 23–24
Educational vulnerability, diversity and, 23–31
EEOA. *See* Equal Educational Opportunity Act, 1974
Elementary and Secondary Education Act, 1965 (ESEA), 44, 99–100
Elementary and Secondary Education Act, 1994 overhaul of, 45–47, 100. *See also* Improving America's Schools Act (IASA)
Embedding context of learning, 217
Emotional needs of students, addressing, 297
Employment, preparing students for, 14
English: dialects of, 197; as language of U.S., 12; standard and nonstandard, 197–200
English as a second language (ESL) programs, 42; and print immersion, 192–193
English as a second language (ESL) teachers, role of, 263
English First movement, 5
Enlarged understanding: elements of, 234–244; as goal of education, 230
Enrollment, public school, 19–20
Environment: and instructional conversation, 234; and self-concept, 139–140
Environments conducive to learning, 277
Equal Educational Opportunities and Transportation Act, 1974 (EEOA), 42–43, 101
Equity in education, 98–101
Errors, attitude toward, 193